KU-201-574

INSIGHT GUIDES

TUSCANY

Discovery
CHANNEL

APA PUBLICATIONS

Part of the Langenscheidt Publishing Group

※ INSIGHT GUIDE
Tuscany

Editor
Cathy Muscat
Art Director
Klaus Geisler
Picture Editor
Hilary Genin
Cartography Editor
Zoë Goodwin
Production
Kenneth Chan
Editorial Director
Brian Bell

Distribution

UK & Ireland
GeoCenter International Ltd
The Viables Centre, Harrow Way
Basingstoke, Hants RG22 4BJ
Fax: (44) 1256-817988

United States
Langenscheidt Publishers, Inc.
36–36 33rd Street 4th Floor
Long Island City, NY 11106
Fax: (1) 718 784-0640

Australia
Universal Publishers
1 Waterloo Road
Macquarie Park, NSW 2113
Fax: (61) 2 9888 9074

New Zealand
Hema Maps New Zealand Ltd (HNZ)
Unit D, 24 Ra ORA Drive
East Tamaki, Auckland
Fax: (64) 9 273 6479

Worldwide
**Apa Publications GmbH & Co.
Verlag KG (Singapore branch)**
38 Joo Koon Road, Singapore 628990
Tel: (65) 6865-1600. Fax: (65) 6861-6438

Printing

Insight Print Services (Pte) Ltd
38 Joo Koon Road, Singapore 628990
Tel: (65) 6865-1600. Fax: (65) 6861-6438

©2006 Apa Publications GmbH & Co.
Verlag KG (Singapore branch)
All Rights Reserved

First Edition 1989
Fourth Edition 2006

ABOUT THIS BOOK

The first Insight Guide pioneered the use of creative full-colour photography in guidebooks in 1970. Since then, we have expanded our range to cater for our readers' need not only for reliable information about their chosen destination but also for a real understanding of that destination. Now, when the internet can supply inexhaustible (but not always reliable) facts, our books marry text and pictures to provide that much more elusive quality: knowledge. To achieve this, they rely heavily on the authority of locally based writers and photographers.

How to use this book

The book is carefully structured to convey an understanding of Tuscany:
◆ To understand the region today, you need to know something of its past. The first section covers its people, history and culture in lively essays written by specialists.
◆ The main Places section provides a full run-down of all the attractions worth seeing. The main places of interest are coordinated by number with full-colour maps. Margin notes provide background information and tips on special places and events.
◆ A special section of photographic features highlights Florentine museums and other aspects of Tuscan culture, such as Chianti and its wine.
◆ Photographs are chosen not only to illustrate the landscape and buildings but also to convey the moods of the region and the life of its people.
◆ The Travel Tips listings section provides a point of reference for information on travel, hotels, shops and festivals. Information may be located

European University Institute in Fiesole, and **Robert John**, former tour guide in the region. Their contributions have been blended with the expertise of writers who contributed to previous editions, much of whose work survives in this edition.

Among the principal authors, **Lisa Gerard-Sharp**, who is knowledgeable about all things Tuscan, from Etruscan grave-robbing to the social habits of the modern populace, contributed to the original Places section and wrote sections on *Wild Tuscany* and *Tuscan Architecture*. **Christopher Catling** expanded the historical chapters, enhancing the fine section on the Renaissance written by **Russell Chamberlin**. **Valentina Harris** describes the pleasures of Tuscan food and wine. **Mark Zakian**, a travel writer specialising in Italy, contributed the new essay on *Tuscany Today*.

Other contributors to previous editions included **Paul Duncan**, **Nicky Swallow**, **Marco de Stefani**, **Lorella Grossi**, **Susan Zucker** and **Yvonne Newman**.

The majority of stunning pictures were taken by **Anna Mockford** and **Nick Bonetti**, regular Insight photographers. They have captured the timeless beauty of the Tuscan landscape and its historic towns.

Thanks also go to **Neil Titman**, who proofread the book, and to **Helen Peters**, who compiled the index.

CONTACTING THE EDITORS

We would appreciate it if readers would alert us to errors or outdated information by writing to:

Insight Guides, P.O. Box 7910, London SE1 1WE, England. Fax: (44) 20 7403-0290. insight@apaguide.co.uk

www.insightguides.com
In North America:
www.insighttravelguides.com

quickly by using the index printed on the back cover flap – and the flaps are designed to serve as bookmarks.

The contributors

This edition of *Insight Guide: Tuscany* was revised by **Cathy Muscat**, who spent a number of years living and working in central Italy. She currently works at Insight Guides as an editor specialising in Italian destinations. This new edition builds on the excellent foundations laid down by editors of previous editions, **Rosemary Bailey** and **Barbara Balletto**.

The Places chapters and Travel Tips section have been comprehensively updated on the spot with the help of **Adele Evans**, a regular contributor to Insight Guides, and **Sarah Birke**, who knows this part of Italy very well after studying law at the

Tuscany

Map Legend

Autostrada	
Autostrada (under construction)	
Dual Carriageway	
Main Road	
Secondary Road	
Minor road	
Track	
Regional Boundary	
Province Boundary	
National Park/Reserve	
Ferry Route	
✈ ✈	Airport
† ⚑	Church (ruins)
†	Monastery
⌂	Castle (ruins)
∴	Archaeological Site
∩	Cave
★	Place of Interest
⌂	Mansion/Stately Home
☼	Viewpoint
⚑	Beach
	Autostrada
	Dual Carriageway
	Main Roads
	Minor Roads
	Footpath
	Railway
	Pedestrian Area
	Important Building
	Park
❶	Numbered Sight
⛟	Bus Station
❶	Tourist Information
✉	Post Office
⊞	Cathedral/Church
☾	Mosque
✡	Synagogue
⚑	Statue/Monument
⌷	Tower
⚱	Lighthouse

Maps

Travel Tips

TRANSPORT

ACCOMMODATION

ACTIVITIES

A–Z

LANGUAGE

FURTHER READING

THE BEST OF TUSCANY

Art, culture, food and shopping...
Here, at a glance, are our
recommendations for
your visit

CHURCHES AND MONUMENTS

- **The Leaning Tower** stands alongside the gleaming Duomo and Baptistery on Pisa's aptly named Campo dei Miracoli – Field of Miracles. *See page 155*
- **Brunelleschi's dome**. An incredible feat of engineering by the father of Renaissance architecture. *See page 89*
- **Florentine churches**. San Lorenzo, San Marco, Santa Croce and San Miniato should all be seen. *See pages 87–96*
- **San Michele** in Lucca, a fine example of the exuberant Tuscan Romanesque style. *See page 135*
- **San Galgano**. The evocative ruins of a Gothic abbey. *See page 190*

- **Siena cathedral**. A magnificent Gothic structure of banded black and white stone. *See page 209*
- **Monte Oliveto Maggiore**. A secluded 14th-century monastery set among groves of cypress trees. *See page 217*
- **Sant'Antimo**. An abbey church built of creamy travertine and set against tree-clad hills. *See page 230*
- **Santa Maria Nuova**. The domed church just outside the Etruscan walls of Cortona is a hidden gem. *See page 255*
- **San Pellegrino in Alpe**. An ancient monastery deep in the Garfagnana mountains, with glorious views. *See page 144*

THE BEST TUSCAN HILLTOWNS

- **San Gimignano.** The medieval skyscrapers are best seen early in the morning or at dusk, when the coachloads have left. *See page 193*
- **Pienza**. The ideal Renaissance city. *See page 219*
- **Monteriggioni**. The Sienese hilltown encircled by walls and 14 towers is a spectacular sight. *See page 197*
- **Cortona**. One of many Tuscan hilltowns rich in attractions out of all proportion to their tiny size. *See page 255*
- **Vinci**. The genius of Leonardo is cele-

brated in his birthplace, a tiny hilltown between Florence and Pisa. *See page 119*
- **Massa Marittima**. The ancient mining capital of the region. *See page 189*
- **Montepulciano** and **Montalcino** deserve long and leisurely exploration with frequent stops to sample their famed wines. *See pages 220 and 229*
- **Pitigliano** is situated above a dramatic cliff of soft tufa in the forgotten corner of Tuscany. *See page 242*
- **San Miniato**. An ancient town straddling three hills. *See page 119*

ABOVE The Leaning Tower of Pisa and **LEFT:** Brunelleschi's dome – two Tuscan icons.

TUSCANY FOR FAMILIES

- **Giardini di Boboli**. The gardens behind the Pitti Palace are fun for children to clamber around. There is an amphitheatre, strange statues and grottoes, and a handy café. *See page 104*
- **Trips to the Tuscan islands**. Ferries and hydrofoils sail from Porto Santo Stefano to Giglio and from Piombino to Elba. *See pages 239, 174 and 260*
- **Giardino dei Tarocchi**. A bizarre garden full of colourful fantasy figures. *See page 240*
- **Pistoia Zoo**. Compact, but one of the region's best. *See page 127*
- **Parco di Pinocchio**. At Collodi near Pisa. A hi-tech theme park it isn't, but Pinocchio's park has a certain old-fashioned charm. *See page 138*

- **Horse-riding**. Excursions on horseback are popular with families visiting Tuscany. There are over 40 equestrian centres. For recommendations *see page 283*
- **Ludoteca Centrale**. This children's centre in Florence provides fun and games for under-sixes. *See page 287*
- **Ice cream**. When all else fails, an ice cream on the town square, most of which are traffic free, rarely fails to win them over.

TOP ETRUSCAN SITES

- **Volterra** has some of the best Etruscan art to be found outside Rome. *See page 185*
- **Chiusi**. Etruscan tombs are the highlight of a visit to Chiusi. *See page 226*
- **Fiesole**. An Etruscan temple and a Roman theatre a 30-minute bus ride from Florence. *See page 113*
- To see some of the most intact Etruscan ruins visit **Roselle** and **Vetulonia**, near Grosseto. *See page 235*
- **Museo Archeologico** in Florence has a fine collection of Etruscan art. *See page 93*

SEASIDE AND SPAS

- **Elba**. A beautiful island with dramatic scenery and a series of small beaches. Perfect for families. *See pages 177–183*
- **The Maremma**. One of the most unspoilt stretches of beach on the Italian coast. *See page 237*
- **Viareggio**. An appealing coastal town with art nouveau architecture, plentiful fish restaurants and an atmospheric harbour. *See page 138*
- **Spas**. Montecatini is the most splendid but Tuscany has many therapeutic spas. *See pages 128 and 287*

FAR LEFT: on the Tuscan Riviera.
LEFT: 5th-century BC Etruscan sculpture, *L'Ombra della Sera* (Evening Shadow).

A TASTE OF TUSCANY

- **Wine-tasting**.
Sample Vino Nobile
in Montepulciano's
Cantine Contucci *(see
page 221)*, sip a glass
of Brunello in Mon-
talcino's Fortezza *(see
page 230)* or visit the
Castello di Brolio,
birthplace of the mod-
ern Chianti industry
(see page 200).
- **Food festivals**.
Tuscans are proud of
their local produce
which they celebrate
with festivals *(sagre)* –
white truffles, chest-
nuts, Valdichiana beef,
wild boar and pecorino
cheese all have festi-
vals dedicated to
them *(informa-
tion from lo-
cal tourist
offices)*.

- **Cookery Courses**
are big business in
Tuscany. The course
at Il Borghetto in the
heart of the Chianti
region is one of the
best. *See page 274*
Badia a Coltibuono is
a "wine resort" where
you can eat, sleep and
learn to cook. *See
page 199*
- **Cacciucco**. The
famous fish stew from
Livorno is best sam-
pled in the port town
and the immediate en-
virons. *See page 107.*
- **Mushrooms**.
Around October time,
mushroom-loving
Tuscans head for the
mountain woods to
forage for *funghi*.
Wild mushrooms, es-
pecially the prized
porcini and *tartufi*
(truffles), are widely
available in restau-
rants in the autumn.
See page 69
- **Sweet treats** include
the candied fruit cake,
Panforte, sweet al-
mond biscuits, *Riccia-
relli* and the irresistible
gelati. *See page 102*

BEST SQUARES

- **Piazza del Campo**.
All roads in Siena
lead to the rose-pink
Campo which spreads
out from the Gothic
town hall like a fan.
See page 207
- **Piazza della Signoria**.
Florence's open-air
museum of statuary,
where a copy of
Michelangelo's *David*
takes centre stage.
See page 84

- **Piazza Grande**.
Arezzo's main square
in the old hilly part of
the city, is the venue
for Tuscany's biggest
antiques market.
See page 245
- **Piazza Anfiteatro**.
Lucca's bustling
square takes the shape
of the Roman
amphitheatre that
once stood here.
See page 136

VILLAS AND GARDENS

- **The Boboli Gardens**.
The regal gardens of
the Pitti Palace, pala-
tial residence of the
Medici and now a vast
museum. *See page 104*
- **Villa Medicea Poggio
a Caiano**. Thought by
many to be the perfect
Medici villa, with
frescoed halls and
beautiful gardens. *See
pages 116 and 118*
- **Villa Demidoff and
Parco di Pratolino**.
The gardens here
contain extraordinary
Mannerist sculpture
and grottoes. *See
page 116*

- **Villa Medici (Fiesole)**.
A delightful villa and
garden with superb
views of Florence.
See page 116
- **Villa Medicea della
Petraia**. An elegant
villa decorated with
wonderful frescoes.
See page 116
- **Villa Medicea di
Castello**. Beautiful
Renaissance gardens.
See page 116
- **Lucchesi villas**. The
area around Lucca is
rich in villas, all
surrounded by
beautiful parks.
See page 137

ABOVE: Arezzo's Piazza Grande. **ABOVE LEFT:** the "rustic"
raffia-wrapped Chianti flask. **LEFT:** Giambologna's *Rape of
the Sabine Women* on the Piazza della Signoria, Florence.
RIGHT: Michelangelo's *Holy Family* tondo in the Uffizi.

TUSCAN LANDSCAPES

- **The Crete Senesi**. The dramatic landscape of rounded hills, stately cypresses and isolated farms, is the Tuscany of postcards and posters. *See page 217*
- **Parco Naturale della Maremma** Beautiful unspoilt beaches backed by steep cliffs, parasol pines and Mediterranean scrubland. *See pages 65 and 236*
- **Chianti Country**. Gentle hills cloaked in vineyards, many centred around medieval castles where winetasting is usually on offer. *See pages 63 and 202–3*

- **Parco dell' Orecchiella**. A wild mountainous area, rich in wildlife – the region's most spectacular park. *See pages 64 and 145*
- **Apuan Alps**. Behind the well groomed beaches of the Versilia is a rugged hinterland of marble quarries, mountain ridges and narrow gorges. *See pages 64 and 146*
- **The Casentino**. Ancient forests of the upper Arno valley. *See pages 63 and 249*
- **Monte Amiata** The site of an extinct volcano with a profusion of thermal springs. *See pages 228 and 242*

FESTIVALS AND EVENTS

- **Giostra del Saracino**. Jousting tournament in Arezzo. *See page 280*
- **Scoppio del Carro**. Amid colourful processions fireworks explode from a moving carriage in Florence. *See page 280*
- **Estate Fiesolana**. Music festival in Fiesole. *See page 281*
- **Effetto Venezia**. Livorno's lively 10-day festival. *See page 281*
- **Il Teatro Povero**. Drama written, acted and directed by the people of Montichiello. *See pages 39 and 281*

- **Luminaria di San Ranieri**. Pisan festival (pictured above) when thousands of candles light up the Arno; ends with a boat race. *See pages 162 and 281*
- **Palio**. Siena's traditional horse race. *See pages 214–5*
- **Puccini Festival**. By the composer's villa on Lake Massaciuccoli. *See pages 139 and 281*
- **Carnevale**. Viareggio's carnival is one of the best in Italy. *See page 138*

RENAISSANCE ART

The Uffizi an overwhelming collection of masterpieces including Botticelli's *Birth of Venus* and *Primavera* and works by Leonardo da Vinci, Raphael, Titian and other masters of the High Renaissance. *See pages 100–3*

The Bargello A major collection of Renaissance and Mannerist sculpture in a former prison. *See pages 110–11*

The Baptistery Ghiberti's doors are so dazzling, Michelangelo called them the "Gates of Paradise". *See page 87*

Lorenzetti's frescoes in Siena's Palazzo Pubblico – an allegory of good and bad government. *See page 209*

The two Davids Michelangelo's *David* is Florence's icon, but Donatello's *David* was the first free-standing nude since antiquity. *See pages 109 and 110*

Masaccio's Florentine frescoes in the Brancacci chapel and Santa Maria Novella display all the characteristics of the Renaissance: the importance of the human form, human emotion and the use of perspective. *See pages 96 and 92*

Giotto's frescoes in Florence's Santa Croce show a departure from the flat Byzantine style. *See page 94*

Piero della Francesca's frescoes in Arezzo are marvels of pastel shades awash in cool light. *See page 246*

Orsanmichele a showcase of statuary paid for by the wealthy guilds. *See page 87*

THE TUSCAN MIRACLE

Birthplace of the Renaissance, a strong tradition of village life, a picturesque countryside: these factors and more contribute to the enigma that is Tuscany

From the top of a village tower, the Tuscan landscape lies below: the most civilised rural scene on Earth. Yet driving through southern Tuscany at night there is little sense of civilisation, still less of domesticity – even farm animals are kept indoors. In the distance, a succession of small lights trail across the black countryside: tenuous links with separate inward-looking communities. The spaces in between are remote, uncivilised. The blackness and emptiness of the countryside go back to medieval times and beyond; the "Tuscan Miracle" only illuminates the cities, leaving the gaps unfilled.

In giving birth to the Renaissance, Tuscany designed the modern world. In his painting, Giotto projected Tuscany into space. Brunelleschi crowned space with his Florentine dome, the greatest feat of Renaissance engineering. In the Carmine frescoes, Masaccio peopled space with recognisably human figures. His *Expulsion from Paradise* reveals Adam and Eve in all their naked beauty. Gone is the medieval coyness; present is the palpable suffering of a couple who have lost everything.

The Tuscan miracle, however, is not a frozen Renaissance portrait but a living procession of Tuscans at ease with their artistic setting and identity. Tuscans do have an innate aesthetic sense but the Tuscan tapestry is a rich weave that has been created by many different threads. Literary Tuscany is a strand that can be clearly traced through Boccaccio, Petrarch and Dante. Republican Tuscany is best glimpsed through its fortified town halls while humanist Tuscany is enshrined in poetry, sculpture and art, the fruits of patronage and craftsmanship. Aristocratic Tuscany still lingers in Medici palaces, villas and sculptured gardens, as well as the ancestral homes of the Rucellai, Corsini and Frescobaldi. Bourgeois Tuscany parades along Florence's Via Tornabuoni, patronises the arts and restores family farms. Peasant Tuscany traditionally takes a little of everything from the land: game, beans, chestnut flour, unsalted bread, olive oil, and, of course, the grapes needed to make Chianti and Brunello. Tuscan cuisine combines proportion and variety. Like the Tuscans themselves, it is of good peasant stock.

PRECEDING PAGES: PRECEDING PAGES: view of the Piazza del Duomo, religious heart of Florence; the skyline of San Gimignano, one of Tuscany's best-preserved medieval towns. **LEFT:** Hidden hill village in the heart of the Garfagnana.

THE MAKING OF TUSCANY

First the Etruscans and Romans left their imprint on the landscape. By the Middle Ages Tuscany had become the scene of fiercely battling city-states. Then the Medici dynasty arrived and dominated Tuscan politics for 300 years. Unification in the 19th century and the two world wars in the 20th forced a somewhat scarred Tuscany into the modern world

The story of Tuscany begins with the Etruscans, its earliest known inhabitants, whose origins are shrouded in myth and mystery. The Romantics and latter-day writers believed that the Etruscans sailed from Asia Minor. However, Dionysius, writing as the Etruscan civilisation neared its end, held that the Etruscans were natives with an indigenous culture too deeply ingrained to be oriental. Most modern scholars believe that the Etruscans migrated from Eastern Europe over the Alps and represent the flowering of the early Italic tribes. What is clear is that between the 8th and 4th centuries BC "Etruria Propria" flourished as a confederation of 12 city-states in central Italy. Northern Etruria, roughly equivalent to modern Tuscany, included Arezzo, Chiusi, Cortona, Populonia, Vetulonia and Volterra.

Etruscan seafarers and merchants first settled on the coast and began smelting iron ore from Elba and importing oriental ceramics, glass and silverware. Greek naval supremacy meant an opening to Hellenistic culture: ships sailed to Corinth with honey, gold and bronze figurines, and returned to Vetulonia and Populonia with perfume and painted wine jars. The inland cities such as Chiusi and Volterra thrived on hunting, farming and internal trade. Over the next two centuries, the Etruscans allied themselves to the developing Roman power, and by the 1st century BC all the Etruscan territory was annexed. Although Etruscan and Latin co-

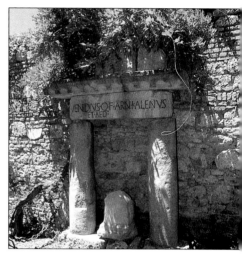

existed, Etruscan culture was crushed; its role degenerated into the provision of soothsayers, musicians, dancers and fighters for Rome.

Etruscan society

The original confederation had a complex urban and social structure: each city was originally run by a king, later by local aristocrats and finally by a priestly oligarchy. The lords owned large landholdings or navies and were served by serfs and slaves. Whereas the serfs were rewarded with agricultural plots, the slaves danced and sang for their supper. With urbanisation, an independent class of artisans and merchants emerged. The granting of the same

LEFT: Etruscan tomb painting.
RIGHT: part of the fortification wall at Chiusi, one of Tuscany's major Etruscan sites.

Roman citizenship to the middle classes as to the aristocratic priests and magistrates was a blow to the Etruscan princely tradition.

The Etruscans were expert builders. Their cities followed the contours of the land and sited the necropolis below the city walls and the living city above. If cities of the dead predominate today, it is by accident and not by design. Public buildings, constructed of wood and clay, did not survive. From what remains of the cities, there was enough to impress Roman and Renaissance architects. Volterra's Porta all' Arco, a deep gateway inspired by Mesopotamian architecture; the huge drystone walls at Saturnia, rebuilt to defend the city against

borrowed from Greek, the language, read from left to right, is part of no known linguistic group and defies interpretation. Many claim to have found a key text equivalent to the Rosetta Stone. In Marsiliana a writing tablet was found engraved with the Greek Euboic alphabet used as a model for Etruscan.

Despite considerable progress, the unintelligibility of Etruscan is part of a glamorous myth. True, there are no external keys such as dictionaries or bilingual texts, but even by the 18th century, the sounds of most letters, names and gods had been identified and simple texts translated. Today, the core grammatical and phonetic structure is known, and, by deduction,

Roman incursions; the neat town plans of Pitigliano and Sovana – all these scattered remains are evidence of the vitality and ingenuity of Etruscan builders.

But it is the tombs that remain as a cultural testimony to the power, wealth and beliefs of their owners. Death reflected life: the poor were often buried in shallow graves or their ashes put in small urns; the rich were buried in chamber tombs and stone sarcophagi decorated with pottery.

Mystery language

The Etruscan language is as mysterious as the people's origins. Although the alphabet is

most of the 10,000 shorter texts can be read accurately. These texts are mostly funerary inscriptions and religious dedications. The one known book, a priest's manual discovered wrapped around an Egyptian mummy, has still only been partially deciphered.

Etruscan influence

The art critic John Ruskin saw an unbroken line of tradition from the tomb paintings of the Etruscans to Giotto and Fra Angelico. Certainly, the Etruscan influence on the Romans was considerable. Apart from introducing to Rome the purple toga, an abundance of gods and competent soothsayers, the Etruscans also added a set of religious, humanistic and regional values which far outlived the Roman Empire.

The Roman legacy

Rome annexed Etruria in 351 BC, and, from the 3rd until the 2nd century BC, as part of the massive road-building programme which was to transform Italy, four great Roman roads were built across the territory: the Via Aurelia, which ran up the western seaboard to Pisae and the naval base at Genua in Liguria; the Via Clodia, which stopped at Saturnia; the Via Cassia, built in 154 BC to connect Rome with Florentia; and the Via Flaminia, built in 220 BC to connect Rome to Umbria and the Adriatic.

Roman roads purposely avoided the great Etruscan cities, which slowly fell into decline, whereas the new Roman cities such as Pistoriae (Pistoia) grew in importance.

New colonies were founded at Ansedonia, Fiesole, Roselle, Populonia, Volterra, Luni and Lucca. The cultural identity of the Etruscans was gradually absorbed into that of the Romans, a process which accelerated in 91 BC when Roman citizenship was extended to the Etruscans. The Romans learned many things from the Etruscans – principally the Tuscan arch, which they developed as a key element in their extraordinary aqueducts, bridges and buildings, relegating the classical

It's hard to imagine the impact these giant engineering projects must have had on the local inhabitants, as surveyors and workmen spanned rivers with elegant stone bridges, built drains to prevent their new roads from flooding and at times even cut through the hills themselves.

Etruscan roads were all designed to connect the interior with the coast, whereas Roman roads all led to Rome, thus the axis was turned 90°, from east–west to north–south. The new

columns of Greece to a more decorative role.

The most complete remains in Tuscany are at Fiesole, Roselle and Cosa (Ansedonia); the best villas are near the coast on Elba, near Porto Santo Stefano and particularly on the Isola di Giannutri, near Grosseto. Most Tuscan cities have something to show, though sometimes a little detective work is required.

By creating the roads and major cities of Tuscany, the Romans left a permanent imprint on the landscape. A millennium later, the ruins of their great bridges, amphitheatres and city walls were the inspiration for the next great blossoming of Italian culture: Tuscany's coming of age, the Renaissance.

LEFT: the Etruscan tomb of Larthia Seianti, Chiusi, 2nd century BC.
ABOVE: the Teatro Romano in Fiesole.

Roman Tuscany

Ansedonia, the Roman Cosa, was founded as a Roman colony in 273 BC. The ancient hilltop city has been excavated, and the site contains a main street, remains of a forum, a walled acropolis and the ruined *capitolium* – a tripartite sanctuary for the triad of Jupiter, Juno and Minerva. The city's 1.5 km (1 mile) of wall is virtually intact, as are many of its 18 guard towers. The site is overgrown, and many of the ruins are covered in brambles, giving it a melancholy atmosphere.

Fiesole, which possibly dates from the 8th century BC, is an Etruscan settlement overlooking the valleys of the Arno and the Mugnone. As Faesulae, it was a Roman military colony from 80 BC and later became the capital of Roman Etruria. The Piazza Mino da Fiesole is built on the site of the Roman forum. The archaeological site, set on a hillside near the Duomo, features a remarkably well-preserved Roman theatre, still used for performances. Near by are Roman baths, and on the other side the ruins of a Roman temple, both 1st-century BC, as well as a 3rd-century BC Etruscan temple, set against the Etruscan city walls.

Detective work is necessary in Florence, the Roman Florentia; the Roman gridiron street plan is clearly visible in maps, with the Piazza della Repubblica following the outline of the old *castrum*. The perimeter of the theatre, outside the city walls to the southwest, is still described by the little streets surrounding the Piazza Santa Croce.

In Lucca, the original street plan is also still evident. Luca, as the Romans named it, began as a military colony in 178 BC and featured a 10,000-seat amphitheatre that was originally to the north of the city, outside the walls. In time, it was largely dismantled, and most of its remains are below street level. During the Middle Ages, however, houses were built using the remaining walls of the amphitheatre, thus fossilising its outline and four main entrances. Fragments of it are still visible from the surrounding lanes, incorporated in the outer walls of the houses.

Luni, called Luna by the Romans, was founded in 177 BC and was the springboard for the conquest of the Ligurian tribes. The Roman city, its forum, a number of houses and its amphitheatre have been excavated.

Another extensively excavated site is at Roselle, the Roman Rusellae. The Etruscan city was taken by Rome early in the 3rd century BC. It was originally an island, dominating the waters of the gulf. The ruins are satisfyingly complete, with a nearly intact circuit of Romano-Etruscan walls, a Roman forum, paved streets, basilicas, villas, amphitheatre and baths.

Volterra was the Etruscan city-state of Velathri. It became the important Roman municipality of Volterra in the 4th century BC. The Porta all'Arco Etrusco has a Roman arched vault on massive Etruscan bases, with three Etruscan basalt heads incorporated into the arch. The ruins of the 1st-century BC Roman theatre are outside the city walls.

Throughout the region, indeed the whole of Italy, perhaps the Romans' most significant legacy, apart from the roads, is the template they laid down for the classic town plan, with the forum – evolving into the piazza – the focal point ❏

LEFT: view from the Teatro Romano, Fiesole.

Feuds of the city-states

Between the ending of the Roman Empire in the 5th century AD and the beginning of the foreign invasions in the 16th century, the story of Italy is a catalogue of conflict between its cities, each of which was a sovereign state. Gradually, the larger absorbed the smaller. In the far south, Naples dominated the area from Rome to Sicily. In and around Rome, the popes built up a power base. In the north, Milan swallowed up all its neighbours on the Lombard plain. And in Tuscany, a three-way battle was conducted between Florence, Pisa and Siena.

In the early stages the battles between the city-states were conducted by the citizens them – dominated its neighbours. Few could control them, however, and that is why the *condottieri* system got such a bad name. The *condottieri* had a vested interest in conflict, and if there were no battles to fight then trouble was created. From being paid to fight on behalf of a city, it was a short step to blackmailing that same city into paying you not to attack them.

Some *condottieri* were bought off – Sir John Hawkwood, the infamous and piratical leader of the much-feared White Company, was given a palatial villa and a substantial estate as his reward for retiring gracefully from the fray. Hawkwood craved immortality

themselves, able-bodied men between the ages of 15 and 50 sallying forth beyond their city's walls to fight the men of the neighbouring city. When Florence crushed Arezzo in 1289 at Campaldino, the bloodshed was so great that thereafter the cities began to fight out their differences with mercenaries, the *condottieri*.

Throughout the 14th century, the *condottieri* held the balance of power. Commanding companies numbering thousands of men, they sold their services to the highest bidder. The city that could afford them – and control

ABOVE: details from Lorenzetti's *Effects of Good and Bad Government* (1338).

and wanted an equestrian statue to be erected in Florence – instead, the miserly Florentines opted for the less expensive solution of an illusionistic fresco, painted by Paolo Uccello to look like a statue, in the Cathedral in Florence.

Siena employed Guidoriccio da Fogliano as its *condottiero*, and his portrait, depicting him in ceremonial battle dress, can be seen on the walls of the Palazzo Pubblico. In the adjoining room of the palace, Lorenzetti's great fresco, *Effects of Good and Bad Government*, served as a reminder to the medieval rulers of Siena of the consequences of their decisions. Under the heading of *Bad Government*, the fresco depicts a countryside ravaged by bandits, fields left uncultivated, churches and other public buildings in ruin, and women being robbed and raped in broad daylight. By contrast, *Good Government* results in a city full of happy, well-dressed people, schoolchildren listening attentively to their lessons, and merchants prospering.

It was on these same merchants that the burden of paying the *condottieri* fell. They were caught on the horns of a dilemma, desiring domination over their trade rivals, and yet aware of the high cost of war, in terms of both taxes and economic instability. When they waged war on neighbouring cities, they often did so in the name of "Guelf" or "Ghibelline"

Outside Tuscany, many city-states fell under the dominion of a single ruler – some of them former *condottieri* who ended up rulers of the cities they once protected, founding dynasties. The Tuscan city-states and republics maintained their independence far longer, but eventually even they fell to a dynastic power, as the Medici transformed themselves from private citizens to grand dukes.

The Medici

Ruefully reflecting on the mistakes that had led him to be imprisoned and tortured before being cast from office, Niccolò Machiavelli, former Chancellor of Florence, wrote his mas-

partisanship. The Guelfs were broadly made up of the rising middle class of merchants, bankers and members of the trades guilds, who nominally supported the papacy in its long battle against the Holy Roman Emperor, and who wanted a greater role in city government. Conversely, the Ghibellines, the old feudal aristocracy, supported the emperor, because he seemed the best guarantor of their virtual autocracy. Since the emperor was often German or Spanish and an absentee ruler, paying nominal allegiance to such a distant figurehead was far preferable to the threat of the pope exercising real and temporal power closer to home.

terpiece *The Prince*, in which he admiringly recounted the ruthless methods used by the Medici to claw their way to absolute power in Tuscany, admitting that they had the gift of ruthless single-mindedness that he lacked. Even more remarkable is the way that this family threw up gifted individuals, generation after generation, and, whilst being masters of realpolitik and military strategy, also performed such an important catalytic role through their sponsorship of the arts, that Florence and Tuscany became the engine of European cultural regeneration that we know as the Renaissance.

The man who laid down the foundations for the family's meteoric rise was Giovanni de'

Medici (1360–1429), founder of the Medici bank. This was just one of 100 or so financial institutions flourishing in Florence in the 15th century, but Giovanni's master stroke was to develop a special relationship with the Church, eventually securing a monopoly over the collection of the papal revenues.

Giovanni's son, Cosimo, developed this relationship still further: one of his great coups was to attract the prestigious General Council of the Greek Orthodox and the Roman Catholic churches to Florence – the equivalent, in today's terms, of being chosen as the headquarters of the European Union, or the headquarters of a worldwide body such as the United Nations. These two great Christian churches had been at loggerheads for six centuries. Their assemblies in Florence were intended to find ways of burying their differences and creating a unified Christian church. This they failed to do, but the meetings had a lasting impact on Florence. Not only did they create a stimulating climate of theological and intellectual debate, out of which the Renaissance was to grow, but also the gorgeous dress and ceremony of the papal entourage – and the even more flamboyant and exotic manners and dress of their Greek counterparts – provided artists with a rich source of exotic subjects – the inspiration, for example, behind Benozzo Gozzoli's richly detailed fresco of the *Journey of the Magi* in the Palazzo Medici-Riccardi.

Cosimo himself eschewed such riches. He was a man who took pride in simplicity, ordering Brunelleschi, the temperamental but gifted architect of the Florence Cathedral dome, to modify his designs for the Medici palace, on the grounds that they were too ostentatious. More to his taste was the work of the architect Michelozzo, who designed the marvellously airy library in San Marco, Florence, as a repository for the Medici book collection, and as the world's first-ever public library. Such generosity was typical of Cosimo, who spent a fortune in endowing Florence with public buildings. Among his friends he counted many

of the greatest minds of the era: humanists who shared his thirst for knowledge, especially classical knowledge, for this was an era in which the lost classics of Greece and Rome – Plato, Cicero and the like – were being rediscovered and translated.

Though a devout Christian who regularly spent time in retreat in his private cell at San Marco, he believed strongly that God's grace was best leavened by a healthy dose of human intellect and reason. This made him an effective and humane ruler of the city – for that is what he was in all but name: following his father's advice to "keep always out of the public eye", Cosimo never sought public office.

Instead, he wielded immense influence behind the scenes, so that no major decision was taken in the city without his being consulted.

Lorenzo de' Medici inherited his father's love of the classical philosophers, and his gift for diplomacy. An outstanding poet in his own right, he promoted the study of Dante's works in Tuscan universities, elevating the Tuscan dialect to equal status with Latin. His greatest gift to the Italy of his day was peace. By using his diplomatic gifts to hold the great rival powers of the papacy and the Holy Roman Empire apart, Tuscany and the whole of northern Italy enjoyed a period of relative prosperity, in which merchants thrived and great

---

LEFT: *The Journey of the Magi*, by Benozzo Gozzoli (*c*.1460), in the Palazzo Medici-Riccardi; the central figure on horseback is a portrait of Lorenzo de' Medici.
RIGHT: Cosimo de' Medici, Lorenzo's father, by Pontormo (*c*.1518).

fortunes were made. With the countryside no longer ravaged by war or held to ransom by lawless mercenaries, wealthy individuals began to build the villas that are still such a characteristic feature of the Tuscan countryside. Lorenzo himself led the way, retreating regularly to his rural retreats at Fiesole and Poggio a Caiano, where he enjoyed breeding racehorses and ornamental hens.

Bonfires of vanity

Prophetically, Pope Innocent VIII declared that "the peace of Italy is at an end" on learning of Lorenzo's death in 1492. From that moment on, the sounds of battle were heard again and again

were collected and smashed, or burned in what Savonarola termed "bonfires of vanity". Botticelli supported the movement, recanting of his past fondness for Neoplatonic ideas, turning from such mesmerising paintings as the *Birth of Venus* and the *Primavera* to equally complex Christian allegories, such as the mystic *Nativity*.

Michelangelo carved his *David*, the boy hero standing up to the bullying giant Goliath, as a symbol of the city's desire to rid itself of the Medici. He also helped to design and build new defences for the city, but when the combined forces of the Medici and Holy Roman Emperor held the city to siege in 1530, he took

at the gates of northern Italian cities, during a period in which the aspirations of small city-states to remain independent were dashed by powerful imperial or papal armies. Lacking the wisdom, intelligence and political acumen of earlier generations of the Medici, Lorenzo's successors were expelled from the city as Savonarola, the firebrand Dominican preacher, filled his fellow Florentines with anti-Medici zeal, shrewdly claiming that their love of pagan philosophers and fondness for the depiction of pagan gods in painting and sculpture would bring God's wrath upon the city.

Erotic art, fine clothing, secular poetry, mirrors, bronzes and sculptures of all sorts

himself off to hide – irony of ironies – in the Medici mortuary chapel, attached to San Lorenzo church. Vasari attributes his cowardice to the artistic temperament, and while he was in hiding he worked the masterly reclining figures of *Dawn*, *Evening*, *Day* and *Night*, which now adorn the tombs of two minor members of the Medici family.

Alessandro de' Medici, who led the victorious siege of the city, rubbed salt in the wounds of his fellow citizens by having himself crowned Duke of Florence, claiming absolute power for himself where his predecessors had been content with influence. When he was murdered in 1537 by his own cousin, with whom he had been having a homosexual affair, the city was relieved of one burden but faced with another – that of choosing a successor, since Alessandro had no natural heir. Various candidates were canvassed, and it was Cosimo, descended from Giovanni de' Medici via the female line, who emerged victor, partly by persuading his fellow citizens that he would appoint counsellors and consult widely before making decisions.

Once in power, Cosimo revealed his true colours, as he systematically set about destroying all opposition. Not only was he unrelenting in his pursuit of the republican leaders who had opposed his election, tracking them down in

cany into political unity and established security in the region, he also set up an effective civil service to administer the dukedom, based in the Uffizi (literally, the "Offices") in Florence, which proved effective right up to the point when Tuscany joined the United Kingdom of Italy in 1861. So effective was this civil service that Tuscany continued to be ruled effectively even when, as so often happened, Cosimo's successors proved to be corrupt, incompetent, self-indulgent or mad. Few made their mark on the city in quite the same way as the earlier generation, though Cosimo II did the world a great favour by patronising Galileo, making him court mathematician to the Medici

their exile and bringing them back to be tried and executed in Florence, he also set about conquering old enemies – Pisa, Siena, Massa Marittima, Montepulciano – with a ruthlessness and brutality that is still remembered and resented to this day. The whole story is told on the ceiling of the Palazzo Vecchio council chamber in a series of bloody frescoes painted by Vasari to honour Cosimo I in 1563–5.

To his credit, Cosimo not only forced Tus-

LEFT: the 15th-century Villa Medicea di Castello.
ABOVE: one of the battle scenes decorating the Hall of the Great Council in the Palazzo Vecchio by Vasari, depicting Florence's victories over Pisa and Siena.

and providing him with a home after his trial and excommunication by the Inquisition.

The family also amassed an astonishing art collection, which Princess Anna Maria Lodovica, the last of the Medici line, bequeathed to the city of Florence at her death in 1743, along with all the Medici palaces and gardens, ensuring that many of the greatest works of the Renaissance were not sold off or dispersed, but would remain in the city that gave them birth. Today, these priceless works form the backbone of Florence's three main galleries: the Uffizi, the Pitti and the Bargello.

For more about Renaissance art and architecture see pages 43–52.

Unification and war

Since the glories of Rome and the Renaissance, Italy has written little history. The head of Italy's Bureau of Statistics likens modern Italian history to a muddle, "a happy antheap where everyone is running about and no one is in control". The alternative is the "strong man" view of recent history, as expressed in the Florentine saying, "Whose bread and cheese I eat, to his tune I dance". But, while Rome danced to martial music, Tuscany sometimes starved or burned.

Tuscany has been buffeted rather than enriched by its recent past. Well-kept war memorials in shabby towns attest to the loss of two generations, one abroad and one at home. Look at Asciano, a village dwarfed by its Carabinieri stronghold, built by Benito Mussolini and still used to this day to maintain law and order. Visit Montisi where, for the price of a drink, locals will describe the German bombing of the village tower, a story complete with sound effects, gestures and genuine sorrow. Ask proud Florentines why the medieval houses on the south side of the Arno are lost for ever.

In 1865 Florence briefly became the capital of the newly united Italy. Although its exalted role would only last five years before Rome was then made the permanent capital, Florence underwent profound and rapid change during

THE GROWTH OF THE GRAND TOUR

Tuscany – particularly Florence – has been a magnet to foreign visitors since the 17th century, when a few adventurous eccentrics ventured forth into this strange land. By the 1700s, rich aristocrats were attracted to the region's alien psyche, perfect climate, low cost of living and undervalued works of art. Florence became an essential stop on any European tour.

But it was only in the 18th century that the middle classes joined the aristocratic dilettanti and literati on the road to Tuscany. Art was well and truly on the agenda, with foreign visitors flocking to see the Uffizi sculptures and Botticelli's *Birth of Venus*. By the 1850s, escapees

from mid-Victorian England had made Florence *"une ville anglaise"*, according to the Goncourt brothers.

At the turn of the 20th century, the Anglo-Florentine community was well established, although World War I chased many away. The Grand Tour resumed in the 1920s and 1930s, but mainly for society figures and intellectuals rather than for leisured young aristocrats. The tradition continues to this day, with sons and daughters of the Establishment coming to learn Italian and attend art courses on the Renaissance – while others come to enjoy the designer labels and the shopping rather than the artistic treasures.

this time. An ambitious plan of expansion and modernisation sadly led to the demolition of among other things the old city walls, and their replacement with a wide ring of avenues punctuated with large piazzas in keeping with the French urban taste of the times. Quarters for the middle classes and the Piazzale Michelangelo were built. Later, old areas of the centre including the Ghetto were declared to be in dangerous condition and unwholesome, and were razed; the soulless Piazza della Repubblica was created partly in their place. The square remains a bold flourish of nationhood, but when the capital was transferred to Rome, Tuscan allegiance unquestionably remained in

enough, but the end result is still only to be seen abroad or at international football matches.

Unification represented a missed chance for Italy. By failing to help shape a national identity, Tuscans also fell victim to the clearer vision of a "strong man". Even before World War I, Mussolini was making inflammatory speeches while a weak parliament practised the art of "timely resignation", a ploy used ever since to stage-manage a new coalition.

Although the pre-war Tuscan economy thrived under weak government, it was no match for growing social pressures and a deepening gulf between society and state. With few real policies, one of the last liberal

Tuscany. Unification, under the leadership of Count Camillo Benso Cavour, a French-speaking Piedmontese, was seen as a foreign threat to the de facto sovereignty of Florence and the smaller city-states. Defenders of the Risorgimento, the Movement for Italian Unification, appealed to nascent patriotism. Critics of unification cited Dante's pleas to Tuscan liberty before both sides settled down to start subverting the power of the new rulers. The welding of Tuscans into Italians started promisingly

governments blundered into World War I. Italy's unpopular late entry cost Tuscan lives and support. The pyrrhic victory was exacerbated by a power vacuum, economic problems and a revolutionary working class. Benito Mussolini, from neighbouring Emilia, wasted no opportunity in proclaiming, "Governing Italy is not only impossible, it is useless," before proceeding to govern it impossibly but fairly usefully for 20 years.

By 1922, the corporate state was literally under construction. The economic benefits lasted until 1929, but the aesthetic effects linger on in functionally "improved" cities all over Tuscany. Florence station, from which trains

LEFT: American Grand Tourist Allen Smith contemplating the Arno, by François-Xavier Fabre (1797).
ABOVE: Montecatini in the early 1900s.

Foreign Writers in Tuscany

The poet Shelley pronounced Tuscany a "paradise of exiles" tempted by art, adventure and escape from persecution. But the exiles' motives were as varied as their prose styles. Tobias Smollett (1721–71), the misanthropic Scottish writer, found nothing to admire in Tuscany. He failed to appreciate the entrepreneurial nature of the Tuscan aristocracy, finding it undignified for "a noble to sell a pound of figs or to take money for a glass of sour wine". The Romantics were more enthusiastic. Lord Byron

threw himself into Renaissance art and was "dazzled, drunk with Beauty" in Santa Croce. His friend Shelley adored Pisan landscapes and Livornese seascapes, tragically drowning near La Spezia. Tuscany soon became a pilgrimage for the later Romantic poets, such as Tennyson and Wordsworth.

Although officially a diplomat in Florence, French novelist, Stendhal, spent most of his time absorbing Renaissance frescoes and planning his novel, *Le Rouge et le Noir* (1830). As with Byron, the Santa Croce Effect sent Stendhal reeling: once outside, "I walked in constant fear of falling to the ground." This aesthetic sickness is now known as the Stendhal Syndrome.

Henry James was one of the few foreign writers able to see through Tuscany's literary and artistic veil, taking a more pragmatic approach. His *Portrait of Places* gives an opinionated but sensitive picture of the region in the 1870s.

The most romantic mid-Victorian couple was undoubtedly the poets Elizabeth Barrett Browning and Robert Browning. Robert brought his wife to Florence because of her poor health. There he cunningly used local Chianti to wean Elizabeth off her long addiction to laudanum. Their 15th-century *palazzo*, redecorated in Victorian style, is now a literary museum and writers' haunt.

The 20th century brought E.M. Forster, with his ironic analysis of the resident English community at play. Forster's *A Room with a View* is famous for its portrayal of the heroine's encounter with alien culture and passions. Virginia Woolf, along with many other writers on Tuscany, saw her own image reflected in the landscape, "infinite emptiness, loneliness, silence…", while D.H. Lawrence, living in his "grave old Tuscan villa", imagined he was communing with the original Etruscans.

World War II prevented further literary flowering, but in *War In Val d'Orcia*, Iris Origo, an Anglo-Florentine, painted a dramatic picture of the Tuscan battlefield. As a young woman Origo was part of Lawrence's artistic circle, but her understanding of the Tuscans set her apart. Soon after the war, the Welsh poet Dylan Thomas came to Tuscany for the first time and was entranced: "The pine hills are endless, the cypresses at the hilltop tell one all about the length of death, the woods are deep as love and full of goats." He apparently enjoyed a hedonistic lifestyle, vegetating in the sun and devouring strawberries and wine at only 20 lire a glass.

Tuscany still draws literary pilgrims. Frances Mayes's recent best-seller, *Under the Tuscan Sun,* has brought a fresh wave of American tourists in search of the Tuscan experience. The irony is that tourism is in danger of destroying the Tuscan idyll visitors have come in search of for centuries.   ❑

LEFT: Virginia Woolf saw "loneliness".

presumably ran on time, was the first Functionalist station in Italy. At the outbreak of World War II, most Tuscans were cautiously neutral. Mussolini, despite having signed the Pact of Steel with Germany, only entered the war in 1940, after the fall of France. By 1943 the north was under German control, but the Allies were progressing northwards from Sicily. Allied bombing, German entrenchment and an emerging Tuscan Resistance transformed Tuscany into a battleground.

Anti-Fascist cells had been secretly set up by the Communists and Catholics in key towns under German and neo-Fascist control. Florence was split: while it was the intellectual centre of

winter behind the so-called "Gothic Line" in the Apennines. Apart from Florence, the partisans were very active in the Monte Amiata area, as well as in the Val d'Orcia where the writer Iris Origo, an Englishwoman married to an Italian *marchese*, sheltered many refugees and prisoners of war in her villa, La Foce.

Writing about it at the time, she grimly observed, "In the last few days I have seen Radicofani and Cortignano destroyed, the countryside and farms studded with shell holes, girls raped, and human beings and cattle killed. Otherwise the events of the last week have had little effect upon either side; it is the civilians who have suffered."

the Resistance it also harboured strong Fascist sympathisers. Even after the city was captured by the Allies, individual Fascists held out, firing from the rooftops. Surprising loyalties emerged: while the director of the British Institute was a known Fascist sympathiser, the German consul risked his life to protect Florentines who had been denounced. After the liberation he was granted the freedom of the city.

Florence was liberated in August 1943, but Mussolini and the German forces survived the

ABOVE: Hitler and Mussolini salute at Florence's Tomb of the Fascist Martyrs.

Nor were the Allies completely blameless. The modernity of Grosseto, Livorno and Pisa today owes much to Allied bombing in 1943. The British War Office reports naturally exonerated the Allies: "No damage of any significance is attributable to Allied action [in Florence]." The Allies issued their troops with booklets listing various buildings to be protected, including the tricky prospect of safeguarding the "living museum" of Florence: "The whole city of Florence must rank as a work of art of the first importance." According to one report, "The great monuments, nearly all of which lie north of the river, escaped practically undamaged because, though the enemy held the northern bank against an advance, our troops deliberately refrained from firing upon them."

Commendable feats of Allied bravery included the penetration of enemy lines via the Vasari Corridor, a secret route used by the Medici in similar crises. Despite Allied concern and care, Florence nevertheless lost innumerable bridges, streets, libraries, churches, *palazzi*, paintings and Tuscan lives. But in contrast to the "mutilated victory" of 1919, Italy lost the war but won the peace.

Massimo Salvatore, a supporter of the partisans in Florence, saw the war as a character-building exercise: "Without it [we] would surely have sunk into a morass of low politics and intrigues." That was still to come.

"Red-belt" Tuscany

Tuscans may be conservative by nature, but they are also fiercely independent. Since World War II, they have tended to vote for right-wing governments nationally but for left-wing councils locally. Until recently, this meant Christian Democracy at national level and Communism at regional level. On the surface, this appeared a rather curious recipe for success.

Given the level of national opposition to Communists, the Communist Party evolved an aggressively pro-regionalist stance. The reward

THE FLOODING OF FLORENCE

When the Arno broke its banks in 1966, the havoc caused to the city's heritage was immediate: Santa Croce was soon under water; the Duomo lost sections of its marble façade; panels from the Baptistery doors were swept away; statues from the Arno bridges were lost; over a million antiquarian books and illuminated manuscripts were destroyed; and countless artworks were damaged. Although most works have been restored to their original state, Cimabue's *Crucifix* in Santa Croce was controversially left semi-restored. Instead of re-creating the missing sections of the work, restorers simply painted in the spaces with patches of neutral colour, intended to symbolise the city's "wound".

Since the flood, attempts have been made to ensure that the disaster will not be repeated; the river bed near the Ponte Vecchio has been deepened, and the river banks around Ponte Amerigo Vespucci have been reinforced by massive walls. Changes in the river's level are scrupulously monitored by computers and video cameras. Throughout the city, both inside and on the façades of buildings, small plaques have been mounted on the walls, showing the 1966 flood levels. This is especially striking in the area around Santa Croce, one of the lowest parts of the city. The actual water marks are still visible on some buildings which have not been repainted since the disaster.

was the "red belt" across central Italy, run by left-wing coalitions since the first regional elections in 1970. Red Tuscany formed the central strand between Emilia Romagna's model economy and rural Umbria. Despite the transformations in the "new Italy", the "red" regions survive under broad left labels as some of the most efficient of regional governments.

The Tuscan left believes in a broad but increasingly secular Church. Civic culture, regional pride and fierce individualism form the real faith. The power of the left is as much a reflection of regional hostility to Roman centralisation as an espousal of social democratic principles. Even in "red-belt" Tuscany,

ments suffered from opportunism, not lack of opportunity. *Partitocrazia* (party influence) supplanted democracy, extending from government to public corporations, infiltrating banking, the judiciary and media, and the public tacitly condoned this "old boys' network".

Corruption and terror

The early 1990s saw a series of political scandals involving bribes, and the result was the *Mani Pulite* ("Clean Hands") campaign under the fiery leadership of Antonio di Pietro, a former magistrate who became Italy's most popular public figure when he spearheaded inquiries into corrupt practices in politics, business and

the region's most popular newspaper is the right-wing but regional *La Nazione*, not the left-wing but national *La Repubblica*. How could a Roman product possibly compete with a Florentine/Sienese masterpiece?

At a national level, however, by the early 1990s, more than 50 post-war "swing-door" governments had come and gone. To many observers, the source of this crisis lay in Italy's administration and dubious morality. Senior party leaders tended to die in office, govern-

LEFT: pictures from the Uffizi laid out for restoration after the 1966 flood.
ABOVE: Craxi and Andreotti shake hands.

state administration. A seemingly vast network was uncovered, in which public contracts were awarded by politicians to businesses in return for bribes. Italian public life was convulsed by the scandal, dubbed *Tangentopoli* – literally, "Bribesville". Dozens of MPs and businessmen came under investigation. A number of these were preventively held in jail; some even took their lives. The Christian Democrat Party, which had dominated Italian politics since the war, collapsed under the weight of its own corruption. Two former prime ministers – the socialist Bettino Craxi and the Christian Democrat veteran and seven times former prime minister Giulio Andreotti – were investigated.

Craxi slipped through the net and died in self-imposed exile in Tunisia in January 2000, with international arrest warrants hanging over his head for a string of corruption charges and convictions. Andreotti, who was instead charged with Mafia ties, was eventually let off after a mammoth trial lasting years. His acquittal was later held up on appeal by state prosecutors. However, in a long report published afterwards to show how they had reached their decision, appeal judges said that Andreotti had been found to have enjoyed "friendly" and direct relations with the Mafia "up until 1980", but not later – meaning that due to statutory time limitations he could not now be prosecuted.

to force the Italian state into submission, and to agree to a deal of mutual convenience with the Mob, as had been enjoyed with the Christian Democrats. The jailed Sicilian Godfather, Salvatore "Toto" Riina, was sentenced to life for the Uffizi bombing, along with other crime bosses in 1998. However, the more refined minds thought to have been behind the attacks have never been brought to book.

Meanwhile, while no area of Italy appeared to have been left untouched by corruption, including Florence which had its share of scandal, in the end few if any *Tangentopoli* politicians served any real time in jail. Many, initially ostracised, were later rehabilitated, while a

In the midst of the political upheaval, in May 1993 Florence suffered yet another devastating blow, when a bomb planted by the Mafia behind the Uffizi gallery rocked the city, both physically and psychologically. Five people were killed, and priceless paintings and sculptures damaged, while a handful were destroyed. The fabric of the Uffizi's buildings was damaged, and several medieval buildings around the corner were virtually destroyed, while the *pensione* used to film the Merchant-Ivory film adaptation of *A Room With a View* was so devastated that it was forced to close for good.

The Mafia's widely perceived aim was to use the attack, and others in Milan and Rome,

number of those originally embroiled have since returned to politics, "running", as the writer Ennio Flaiano once said of Italians in general, "in aid of the winner".

In a frank interview in July 2005, film director Bernardo Bertolucci told the *Corriere della Sera*: "Italy lost a great opportunity after *Tangentopoli*. It should have had a real examination of conscience, in order to understand how on earth it could be that there were so many corrupt figures populating our landscape, accomplices of a system which goes from small tips in return for small favours, to large *tangenti* [bribes] for big contracts. And instead we have wound up with an illegal prime minister, who was elected amid conditions of almost complete control of the media." He was referring to Silvio Berlusconi, the media tycoon turned prime minister.

Silvio Berlusconi

Elected in March 1994 on an anti-corruption ticket and depicting himself as the new face of Italy, his centre-right coalition – including neo-Fascist elements – resoundingly collapsed in November the same year, after he came under investigation himself for graft. Following his extraordinary return to power in June 2001 with the largest majority in post-war history – despite the by now many accusations of corruption against him – he immediately set about

house, Mondadori, leading daily paper *Il Giornale*, the popular news magazine *Panorama*, and three commercial TV channels representing nearly half of Italy's viewing figures. Thanks to his indirect control also of state broadcasting, from where his satirical opponents have meanwhile been banished, he is thought to control one way or another some 95 percent of Italian television. Berlusconi's opponents point to a glaring conflict of interests between his roles as businessman and prime minister, and say he shamelessly uses his TV channels to promote his cause. Berlusconi the populist shrugs this off: "The people decide," he says; and the people have, until now, over-

pushing through a series of laws to spare himself and his cronies from prosecution. A number of politicians whose career had appeared to be finished in the wake of *Tangentopoli* had meanwhile joined his coalition, including from apparently opposed and incompatible parties at the other end of the spectrum.

Berlusconi heads an empire that spans telecommunications to insurance and building. It includes top football club AC Milan, the Mediolanum bank, Italy's largest publishing

looked everything in favour of political stability and strong, if idiosyncratic, leadership.

But in the face of a failing economy and continued allegations of bribery and corruption, Berlusconi will struggle to win the population over before the April 2006 election. Italians are now vowing that never again will they make the same mistake of voting him into power. However, despite opinion polls being strongly in their favour, the centre-left opposition, led by ex-prime minister Romano Prodi, have so far done everything possible to hurt their own cause, especially due to internal divisions. A defeat for Berlusconi, while it should be the logical outcome, is by no means certain.   ❑

LEFT: aftermath of the 1993 bombing of the Uffizi.
ABOVE: anti-war demonstrators at the European Social Forum, held in Florence in 2002.

Decisive Dates

Etruscans and Romans

800–500 BC Etruscan civilisation flourishes. Etruria Propria, a confederation of 12 states, includes Arezzo, Cortona, Chiusi, Fiesole, Populonia, Roselle, Vetulonia, Volterra.

480–290 BC Romans in power; they annex Etruria and found colonies at Ansedonia, Roselle, Volterra, Luni and Lucca.

80 BC Faesulae (now Fiesole) becomes a Roman military colony.

59 BC A colony of Roman army veterans founds Florentia (Florence) on the banks of the Arno.

AD 200–600 Region invaded by Lombards, Goths and Franks.

AD 306 Constantinople becomes capital of Roman Empire; the Byzantine period follows.

AD 476 The Fall of Rome.

Medieval Tuscany

1000–1300 German emperors conquer Italy, followed by constant warring between Guelfs (supporters of the papacy) and Ghibellines (supporters of the Holy Roman Empire).

1062 Pisan navy wins an overwhelming victory over the Saracens in a battle off Palermo.

1115 Florence is granted the status of a *comune* – an independent city governed by a council drawn from the mercantile class.

1118 The consecration of Pisa Cathedral.

1125 Florence begins its expansion with the takeover of Fiesole.

1173 Bonnano Pisano begins work on Pisa Cathedral's campanile, now known as the Leaning Tower.

1246 Work on Florence's Santa Maria Novella begins.

1250 Florence's Bargello built.

1260 Sienese defeat the Florentines in battle of Montaperti.

1289 Florence crushes Arezzo.

1294 Arnolfo di Cambio begins work on Florence's Santa Croce church.

1296 Di Cambio begins work on Florence's Duomo, which – excepting the dome – was completed in 1369.

1301–11 Giovanni Pisano sculpts the pulpit in Pisa cathedral.

1310 Siena's Palazzo Pubblico is completed.

1314 Dante Alighieri begins work on *The Divine Comedy*.

1330 Andrea Pisano is commissioned to design and cast bronze doors for Florence Baptistery.

1334 Giotto di Bondone begins work on the Florentine Campanile.

1338 Pietro Lorenzetti paints the *Good and Bad Government* fresco in Siena's Palazzo Pubblico.

***c.*1345** Florence's Ponte Vecchio is erected by Taddeo Gaddi.

1348 Black death strikes Florence, killing a third of the population.

1350 Boccaccio starts work on *The Decameron*.

1390 John Hawkwood, *condottiero*, becomes Captain General of Florence; inter-city wars fought.

The Renaissance

1406 Pisa is defeated and becomes part of the Florentine state.

1420 Papacy returns to Rome from Avignon.

1421 Florentines pay the Genoese 100,000 florins for Livorno.

1425 Masaccio paints the *Life of St Peter* frescoes in Santa Maria del Carmine.

1434–64 Cosimo de' Medici rules Florence.

1436 Brunelleschi's dome for Florence's Duomo is completed.

1452 Alberti's *Ten Books on Architecture* is published.

1469–92 Lorenzo de' Medici rules Florence.

1478 Sandro Botticelli paints *La Primavera*.

1498 "Mad monk" Savonarola is hanged for heresy in Florence's Piazza della Signoria.

1504 Michelangelo completes *David*.

1513 Niccolò Machiavelli writes *The Prince*.

1527 The sack of Rome.

1530 The Republic of Florence ends as armies of Pope Clement VII and Emperor Charles V besiege the city.

1537 Alessandro de' Medici is murdered by his cousin.

1550 Giorgio Vasari's *Lives of the Most Excellent Architects, Painters and Sculptors* first published.

1554 Florence defeats Siena and incorporates its rival into the Florentine state.

1564–1642 The Pisan Galileo Galilei discovers the principles of dynamics.

Grand Duchy Tuscany

1716 Decree issued by the Grand Duke of Tuscany defines boundaries of Chianti and establishes laws governing production and sale of wine.

1737 Gian Gastone, the last male Medici, dies.

1796 Napoleon's first Italian campaign.

1815 The Grand Duchy is absorbed into the Austrian Empire.

Wartime Tuscany

1848 The War of Independence.

1861 The proclamation of the Kingdom of Italy.

1865–71 Florence is briefly capital of Italy; the Piazza della Repubblica is built in 1865 to celebrate.

1915 Italy enters World War I on the Allies' side.

1922 Benito Mussolini comes to power.

1940 Italy forms pact with Germany and Japan, and enters World War II against Britain and France.

1943 The fall of the Fascists. Mussolini is executed at the end of the war, in 1945.

1946 Italy becomes a republic.

LEFT: Lorenzo de' Medici.
RIGHT: debris from the 1966 flood outside Santa Croce, Florence.

Modern Tuscany

1957 The Treaty of Rome; Italy is a founder member of the EEC (now the European Union).

1966 Massive flooding: the Arno overflows in Florence and many works of art are damaged.

1970 The first regional elections held.

1989 The Leaning Tower of Pisa is closed in response to its increasing tilt.

1993 A terrorist bomb in Florence kills five people and damages the Uffizi.

1994 Italy adopts a first-past-the-post electoral system. A right-wing government ushers in the Second Republic.

1996 The electorate does an about-turn and elects Romano Prodi's left-wing Ulivo Party.

1996–7 Freak fires and floods ravage much of the region, killing at least 14 people.

2000 Top Mafia bosses Filippo Graviano and Leoluca Bagarella are imprisoned for their part in the Uffizi bombing.

2001 Silvio Berlusconi is elected prime minister. His Forza Italia party governs in coalition with the National Alliance and the Northern League.

2001 Tower of Pisa reopens to the public.

2002 The euro replaces the lira.

2005 Pope John Paul II dies and is succeeded by Cardinal Joseph Ratzinger, elected 265th pope, who takes the name Benedict XVI.

2006 General election scheduled for April. ❏

TUSCANY TODAY

The challenges facing modern Tuscans are many, and include
achieving a successful blend of the old and the new

Pienza is typical Tuscany. This tower-capped 15th-century village gazing imperiously over lush valleys is everything an Italophile could wish for – so much so that this town of 2,300 has 100,000 visitors a year. In the rush to enjoy rustic perfection, tourism has turned high-season Pienza into an elbow-to-elbow mêlée. And this is Tuscany's dilemma. Her beauty is in danger of becoming her beast. While Rome does government and Milan does commerce, La Toscana does cypress-lined rolling hills and the Renaissance. The region's wealth is her landscape and heritage, and the question for the 21st century is how to preserve this and at the same time find room for 10 million tourists a year.

The price of tourism

Florence's long-standing relationship with tourism is finely balanced. The city that invented the Stendhal Syndrome – the dizzying disorientation some visitors experience when they overdose on Florentine Renaissance masterpieces – is in danger of sending tourists' heads spinning from hours spent queuing to enter its famous sites.

There are also concerns that tourism could affect the city's character. Historic artisan shops are struggling with rent hikes, as landlords try to maximise profits. And landmark stops on the Grand Tour itinerary are striving to keep their dignity; Piazza Donatello's cemetery – the burial place of English poet Elizabeth Barrett

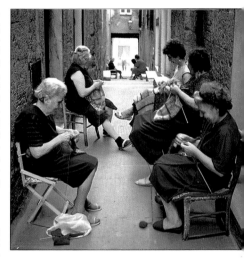

Browning – is now visited to the honking soundtrack of traffic on roads which threaten to overwhelm this once quiet oasis.

For residents and visitors alike, traffic pollution is a blot on the landscape. On hot, windless days the city is shrouded in a cloudy pall. The traffic police complain that their 600-strong force was designed to cope with Florence's 400,000 residents, not the summer population of millions. Noise and air pollution harm major buildings and modern sensibilities. In the historic centre, pollution has been reduced, but some residents complain that restrictions on traffic in the centre merely lead to the clogging of the *viali*, Florence's arteries.

LEFT: Florence draws huge crowds all year round.
RIGHT: in Tuscan villages domesticity still reigns.

On the positive side, despite rising rents, the sons and daughters of the artisan community continue to run the family businesses. And swathes of Florence resist "Macdonaldisation", remaining as they did when Barrett Browning took refuge in the city in the 1800s. At the same time the local council is spending on the infrastructure of the city, which is in a constant state of restoration. And as any Tuscan not from the region's capital will tell you, the Fiorentini are far too proud to let their heritage disappear.

Tuscany's second city, Pisa, is also grappling with the quick-fire habits of the modern tourist. With day-tripper coaches decanting passengers on a racing schedule to take in the

The city's recent tourist trump card is the budget airlines' choice of Galileo Galilei airport as their regional hub; but the town doesn't want to be Tuscany's airport lounge – Pisa needs visitors to come for more than just a photo of the tower.

In the countryside, the same problems which face Florence and Pisa are played out on a smaller scale. But for Tuscany's hill towns there is an extra resonance to the money and opportunities tourism brings.

The countryside revival

World War II shattered rural life in Tuscany – ending the feudal *mezzadria* system, with land governed by a few rich aristocrats. With the

highlights of the Campo Dei Miracoli in as short a time as possible, the rest of Pisa often goes unnoticed. This is not surprising. No city in the world is as closely associated with one single monument as Pisa is with her tower. Even during the 1990s, when the marble miracle was in architectural intensive care and out of bounds to visitors, most tourists still failed to notice that there was life outside the Campo.

To encourage visitors to enjoy the unhurried, bookish atmosphere of the Pisa beyond the Tower, local government has refurbished the market area around Piazza delle Vettovaglie. And the Arno river, with its boat tours and festivals, is being touted as the Pisan "left bank".

paternalistic social structure that had sustained the countryside for centuries gone, thousands of farmers and villagers abandoned their homes and headed for the towns and cities in search of jobs. Many left Italy never to return. Villages which had been the hub of rural life for thousands of years became ghost towns overnight.

To generate local jobs, some areas turned themselves over to industrial production. Textiles, chemicals, petroleum and fertiliser factories spread though the region. And though they provided much-needed employment for the now landless peasantry, the visual impact on the countryside was less than welcome. Today they sit uncomfortably alongside the rustic charm that characterises the region. For those who remained in their villages and farms, life was hard. Typically the older ones clung on – and with no children in the schools, or young blood to energise the economy, the countryside was drifting into a decaying slumber.

Monticchiello's response to these seismic changes was unique. Thirty-five years ago this village of 500 people in the bobbing hills of the Orcia valley decided to write and perform a play about their plight. Four decades on, the *teatro povero* is an annual event. The plays' themes have charted the fall and rise of rural Tuscan life. Early productions were pleas to the young people not to leave, and calls for the

'70s, saw the empty farmhouses as an opportunity to create a rural idyll. Not surprisingly, the peasant farmers who had abandoned their homes to posterity could not believe their luck, and news soon spread that foreigners were prepared to pay good money for crumbling piles.

The few became many, and now over 100,000 farmhouses have been brought back to life. The British presence gave birth to the nickname Chiantishire. Residents of this very English Italy include writers John Mortimer, Muriel Spark and Harold Pinter, while political Italophiles include multi-millionaire Labour MP Geoffrey Robinson, who regularly hosts the Blair family at his home near San Gimignano.

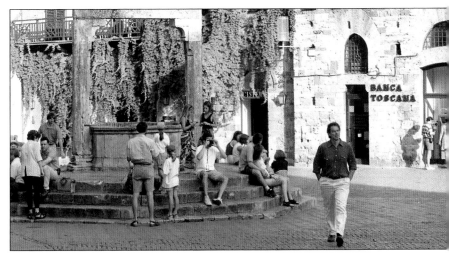

government to sustain traditional rural life. More recent dramas have dealt with the reverse phenomenon: wealthy people moving from the cities in search of an idealised Tuscan rural "lifestyle". This constant flow of newcomers into the region's peasant heartland threatens to overwhelm the character of the area. As Monticchiello's director Andrea Cresti puts it, rural Tuscany is in danger of becoming "a brand too successful for its own good".

The early days of this "brand" was pioneered by Germans and Britons who, in the 1960s and

Tuscans protest that the Chiantishire commuters have pushed prices so high that locals can't afford to live in their native villages. Foreigners counter this by pointing out that they saved places like Sovicille near Siena, or Bugnano near Lucca from total abandonment, and that blaming *"stranieri"* is simply passport prejudice, because wealthy Florentines and Pisans are just as busy buying second homes as foreigners. Tuscan landowners themselves have benefited from the revival of the countryside. *Agriturismo* – farm stays – are increasingly popular, both as a way of making the farm pay, and as an opportunity for locals to restore or convert outhouses and barns.

LEFT: Florence in seven languages.
ABOVE: Tony Blair is a regular visitor to 'Chiantishire'.

Though the medieval *mezzadria* system of share-cropping was officially banned in 1978, old traditions die hard. The scale of farming in most of the region is small; apart from some large wheat and cattle farms in the Val d'Arno and Val di Chiana, much of the farming is labour-intensive, relatively unmechanised and organic. Partly through poverty and partly through tradition, Tuscany has gained itself a reputation as Europe's leading region for small-scale sustainable farming.

Tuscany's countryside traditions have deep roots. Lucca's olive trees date back to Roman times, and the region's ancient vineyards are terraced onto slopes which have been cultivated for wine for centuries. And, after decades of intensive logging which left some parts of the Casentino forest slopes bare, official protection has seen the fir, beech and maple trees recover. Even the wild wolves which were once lost to this part of the country are back.

Environmental issues

But there is still much work to be done if tourism and the environment are going to co-exist. The *legambiente* (environmental league), which monitors pollution on Italy's beaches, gives the Tuscan Riviera a mixed report: while some of the beaches are clean, others exceed pollution levels by 10 times the acceptable level.

A TUSCAN HALL OF FAME

There's a saying that Tuscany is "equally blessed by the genius of man and nature". And history has proved the proverb, with the greatest of the region's greats achieving worldwide fame. Not surprisingly, many of the province's superstars are from the world of art: Giotto, Leonardo da Vinci, Michelangelo, Donatello, Masaccio and Cellini were all born in or near Florence. And Giorgio Vasari – also a painter – is famed for his much-read *Lives of the Artists*.

Literary celebrities include the writer triumvirate Dante, Petrarch and Boccaccio (born in Paris, but raised in Florence). While in the field of music, the composer Puccini hailed from Lucca, and opera itself was born in Florence in the late 1500s. Tuscany was also home to the astronomer Galileo, father of modern mathematics, Leonardo Fibonacci, the philosopher Machiavelli, architect Brunelleschi and merchant-turned-explorer Amerigo Vespucci.

Many famous modern-day Tuscans are associated with the fashion world, such as Emilio Pucci, Guccio Gucci and Salvatore Ferragamo (a transplanted Neapolitan). While showbiz representatives include singer Andrea Bocelli, film-makers Franco Zeffirelli and the Taviani brothers, producer-cum-politician Vittorio Cecchi Gori and the Oscar-winning film-maker and comedian Roberto Benigni.

The river Arno, which flows 240 km (150 miles) through the heart of Tuscany, has suffered from decades of industrial development. A critical problem for people living near the Arno is flooding. Heavy rains bring the water up to dangerous levels, most notoriously in 1966 when it rose 6 metres (20 ft), causing death and destruction and compromising Florence's cultural heritage. After years of debate, the authorities are finally taking action by building expansion chambers to reduce the risk of future floods.

Engineers are also constructing Florence's first-ever sewage-treatment plant. Currently, waste from Florence flows directly into the Arno, in stark contravention of EU directives. have suffered far less from the Disneyfication that has infected central Tuscany. And to the west, the Maremma is still imbued with a sense of mystery and rural isolation, its wild pine woods a reminder that Tuscany is blessed with more forest than any other region in Italy. And in these unspoilt environments lies the region's magnetic charm. True Tuscans are provincial, conservative and independent; civic culture and regional pride are their touchstones, and as a consequence the quality of life – both urban and rural – is generally good; nobody is prepared to jeopardise this by turning the region over to heavy industry. The industries Tuscans speak of with pride, such as Siena's

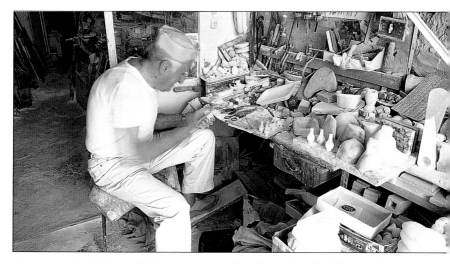

A treatment plant is being built at Lastra, just outside Florence, and it is hoped that a cleaned-up river will be an opportunity to revive the river banks for leisure.

Tuscany's allure

Outside the Florence–Siena axis the effects of modern tourism are far less visible. Here another Tuscany emerges; the Apuan Alps and Garfagnana region in the north with their rugged mountains, plunging valleys and marble mines,

LEFT: Tuscan-born Roberto Benigni with fellow Oscar-winning actors. **ABOVE:** alabaster craftsman in Volterra.

panforte, Carrara's marble, Volterra's alabaster and Arezzo gold, date back to medieval times.

For all its Dantesque grandiloquence and Renaissance finery, Tuscany's heart is rural. Its largest city is home to less than half a million people, and the nickname for Tuscans is *"Mangiafagioli"* (bean eaters). So it is perhaps not surprising that the province's most loved son is a child of countryside Arezzo. Italy's tragicomic clown prince – Oscar-winning film-maker and actor Roberto Benigni – speaks lovingly of his homeland as "a region of hunters and hares, of large peasant women and wild and poetic beauty". And who would argue with Tuscany's "grande Roberto"? ❑

RENAISSANCE ART

Art historians divide the Renaissance into three sub-periods:
the Trecento (1300s) was the era of the workshop and fresco;
the Quattrocento (1400s) welcomed a new realism featuring
perspective and emotion; the Cinquecento (1500s), or High
Renaissance, was a peak period followed by a sharp decline,
as political and economic decay eventually took its toll

One of the great myths of history provides a kind of Hollywood scenario for the "birth of the Renaissance", linking it to the fall of Constantinople in 1453, when scholars were supposed to have escaped, clutching their precious Greek manuscripts, to Italy. There, these manuscripts became a kind of magical seed, taking root, growing and bearing fruit almost immediately as "the Renaissance".

Of course, this is nonsense; like any other human phenomenon, the Renaissance had roots deep in history. It was the political fragmentation of Italy which created the Renaissance, each little city-state contributing something unique to the whole. But the process certainly started in Florence, and the city dominated the cultural scene until the early 16th century. Again and again over the centuries, attempts have been made to analyse the causes of the Florentine flowering, with reasons ranging from the poverty of the soil to the quality of the light. But it is no more possible to "explain" this than any other mystery of the human spirit.

Defining the Renaissance

The very word "renaissance" is a Florentine invention. In his book *Lives of the Most Excellent Architects, Painters and Sculptors*, first published in 1550, Vasari, first of the art historians, remarks that the reader "will now be able

to recognise more easily the progress of [art's] rebirth *(il progresso della sua rinascita)*".

But what, exactly, did Vasari mean by *rinascita*? What was being "reborn"? Vasari was referring to a rebirth of the art and architecture of classical times, that is, before Emperor Constantine transferred the seat of empire to Constantinople at the beginning of the 4th century AD, causing Byzantium to become the centre of art and culture. A distinctive architecture, based on Roman models, using bricks and featuring domes and cupolas, was developed. Byzantine artists covered the interiors with mosaics, a Roman decorative form which they developed into a sumptuous art form, the thousands of

LEFT: portrait of a young man (*c.*1475), probably a member of the Medici dynasty, by Botticelli (Uffizi).
RIGHT: *The Awakening Slave* (1519–20), one of four "unfinished" *Slaves* by Michelangelo (Accademia), intended for the tomb of Pope Julius II in Rome.

glazed-stone fragments catching the light in a way no fresco ever could. The best examples in Italy are in Ravenna, made in the 5th and 6th centuries, but the style prevailed in the 11th century in San Marco, Venice, and even in the 13th century in the magnificent Baptistery in Florence. It was the stiff formalised work of Byzantine artists that Vasari, who dismissed them as "a certain residue of Greeks", was attacking, and which was completely overthrown by the new naturalism of the Renaissance artists.

Architects drew and measured the ruins of the Roman cities, rediscovering their building techniques and their rules of proportion, the "classical orders". Vitruvius' *Ten Books on*

Architecture, the only surviving manual from classical times, was studied anew and became the basis, in the 15th century, for Alberti's treatise of the same name.

Painting, which of all the arts is preeminently *the* art of the Renaissance, owed little to antiquity, partly because no Roman examples survived to be used as models. Renaissance artists broke new ground, discovering perspective and observing the natural world which surrounded them. The 14th-century Florentine artist Cennino Cennini gave good advice to his fellow artists. "If you wish to draw mountains well, so that they appear natural," he wrote, "procure some large stones,

rocky, not polished, and draw from these." The idea of a handful of stones standing in for the Alps or the Apennines might seem ludicrous, but it was a pointer to the new road the artist was taking, the road to reality in nature.

The classical world provided the inspiration for the artist to rise above the narrow medieval world, with its emphasis on theological studies. But, once he had started, he went his own way. What was reborn was an artistic sensibility but not a re-cycled past.

The Trecento

Until the Quattrocento (15th century), the term "artist" had no particular significance, being virtually interchangeable with "artisan" or "craftsman". All were members of guilds, or *arti*: there was an *arte* for the shoemaker, no more and no less valid than the *arte* for the goldsmith, itself a sub-division of the immensely powerful Silk Guild. The guilds extended their control, as a matter of course, over the decorative as well as the useful arts. Sculptors and architects were enrolled with the masons, and painters formed a subdivision of the apothecaries, on the general principle that they had to have some acquaintance with chemistry to prepare their colours.

Far from resenting the obligation to join associations, painters and sculptors formed their own groups, or *compagnie*, created both within and across the boundaries of the larger guilds. The reasons were both social and technical. Socially, members could help each other, the group as a whole sharing both profits and losses. Technically, an increasing amount of work was done in cooperation, either on a kind of conveyor-belt system (two or three men might be engaged at successive stages in the shaping of a pillar, from rough hewing to final carving) or working side by side.

The growing popularity of the process known as *buon fresco* demanded this cooperative approach. The medium of fresco painting had been introduced about a century earlier, and time had shown that it was the most permanent of all forms of mural art, since the colouring became an intrinsic part of the plaster itself.

In addition to these large, set tasks, the workshop (or *bottega*) would produce a variety of smaller articles for sale, either on speculation or on commission, ranging from painted scabbards and armorial bearings to holy pictures and statues. There was widespread demand for religious art, which provided the bread and butter for hundreds of small *botteghe*. A peasant may have scraped together a few lire for a picture; a parish priest might have a large sum at his disposal and commission a mural or even an altarpiece, or a merchant who had made his fortune might be anxious to propitiate fate and show appropriate piety.

The potential client had little interest in the identity of the craftsmen producing his order. But, if expensive colours were used (gold, silver, or blue made from the semi-precious lapis lazuli), then the fact was clearly stated in the contract, along with the date of delivery of the finished piece. Commissioned work was almost invariably done on these written contracts which, in addition, usually specified how many figures were to appear in the finished painting, their activities and attributes. Religious paintings touched on the delicate area of religious orthodoxy, and the wise craftsman ensured that his client stated exactly what he wanted.

The identity of most of the workers in these workshops is unknown. They were conscientious and skilled, rather than brilliant, but they formed the subsoil from which the genius of the Quattrocento could flourish. The actual working pattern of the *bottega*, whereby a group of lesser men would paint the main body of a picture, leaving it to the identified master to put the finishing touches to it, would continue into the so-called High Renaissance of the Cinquecento, making it difficult and at times impossible for the most skilled art critic to say that such a painting is, beyond a doubt, the work of a particular famous artist.

Early Renaissance art

Comparing Trecento (or Gothic) paintings in any Tuscan art gallery with the work of Quattrocento (or early Renaissance) artists reveals a compelling difference: whereas Gothic paintings are iconographic, revelling in the use of celestial gold and presenting a spiritual Madonna and Child for worship and contem-

plation, the same subject in the hands of Renaissance painters becomes a study in living flesh, the figures of mother and child endowed with attitudes, character, emotions and psychological motivation. Scholars argue endlessly about why this great change occurred, but there is near-universal agreement on who started it: Giotto di Bondone (1267–1337), who, according to Vasari, "restored art to the better path followed in modern times".

Tradition has it that Giotto was working as a shepherd boy until Cimabue, himself a pioneer of greater naturalism in art, discovered that Giotto could draw a perfect circle freehand, and offered to train him as an artist. Pupil soon

surpassed master, and Giotto went on to create the great *St Francis* fresco cycle in the Upper Basilica in Assisi and the *Life of Christ* fresco series in the Scrovegni Chapel in Padua. In Florence his main masterpiece is in the Franciscan church of Santa Croce, where his work (and, of course, that of the *bottega* that assisted him) covers the walls of the two chapels to the right of the choir.

Despite his supposedly rural experience, even in Giotto's work nature is formalised and in the background. It is the humans who occupy the foreground, vibrantly alive.

Giotto, who died in 1337, was ahead of his time in introducing character and individuality

LEFT: detail from the *Coronation of the Virgin* (*c*.1330) altarpiece by Giotto (Santa Croce, Florence).
RIGHT: scene from the *Life of St Nicholas* (*c*.1327–30) by Lorenzetti (Uffizi).

to his art. He was not, however, entirely alone in these endeavours. Nicola (1223–84) and Giovanni (1245–1314) Pisano, the father and son team, were achieving similar advances in sculpture at the same time as Giotto was breaking new ground in art.

At the time when the Pisani were living and working in Pisa, it was the fashion for Pisan merchants to ship home Roman sarcophagi from the Holy Land or North Africa for eventual reuse as their own tombs. Scores of them still line the cloister surrounding Pisa's Campo Santo cemetery. Inspired by the realistic battle scenes carved on these antique marble tombs, the Pisani created their own versions: great

pulpits sculpted with crowded and dramatic scenes from the life of Christ, which can be seen in Pisa's Cathedral and Baptistery, and in Sant'Andrea church in Pistoia.

In architecture, the classical inspiration that helped to define the Renaissance had never disappeared to quite the same degree as it had in art. The very name Romanesque – meaning derived from or in the Roman style – indicates the essential continuity between the architecture of Rome and that of Tuscany in the 1300s. Churches were still built to the same basilican plan as those of the late Roman period, and, though the façades of many Tuscan churches look quite unclassical, they are still based on the

geometry of the Roman hemispherical arch, as distinct from the four-centred arches of Venice or the pointed arches of French Gothic. What distinguishes Tuscan Romanesque from Lombardic or Piedmontese is the exuberant use of polychrome marble to create complex geometrical patterns. Pisa was the seminal influence here – trade links with Spain and North Africa led to the adoption of arabic numerals in place of Roman, and to the fondness for surface patterning in architecture, copying Moorish tilework and textiles.

From Pisa the oriental influence spread to Lucca, Prato, Pistoia and even to Florence, where it was to pave the way for the great polychrome Campanile built by Giotto. Straddling two ages, Giotto has been claimed by rival art historians both as a Gothic artist and as the pioneer of the Renaissance. Perhaps if war and the Black Death had not ravaged Europe from the 1340s, the Renaissance might well have blossomed sooner than it did. As it was, another 60 years were to pass before the naturalism pioneered by Giotto and the Pisani was to reemerge, this time as a mass artistic movement.

The Quattrocento

A great breakthrough took place in Florence at the beginning of the 15th century, a moment so important that it can be dated to within a few years, and a new philosophy of life flowed through the city. Until the 1470s, Florence was a kind of dynamo, providing light and energy for the entire peninsula. The city retained its dominance in art for barely a lifespan, however, because it exported so much of its native talent – which ensured the spread of Renaissance values but, with it, Florence's own relative eclipse.

The breakthrough began when the Florentine *Signoria*, or government, decided to refurbish the ceremonial centre of Florence: the group of buildings consisting of the Cathedral, the Campanile – begun by Giotto in 1334 and finished after his death but to his design in 1359 – and the octagonal Baptistery. This little black-and-white building had a special place in Florentine affections, and when, in 1401, it was decided to offer a thanksgiving for the city's escape from plague, the Baptistery was chosen to benefit. The wealthy Wool Guild announced that they would finance the design and casting of a second set of bronze doors that would be even grander than those of Pisano. The design for it was thrown open to competition.

Out of the many entrants, seven were chosen each to execute a panel on the same subject: the sacrifice of Isaac. Two of the entrants, the 21-year-old Brunelleschi, later credited as the creator of the "Renaissance style" in architecture, and the 20-year-old Lorenzo Ghiberti, produced work which caused considerable difficulty to the judges. Both the panels exist today, one preserved in the Museo dell' Opera del Duomo, the other in the Bargello museum. Comparing the two, posterity finds it impossible to say which is "better". The *Syndics*,

expected to put in a full day's work "like any journeyman".

In the later contracts, he is treated far more as a free agent, permitted to undertake other commissions. Ghiberti, too, made explicit the change by boldly including his own self-portrait among the sculptures of the door.

Learning from the ancients

Meanwhile, in Rome with his friend Donatello, Brunelleschi was discovering how the ancients had built their enormous structures. In an entirely new approach to the past, he examined originals rather than copies of copies. One of his findings – or possibly, inventions – was the

at a loss to choose, came up with a compromise, suggesting that the artists should share the work. Brunelleschi declined and took himself off to Rome, while Ghiberti began work on the doors, completing them 22 years later.

He was offered the commission to produce a second pair: these took him 27 years. During the almost half-century that he worked on the project, it is possible to see in his contracts the changing status of the artist. In the first contract he is treated essentially as an artisan,

ulivella. Intrigued and puzzled by the existence of regular-shaped holes in the huge stone blocks of the ancient buildings, he assumed that they had been made to allow the block to be gripped by some device, and designed a kind of grappling iron to fit. Whether or not the Romans had actually used such a device, it was very useful – and a demonstration of the benefits to be gained by studying the past.

Brunelleschi returned to Florence at about the time that the *Syndics* of the Wool Guild, who also had the responsibility for the Cathedral, were puzzling over the problem of completing it. Arnolfo di Cambio had begun it in 1296, and it had been completed, all except for the dome,

LEFT: *Adoration of the Magi* (1423) by Gentile da Fabriano (Uffizi). **ABOVE:** *The Battle of San Romano* (1432) by Paolo Uccello (Uffizi).

by 1369. Nobody knew how to bridge this immense gap which, for half a century, had been covered by a temporary roof.

In 1417 a special meeting was called to debate the problem and consider suggestions, and Brunelleschi put forward his solution. He was mocked for it because it dispensed with the wooden centring over which architects traditionally built their arches and vaults, supporting their weight until the keystone was in place. But, in desperation, the *Syndics* offered him the job. Brunelleschi solved the problem by building a dome that was pointed in sections, supported by ribs with the lightest possible in-filling between them. He built two

Brunelleschi introduced the columns, pediments and cornices he copied from Roman ruins into his churches, there were no surviving examples of Roman domestic architecture for the 15th-century Florentines to copy. When Rucellai, a wealthy Florentine merchant, asked Alberti to design a palace for him, Alberti took as a model the Colosseum in Rome and applied its tiers of arches to the façade of a three-storey *palazzo*. Though it was the only *palazzo* he built, and though Brunelleschi's design for the Medici Palace never got beyond the model stage, these two architects developed a new type of building, a system of proportion and an elegance of line which is still in use today.

shells, an outer skin and an inner one: one way in which the crushing weight of the dome, the problem which had prevented its construction, was considerably reduced.

The work took 16 years, and was completed on 31 August 1436. This was the first Renaissance dome in Italy, the largest unsupported dome in Europe, bigger than the Pantheon in Rome which Brunelleschi had studied, bigger even than the great dome which Michelangelo raised a century later over St Peter's in Rome.

It was Brunelleschi's successor, the scholar Alberti, who first applied the classical orders to domestic architecture and created what we now think of as the Renaissance *palazzo*. Whereas

Brunelleschi's other major breakthrough was his use of perspective. Alberti described its effect to a generation for whom it appeared almost a magical technique: "I describe a rectangle of whatever size I wish, which I imagine to be an open window through which I view whatever is to be depicted there." Donatello (1386–1466) eagerly used the technique in his bas-relief of *Salome offering John's head to Herod*. The observer is looking at a banquet where the diners are recoiling in horror from the offering. Beyond the banqueting rooms can be seen a succession of two more rooms, giving a remarkable and, for contemporaries, almost eerie sense of depth.

A new perspective

Like the difference between Giotto's mobile, dramatic figures and their static, formal predecessors, perspective gave a new vista to civilisation. Its most dramatic form was that employed by the young Masaccio. His great painting of the *Trinity*, in the church of Santa Maria Novella, is an intellectual exercise in the use of perspective that is also infused with religious awe. Beneath a *trompe l'oeil* classical arch stands the immense figure of God the Father, half supporting a cross on which there is an equally immense figure of Christ; below them are various saints and donors and a memento mori of a skeleton in a sarcophagus revealing an ancient warning: "I am what you are, and what I am, you shall be."

The huge figures stand out from the background and appear to loom over the observer. As a young man, Michelangelo used to stand before these, copying them again and again to fix the style in his mind. Eventually, therefore, some essence of this experimental period of the Renaissance found its way into the Sistine Chapel, that shrine of the High Renaissance dominated by Michelangelo's work.

The classical arch in Masaccio's painting is a pointer to a curious development which took place during the Quattrocento – the clothing of Biblical figures in a totally anachronistic way, either in classical Roman attire or in contemporary Florentine dress. The frescoes which Ghirlandaio (1449–94) painted in the Sassetti Chapel within the church of Santa Trinità supposedly concern the prophecies of Christ's birth, and the location should be Augustan Rome. But it is an Augustan Rome which bears a remarkably close resemblance to 15th-century Florence, and the people standing round waiting for the awesome news are all citizens of Florence wearing their normal clothes. Lorenzo de' Medici is there, as is his mother, his children, friends and various colleagues.

Mythological elements

Early Renaissance painters were preoccupied with technique. Their subject matter remained largely unchanged: religion was still the most important concern. But in the second half of the Quattrocento a new, exciting and somewhat disturbing element began to appear: the mythological and the allegorical.

The supreme practitioner in this field was Sandro Botticelli, who worked with Leonardo da Vinci in Verrocchio's workshop but developed in a totally different direction. His most famous painting – certainly the most mysterious of the early Renaissance – is *La Primavera*, painted in 1478 and hung in the Uffizi.

Nine supernatural creatures are placed in an exquisite natural setting. On the left, a young man is aiming at, or pointing at, something. Next to him a group of beautiful, grave-faced

women are performing a solemn ritual dance. On the right is the only figure who seems to be aware of the observer: Botticelli's stunningly beautiful "mystery" woman with a provocative half-smile. Beside her what appears to be an act of violence adds a discordant note: a bluish figure is leaning out of the trees and clutching a startled girl.

In the background, but dominating the whole, is the most enigmatic figure: a pale woman whose expression has been variously described as frowning, smiling, gay and melancholy; whose stance has also been described in conflicting ways, as dancing, as that of a consumptive, as pregnant and as offering a blessing. The

---

LEFT: *Birth of John the Baptist* by Ghirlandaio (1485).
RIGHT: *Trinity* (*c.*1425) by Masaccio, the pioneer of perspective (both in Santa Maria Novella, Florence).

figure itself has been "firmly identified" as both Venus and the Virgin Mary. What Botticelli was trying to do was to restate classical mythology in Christian terms while remaining true to the original – and true to his own quirky self. However, he was later influenced by the gloomy, savage friar Savonarola – who turned Florence into a puritan reformatory in the 1490s – and, almost overnight, ceased his joyous mythological paintings, concentrating instead on orthodox religious subjects.

The High Renaissance

Even to the untutored eye, there is a profound difference between the work produced before for Rome with Raphael to work for Pope Julius II. Other artists followed suit: the major Florentine families – other than the Medicis – could no longer afford to make commissions, so there was no longer any kind of independent art scene.

Shortly after the sack of Rome, the Medici Pope Clement VII clamped down on his native city of Florence, ending republicanism and preparing the way for the first dukedom. Meanwhile, in the world of art, the glory was departing from Florence, as the impetus of the Renaissance shifted to Rome and Venice. From the middle of the 16th century, Florentine artists tended to be court artists, dancing

and after the 1520s in Tuscany and elsewhere, most noticeably in Florence. Partly this was the result of an immense political crisis. Italy had become a battleground invaded again and again by warring foreigners. In 1527 a savage army, composed partly of mercenaries, sacked Rome and held the pope to ransom. Italy was never to recover from that experience, which was the curtain-raiser for a period of foreign domination that would not end until the 1800s.

The peak phase of the Renaissance – in Florence, at least – was entered with the advent of Leonardo da Vinci and Michelangelo, but the decline came very soon afterwards, particularly when Michelangelo left attendance on the Medici dukes. Among them was the artist-cum-historian Giorgio Vasari.

Until recently, Vasari's work as an artist was dismissed almost as contemptuously as his work as an art historian was received enthusiastically. However, posterity owes him a debt of thanks, both as an architect and as a painter. Not only did he build the Uffizi for Duke Cosimo I, but in his paintings in the great Salone dei Cinquecento, the parliamentary chamber of the Palazzo Vecchio, he created outstanding contemporary representations of the city and its surrounding countryside. Equally fine is his frescoed interior of Brunelleschi's dome, revealed in 1994 after a five-year restoration programme.

Leonardo

Although the glory was departing from Florence, the sunset was stupendous. It could scarcely be otherwise with two such giants as Michelangelo and da Vinci still working in the city. Leonardo, born in 1452, trained in the *bottega* of Verrocchio, thus carrying the medieval systems on into the new era. One of Vasari's anecdotes claims that Verrocchio, on seeing his young apprentice's work, laid down his brush and never painted again. Unlikely though the incident is, the anecdote shows that Leonardo was recognised as being almost a freakish genius in his own lifetime.

Leonardo left Florence for Milan at the age of 30. He came back again in 1502 when he was commissioned by the *Signoria* to create the great mural, the *Battle of Anghiari* in the Council Chamber, returned to Milan in 1506, then finally crossed the Alps and became court painter to François I of France. His contribution to the history of ideas is incalculable, but his physical contribution to Tuscan art history is relatively small. Typically, both the *Battle of Anghiari* and the *Adoration of the Kings* in the Uffizi are unfinished. And his two most famous paintings, the *Mona Lisa* (a portrait of a virtuous but otherwise undistinguished Florentine housewife) and the *Virgin of the Rocks*, are in Paris and London respectively.

Michelangelo is very different. His greatest work, the Sistine Chapel frescoes, is also outside Florence, but he did leave an enduring imprint upon his home city, in the form of the walls that gird it and the sculptures that grace it.

Michelangelo

Michelangelo was nearly a generation younger than Leonardo, born in 1475 when the Renaissance was approaching its apogee. His father was a poor but proud country gentleman who thoroughly disapproved of the idea of his son becoming an artisan or artist; in his mind there was no clear distinction. Michelangelo, too, was apt to be a little touchy on the subject. Although he served his apprenticeship in a *bottega*, he later rejected the idea that he touted for trade: "I was never a painter or a sculptor like those who set up shop for the purpose."

A Vasari anecdote describes how the young Michelangelo, then around 13 years old, made a drawing of the various tools in the workshop. His master, Ghirlandaio, was so impressed that he drew Lorenzo de' Medici's attention to the talented boy. As a result, Michelangelo entered the princely Medici household, eating at the same table and studying with the same scholars as Lorenzo's own children.

Michelangelo was just 18 when Lorenzo de' Medici died in 1492. Florence was plunged into chaos, because Lorenzo's son, Piero, was extravagant and unpopular, and the Florentines chased him out of the city. Michelangelo's ties with the Medici were no longer so advanta-

geous, and he took the road to Rome. There he undertook the work by which he is best remembered. He also worked for the next 40 years on a task he never completed: the great tomb for his patron and taskmaster, Pope Julius II. The unfinished statues for this tomb, the famous *Slaves*, are now in Florence's Accademia gallery. In them it is possible to see, five centuries later, the sculptor's technique.

As in a *bottega*, the roughing out of the figures was done by apprentices, the master giving the finishing touches. It is profoundly moving to see in some of them the shallow depressions surrounding the figure, made by the rounded head of a chisel, which seems to be "freeing" the figure, as though it already existed and was simply trapped in the stone.

Florence has many statues by Michelangelo; although often unfinished, they always reveal the chisel strokes of a master. They include the famous *David*, and the statues of *Dawn*, *Evening*, *Day* and *Night* in the Medici Chapel.

In the Casa Buonarroti in Via Ghibellina are displayed some of the sculptor's working drawings and a few of his earliest works. Although Michelangelo is remembered as a painter and sculptor, he was also an engineer of very considerable skill and a poet of sensitivity and insight.

on the Piazza della Signoria – a message to anyone in Florence who dared to resist the might of the Medici. But it is indicative both of Cellini and of the phase into which the art of the Renaissance was moving that his best-known work would be the elaborate golden salt cellar which he made for François I of France.

Raphael

Raphael was a gentle, handsome young man who seemed to have no enemies. He was born in Umbria in 1483 and received his basic training in the workshop of Perugino, working on frescoes in Perugia. In 1500, at the impressionable age of 17, he came to Florence, where

Cellini

Michelangelo was just 25 when Benvenuto Cellini was born in 1500. Like so many of the artists of his time, he was skilled in a number of crafts – he was, improbably enough, a gunner. He played a role in the tragic sack of Rome which, in effect, brought the Renaissance to an end. Acting as gunner in defence of the Vatican, he assured his supporters that the pope promised him absolution "for all the murders that I should commit".

In Florence, his most famous work is that beautiful but curiously heartless statue of *Perseus Slaying Medusa* commissioned by Cosimo I for the statue-filled Loggia dei Lanzi

he absorbed the works of Leonardo da Vinci and Michelangelo.

He left Florence in 1508, attracted to Rome by the fiery Pope Julius II, who was planning a series of architectural embellishments to the Vatican. There the young Raphael easily proved himself. He painted the series of rooms known as the Stanze della Segnatura and, under the Medici Pope Leo X, was placed in charge of archaeological excavations in Rome itself.

Thus, the last true artist of the Renaissance introduced into the mother city of Europe that passionate search for the past which had triggered off the Renaissance in Florence nearly two centuries earlier. ❏

decorative details were added, notably graceful courtyards complete with sculpted wells, coats of arms, ornate arches and a loggia on the first or top floors. Despite 16th-century modifications, the Florentine Palazzo Davanzati preserves much of its medieval atmosphere. The palace is impressive, from its iron-bolted doors and formidable façade pierced by numerous small windows to an internal courtyard boasting a well with a pulley system designed to supply water to each floor. The interior presents a charming portrait of domestic life, from 15th-century frescoes and tapestries to the *cassoni*, Tuscan wedding chests, and even a privileged child's bathroom.

home and banking headquarters, a massive mansion with an arcaded inner courtyard. He also designed Palazzo Pitti (1444), the prototype of a patrician palace, boasting strict classical proportions and a rusticated façade. Yet there are lingering traces of feudal times in the Gothic windows and heavy cornices. Built for Cosimo de' Medici, Palazzo Pitti clearly symbolises the power and prestige of the owner.

However, some nobles simply modernised their feudal seats. Palazzo Spini-Ferroni, a crenellated three-tiered fortress close to the Arno, was a 13th-century watchtower before becoming a palatial home. Just around the corner looms the grandiose Palazzo Strozzi, a

Renaissance palaces

The Florentine *palazzo* was a direct descendant of the tower-house, but without an outmoded defensive function. In keeping with the new humanist spirit, architects designed gracious private palaces as proof of their revivalist skills, not simply as symbols of patrician pride. Foremost amongst the trailblazers was Michelozzi (1396–1472), who pursued the architectural principles of Alberti and Brunelleschi. Michelozzo designed the Florentine Palazzo Medici-Riccardi, the Medici

LEFT: woodcut of Florence, *c.*1470.
ABOVE: the fortified town of Monteriggioni.

rusticated stone cube of mammoth proportions built for the greatest banking dynasty. Rustication was intended to underline the Strozzi's power. Whereas Palazzo Strozzi emphasises strength and stability, homes such as Palazzo Rucellai were more harmonious, embellished with elegant loggias, classical motifs and decorative friezes.

Florence may be the most innovative Renaissance city, but Pienza is the best-preserved. Pienza was built by Pius II as a papal city, offering both an echo of imperial patronage and a humanist memorial to his papacy. In 1462, the architect Rossellino grafted a monumental Renaissance core onto medieval grandiosity. All the elements of civic life were set on one tiny square, its geometric shape giving tension to the whole. Using a well-head as the lynchpin, the piazza embraces an episcopal palace, a dignified town hall with an open loggia, and a tower embodying Tuscan pride. In his private palace here, the pope delighted in hanging gardens, delicate loggias and rooms for every season.

Renaissance architects

As the cradle of the Renaissance, Tuscany is where the profession of architect first came into its own. Imbued with a new humanist spirit, architects of the stature of Brunelleschi, Alberti, Michelozzo, Rossellino and Sangallo made their mark on churches, palaces and villas. Florence, which saw itself as the inheritor of Roman grandeur, is the city with the greatest concentration of Renaissance monuments. Strongly influenced by Tuscan Romanesque, the buildings were models of visual restraint, dedicated to proportion, perspective and classical motifs. Brunelleschi (1377–1446), the father of Renaissance architecture, left his masterpiece on the Duomo in Florence. His dome was the fulfilment of the Renaissance ideal, a feat of Florentine engineering *(see page 48)*.

Alberti (1404–72) is considered the archetypal Renaissance man, a patrician playwright,

SACRED SITES

Religious architecture represents one of the highlights of Tuscany. Any tour would certainly include the cathedrals of Florence, Lucca, Pisa and Siena. Lesser-known gems include Barga's Romanesque Cathedral, Montepulciano's Renaissance San Biagio and the Romanesque San Miniato al Monte in the Florentine hills. In many cases, the architecture is inextricably bound up with the artistic wealth on the walls. This is true of the Gothic church of Santa Maria Novella in Florence or Arezzo's San Francesco, with its poignant fresco cycle by della Francesca. By contrast, exteriors can be austere or even unfinished, a sign that patrons squabbled or ran out of funds.

The siting is also significant, with cathedrals usually constructed on sacred spots hallowed since Roman or Etruscan times. Mendicant churches were often built outside city walls, with the surrounding square often becoming a major city market. Abbeys and monasteries, which could be as large as medieval towns, were built on virgin sites, and blended civic and Christian concerns.

Some of the most intriguing architecturally are the Romanesque abbey of Sant'Antimo, the baroque Certosa di Pisa, the Carthusian foundation of Camaldoli, the hilltop monastery of La Verna and Monte Oliveto Maggiore, a Benedictine foundation in the woods south of Siena.

humanist and philosopher, composer and lawyer, athlete and architect. He rivalled Brunelleschi in his gift for geometry and desire to revive "the immutable laws of architecture", yet also sought to respect the Tuscan taste for decoration. As an architectural historian, he revived Vitruvius' theories and put them into practice in Florence. The laws of proportion, perspective and the use of the classical orders all came into play in the Duomo and in the Florentine Palazzo Rucellai (1446). This landmark palace was inspired by the Colosseum and the buildings of classical Rome. The Roman influence is present in the porches and panelled doors as well as in the frieze, which bears the crests of the Medici and Rucellai families. The magnificent Rucellai loggia was the last to be built in 15th-century Florence, such was the profligacy it engendered. Weddings and festivities in the loggia may be no more, but the family remains ensconced in part of the palace.

Rural retreats

Tuscany's rich urban heritage risks overshadowing the delightful rural legacy of sunny villas and picturesque hilltop farmhouses. In medieval Tuscany, the traditional manor or fortified seat was bound by solid walls or battlements. This country refuge evolved into the gracious villa-residence of Renaissance times. In the 13th century, there were two forms of rural retreat, the feudal domain – the grand preserve of the landed nobility – and the *casa da signore*, the busy hub of a country estate. This was a crenellated property with a watchtower, surrounded by farm buildings and cottages, and owned by the gentry or bourgeoisie.

The villa as a country retreat was a Renaissance concept, reflecting the gracious rural lifestyle cultivated by the Tuscan nobility. The villas were generally elegant but not ostentatious, in keeping with the cultural conservatism of the Florentine nobility. However, the grandest Medici villas, such as Cafaggiolo, designed by Michelozzo, were sumptuous princely estates. Poggio a Caiano *(see Villas and Gardens, page 116)* is the model Renaissance villa, with its harmonious design and colonnaded loggia harking back to the grandeur of classical times. The rural

design reflected a desire for symmetry and a rationalisation of form and function. Embellished by porticoes, the villa was built on a square plan around an inner courtyard, with a loggia on the first floor. Set in ornamental gardens and encircled by walls, the villa enjoyed superb views, often from a hilltop.

At a time when peace reigned in the Tuscan countryside, the gardens were regarded as a bucolic retreat, an essential part of the architectural composition. The grounds consist of a *giardino segreto*, a geometrical walled garden, with formal parterres and topiary, kitchen and herb gardens, lined by stately avenues of cypresses or lemon trees. The design, enlivened

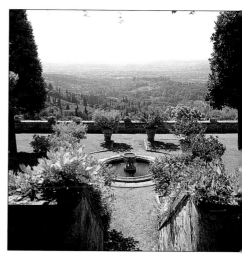

by water gardens, was set in the 16th century, when the Mannerist style acquired colonnades and statuary, grottoes and follies.

By the 17th century, the crisp geometry of the gardens was matched by formal terraces, virtuoso waterworks and sculptures of sea monsters cavorting with mythological figures. In their ease and openness, the gardens were in harmony with the house and with the patrician owner. As the Renaissance architect Alberti declared, "Only the house of a tyrant can look like a fortress: an ideal home should be open to the world outside, beautifully adorned, delicate and finely proportioned rather than proud and stately". ❏

LEFT: Arezzo's stately main square.
RIGHT: Villa Medici, a rural retreat built by Michelozzo.

WILD TUSCANY

Nature-lovers sated by the art treasures of the region will find plenty of wild refuges in which to rest or roam

lassic Tuscany is a civilised scene of silvery olive groves, vine-cloaked hills, sunflowers shimmering in the heat and dark silhouettes of cypresses, arranged in double file along timeless avenues. The Welsh poet Dylan Thomas, who was no stranger to life on the wild side, praised the Florentine countryside – "The pine hills are endless, the cypresses at the hilltop tell one all about the length of death, the woods are deep as love and full of goats" – a seductive rural image that has lured so many visitors to find their version of earthly paradise.

Given the civilisation of the landscape, "wild Tuscany" might seem a misnomer. Yet, beyond the classic chessboard of vineyards, a rugged wilderness awaits. Tuscany is Italy's most thickly wooded region. Mountains soar, and in the northwest there are woods as thick as rainforests, while on the west coast the Maremma marshlands remain the emptiest and ecologically purest stretch of Italian coastline. The south, meanwhile, has the primeval emptiness of the Sienese moonscape.

The animals are indeed in flight given Italian hunters' fondness for the chase. The power of the hunting lobby has severely depleted their numbers, with the exception of wild boar. Outside designated reserves, bird-watchers and animal-lovers fare less well than botanists and nature-lovers. Hawks and golden eagles still enjoy the majesty of the mountains, but life is no pastoral idyll for deer, ravaged by hunting. But, against the odds, Apennine wolves have

made a comeback in mountainous regions, encouraged by the profusion of their favourite dish, shaggy mouflons (mountain sheep).

Rural pursuits

Away from the cultural crowds, nature-lovers and adrenalin junkies can indulge in trekking and skiing, horse riding and mountain biking, climbing and caving, gliding and paragliding, sailing and surfing. Riding is very popular in Tuscany, with more riding stables and well-trodden mule tracks than anywhere else in Italy. It is also a rambler's paradise. Better mapped than most Italian regions, the variety of trails from relaxed to rigorous is vast. Serious hikers

LEFT: Evening primrose in the Apuan Alps.
RIGHT: negotiating a suspension bridge near Pistoia.

can follow the long-distance trails run by the Italian Alpine Club (CAI). Garfagnana Trekking and Apuane Trekking are key paths in the Apuan Alps, while the Grande Escursione Appenninica (GEA) is a 25-day trek to Emilia and Umbria along the ridges of the Apennines.

The Apuan Alps, Lunigiana and Garfagnana

This mountain chain, with its awe-inspiring landscape, runs parallel with the coastline and the Apennine ridge. Behind the well-groomed beaches of Versilia, on the western side of the chain, lurks a rugged hinterland of marble quarries and mountain ridges, narrow gorges

Lunigiana, the mountainous area north of Carrara, is wedged between Emilia and Liguria. The region is criss-crossed by streams, with canoeing carried out in the clear waters of the river Magra. From Aulla, a convenient base, there are organised tours of glacial moraines, karst gorges, caves and botanical gardens.

Garfagnana lies on the borders of Emilia Romagna and northern Tuscany, between the Apuan Alps and the Apennines. Parco dell' Orecchiella is the region's most spectacular park. While closely resembling the Apuan Alps, it is higher and wilder, with a mixture of woodland and pasture, picturesque clearings and mountain streams.

and thermal springs. This desolate landscape was devastated by floods in 1996, but has recovered. Lago di Vaglia, in the heart of the mountains, is a reservoir containing a drowned medieval village that can be seen periodically. The underground landscape is equally inspiring, with caves often as deep as mountains are high, and notoriously long and labyrinthine. In Fornovolasco, east of Forte dei Marmi, the Grotta del Vento represents the region's most fascinating caverns, riddled with steep gorges and secret passages, slowly revealing stalagmites and stalactites, fossils and alabaster formations, crystal pools and echoing chambers.

The Apennines

While the Apuan Alps are more varied, the Apennines have not been ravaged by quarrying. They include the range on the Emilian border, the loftiest in the northern Apennines, as well as those in the Casentino and Mugello. Centred on the resort of Abetone, the rugged northern range is ideal hiking country.

Abetone, commanding the mountain pass separating Tuscany and Emilia, is the most important winter-sports resort in central Italy. Fortunately, the mountain air also makes Abetone invigorating in the most stifling Tuscan summer, when the cable car takes walkers up to the leafy heights. Despite the ravages of hunting, the forest is home to roe deer, mouflons and marmots, with golden eagles swooping over the crags. One of the most rewarding stretches of the rugged long-distance path (GEA) lies between Abetone and Cisa. Yet Abetone is also suitable for less energetic walkers, who can stroll along well-marked paths in the woods.

The Casentino, north of Arezzo, forms a series of razor-like crests and deep woods which straddle Emilia and northeast Tuscany. Centred on Bibbiena in the Upper Arno, these ancient forests are the region's finest. While the Emilian side is characterised by steep bluffs and stratified outcrops, the Tuscan side is softer, with picturesque waterfalls and streams. Hikers and pony-trekkers can follow the long-distance trail (GEA), but should bear in mind that the rescue services are often required in these treacherous forests. Fallow deer and mouflon were introduced in 1870 for hunting purposes, and again in the 1960s after local depredations. Today, sightings of the shaggy sheep, badger or porcupine are more frequent than glimpses of the eagle owl, deer, weasel, wildcat or wolf.

The Mugello, the hilly region north of Florence, resembles a landscape painted by Giotto, whose homeland this was. The Mugello can be explored on horseback, by following the old bridle paths between Bologna and Florence. The valleys along the Sieve, the main tributary of the Arno, are dotted with villages, olive groves and vineyards. The transition from valley to mountains means that olive groves give way to chestnut and oak forests before culminating in beech woods and waterfalls. Upper Mugello is a harsh, wild landscape of mountain peaks and passes, with ridges and ravines carved by rivers over the years.

Classic Chianti

While the Florentine Chianti is devoted to wine, the Sienese side is wilder, with vineyards gradually giving way to slopes covered in holm oaks, chestnuts and juniper. A 15-km (9-mile) hilly hike from Greve in Chianti to Panzano covers the Via Chiantigiana and its offshoots, passing farms, cypresses and chestnut groves.

In subtle Siena province, much is classic Tuscany, with olive groves, gently rolling hills

and dark cypresses standing sentinel. However, stretching from Siena to Montepulciano is a singular moonscape known as Le Crete Senesi, the strange hillocks marking the Sienese badlands. Barren or virtually treeless, this is beguiling territory nonetheless, with solitary farmhouses marooned on the crests of hills. This seemingly empty terrain is home to foxes, badgers and wild boar. Monte Amiata, the site of an extinct volcano further south, presents the province's wilder face, with a profusion of thermal springs bubbling amidst the beech and chestnut groves. With its mossy banks and majestic grandeur, the mountainous setting is suitable for hiking, horse riding and skiing.

Marshy Maremma

Maremma, the southern coastal strip, is a composite of natural Tuscany. The Parco Naturale della Maremma, with its soft whale-backed hills parallel to the coast, is dotted with Spanish watchtowers, parasol pines and coastal dunes. Waymarked paths connect the shoreline and steep cliffs. On La Spergolaia ranch near by, the legendary *butteri*, the last of the Maremman cowboys, break in sturdy wild horses. The Maremma sustains around 600 beasts, a mixture of semi-wild ponies and white long-horned cattle. The park can be explored on horseback, on foot or by bus from Alberese *(see page 237)*. ❑

LEFT: The Garfagnana.
RIGHT: Le Crete Senesi, after the harvest.

Nature Parks

Parco Nazionale Appennino Tosco-Emiliano

The Apennine ridges that form the border between northern Tuscany and Emilia Romagna are rich in contrasting landscapes, from moorlands and lakes to craggy summits and waterfalls. Golden eagles, wolves, mouflons and roe deer roam, and rare botanic species transform whole areas into wild botanical gardens. *The visitor centre is in Reggio Emilia (Via Emilia All'Ospizio 2; tel: 0522-434366, freephone 800-945007). www.appenninopark.it*

Parco Nazionale delle Foreste Casentinesi, Monte Falterona, Campigna

This protected area lies along the Apennine ridge forming the border between eastern Tuscany and Emilia Romagna. Its beech and chestnut woods are among the largest and best-preserved in Italy. They are home to a rich variety of flora and fauna, such as deer, wolves and golden eagles. Also of interest are the secluded monasteries of Camáldoli and La Verna. There are eight waymarked nature trails – "Sentieri Natura" – within the park. A small and practical guide (on sale in the visitor centres) highlights the region's wildlife and points of interest.

The park headquarters is in Pratovecchio (Via G. Brocchi 7; tel: 0575-50301). There are information offices at Camáldoli (tel: 0575-556130) and Campigna (tel: 0543-980231). Outside the park, the Arezzo tourist office (by the train station; tel: 0575-377678) also has information on the park. www.parks.it

Parco Alpi Apuane

The park extends for over 20,000 hectares between the coastal plain and the rivers Magra, Aulella and Serchio. The Apuan Alps differ from the Apennines, with deep valleys, steep slopes and mountains of glistening white marble. Forests of chestnut and beech give cover to some 300 species of birds and a rich diversity of wild flowers. Shy marmots can often be spotted on the higher slopes. It is an ideal environment for trekking, walking, mountain climbing, cycling and horse riding.

The park headquarters is at Seravezza, (Via Corrado del Greco 11; tel: 0584-757325). Visitor centres are at Castelnuovo di Garfagna (Piazza Erbe 1; tel: 0583-644242) and Forno (loc. Filanda; tel: 0585-315300). Park guides are available for hikes and visits to caves. www.parcapuane.it

Parco Naturale dell'Orecchiella

The mountains of the Orecchiella park in the Garfagnana region are higher than the neighbouring Apuan Alps, but the landscape is tamer, though no less beautiful for that, and criss-crossed by a network of hiking trails. The area is centred on the high broad plain of Pania di Corfino, overlooked by a dramatic limestone peak that dominates the Serchio valley. There is a wide variety of rare flora, and the wildlife includes deer, wild boar, mouflons, badgers, otters, weasels and wolves. The monastery of San Pellegrino offers fabulous views and houses a folk museum. San Romano in Garfagnana is a good base for exploring.

The visitor centre is near Corfino (tel: 0583-619002). For walks, contact the Club Alpino Italiano – www.cai.it

Parco Regionale di Migliarino, San Rossore, Massaciuccoli

This regional park covers the coastal hinterland behind the beach resorts and campsites between Viareggio and Livorno, and includes the forest of San Rossore and Lake Massaciuccoli. Huge holm oaks, maritime pines and common oaks grow right up to the beach and are home to wild boar, fallow deer and countless species of native and migratory birds. While the Macchia Lucchese, Lago di Massaciuccoli and Tenuta Borbone are freely accessible, entrance to other areas is restricted. The archaeological area of San Rossore, where a fleet of Roman ships was unearthed, can be visited by appointment.

There is a visitor centre at Coltano (Villa Medicea, Via Palazzi 21; tel/fax: 050-989051), and the Tenuta San Rossore organises walking and cycling tours (tel/fax: 050-530101). Boat tours of Lake Massaciuccoli depart from Torre del Lago. www.parcosanrossore.it

Parco Regionale della Maremma

This beautiful, unspoilt nature park covering over 100 sq. km (40 sq. miles), stretches along the Tyrrhenian coast from Principina a Mare to Talamone. It is centred on the Monti dell'Uccellina (Mountains of the Little Bird), which rise from the sea. The rugged landscape is a mixture of marshland, mountains and virgin coast backed by umbrella pines, interspersed with rocky outcrops and coves. There are no human settlements, and just one access road links Alberese (the main point of entry) to Marina Alberese, a beautiful seaside stretch. A variety of migratory birds stop here en route to Africa. The dense vegetation provides the perfect habitat for wild boar, symbol of the Maremma, while herds of Maremma cattle and horses of the *butteri* (local cowherds), roam on its plains. Waymarked paths connect the shoreline and steep cliffs.

The main entrance and visitor centre are at Alberese (tel: 0564-407098), but Talamone also has an access point.

Parco Nazionale Arcipelago Toscano

This protected area is Europe's largest marine park. It covers the seven islands of the Tuscan Archipelago: Elba, Capraia, Gorgona, Pianosa, Montecristo, Giglio and Giannutri *(see page 182)*. The coastline and seabed vary enormously from island to island, hence the variety of flora and fauna. Seabirds such as shearwaters and black-headed gulls proliferate. More rare is Audouin's gull, an endemic species. These waters, which are popular among

divers, are home to a great many species of fish, including swordfish and tuna. Dolphins, sperm whales and even the rare monk seal may also be sighted by the lucky or the very patient.

The main office of the marine park is on Elba (Via Guerrazzi 1, Portoferraio; tel: 0565-919411; fax: 0565-919428). www.isoleditoscana.it

Useful References

www.parks.it (official website of the Italian Federation of Parks and Nature Reserves)
www.wwf.it/oasi (World Wildlife Fund reserves in Italy) ❏

LEFT: horses can be hired in many locations.
RIGHT: poppies brighten the fields in spring.

A TASTE OF TUSCANY

Purity and simplicity: Tuscan cooking makes full use of
bountiful local products to create dishes that are as
much a joy to prepare as they are to taste

Tuscany has everything to offer the visitor in terms of food. There is a rich selection of fruit and vegetables from the prolific countryside, and a fantastic bounty from the sea – everything from red mullet to mussels, tender beef and pork, excellent oil with which to cook and dress it and superb wines with which to wash it down. To finish off, there are hearty cheeses and divine cakes and desserts.

What is immediately striking about Tuscan food is that, no matter what you are eating or where you are eating it, it is always very rustic, very simple, designed to nourish the soul and the spirit as much as the body. Tuscan cooking is never elaborate or excessive; there are no fussy decorations, complicated reductions of sauces or subtly blended flavours. But there is a basic, honest simplicity about the dishes which has made them popular for centuries the world over.

Tuscany produces its own inimitable versions of Italian staples: pasta dishes with gamey sauces of hare, wild boar, even porcupine; polenta with fresh *funghi*; rabbit or roast baby goat. But along with a particular attitude to food, Tuscany also has many dishes and delicacies unique to the region, most available the year round, others – such as chestnuts, truffles and wild mushrooms – more seasonal.

Hunting is a popular local sport, resulting in plentiful offerings of *cinghiale* (wild boar), which comes in many guises. Despite conservationists' pleas, numerous small birds, from sparrows to quail, are still considered fair game.

Hearty stews and barbecues

Legumes are used widely throughout Italy, but are a particular mainstay in Tuscany, where *cannellini*, or white kidney beans, are favoured. Tuscans, in fact, are known as *Toscani Mangiafagioli* – bean eaters, because the pulse is used so much in local specialities, adding a smooth texture as only well-cooked beans can. Thick soups and hearty bean stews are served in terracotta pots often enhanced by a trickle of olive oil which is added at the table.

Tuscan cooks favour methods that can be carried out on a large scale and preferably out of doors – a grill over an open wood fire is something you will come across behind chic

LEFT: ingredients for a perfect holiday.
RIGHT: preparing *bistecca alla Fiorentina*.

Florentine restaurants or in the garden of rural *trattorie*. Fresh herbs like sage, rosemary and basil are used, as they grow, in abundance.

The most important Tuscan meat dish is the excellent *bistecca alla Fiorentina*, a vast, tender, juicy and succulent beef steak – preferably from cattle raised in Val di Chiana. It is brushed with a drop of the purest virgin olive oil and grilled over a scented wood fire of oak or olive branches, then seasoned with salt and pepper before serving. In good Florentine and Tuscan restaurants in general, you will be able to see the meat raw before you order.

Another famous Tuscan meat dish is *arista alla Fiorentina*, consisting of a pork loin highly

seasoned with chopped rosemary and ground pepper. The origin of this dish goes back to the 15th century. At the Ecumenical Council of 1430 in Florence, the Greek bishops were served this dish at a banquet and pronounced it "*aristos*", which in Greek means very good. The name stuck, and it has become a feature of Tuscan cuisine ever since. It is a particularly useful dish because it keeps very well for several days and is even better cold than hot.

Soups are made of the ubiquitous beans, and include *acquacotta*, a vegetable soup with an egg added before serving, and *pappa al pomodoro*, a thick soup of bread and tomatoes. Also well known in this category is the Florentine speciality *ribollita*, meaning "boiled again": a second boiling of the soup increases the density and improves the flavour.

Although beef- rather than bean-based, a special stew is *peposo*, a fiery blend of meat and vegetables from Impruneta, a town near Florence that is famous for its terracotta.

The coastal province of Livorno produces the delicious *cacciucco*, an immense seafood-and-fish soup claimed to be the original bouillabaisse. The story goes that the soup originated in the port after a tremendous storm that left a widowed fisherman's wife desperately trying to feed her many children. The children were sent begging for something to eat. As the fishermen had nothing else to give, the children came home with handfuls of mussels, a few shrimps, half a fish and some fish heads. The clever mother put them all in a pot, added herbs and tomatoes from her garden and created the glorious *cacciucco*. While *zuppa di pesce* can be eaten all over Italy, *cacciucco* can be eaten only in Livorno and surrounding areas. It is ladled over a thick slice of toasted bread flavoured with garlic.

OLIVE OIL

Tuscany's olive oil has long been famous for its quality and excellent flavour and texture. In recognition of this outstanding quality it is even accorded DOC status. Tuscans are passionate about olive oil; it is an important cooking ingredient, and its flavour and strength fundamentally affect the final dish. Quality is measured by acid content, the finest oil being Extra Vergine with less than 1 percent acid content. A few excellent oils from Florence and the surrounding area are Extra Vergine di Scansano, Extra Vergine di Seggiano cru Querciole, Extra Vergine del Chianti, Extra Vergine di San Gimignano cru Montenidoli, and Extra Vergine Badia a Coltibuono.

Cheese

The cheeses available in Tuscany are plentiful and varied. There is a delightful overspill of cheeses from neighbouring Emilia Romagna, including, of course, the King of Cheeses, *parmigiano reggiano*. It is used extensively to complement Tuscany's marvellous pasta dishes and soups. Other cheeses made locally include *marzolino*, a ewe's-milk cheese made in March, when milk is most plentiful in the Chianti valley; *mucchino*, cow's-milk cheese made in

and around Lucca by the same procedure as pecorino; *brancolino* from the town of Brancoli; the delectable *formaggette di Zeri*, made with half ewe's and half cow's milk in Massa Carrara; and all the local rustic *cacciotte* and ricotta made with cow's, goat's and ewe's milk.

Chestnuts, mushrooms and truffles

Chestnuts are a staple of the region, particularly in mountain areas, where they are made into flour, pancakes, soups and sweet cakes like *castagnaccio*, flavoured with rosemary and pine nuts. The season peaks around mid-October, when chestnut – and steam-train – lovers can travel on a restored 1920s steam

is awaited impatiently, as the spoils are highly prized both for their pungent flavour and the handsome price they will fetch in the market.

There are many different varieties of wild mushrooms growing in abundance amongst the trees in the Tuscan hills – although the type of mushroom found will depend very much upon the type of tree it is growing next to or under – but the most sought after is the perfect *porcine (boletus edulis)*, which grows to enormous size and thickness.

If you want to try your hand at picking them yourself, make sure you go with someone who knows what they are doing, as many types are poisonous. If you don't want to take the risk,

train from Florence's Santa Maria Novella station to Marradi's *Sagra delle Castagne*, or chestnut festival, to partake in the celebrations.

In the autumn, when the rains fall, the hills become a target for family outings. Long lines of cars park along the side of the mountain roads – particularly in the Maremma, Garfagnana and Mugello areas, where little groups of people don stout shoes and arm themselves with baskets and hooked knives, searching for the delectable harvest of *funghi*. The wild-mushroom season

LEFT: picking olives, as pictured by a 15th-century artist. **ABOVE:** *The Fruit Vendor*, a 16th-century still-life by Vincenzo Campi, shows the region's harvest.

just purchase some from a roadside market during the August–October season.

Fresh wild mushrooms can be prepared in a number of ways, but perhaps the best is to grill the large *porcini* in the Tuscan way, like a steak: rub each with a slice of lemon, stick them with slivers of garlic and sprigs of thyme – or, even simpler, just brush them with olive oil and salt. Dried *porcini* are even tastier, as the dehydration concentrates the flavour. When regenerated by soaking in lukewarm water, they are ideal for use in risottos or pasta sauces.

If there is one food item that causes more excitement in Italians than wild mushrooms, it is the *tartufo*, or truffle – particularly the white

truffle, which begins to form in early summer and matures by the end of September, with a season lasting until the middle of January. Truffles are "underground fungi", developing close to the roots of oaks, poplars, hazelnut trees and certain pines. But the exact location of a "truffle trove" is a well-guarded secret, with truffle hunters regarding their talented dogs, who unearth the strong-smelling delicacy, as highly important members of their families.

Truffles are sold by the gram and handled as carefully as if they were gold nuggets – and expect to pay as if they *were* gold, for these are precious commodities. Although it is nearly impossible to describe the taste, true Italian

food connoisseurs will tell you that there is nothing on earth like a plate of plain, buttered tagliatelle with a sprinkling of parmesan and liberal shavings of white truffle on top.

While the most highly prized (and strongest-smelling) white truffles are to be found in the Piedmont region, Tuscany also has its share, mainly centred around the town of San Miniato, which produces 25 percent of Italy's crop and hosts a truffle festival in November.

Other truffle-related activities and fairs held in the San Miniato area at this time include the *Sagra del Tartufo Bianco* at Corazzano and, at Balconivisi, *Il Palio del Papero* (a parade culminating in a goose race).

EATING ITALIAN-STYLE

Italians love their food, and Tuscans are no exception. But there are "rules" to be followed if you want to "eat as the Italians do". Cappuccino in the afternoon? You'll be branded a tourist. Salad *before* the main course? Never.

Usually, breakfast consists of just an espresso or cappuccino, drunk on the hoof in a local bar if not at home, perhaps with a *panino* (filled bread roll) if you are really hungry. Dinner, too, is generally a fairly minor event, with perhaps a light soup or *frittata*, sometimes eaten as late as 10 or 11pm. Lunch, however, is a different story. This is a truly gastronomic event, to be shared and savoured with friends and family at leisure – which is why for sev-

eral hours in the middle of the day you'll find churches locked, museums shut, shops closed and streets empty. All attention is on the table.

Traditionally, a full-blown, no-holds-barred Italian meal will begin with an antipasto – a bit of salami or some roasted peppers, for example. Then follows the first course, *il primo*, usually a pasta, risotto or soup. *Il secondo* is next, consisting of meat or fish accompanied by vegetables. Salad is always served after this, effectively cleansing the palate in preparation for *i formaggi* (cheese) and *i dolci* (dessert), the last often being fruit-based. Top it off with an espresso. *Buon appetito!*

Sweetmeats

Siena is famous for the Palio, for its Gothic beauty, and for its incredibly wide selection of sweetmeats. *Cavallucci* are delicious little hard biscuits which are usually served at the end of a meal and dipped into glasses of Vin Santo.

Panforte, an Italian Christmas speciality, is unmistakable in its brightly coloured octagonal cardboard box. It is a rich, sweet cake of candied fruit, nuts, spices, honey and sugar, sandwiched between sheets of rice paper.

Ricciarelli are delightful, diamond-shaped almond cakes, also saved for the Christmas celebrations, along with the delicious, rich, golden rice cake called *torta di riso*. The local

receive a blessing from the saint. Prato has *biscottini di Prato* made from almonds, eggs, flour and sugar, delicious dipped into the local Vin Santo. In Livorno they make gorgeous, light, golden buns called *bolli*. A speciality of Lucca is a ring-shaped plain cake known as *buccellato*, and an unusual sweet tart of spinach and chard with pine nuts. Finally, in Florence, around carnival time you find *schiacciata alla Fiorentina*, a simple, light sponge cake.

No visit to Florence would be complete without a taste of its ice cream. You can see why Florentines claim to have invented *gelato*, for the city is awash with a rainbow of flavours. Always look for the sign *Produzione*

pasticcerie are filled with these and many other delectable varieties. In other areas of the region, different specialities appear. At Castelnuovo della Garfagnana they make a wonderfully simple cake of chestnuts called *torta garfagnina*; on the borders with Emilia Romagna they bake a delicious apple cake, the *torta di mele*.

Pistoia produces the pretty *corona di San Bartolomeo* for the feast of St Bartholomew on 24 August, when mothers lead their children to church wearing this cake "necklace" to

Propria (home-made). But taking pride of place amongst Tuscany's sweet specialities is the *zuccotto*, a sponge cake mould with a filling of almonds, hazelnuts, chocolate and cream. Once eaten, it is never forgotten. Literally translated as "small pumpkin", *zuccotto*, being a dome-shaped Florentine speciality, is thought by some to refer affectionately to the Duomo – or is perhaps a slightly irreverent allusion to the clergy. In the Tuscan dialect, a cardinal's skullcap is also called a *zuccotto*.

Tuscany is truly a food-lover's paradise. But remember, this is not the region to seek out complicated or intricate dishes. The food of Tuscany is a pure and simple art.   ❑

LEFT: *bruschetta*, the ubiquitous appetiser; fresh *funghi*. **ABOVE:** making a meal of your ice cream – one of the great pleasures of a Tuscan holiday.

PLACES

A detailed guide to the region, with the
principal sites clearly cross-referenced by
number to the maps

tretching from Carrara marble quarries, to the Maremma wilderness;
from Livorno's rugged coastline to the mountainous Casentino,
through the wooded slopes of Monte Amiata, the Sienese craters, the
Chianti hills and Mugello valley – Tuscany's evocative landscapes are a
powerful mixture of the wild and the tamed. For many travellers, Tuscany
is the true Italy – that is the Italy they know from romantic novels, glossy
brochures and the Merchant-Ivory film adaptations of E.M. Forster novels
– a land of swaying cypress trees, olive groves and vineyards, scattered
with medieval castles and Medici villas. Tuscans themselves are more
pragmatic about the rural idyll so beloved of foreign visitors. They have a
deep relationship with the land, but recognise the tough realities of rural
life. They are also innately sociable and will always prefer living in large
villages or small towns to an isolated farmhouse, however idyllic.

The appeal of Tuscan towns is that they appear to go against the current of modern homogeneity and internationalism and remain much as
they were a few hundred years ago. Florence, the city that gave birth to
the Renaissance, retains a huge number of the art works that were created
there. Gazing at its skyline from the Piazzale Michelangelo it is evident
how little the cityscape has changed since its artistic heyday. Variety is
also the secret of Tuscany's townscapes: from medieval hill-top towns to
Etruscan villages; from *fin de siècle* spa towns to sophisticated mountain
resorts; from the splendour of a Renaissance cathedral to a stark
Romanesque church.

But for all its artistic and architectural riches, most visitors to Tuscany
would agree that as much, if not more pleasure can be derived from a simple lunch on the shady terrace of a rustic trattoria and a bit of banter with
its owner, as a meeting with Michelangelo's *David* and Botticelli's *Venus*.
As Forster observed: "The traveller who has gone to Italy to study the tac-
tile values of Giotto, or the corruption of the papacy, may return remem-
bering nothing but the blue sky and the men and women who live under it."
And there's nothing wrong with that.   ❏

PRECEDING PAGES: a lone farmhouse and cypress trees – a classic Tuscan scene;
Porto Santo Stefano, on the Argentario peninsula. **LEFT:** a cypress copse in Le Crete.

Tuscany

0   15 km

0   15 miles

8 1

0   200 m
0   200 yds

Corte d'Appello
Museo Botanico
acolo
apollonia
Piazza San Marco
19 San Marco
Museo di Litologia e Mineralogia
Pal. Capponi
GIARDINO DELLA GHERARDESCA
Piazzale Donatello
CIMITERO DEGLI INGLESI
zi
Università
V. Cesare Battisti
S.S. Annunziata
Galleria dell' Accademia **20**
Accademia di Belle Arti
Pza d. S.S. Annunziata
Opificio delle Pietre Dure **21**
Spedale degli Innocenti
Museo Archeologico **22**
Pal. Paneiatichi Ximenes
Pal. Gerini
S. Maria d. Angeli
Pal. Niccolini
tichi
S. Maria d. Angeli
PIAZZA MASSIMO D'AZEGLIO
Pal. Pucci
V. del Castellaccio
Ospedale S. Maria Nuova
Piazza S. M. Nuova
Via degli Alfani
Via Maurizio Bufalini
Pal. Niccolini **14**
Museo dell'Opera del Duomo
Museo di Firenze Com'Era **15**
Teatro della Pergola
S. Maria Maddalena dei Pazzi
Sinogoga
Museo di Antropologia e Etnologia
Sant' Coldo
Pal. Salviati
Pal. Albizi
Piazza Salvemini
Corso
Borgo degli Albizi
Pal. Pazzi
Pal. Alessandri
Piazza S. Ambrogio
Piazza Sant'Ambrogio
ghieri
Via dei Pandolfini
Via Ghibellina
Quaratesi
Pal.
Via della Vigna Vecchia
6 Bargello
Casa Buonarroti
Piazza Pietrapiana
Borgo la Croce
Piazza dei Ciompi
ondotta
V. d. Burella
Teatro Verdi
Mercato di Sant' Ambrogio
Carceri S. Verdiana
Piazza Cesare Beccaria
Porta alla Croce
Via Vincenzo Gioberti
Via dell'Agnolo
Borgo dei Greci
Pal. Serristori
Piazza Santa Croce **23**
Carceri delle Murate
Casa d. Peruzzi
Pal. Rasponi
Pal. Corsini
Santa Croce **24**
Cappella de' Pazzi
Via Ghibellina
Pal. Vita
Museo Horne
Biblioteca Nazionale
Via dei Malcontenti
Piazza del Cavalleggeri
Via Tripoli
Piazza Piave
Lungarno delle Grazie
Lungarno della Zecca Vecchia
Lungarno Pecori Giraldi
Lungarno del Tempio
Arno
rrigiani
Pal. Museo Bardini
Pal. Serristori
Pal. Alamanni
S. Niccolò
Piazza G. Poggi
Lungarno Benvenuto Cellini
Pescaia S. Niccolò
Arno
S. NICCOLÒ
Porta San Niccolò
Porta S. Miniato
Viale Giuseppe Poggi
Villa Rusciano
L. F. Ferrucci
V. G. Orsini
RICORBOLI
Via di Belvedere
32 Piazzale Michelangelo
Convento delle Stimmatine
San Salvatore al Monte
Ricorboli
San Miniato al Monte **31**
MONTE ALLE CROCI
Istituto del Sacro Cuore

THE CITY OF FLORENCE

The throbbing heart of Tuscany and the cradle of the Renaissance, Florence is a truly outstanding city – in a country full to bursting with spectacular sights

Viewed from the surrounding hills, Florence seems to be floating in a bowl which, at dusk, is tinged violet. The honey-coloured walls and myriad, rose-coloured roofs of the city combine to make a unity which is dominated by a single, vast building, the Cathedral, or Duomo. It is by far the biggest building for miles around, with its roof and dome in the same subtle colour-range as the surrounding smaller buildings, above which it seems to float like a great liner among tugs. There are few towers or spires. Giotto's multicoloured Campanile next to the Duomo, plain in outline but intricate in detail, and the thrusting tower of the Palazzo Vecchio, elegant and sombre, soar above a generally low profile. The overall impression is not that of a city, composed of tens of thousands of units, but of one single, vast building, a majestic palace.

Close contact with the city can be at first disconcerting, even disappointing and claustrophobic. The streets are narrow, hemmed in by towering, plain buildings. There is no delicate filigree, as in Venice, or cheerful baroque, as in Rome, to tempt the eye. Some of the buildings resemble 19th-century warehouses – grim structures that were erected at a time of social unrest, their primary function being as fortresses. In any case, Florentine taste runs to the understated and the restrained.

However, gradually, the visitor comes to terms with a city which, though sharing basic characteristics with the larger family of Italian cities, is a unique mixture. The no-traffic laws in the historic centre – while often abused – have, for the most part, given Florence back to pedestrians. The streets are again part of the city's fabric, simultaneously discharging the role of stage-set and

Map on pages 80–1

LEFT: the rooftops of Florence seen from Brunelleschi's dome.
BELOW: San Miniato by moonlight.

communication link. It's a liberating atmosphere: you are free to wander, stop, and wander again, absorbing all the city has to offer.

For the visitor to attempt a comprehensive survey of Florence on a single visit will simply invite fatigue, then boredom. The monuments and localities which figure in the following bird's-eye view are chosen on a necessarily arbitrary basis. Some, of course, select themselves; others have been included because they can stand as an example for their class as a whole, or illustrate some particular point of the Florentine story.

The city has been grouped into four sections, starting with the area around the Palazzo Vecchio, followed by the area around the Duomo and then by three important religious foundations (which, though physically scattered around the city, have been grouped together in this chapter). The final section is the river Arno and beyond. Nearly all the places are within easy walking distance of one another – despite Florence's size, its historic centre is reasonably compact.

BELOW: crowds outside the Uffizi.

The civic heart

Of all the great Italian city squares, Florence's is the most perversely irregular. There is nothing in the **Piazza della Signoria ❶** to compete with the harmony that makes Venice's San Marco a vast, unroofed hall. There is nothing here of the grace of Siena's curved Campo, or the simple majesty of Rome's Capitol. Instead, the buildings follow each other around the perimeter of the piazza in no particular order. Tucked on one side is the **Palazzo Vecchio ❷** (open Fri–Wed 9am–7pm, Thur until 2pm; in summer Fri and Mon until 11pm; entrance fee; tel: 055-2768224), the seat of government for the past six centuries. Next to it is the elegant **Loggia dei Lanzi ❸**, crammed with statues. The huge fountain in the centre is the subject of amiable mockery by the residents of Florence themselves, and no two buildings in the piazza seem to have the same façade.

With a despot's love of order, Cosimo I tried to impose an artificial unity on the square, and Michelangelo even came up with a scheme to continue the shape of the Loggia all the way round. Such schemes came to nothing, leaving the piazza as a perfect illustration of Florentine "unity in diversity". Despite the absence of an overall plan and the individuality of the buildings, the piazza as a whole does come together. It has changed little over the centuries, as can be seen by comparing the contemporary painting (in the Museo di Firenze Com'Era) of the execution of Savonarola in the piazza in 1498 with the square today. The narrow platform in front of the Palazzo Vecchio sums up the function of the Piazza della Signoria: it is all that remains of the original *Ringheria* – literally, the "Haranguing Place", where orators could address the assembled citizenry.

The **Marzocco**, the lion symbol of the city which prisoners were forced to kiss, can be found here, as well as a copy of Michelangelo's immense statue of *David* (the original is in the Accademia, *see page 109*), commissioned in 1501 to mark an important change in the constitution.

Near by is a statue of the first Medici duke – and the first Medici so to aggrandise himself – Cosimo I. The Loggia dei Lanzi (named after the *landsknechts* or mercenaries employed by Cosimo) has a statue of a triumphant Perseus holding the head of Medusa *(see page 52)*, which Cosimo commissioned from Cellini. Both this bronze masterpiece and Giambologna's *Rape of the Sabine Women* on the opposite side have recently been restored and are due to be transferred to the Accademia.

The interior of the Palazzo Vecchio itself, begun in 1299 and finished in 1314, belies its grim exterior. The courtyard, with its copy of an enchanting fountain by Verrochio, is a delight. The portentous **Salone dei Cinquecento** was built for the Republican Council of 500 introduced by Savonarola in 1496. It was transformed into a throne room for Cosimo I by Vasari, who produced vast, rather tasteless but historically fascinating frescoes lauding the exploits of the Medici. Finally it served as the first parliament of a united Italy when Florence briefly became the Italian capital in 1865.

Although the Palazzo still functions as Florence's town hall – you might even catch the incongruous sight of a wedding party, as it is very much a working building – most of the historic rooms, including the Medici suite and the grim little cell where Savonarola was held before his execution in the piazza below, are usually open to the public.

The Uffizi

Adjoining the piazza are the immense galleries of the **Uffizi ❹** *(see pages 100–103)*. Originally built to house the city's administration offices *(uffici)*, the building now contains the world's greatest collection of Renaissance art, with paintings by Giotto, Botticelli, Michelangelo, Leonardo, Raphael, Titian and Caravaggio among other great masters.

Map on pages 80–1

The intricately decorated ceiling in Palazzo Vecchio's Sala d'Udienza.

BELOW: A copy of Michelangelo's *David* outside the Palazzo Vecchio.

Milan may be the fashion capital, but Florence has its fair share of home-grown designers of international repute. Nearly all have their outlets at the southern end of Via de' Tornabuoni, including the shoemaker, Ferragamo.

BELOW: arcades on the Piazza della Repubblica.

Just behind the Uffizi is the **Museo di Storia della Scienza ❺** (open Mon, Wed–Sat 9.30am– 5pm, Tues 9.30am–1pm, late opening last Thur in June and Aug, first Thur July and Sept 8–11pm; entrance fee). This museum, housed in the 14th-century Palazzo Castellani, is a refreshing change after an over-indulgence in the arts. The collection of scientific instruments shows that Renaissance Florence was pre-eminent in Europe as a centre of scientific research as well as of painting and sculpture. Amid the museum's prized collection of Galileo's instruments, the mathematician's middle finger of his right hand is displayed like the relic of a Christian saint.

The Bargello

Chronologically, the Palazzo Vecchio is the second city hall of Florence. Its predecessor, the **Bargello ❻** *(see pages 110–11)*, was built 50 years earlier in 1250 as the seat of the chief magistrate, the *Podestà*. The Bargello was, in effect, the police headquarters, and its courtyard was often the scene of public executions.

The building is now a wonderful museum specialising in sculptures; it has a rich collection of works by artists such as Brunelleschi, Michelangelo, Cellini, Donatello and many others – and is not nearly as bewildering as the Uffizi.

Four centuries of history

Just west of the Piazza della Signoria is a loosely associated group of three buildings which takes you across some four centuries of Florentine history, from the embattled Middle Ages to the era of ducal control. The **Palazzo di Parte Guelfa ❼** (just off the Via del Terme) was the headquarters of the all-powerful Guelf Party which, after the defeat and expulsion of the Ghibellines, completely ruled the city. The Palazzo was built in the 13th century, but was subsequently enlarged on a number of occasions – an indication of its expanding status in Florence.

Also referred to as the Museo dell' Antica Casa Fiorentina, the **Palazzo Davanzati ❽** (only partially open owing to restoration; daily 8.15am–1.50pm; closed 1st, 3rd and 5th Mon, 2nd and 4th Sun of the month; entrance free during restoration) is the earliest example of a patrician's home adapted to a safer age. Built about 1330, its painted walls and ceilings are excellent examples of Trecento work serving to soften and brighten domestic architecture, turning a fort into a home.

Near by, is the lively **Mercato Nuovo ❾** – also known as the "Straw Market". "Nuovo" is only relative, for the elegant covered market was built in around 1550. It is still a popular shopping place, full of high quality leather goods and tourist "tat". Here is the **Porcellino**, the amiable bronze boar whose snout is polished to gleaming gold by the rubbing of visitors, who touch it as a means of ensuring a return to the city on the Arno.

Just north of here is the **Piazza della Repubblica** , created after the medieval market quarter and Ghetto were demolished in the 19th century. The plan to develop central Florence was conceived between 1865 and 1871, when the city was briefly the capital of Italy. The ancient and "squalid" buildings were to be swept away and replaced by broad avenues, symbolic of the new age of the United Kingdom of Italy. Thankfully the scheme was abandoned. The square, with its swish cafés, department stores and billboards, remains a modern intrusion into the heart of the city.

The religious centre

The main artery of the city, the street which links the two great monuments of the Palazzo Vecchio and the Duomo, is still known as the Street of the Hosiers – Via Calzaiuoli – after the trade of the stocking-knitters who were concentrated here. It still specialises in footwear. The guilds were concentrated in this area: on the left of the street is **Orsanmichele** ⓫ (open Mon–Fri 9am–noon, 4–6pm,

Sat–Sun 9am–1pm, 4–6pm – these times may vary; closed 1st and last Mon of the month), the guild church, built on the site of the 9th-century San Michele ad Hortum. Its exterior is in effect an open-air sculpture gallery, with various statues displayed in individual niches set into the wall of the building.

Holding up to 20,000 people, the enormous size of the **Duomo** ⓬ (open daily) is emphasised by the smallness of the square in which it is placed, and the narrowness of the streets which enter it. At no point can one take in the whole.

Despite the Duomo's dominating presence, the little **Battistero** ⓭ (open Mon–Sat noon–7pm, Sun 8.30am–2pm; entrance fee) in front of it easily holds its own. The oldest building in the city, it was built on, or reconstructed from, a 7th-century building sometime between 1060 and 1120 and served as the cathedral of Florence until 1228, when it was relegated to the role of baptistery. Dante was among the eminent Florentines baptised there, and the wealthy Wool Guild *(Calimala)* lav-

TIP

In peak season, to avoid queuing for hours for the Uffizi, Bargello or Accademia, you can book your ticket and a time slot for entry either online (www.firenzeart.it), through your hotel or by phoning the museum directly. For up-to-date information on all the state museums in Florence, visit www.polomuseale.firenze.it

BELOW: the cupola mosaics of the Baptistery.

The south doors of the Baptistery were the work of Andrea Pisano (c.1270–1348) – goldsmith, sculptor and architect rolled into one.

BELOW: Moses receiving the Commandments, as depicted on the Baptistery's east doors by Ghiberti.

ished vast sums on its interior. In particular, they commissioned the superb Venetian mosaics decorating the cupola.

The Baptistery doors

The *Calimala* then turned its attention to the three great doors, first commissioning Andrea Pisano to create bronze doors for the south entrance, then initiating a competition for the other doors, which was won by Lorenzo Ghiberti. There is no mistaking the second pair (the east doors, facing the Duomo) – which took Ghiberti 27 years to create, and which Michelangelo described as the "Gates of Paradise" – for there is always a little knot of people standing staring at them. But the present panels are copies. The original panels are in the **Museo dell'Opera del Duomo** on the east side of the Piazza del Duomo (open Mon–Sat 9.30am–7.30pm, Sun 9am–1.40pm; entrance fee), while the competiton panels are in the Bargello.

The two doors are divided into 10 panels, each representing a scene from the Old Testament. Round the

panels are heads of the Sibyls and the Prophets. To get an idea of the incredible detail, and the precision to which Ghiberti worked, look for his self-portrait. It is halfway down on the right-hand side of the left-hand door and, though only a few inches high, is a perfect portrait – a little, balding man peering knowingly out.

It took the Florentines over 400 years to decide just what kind of façade they wanted for the west front of the Duomo – the side immediately facing the Baptistery. Again and again both artists and the city fathers came up with some scheme which satisfied nobody (when the first Medici pope, Leo X, visited his native city in 1515, they even erected a cardboard front for it). The present front was designed in 1887 and has inevitably come in for criticism.

Inside the Duomo

After the multicoloured splendour of the freshly restored exterior, the interior of **Santa Maria del Fiore** (the Duomo's official name) comes at first as a disappointment. Many of the treasures have been removed and are now in the Museo dell'Opera del Duomo. The overall colour scheme of the interior is muted, coming to life only at the time of religious festivals, when immense crimson banners are hung on the walls and pillars.

But the relative lack of architectural detail allows the eye to pick out the remaining treasures which highlight the city's history. High on the wall immediately to the left of the entrance are two large murals of soldiers. The right-hand one is of an Englishman, John Hawkwood, a mercenary soldier or *condottiero* who first attacked Florence for his paymasters and then became the city's Captain-General in 1375. The original intention was to erect a monument to him, but thriftily the *Signoria* settled for this clever chiaroscuro imitation, painted by Uccello in

1436, which gives the impression of a three-dimensional monument.

Further along the aisle is the painting *Dante Declaiming the Divine Comedy* by Michelino. On Dante's right in the painting are Hell and Purgatory, while on his left is a contemporary view of the city's major monuments. For years, readings from the *Comedy* used to be given in the Duomo during Lent, a fact which would doubtless have given Dante wry amusement, and in 1465 this painting was commissioned to mark the second centenary of his birth.

The Duomo's greatest treasure is Michelangelo's *Pietà*, which is now in the museum. He sculpted it for his own tomb in 1550, though it was never finished. It is entirely different from his earlier, more famous *Pietà* in St Peter's in Rome; where that is all calm, resigned acceptance, this is simply the utter defeat of death.

Lorenzo the Magnificent took refuge in the nearby **New Sacristy** on Easter Sunday morning in 1478 when the Pazzi Conspirators wounded him and murdered his brother Giuliano during High Mass. Although you can't actually walk in the New Sacristy, you can observe the artwork (including a Lucca della Robbia terracotta relief) through glass doors.

The dome and bell tower

If you have a head for heights, ascend to the gallery of the **dome** (open Mon–Fri 8.30am–7pm, Sat 8.30am–5.40pm, 1st Sun of month 8.30am–6pm; entrance fee). It is not for vertigo sufferers: the gallery is narrow and the balustrade low, but only here can Brunelleschi's stupendous achievement be fully appreciated. The original intention was to cover the interior of the dome with mosaic, which would have emphasised its soaring majesty; instead Vasari was commissioned to cover it with bold allegories.

Scarcely less tall, at 85 metres (278 ft), is the **Campanile** (open daily 8.30am–7.30pm in summer, until 4.30pm in winter; entrance fee) alongside, begun by Giotto shortly after he was appointed chief architect in 1331 and finished off after his death in 1337 by Andrea Pisano and then Talenti. Work was eventually

Map on pages 80–1

TIP

If you're thinking of climbing up to the dome, it is probably best to do it early in the day, when you still have some stamina: there are 464 spiralling stairs to negotiate before reaching the top. But once there, the view of the city is fabulous.

BELOW: the magnificent outline of Giotto's Campanile and Brunelleschi's dome.

BELOW: San Lorenzo's unfinished façade.

completed in 1359. The climb to the top is worth the effort for intimate views of the Cathedral's upper levels and the panoramic city views.

East of the Duomo, on Via dell' Oriuolo, is the **Museo di Firenze Com'Era** ⓑ (open Fri–Wed 9am–2pm; entrance fee). The historical-topographical museum of "Florence as it was" is best seen once you have familiarised yourself with the city, so you can recognise the buildings depicted in the collection. One of the most fascinating exhibits here is a 19th-century copy of the huge and famous woodcut *Pianta della Catena* made around 1470, which shows an early view of the city (*see page 56*).

Memories of the Medici

A few streets to the northwest of the Duomo is the heartland of Medicean Florence: the **Medici Palace** and the church of **San Lorenzo**. The main façade of the palace is on the Via Cavour, one of the few streets in Florence to have changed its name – it was known as the Via Larga at the time of the Medici.

The palace – now known as the **Palazzo Medici-Riccardi** ⓰ (open Thur–Tues 9am–7pm; entrance fee) – is dignified but not ostentatious. It still has the look of a fortress about it, particularly in the façade of the ground floor, with its massive blocks of "rustic" masonry. Today it is the Prefecture of Florence, but the **Cappella dei Magi** and the Medici Museum are open to the public.

The museum contains various mementoes of the family, including the poignant death-mask of Lorenzo, but it is the Capella which contains one of the brightest jewels in the Medici crown, *The Journey of the Magi* by Benozzo Gozzoli (*c.*1460; *see page 22*). This painting has been reproduced again and again, for it breathes the spirit of the Florentine Renaissance in its mixture of real figures of identifiable people, historical recreation and delight in colour. The immense procession, winding its way through a delightfully improbable landscape, is led by a handsome, richly dressed youth on horseback – the young Lorenzo. Behind him comes his grandfather, Cosimo, soberly dressed, attended by a black servant. Other members of the family are in the group – which includes the painter himself, with his name inscribed on his hat. In the distance is the Medici country Villa Cafaggiolo – and a couple of camels to remind the observer that the picture is set in the Middle East!

San Lorenzo ⑰ (open daily; entrance fee), although consecrated in 393, had its present structure commissioned by the Medici from 1420 onwards, according to designs by Brunelleschi. After the latter died, the work was continued by Antonio Manetti and then by Michelangelo, who built the new sacristy as well as the Cappelle Medicee and the Biblioteca Medicea-Laurenziana. Of particular note in the basilica are Donatello's pulpits with bronze relief of the Passion, and the Old Sacristy with sculptures by Donatello. The cloister leads to the **Biblioteca Medicea-Laurenziana** (open Mon, Fri, Sat 8am–2pm, Tues–Thur 8am–5pm), commissioned by Cosimo de' Medici, housing 10,000 volumes of the Medici library and featuring a staircase designed by Michelangelo.

The entrance to the **Capelle Medicee** (open daily 8.15am–4.50pm; closed alternate Sun and Mon; entrance fee) is outside the church, in the Piazza della Madonna degli Aldobrandini. You go in via the crypt, where a floor slab commemorates Anna Maria Ludovica (died 1743), the last in the Medici line. Stairs lead to the **Capella dei Principi** (the mausoleum of the Medici grand dukes) and the **New Sacristy** (the Medici tombs), the latter Michelangelo's first architectural commission. The two New Sacristy tombs of Giuliano and Lorenzo de' Medici are graced with the symbolic figures of *Dawn*, *Evening*, *Day* and *Night*, conveying to the observer an unforgettable feeling of uneasiness, of sadness, of loss.

Santa Maria Novella

The three great buildings of Santa Maria Novella, San Marco and Santa Croce are widely separated in the city – the first near the Stazione Centrale, the second on the far eastern side of the city, and the last in the north. They are grouped together here be-

Map
on pages
80–1

The Mercato Centrale, Florence's main food market, open Mon–Fri 7am–2pm.

BELOW: a Florentine news-stand.

*St Thomas Aquinas,
depicted on one of
the stained-glass
windows of Santa
Maria Novella.*

BELOW: Giotto's
Crucifix in Santa
Maria Novella.

cause they illustrate a truth about Florence, in the absence of which even the most splendid buildings lose something of their significance. The truth is that religion was a driving force – probably even stronger than commerce or the desire for self-aggrandisement – a force that nearly drove the city to destruction.

The church of **Santa Maria Novella** , begun in 1246, was designed by Dominican monks. Though dignified and indeed majestic, it reflects their gloomy preoccupations: striped like a tiger, the family chapels are sombre and overwhelming, their murals little more than illustrations of sermons. The **Spanish Chapel** carries this to extremes, with its murals dedicated to the 13th-century theologian, Thomas Aquinas, who was, of course, a Dominican. The chapel now lies within the **Cloister Museum** (open Mon–Thur, Sat 9.30am–5pm, Fri and Sun 1–5pm; entrance fee) adjoining the church, as do Uccello's frescoes. In the church itself is Masaccio's *Trinity (see page 49),* and the chapel is frescoed by Fra Filippino Lippi and Ghirlandaio.

Decorations in the church were carried out well into the Renaissance, with work by Brunelleschi, among others, so there is a lightening of the spirit. But the overall impression is a somewhat gloomy one, with a rather threatening air. It was in Santa Maria, incidentally, that Boccaccio's seven young maidens met in the spring of 1348, where they were joined by three young men and launched the comedy of *The Decameron.*

San Marco

Ironically, the convent of **San Marco** ⑲ was almost entirely rebuilt with money provided by Cosimo de' Medici; the irony lies in the fact that San Marco became the headquarters of the friar Girolamo Savonarola, who was the greatest and most determined enemy of Cosimo's grandson, Lorenzo. Cosimo engaged his own favourite architect, Michelozzo, who had designed the Palazzo Medici, to build San Marco, and spent more than 50,000 florins on it, as well as presenting it with a magnificent library.

Savonarola was Prior of San Marco from 1491 until his execution in 1498. During those years he totally dominated Florence, nearly succeeded in overthrowing the Medici and even presented a challenge to the papacy. The vivid portrait of him by Fra Bartolomeo, which can be seen in San Marco, shows a man with a forceful but ugly face, a great beaked nose and burning eyes.

Contemporary reports of his sermons show that they were only average in content and delivery. It was their burning sincerity which moved his audience, coupled with the fact that his prophecies of damnation seemed to come true with the French invasion of Italy and occupation of Florence in 1494. The people of Florence – ever responsive to novelty – reacted positively to this harsh, austere retainer. When he ordered them to cleanse their bodies and homes of the Devil's frivolities, they proceeded to burn their precious ornaments on a bonfire in the Piazza della Signoria.

There was, naturally, a strong reaction. Just a year later, Savonarola's power crumbled. The people abandoned him to the powerful enemies who had been waiting for this moment. He confessed that he had been deluded and that his visions were false. They hanged him, with two of his disciples, in the Piazza della Signoria, and burned the bodies afterwards. There is a plaque in the pavement commemorating the spot.

The convent of San Marco is now a **museum** (open Mon–Fri 8.15am–1.50pm, Sat and Sun until 6.50pm; closed alternate Sun and Mon; entrance fee). The prize exhibits are the murals of Fra Angelico, himself a Dominican, but one who brought a delicacy to his work quite at variance with the austere tenets of that order. Each of the friars' cells is graced by one of his murals, and at the head of the stairs is the most famous of them all, the *Annunciation*, where he almost achieves the impossible in showing how a young girl receives the news that she is to be the Mother of God. Savonarola's cell is laid out as he knew it, complete with desk and elegant but rather uncomfortable-looking chair.

In the immediate vicinity of San Marco are several sites of note, the first and foremost being the **Galleria dell'Accademia ㉕** (*see pages 108–9*), often identified by the enormous lines outside (at times even longer than those at the Uffizi). Its star attraction – and the focal point of the entire museum – is the colossal statue of *David*, which was carved between 1501 and 1504 from a single piece of marble, and established Michelangelo as the foremost sculptor of his time before the age of 30. The statue now standing in front of the Palazzo Vecchio is an equally impressive copy.

Near to the Accademia, with its entrance on the Via Alfani, is the museum **Opificio delle Pietre Dure ㉑** (open Mon–Sat 9am, 10.45am, 12.30pm, also Thur 2pm, 3.45pm, 5.30pm; entrance fee), where restoration of artistic treasures takes place. Exhibits include inlaid semi-precious stones used in *pietra dura*, as well as workbenches and instruments once used by the craftsmen.

The **Museo Archeologico ㉒** (open Mon 2pm–7pm, Wed, Fri–Sun 8.30am–2pm, Tues and Thur 8.30am–7pm; entrance fee) on Via della Colonna features an important collection of Greek, Egyptian, Etruscan and Roman art.

Santa Croce

The great **Piazza Santa Croce ㉓** was a favoured place for such large-scale activities as horse races and tournaments. *Calcio in Costume*, a historic football match, continues to be played here. And it was here that Lorenzo de' Medici held the most sumptuous tournament of all on the occasion of his marriage. "To follow the custom, and do like others, I gave

Map on pages 80–1

TIP

One little-known sight worth discovering is the Cenacolo di Sant' Apollonia (Via XXVII Aprile; open daily 8.30am–1.50pm; closed 1st, 3rd and 5th Sun, 2nd and 4th Mon of the month), a Renaissance refectory *(cenacolo)* set in a Benedictine convent now occupied by the University of Florence. On the main wall is Andrea del Castagno's dramatic version of The Last Supper.

BELOW: Fra Angelico's *Last Judgement* in San Marco.

TIP

From 6.30–9pm most bars in Florence offer a set price for drinks and free access to a buffet. The buffet laid on in some bars is substantial enough to provide a cheap substitute for supper, for those with smaller appetites or following a big lunch.

BELOW: Ponte Vecchio.

a tournament on the Piazza Santa Croce at great cost," he recorded complacently. "I find that about 10,000 ducats was spent upon it." Featuring many souvenir and leather shops, the square is now dominated by a statue of Dante.

Although the façade of **Santa Croce** ㉔ dates from the mid-19th century, Arnolfo di Cambio began work on the church in 1294. With the lightness and elegance associated with Franciscan churches, it is the Pantheon of Florence – and, indeed, of Italy, since this is where so many of the country's illustrious dead were laid to rest. The tomb of Michelangelo, designed by Vasari, is here and invariably has a little bunch of flowers laid upon it. Here also are the graves of Ghiberti and Galileo; and of Machiavelli, who died in 1527. Crowning all are the frescoes painted by Giotto and his school.

This area, which is the lowest in the city, recorded water levels in the piazza itself as high as 6.2 metres (20 feet) in the 1966 flood. The watermarks are still visible today on some buildings. The cloisters, designed by Brunelleschi, lead to the highly original **Pazzi Chapel**, which contains 12 terracotta roundels of the Apostles by Luca della Robbia.

The **Museo dell'Opera di Santa Croce** (open Mon–Sat 9.30am–5.30pm, Sun 1–5pm; entrance fee) houses the beguiling *Tree of the Cross* by Taddeo Gaddi and Cimabue's world-famous 13th-century *Crucifix*, which has badly damaged in the flood. It has only been partially restored, but this was intentional, so that the work remains a poignant reminder of the city in peril.

Across the river

The Florentines look upon their river with decidedly mixed feelings. It has brought wealth but it has also brought danger, for it is entirely unpredictable. In summer it can shrink to nothing more than a trickle along a dried-up bed. In winter, however, the Arno becomes a raging brown torrent.

The **Ponte Vecchio** ㉕ was erected by Taddeo Gaddi sometime after 1345 and has become virtually a symbol of Florence itself. Fortunately, the Germans spared it when they blew up every other Florentine bridge during World War II. It bears the same appearance that it has borne for six centuries. Even the goldsmiths and jewellers who throng it today were established there in the mid-16th century. Before the goldsmiths, the shops on the bridge were occupied by butchers and tanners, who used the river as a dumping ground until they were evicted in 1593.

It was for Ferdinando's father, Cosimo I, that Vasari built the extraordinary **Vasari Corridor** *(see page 100)* in 1565. Running from the Uffizi to the Pitti across the Ponte Vecchio, the private walkway made a physical as well as symbolic link between the two centres of Medicean power. In his film *Paisà*, Roberto Rossellini shot an unforgettable sequence of the fighting that took place along this gallery during the German retreat, which caused damage so severe that the gallery has been closed until recent years.

The Pitti Palace

The part of Florence beyond the river, the **Oltrarno**, has a character all of its own. It was not even a part of the city until an expansion of the walls in the 12th century encompassed it. Here the nobles gathered in the 14th century to make their last stand against the victorious populace who would henceforth run the city until the Medici grip tightened.

In the 15th century, this area was the centre of opposition to the Medici, spearheaded by the Pitti family. It was they who built the **Palazzo Pitti ㉖** *(see pages 104–7)*, the most grandiloquent of all Florentine buildings, which, by the irony of history, eventually became the seat of government for the Medici dukes themselves. Today it is home to museums and art galleries, the foremost of which is the **Galleria Palatina**. Here, in an opulent setting, are hung some masterpieces of the Medici collection

by artists such as Raphael, Rubens, Van Dyck and Titian. Adjoining the gallery are the **Appartamenti Monumentali** or **Reali** (State Apartments), lavishly decorated with impressive works of art. The palace also contains the **Galleria d'Arte Moderna**, the **Galleria del Costume** and the **Museo degli Argenti**.

An excellent antidote to the overwhelming splendours of the Pitti are the enchanting Boboli Gardens or **Giardino di Boboli ㉗** *(see page 103)*, attached to them.

The Porta Romana

The **Via Romana**, which begins just past the Palazzo Pitti in Piazza San Felice, goes to the **Porta Romana ㉘**, providing an artery from the city centre, via the Ponte Vecchio, to the outside world. The gates of Florence were more than a means of entry and exit. The larger ones, like the Porta Romana, built in 1328, were both a garrison and a customs post, collecting dues on all the goods that came into the city. You can now walk a section of the ramparts near Porta Romana.

Map on pages 80–1

Resting outside the Palazzo Pitti – much time and energy are needed to do this vast repository of art and the adjacent Boboli gardens justice.

BELOW: fountain on Piazza Santa Trinità.

Map on pages 80–1

The Expulsion from Paradise *by Masaccio (c.1427) in the Brancacci Chapel. They are among the most powerfully emotive figures ever painted in Western art.*

BELOW: café on Piazzale Michelangelo.

Oltrarno churches

Three churches of note are also situated on this south side of the city, each remarkable in its own way. The first, not far from the Ponte di Santa Trinità, is **Santo Spirito** ㉙, its modest 18th-century façade masking the beautiful and harmonious interior designed by Filippo Brunelleschi in the 15th century. The numerous paintings inside provide an insight into the work of some of the lesser-known masters of the Renaissance period.

To the west of Santo Spirito is the church of **Santa Maria del Carmine** ㉚, which contains one of the greatest treasures of Italian painting – the **Brancacci Chapel** frescoes (open Mon and Wed–Sat 10am–5pm, Sun 1–5pm; entrance fee). Considered by many to rival even Michelangelo's Sistine Chapel in Rome, the work of Masolino (including *The Temptation of Adam and Eve*), Masaccio (including *The Expulsion from Paradise* and *The Tribute Money*) and Filippino Lippi is truly magnificent. Unfortunately, due to the popularity of the frescoes, visitors are only allowed 15 minutes to see them.

Further east, dominating a hilltop (and battling a subsidence crisis), is **San Miniato al Monte** ㉛ (open daily). A building stood on this site as early as the 4th century; the present structure was started in 1018 and is a fine example of Florentine Romanesque architecture. Of particular interest inside are the **Capella del Crocifisso**, a tiny vaulted temple with pillars, terracotta and paintings, and the 11th-century crypt, which houses the relics of St Minias. You can hear the monks chanting each afternoon at 4.30pm.

San Miniato towers above the **Piazzale Michelangelo** ㉜, which is most easily reached from the Porta Romana along the enchanting Viale dei Colli, or else by climbing up from the river, past the Porta San Niccolò, taking the winding paths through the gardens to the piazzale.

Adorned with bronze copies of Michelangelo's statues, the piazzale is one place that no visitor should miss. From it the entire city is visible.

On the edge of the city

This southern section of Florence outside the remainder of the city wall is doubly poignant; it was here that the Republic of Florence came to an end in 1529 when the combined armies of Pope Clement VII and Emperor Charles V besieged the city. The area is a reminder, though a rapidly fading one, that Florence is a country town: a brisk walk along Via di San Leonardo will take you from the very heart of the city out into vineyards, olive groves and maize fields.

The area north of Florence is also succumbing to "urban sprawl". Fiesole *(see page 113)* is a prime example. In its heyday it was one of the chief towns of the Etruria Propria and could claim to be the mother of Florence itself; now it is little more than a refined suburb of the spreading city it overlooks from its steep hilltop vantage point. ❏

RESTAURANTS & BARS

Restaurants

VERY EXPENSIVE (€€€€)

Alle Murate
Via Ghibellina 52r
Tel: 055-240618
www.caffeitaliano.it
Cosy restaurant, very fashionable with young Florentines. Creative Tuscan and international dishes; elegant but relaxed atmosphere. Fine wines too. Closed Mon.

Enoteca Pinchiorri
Via Ghibellina 87
Tel: 055-242777
www.enotecapinchiorri.com
Reservations are essential at "Italy's finest restaurant" (three Michelin stars), as is elegant dress. It occupies a 15th-century palace with a fine courtyard for alfresco meals. Expect excellent nouvelle cuisine and very rare wines. Closed Sun and Mon, and lunchtime on Tues and Wed.

Il Cibrèo
Via Andrea del Verrocchio 8/r
Tel: 055-2341100
www.cibreo.com
Justly famed, elegant but relaxed restaurant, one of the most popular in the city. Pure Tuscan cuisine, with a creative twist. No pasta, but a selection of superb soups and other *primi* (first courses). Closed Sun and Mon.

Relais Le Jardin, Hotel Regency
Piazza Massimo d'Azeglio 3
Tel: 055-245247
www.regency-hotel.com

Top-notch food in exclusive hotel restaurant, overlooking a garden. Elegant dress and reservation required.

Sabatini
Via de' Panzani 9a
Tel: 055-282802
Fax: 055-210293
www.ristorantesabatini.it
No longer a fashionable hotspot, this very traditional restaurant remains a sophisticated choice for classic Tuscan cuisine and sober international dishes. Closed Mon.

Targa Bistrot
Lungarno Cristoforo Colombo 7
Tel: 055-677377
www.targabistrot.net
Very pleasantly set restaurant on the north bank of the Arno, some way from the centre, with a wood-panelled interior. Imaginative food. Closed Sun and mid-Aug.

Taverna del Bronzino
Via delle Ruote 25/27r
Tel: 055-495220
Classically comfortable restaurant in a quiet side street, some way from the centre. Elegantly served traditional food. Try the black *tortellini*, flavoured with truffle. Closed Sun and Aug.

EXPENSIVE (€€€)

Beccofino
Piazza degli Scarlatti 1r
Lungarno Guicciardini
Tel: 055-290076
www.beccofino.com
A newish restaurant

owned by the same couple as Baldovino. The wines and desserts are good. Closed Mon.

Cantinetta Antinori
Piazza Antinori 3
Tel: 055-292234
www.antinori.it
Restaurant in a 15th-century *palazzo*, serving typical Tuscan snacks and meals with wines from the well-known Antinori estates. A good place for a light lunch at the bar or a fuller meal in the elegant dining room. Closed weekends and Aug.

Garga
Via del Moro 48
Tel: 055-2398898
This cosy, cramped trattoria is run by an Italian-Canadian couple. Against a background of frescoed walls and cut flowers, the trendy clientele enjoy *bistecca alla Fiorentina*, fish dishes and other varied fare.

Godò
Piazza Edison 3–4r
Tel: 055-583881
A little out of town, but on the bus route to Fiesole, Godò lays on a wonderful breakfast, lunch and dinner. The *gnocchi al pomodoro* are sumptuous and the salads generous. Closed Sun.

Osteria Caffè Italiano
Via Isole delle Stinche 11/13r
Tel: 055-289368
www.caffeitaliano.it
One of the new "in" places, under the same directorship as Alle

Murate *(above)*. Short menu but high standards. Open 10am "till late". Closed Mon.

Osteria dei Centopoveri
Via Palazzuolo 31r
Tel: 055-218846
Don't be put off by the number of tourists in this cosy osteria: the food, a mixture of Tuscan and Pugliese, is excellent. Closed Mon and Tues.

MODERATE (€€)

All'Antico Ristoro di Cambi
Via S. Onofrio 1r
Tel: 055-217134
www.anticoristorodicambi.it
Busy, rustic trattoria serving genuine Florentine food, popular with local academics. Terrace in summer. Closed Sun, and a week in mid-Aug.

Alla Vecchia Bettola
Viale Ludovico Ariosto 32–34r
Tel: 055-224158
South of the river, away from the centre: the marble-topped tables, wooden benches and convivial atmosphere make this a popular place with Florentines filling up on good, rustic food. Closed Sun and Mon.

PRICE CATEGORIES

Average cost of a three-course meal per person with a half-bottle of wine:
€ = under €25
€€ = €25–€40
€€€ = €40–€60
€€€€ = more than €60

Acqua al Due
Via della Vigna Vecchia 40r
Tel: 055-284170
www.acquaal2.it
A real dining experience which requires booking ahead due to its popularity. Try the *assaggio di primi* (five pasta dishes as chosen by the chef) followed by the *assaggio di dolci* (a selection of the desserts of the day).

Baldovino
Via S. Giuseppe 22r
Tel: 055-241773
www.baldovino.com
Located just off Piazza Santa Croce, at Baldovino you can eat anything from a salad to a full meal, without sacrificing quality. Refreshingly modern decor, young Scottish owner. Closed Mon in winter.

Buca Mario
Piazza Ottaviani 16r
Tel: 055-214179
www.bucamario.it
Cellar restaurant with good home-made pasta and grilled meats. Very popular with tourists. Closed Wed and Thur lunch, and three weeks in July.

Coco Lezzone
Via del Parioncino 26
Tel: 055-287178
Traditional food of the highest quality. Ingredients are always very fresh, and the menu changes with the seasons. Closed Sun and Tues evening.

Da Zà Zà
Piazza del Mercato Centrale 26r
Tel: 055-215411
www.trattoriazaza.it

Good, earthy food and delicious home-made puddings. The riotous atmosphere is enjoyed by both locals and tourists. Closed Sun.

Gustavino
Via della Condotta 37r
Tel: 055-212421
www.gustavino.it
New classy restaurant whose open kitchen allows you to see your meal in preparation. The food is creative without being too fancy and is beautifully presented. Look out for the speciality food-and-wine evenings, which can be booked via the website. Closed Mon.

La Pentola dell'Oro
Via di Mezzo 24–26r
Tel: 055-241808
www.lapentoladelloro.it
As well as being unique, this is one of the friendliest restaurants in the city. Chef Giuseppe Alessi is more than willing to explain the dishes; the recipes – published in the restaurant's book – are inspired by medieval and Renaissance cookery. Closed Sun.

Latini
Via dei Palchetti 6r
Tel: 055-210916
www.illatini.com
You can't book for this popular, noisy trattoria, and there is often a long queue. Communal tables; enjoyable atmosphere. Not a good choice for vegetarians: huge plates of meat are specialities. Closed Mon.

Mamma Gina
Borgo San Jacopo 37r
Tel: 055-2396009

www.mammagina.it
Set in a Renaissance *palazzo*, this trattoria produces hearty Tuscan dishes. Closed Sun.

Pane e Vino
Via San Niccolò 70r.
Tel: 055-2476956
Pleasant, informal restaurant with an interesting menu (including a daily "Menu Degustazione" with six courses) and excellent wines. Closed Mon.

Trattoria del Carmine
Piazza del Carmine 18r
Tel: 055-218601
Small, traditional trattoria in the Oltrarno. Part of the long menu changes seasonally; all tastes catered for. Good Tuscan soups; huge portions of home-made lasagne. Closed Sun.

INEXPENSIVE (€)
Borgo Antico
Piazza Santa Spirito 6r
Tel: 055-210437
A cosy restaurant where a standard menu is supplemented by an extensive range of daily specials. Try the ravioli for a rich filling pasta dish, or one of the *secondi* from the specials menu. Lovely terrace for summer dining.

Cantinetta da Verrazzano
Via de' Tavolini 18–20
Tel: 055-268590
Pleasant, wood-panelled coffee house and wine bar in the centre of town. Delicious sandwiches and snacks; wines from the Verrazzano estate. Closed Sun.

Da Nerbone
Mercato di San Lorenzo
Tel: 055-219949
Authentic, very good market eatery as old as the market itself. Dishes like tripe and *lampredotto*, as well as the usual trattoria fare. There are few tables. Closed evenings and Sun.

Da Sergio
Piazza San Lorenzo 8r
Tel: 055-281941
Big, airy trattoria, hidden behind a row of stalls. A haunt of market workers and discerning tourists. Short, simple, seasonal menu; fish is featured Tues–Thur. No desserts served. Open for lunch only; closed Sun.

Enoteca de' Giraldi
Via de' Giraldi 4r
Tel: 055-216518
www.vinaio.com
A pleasant wine bar in a high-ceilinged, former stable building, which once formed part of the Palazzo Borghese. There is an interesting selection of Tuscan wines. Handy for the Bargello. Closed Sun.

I Tarocchi
Via dei Renai 12r
Tel: 055-2343912
Pizzeria with lively, friendly atmosphere. Closed Mon and lunchtime on Sat and Sun.

Il Pizzaiuolo
Via dei Macci 113r
Tel: 055-241171
The pizzas are wonderful, but there's plenty more besides. Try the *antipasto della casa*. Popular. Closed Sun and Aug.

Il Vegetariano
Via delle Ruote 30r
Tel: 055-475030
The imaginative use of fresh vegetables in its dishes makes Il Vegetariano the main contender for the city's best vegetarian eatery. The atmosphere is informal and unassuming. Closed Mon.

La Casalinga
Via del Michelozzo 9r
Tel: 055-218624
One of the best-value eateries in town. Plentiful helpings of home cooking attract locals as well as visitors. Family run. Closed Sun.

Le Belle Donne
Via delle Belle Donne 16r
Tel: 055-2382609
Hole-in-the-wall restaurant with a marvellous counter display of fresh fruit and vegetables. Always crowded. The menu, written on a board, features Florentine standards with some variations. Closed weekends and Aug.

Le Mossacce
Via del Proconsolo 55r
Tel: 055-294361
Trattoria between the Cathedral and the Bargello, serving pasta dishes and basic Tuscan fare. Popular lunchtimes with office workers. Closed Sat and Sun.

Mario
Via delle Rosine 2r
Tel: 055-218550
www.trattoriamario.com
Intimate and down to earth, this is a great place to experience fast food, Tuscan-style. A good selection of meals. Open for lunch Mon–Sat.

Ruth's
Via Carlo Farini 2a
Tel: 055-2480888
Pleasant and airy restaurant serving kosher Middle Eastern food. Closed Fri pm.

Santa Lucia
Via Ponte alla Mosse 102r
Tel: 055-353255
Authentically Neapolitan, no-frills trattoria, serving the best pizzas in town. Good seafood, too. Booking essential.

Trattoria Cibrèo
Via dei Macci 122r
Tel: 055-2341100
www.cibreo.com
Annexe of Il Cibrèo (see above), but with meals at half the price. Few frills, but the food is basically the same as in the main restaurant. No bookings. Closed Sun and Mon.

Bars, Cafés and Ice-Cream Parlours

A frothy cappuccino and a buttery brioche at **Robiglio** (five branches including Via dei Servi and Via dei Tosinghi) is a must in Florence. A hot chocolate or aperitivo at **Rivoire** (Piazza della Signoria) is also worth experiencing just once. People-watch at **Paszkowski**, **Gilli** or the **Giubbe Rosse** (Piazza della Repubblica), or for a view of the rooftops and Brunelleschi's dome, go to the bar at the top of **La Rinascente** department store. **Caffè Italiano** (Via della Condotta), just behind Piazza della Signoria, is a cosy place to indulge in a slice of cake or cocktail. Choose from the vast range of ice creams at the neon-lit **Festival del Gelato** (Corso). Follow the street on down to **Chiaroscuro**, for a buffet lunch, evening aperitivo and coffee from all over the world. Further along is **I Visacci** (Borgo degli Albizi), a cheerful place in which to relax and drink a prosecco. On the street behind (Via San Egidio), **Oleum Olivae** makes delicious panini to order, washed down with a glass of wine. North of Santa Croce, **Caffè San Ambrogio** (Piazza San Ambrogio) is suitable at any time of day and has outside seating in the square. **The Jazz Club** (Via Nuova de'Cascini, off Borgo Pinti) is an underground cavern with live music. Near Piazza Santa Croce, **Finesterrae** (Via dei Pepi) is a Moroccan restaurant and bar with a sultry atmosphere. **Gelateria dei Neri** (Via dei Neri) makes creamy ice cream and granite to beat the summer heat. In the other direction, towards the Arno, **Moyo** is a chic bar and restaurant. The elegant and pricey bars lining the river are where Florentines go to be seen. On the south bank, drink wine at **Caffè Pitti** (Piazza Pitti) or have a cocktail at **Il Rifrullo** (Via San Niccolò).

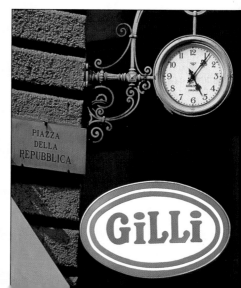

GLI UFFIZI

The greatest collection of Renaissance art to be found anywhere in the world

Florence's most famous gallery (open Tues–Sun 8.15am–6.50pm; entrance fee) is housed in a U-shaped building whose former use as administrative buildings gave it its name "The Offices". It now holds the highest concentration of Renaissance art in the world, including famous works by Botticelli, Leonardo, Michelangelo and Raphael. The majority of the collection originates from the Medici family, dating from the latter half of the 16th century, when Francesco de' Medici decided to convert the second floor into a museum.

The gallery was left to the city at the end of the dynasty line, and also contains the **Gabinetto Disegni e Stampe degli Uffizi** (Collection of Prints and Drawings; entrance included) and the **Contini Bonacossi Collection** (temporarily closed, normally on request only; tel: 055-2388651; entrance included) and the **Corridoio Vasariano** (Vasari Corridor; by appointment only; tel: 055-2654321 for information), which passes over the Ponte Vecchio and connects the Uffizi to the Palazzo Pitti. There are three different entrances into the museum for groups, individuals and individuals with tickets. The frequent long lines make it worthwhile buying tickets with a scheduled entry time in advance (055-294883 or www.florenceart.it).

The main collection is on the second floor, with some important rooms on the first and temporary exhibitions on the ground floor. The paintings are largely arranged chronologically by schools – moving from the predominantly Italian collection to some works by German, Flemish and Dutch masters.

ABOVE: The Botticelli Rooms (10–14) are the most popular exhibit in the Uffizi, containing the world's best collection of work by the artist. Here are the famous mythological paintings which fused ideas of the spiritual and the secular: the *Birth of Venus*, painted around 1485, and *La Primavera*, painted some five years earlier. The meaning of the latter remains a subject of fervent discussion, while Venus has overtones of the Virgin Mary.

ABOVE: Room 15 exhibits Leonardo da Vinci's early works – including the *Annunciation* (1475) and the unfinished *Adoration of the Magi* (1982) – and also paintings by Perugino and Signorelli.

BELOW: Rooms 5–6 form the International Gothic Rooms, whose paintings exhibit a more conservative and less lavish approach, in keeping with the medieval mindset. Lorenzo Monaco's *Crowning of Mary* provides a good example of this by one of the main practitioners of the era.

THE EASTERN CORRIDOR

The two corridors from which the 45 rooms lead off are filled with sculptures, while the strip connecting the sides allows magnificent views down the river and towards the Ponte Vecchio. Rooms 2–4 are dedicated to works from Siena and Florence during the Duecento and Trecento (13th and 14th centuries), exhibiting the decorative and iconographic pre-Renaissance style. Notable works are the interpretations of the Madonna by Giotto and Duccio, as well as that of Cimabue, Giotto's master.

Room 7 is dedicated to the early Renaissance and its founders and leading figures, who include Masaccio and Uccello and, later, Fra Angelico. The Filippo Lippi Room (8) holds the Franciscan monk's lovely *Madonna with Angels*, as well as a number of other celebrated works, and is worth visiting for Piero della Francesca's portraits of the Duke and Duchess of Urbino I *(pictured above)*. Room 9 holds works by the Pollaiuolo brothers, whose paintings show no distinctive style but are nonetheless decorative.

After a room of sculpture, the Tribuna (Room 18) is an octagonal room lit from above, with a mother-of-pearl-encrusted ceiling, designed by Buontalenti. This room's structure, decor and holding was designed to allude to the four elements and used to exhibit the objects most highly prized by the Medici. It holds a collection of portraits and sculpture, as well as Rosso Fiorentino's super-famous *Putto che Suona*, or *Angel Musician (pictured opposite)*. The circular route around the room unfortunately renders it somewhat difficult to appreciate the art from a good distance or to linger in front of the portraits.

ABOVE: The High Renaissance continues in Room 19, which exhibits Perugino and Signorelli's work. These Umbrian artists worked during the 15th and 16th centuries, and the latter's tondo (circular painting) *Holy Family* is reputed to have inspired Michelangelo's version. Room 20 is a break from Italian art, with work by Dürer (including his *Madonna and the Pear* pictured here) and Cranach. The last few rooms on the eastern corridor hold works from the 15th and 16th centuries: the Venetian school in Room 21, followed by Holbein and other Flemish and German realists (22) and more Italian work by Mantegna and Correggio in Room 23. Room 24 contains a collection of miniatures.

THE WESTERN CORRIDOR

The western corridor starts with the Michelangelo Room and his vivid *Holy Family* tondo *(below)*. This prelude to Mannerism was produced for the wedding of Angelo Doni to Maddalena Strozzi, and the depth of the figures betrays Michelangelo's penchant for sculpture. Early works by Raphael – such as the glowing *Madonna of the Goldfinch* – and Andrea del Sarto's *Madonna of the Harpies* can be seen in this room. The subsequent room (27) is the last to focus on Tuscan art before moving on to other regions of Italy.

LEFT: Room 28 displays work by Titian, including the erotic *Venus of Urbino (left)*. Rooms 29–30 focus on Emilia Romagnan art and the Mannerists Dosso Dossi and Parmigianino. Veronese's *Annunciation* is in Room 31, while Tintoretto's sensual *Leda and the Swan* hangs in Room 32. A number of rooms are now dedicated to minor works of the Cinquecento (16th century) before the Flemish art of Rubens and Van Dyck in Room 41. The Sala della Niobe has reopened and holds sculpture, while Room 43 has works by Rembrandt.

On the first floor are five rooms of paintings, as well as the Verone sull'Arno – the bottom of the U-shaped corridor which looks over the Arno and the Piazza degli Uffizi the other side.

The Sala del Caravaggio holds three paintings by the troubled artist whose style is characterised by his realism and use of light *(see his* Sacrificing of Isaac, *right)*. His method inspired the works by other artists contained in the same room and the next three: the Sala di Bartolomeo Manfredi, the Sala di Gherardo delle Notti and the Sala dei Caravaggeschi.

The last room adjacent to the Verone is the Sala di Guido Reni, where three paintings by the classicist artist of the first half of the 17th century are displayed.

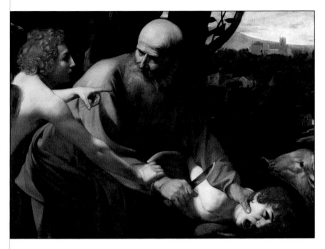

Gabinetto and Contini Bonacossi Collection

The Gabinetto, recently situated on the second floor, holds a number of important and precious drawings – including works by Renaissance masters (such as Fra Bartolommeo's *Portrait of a Young Woman, right*), some of which are only viewable for academic study purposes. The Contini Bonacossi Collection was recently installed in the Uffizi (moved from its previous home in Palazzo Pitti) and contains paintings, furniture, majolica and coats of arms.

Galleria degli Uffizi

PALAZZO PITTI AND GIARDINO DI BOBOLI

The gigantic Palazzo Pitti and the Boboli Gardens were once the royal residence

The Pitti houses seven museums, and provides access to the splendid gardens that became a model for Italian landscaping. The imposing Renaissance palace is built of large, rough-hewn stones; set in its own piazza, it dominates the area to the south of the Ponte Vecchio. The gardens, which lead up to Forte Belvedere, escape being overshadowed thanks to the hill, which allows them to rise, to give glorious views over the city to the north and countryside to the south.

A visit to one or two museums combined with the gardens will take up at least half a day, and a three-day ticket offers value for money. Tickets are purchased in the right wing of the palace, and entrance to all the museums is from the internal courtyard. The **Appartamenti Reali** and the **Galleria Palatina** (Royal Apartments/ Palatine Gallery) combine luxurious rooms with spectacular works of art. A ticket to the **Giardino di Boboli** (Boboli Gardens) includes admission to the **Museo degli Argenti** and the **Museo delle Porcellane** (Silver Museum/Porcelain Museum). These smaller museums are worthwhile for a second visit or if you have a specific interest. The **Galleria d'Arte Moderna** and the **Galleria del Costume** (Gallery of Modern Art/ Costume Gallery) are accessed by another joint ticket. The **Museo delle Carrozze** (Carriage Museum) is closed at present for restoration.

ABOVE: At the end of the Medici reign in 1737, the *palazzo* became the home of the Lorraines, and its elongated cubic form was further extended by the wings which curve round to frame the paved square at its front. Work on the outside was paralleled by alteration to the interior decor, which exhibits the ostentatious tastes of the period of the Lorraines and the Savoys, the next to take up occupancy within its walls. The history of the *palazzo* includes brief tenure by the Bourbons and the Emperor Napoleon before the last ruling monarch, Vittorio Emmanuele III, transferred the house to the public.

THE GARDENS

The gardens (open daily 8.50am–sunset; closed 1st and last Mon of the month; entrance fee) were commissioned by Cosimo I and created by a range of prolific figures of the day, from Vasari and Ammannati to Buontalenti. One of the most compelling characteristics of Boboli is the shadowy dark-green colour of the cypress and box which serve to highlight the numerous statues of amorous nymphs, satyrs and statuesque deities, as well as the grottoes and fountains. The steps lead up to the terrace behind the palace and in front of Susini's fountain of 1641. The amphitheatre surrounding the fountain occupies the site of a quarry used to obtain much of the stone for the palace, and contains an Egyptian obelisk. A series of terraces leads up the hill to the Neptune Fountain, round to the Rococo Kaffeehaus and up to the statue of *Abundance*. At the summit lies the Giardino del Cavaliere, or Knight's Garden. This delightful garden – with its low hedges, rose bushes and little cherub fountain – gives open views of San Miniato to the left and the village of Arcetri to the right, rising above a valley dotted with villas and olive groves. This is where the Museo delle Porcellane is located.

ABOVE: The Palazzo Pitti was commissioned in the 15th Century by Luca Pitti, and was designed by Brunelleschi, although he never lived to see the final results. The Medici family took over ownership in 1549, when Eleonora di Toledo, wife of Cosimo I, purchased the *palazzo* when the Pitti family ran into financial strife. She transferred her family from the Palazzo Vecchio to this more tranquil location, though still close to the political heart of the city. This link was strengthened by the Vasari Corridor, which directly connects the residence with Piazza della Signoria by way of the Uffizi and the Palazzo Vecchio. Under the Medici family work on the *palazzo* continued, substantially increasing its size and grandeur. Ammannati was given architectural control, and he constructed the inner courtyard and redesigned the outer façade, which was later further extended.

The cypress-statue-lined avenue known as il Viottolone *(see left)* leads to the Vasca dell'Isola (Island Pool) with its Oceanus Fountain (by Giambologna), murky green water, ducks, fish, strange mythical creatures and circular hedge. The route from here to the exit leads past the Grotta di Buontalenti, named after the sculptor who created this cavern in 1583–8. Copies of Michelangelo's *The Slaves* (the originals are on display in the Accademia; *see page 109*) are set in the four corners. Finally, on the right as one exits and nestling below the wall of the corridor, is the naked, pot-bellied Pietro Barbino, Cosimo I's court dwarf, seated on a turtle *(see opposite)*.

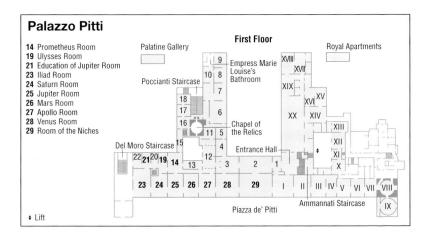

Palazzo Pitti

First Floor

14 Prometheus Room
19 Ulysses Room
21 Education of Jupiter Room
23 Iliad Room
24 Saturn Room
25 Jupiter Room
26 Mars Room
27 Apollo Room
28 Venus Room
29 Room of the Niches

Palatine Gallery

Poccianti Staircase

Del Moro Staircase

Empress Marie Louise's Bathroom

Chapel of the Relics

Entrance Hall

Royal Apartments

Piazza de' Pitti

Ammannati Staircase

✦ Lift

The **Galleria Palatina** on the first floor (open Tues–Sun 8.15am–6.50pm; closed Jan; entrance fee) houses an extraordinary range of paintings collected by the Medici family. In the west wing of the building are the rooms comprising the **Royal Apartments** (same times as the gallery). They are garish and ostentatious, decked out in heavy carpets, wallpapers, fabrics and furnishings, and overstuffed with treasures. Several of the rooms are named after the colour in which they are themed, and contain paintings and portraits fitting with the mood, followed by the Queen's Apartments, the King's Apartments and a ceremonial room, all filled with exquisite furniture.

ALLEGORICAL FRESCOES

The most important rooms, named after the planets, are frescoed by Pietro da Cortona to allegorise the stages of Prince Ferdinando's education: Sala di Saturno, Sala di Giove, Sala di Marte (during restoration paintings have been moved to the Sala delle Nicchie) and Sala di Venere. These contain works such as Rubens's *The Consequences of War* (Sala di Marte), Raphael's *Portrait of a Lady* (*see left*: Sala di Giove). Other important paintings, such as Raphael's *The Pregnant Lady* (Sala dell'Iliade), Lippi's tondo of *The Madonna and Child* (*see above*: Sala di Prometeo) and *Sleeping Cupid* by Caravaggio (Sala dell'Educazione di Giove) are found in smaller rooms.

SILVER AND PORCELAIN

On the ground floor, the Museo degli Argenti is in the left-hand corner of the courtyard, whilst the Museo delle Porcellane is situated in the Boboli Gardens (both open daily 8.15am–sunset; closed 1st and last Mon of the month). The former contains much more than silver, ranging from antique vases much loved by Lorenzo the Magnificent to baubles encrusted with semi-precious stones and jewellery. The frescoed rooms alone make a visit worthwhile – in particular the Sala di San Giovanni which formed part of the summer apartments. The frescoes by the artist after whom the room is named depict the reign of Lorenzo de' Medici, portrayed as a great patron of the arts. The latter museum displays pottery as well as objets d'art.

The **Galleria d'Arte Moderna** contains mainly Italian works from the neoclassical and Romantic movements, dating from the 18th century to the period after World War I (including this fine portrait of *The Artist's Daughter-in-Law* by Giovanni Fattori). The most notable feature of the second-floor collection is its holding of paintings by the Macchiaioli, late 19th-century Italian Impressionists. Also situated on the second floor is the **Galleria del Costume** (both open daily 8.15am–1.50pm; closed 1st, 3rd and 5th Mon, 2nd and 4th Sun of the month; entrance fee), whose 6,000-piece holding of clothing, theatrical costumes and accessories is supplemented by frequent special exhibitions.

ABOVE AND RIGHT: One of the finest rooms is the Sala di Apollo, in which hang important works by Andrea del Sarto (including his *Lamentation of Christ*, 1522–3, *above*) and another master of the High Renaissance, Titian (notably his *The Interrupted Concert*, c.1510, *right*).

THE ACCADEMIA

Originally the world's first
school of art, the gallery is now
home to Michelangelo's most
famous work, *David*

Michelangelo's *David* is the main attraction of
the Galleria dell'Accademia (open Tues–Sun
8.15am–6.50pm; entrance at No. 60; entrance
fee includes entry to the Museo degli Strumenti
Musicali), but the rest of the art is equally
worthy of attention.

The museum was originally part of
the world's first art school, the
Accademia delle Belle Arti, an institution established by Cosimo I de'
Medici and of which Michelangelo
was a founding academician. The
current gallery was consolidated in
the late 18th century by Grand
Duke Pietro Leopoldo next to the
art school housed in the same row
of buildings.

The collection contains
sculpture and early Renaissance religious art, and has
recently been expanded to
incorporate a display of musical instruments. On entry, the
Sala del Colosso contains
the plaster cast of Giambologna's *Rape of the Sabines*
(on display in the Loggia
dei Lanzi – *see pages 84,
111*) and a collection of
colourful religious art from the
early Cinquecento (16th century).

While the exit to the right of the entrance
leads to the Museo degli Strumenti Musicali, the
Accademia continues through the door to the
left. The view of Michelangelo's *David* from the
end of the corridor-shaped Galleria dei Prigion-
ieri is stunning, the domed Tribuna di Michelangelo at its far extent framing the huge statue.

ABOVE: A double bass made by Bartolomeo Castellani in 1792.

ABOVE: Among the most notable pieces is Fillipino Lippi's
striking *Deposition from the Cross*, which was finished by
Perugino on the former's death. Other highlights are *Christ as
a Man of Sorrows* – a poignant fresco by Andrea del Sarto –
and Fra Bartolomeo's *Prophets*.

Off to the left of the Tribuna di Michelangelo are three small rooms – the Sala del Duecento e Prima Trecento, the Sala dei Giotteschi
and the Sala degli Orcagna. These all hold
early Florentine works, including works by
Taddi and Daddi. The *Tree of Life* by Buona-
guida is one of the best-known and most
impressive works in the small collection.
Stairs lead to the first floor and four further
rooms. The first two contain attractive work
from the late 14th century. The following room
is dedicated to Florentine painter Lorenzo
Monaco, whose work shows the bridge
between Gothic and Renaissance art – the key
to understanding the Florentine style.

LEFT: The approach to the Tribuna is lined with four unfinished sculptures by Michelangelo. Known as *The Prisoners* or *The Slaves*, the pieces were intended for the tomb of Pope Julius II, but became the property of the Medici family instead.

DAVID

Standing at over 4 metres (13 ft), Michelangelo's *David* is the most famous sculpture in Western art. It was sculpted between 1501 and 1504 as a symbolic commemoration of the start of republican Florence, through its depiction of the young boy who slew Goliath. Originally placed in front of the Palazzo Vecchio (a copy stands in the former position), the statue was moved to the Accademia in 1873 for reasons of preservation – a decision which was heavily criticised by many at the time. The marble from which *David* was carved was famously rejected as faulty by other artists, but the then 29-year-old Michelangelo sought to embrace its faults and patches of discoloration.

David is celebrated for being of perfect proportions – hailed as a testament to Michelangelo's eye for detail. The artist's attention to minutiae is evident in the muscle contour of the legs and the veins in the arms, which can be appreciated from every angle thanks to the way in which the statue is displayed. The eyes are of particular interest for their heart-shaped pupils – a feature which the visitor could well believe was a computer-generated alteration for the many postcards and souvenirs featuring *David*.

Surrounding *David* in the main room are works by contemporaries, including di Tito and Allori. The first floor is also the location of the Salone del Ottocento, a cluttered room of more modern and less attractive sculptures and busts, primarily by Lorenzo Bartolini, and the rooms known as the Sale del Quattrocento *(see left)*. The latter display a holding of 15th-century Florentine paintings, but unfortunately they are often closed.

The gallery ends with a small

ABOVE: Botticelli's delightful *Madonna and Child* is in the Sale del Quattrocento Fiorentino, as is Paolo Uccello's masterpiece *Scenes of a Hermit Life*.

THE BARGELLO

The Bargello holds Florence's most important collection of sculpture from the Medici and private collections

The *palazzo* was transformed into a museum in 1865, its previous uses as the seat of the city's chief magistrate and later as a prison reflected in features of the building such as the decor, and in the street names of the surrounding area. Entry into the rooms of the museum (open Mon–Sun 8.15am–1.50pm; closed 2nd and 4th Mon, 1st, 3rd and 5th Sun of the month; entrance fee) takes the visitor through the medieval courtyard, whose walls are adorned with emblems of the city wards, magistrates and governors. *Oceanus* by Giambologna is one of the sculptures housed under the vaulted cloisters, which lead off to the right of the staircase into the Sala del Cinquecento. The entrance to this room – which contains a range of Renaissance statues, busts and bas-reliefs in marble and bronze – is flanked by two lions. Of particular note in the room are a number of works by Cellini, a Florentine bronze sculptor of lesser fame, while 16th-century contemporaries such as Ammannati and others complete the collection in this room. An external staircase leads to the second floor and a number of bronze sculptures of birds on display in the loggia, originally made by Giambologna for the Medici Villa di Castello.

ABOVE AND BELOW: The Bargello museum (above in an 18th-century painting by Giuseppe Zocchi) is situated in an impressive Gothic *palazzo* constructed in the mid 13th-century on Via del Proconsolo, the heart of the ancient city.

ABOVE: Donatello's famous version of *David* (from 1430–40) is on display in the Donatello Gallery – a small bronze most renowned for being the first nude since antiquity. It differs dramatically from Michelangelo's masterpiece not just in size and material, but also in its coyness and melancholy, which some view as more faithful to David's youth.

THE DONATELLO AND BRONZE GALLERIES

The Salone del Consiglio Generale is often nicknamed the Donatello Gallery. Apart from *David*, other works by Donatello in the room worth paying attention to are *Saint George*, which was designed for the Orsanmichele church, and *Cupid*. The walls and ceiling of the room figure several glazed terracotta works by Luca della Robbia, while the adjoining chapel (the Cappella Maddalena) features attractive frescoes depicting hell: look out for the figure on the right dressed in maroon thought to be a depiction of Dante. Also on the first floor is a corridor displaying an eclectic group of 5th- to 17th-century objets d'art, including ivories and Islamic treasures.

Upstairs, the Verrocchio Room displays Tuscan sculpture from the late 15th century, including portrait busts of notable Florentines and an interpretation of *David* by the artist who lends his name to the room, Andrea del Verrocchio. The adjoining rooms are filled with work by members of the della Robbia family – predominantly Andrea and Giovanni – dominated by the often overbearing large reliefs coloured in yellow, green and blue.

The last major room in the museum is the Bronze Gallery. This has one of the most rewarding displays in the Bargello. The sculptures generally depict mythological tales or Greek history, in the form of both models and more functional articles such as candelabra. The model for Giambologna's *Rape of the Sabines* (on display in the Loggia dei Lanzi) stands out, as do two other of his statues: *Kneeling Nymph* and *Hercules and Antaeus*. Completing the second floor is a collection of medals.

ABOVE RIGHT: Four of Michelangelo's early sculptures are on display in the Sala del Cinquecento: *Bacchus Drunk*, the Pitti Tondo – a depiction of the Madonna and Child shown here – *Apollo-David* and *Brutus*.

ABOVE: In the Donatello Room are the bronze panels submitted by Ghiberti and Brunelleschi *(above)* for the Baptistery doors.

RIGHT: Giambologna's bronze of Mercury is in the Sala del Cinquecento.

AROUND FLORENCE

The region surrounding Florence was the most advanced in Europe throughout the Middle Ages and the Renaissance, resulting in an important agricultural, historical and artistic heritage for its people

The province of Florence is full of towns and villages perched on steep, cypress-covered hills. Below them, straggling down to the bottom of the valleys, are the vineyards that have been producing some of the most famous wines in Italy since the Renaissance – red Chianti and Carmignano and white Malvasia and Trebbiano. Just north of the city lies the Mugello, the fertile Apennine region that forms the border between Tuscany and Emilia Romagna. The best view of the mountains is a seat in the Roman theatre of Fiesole, a delightful hill town 8 km (5 miles) northeast of Florence.

Hilltop retreat

Fiesole ❶ was first settled by Etruscans probably in the 8th century BC. The Romans who followed named the place Faesulum – praising it for its freshwater springs and its ideal location for controlling the entire valley. Despite this, the town was repeatedly attacked by the Goths and the Byzantines, and in 1125 it was destroyed by Florentine troops – only the Cathedral and the bishop's palace were saved. During the 15th century Fiesole became a city suburb where wealthy Florentines built their villas. Today, a villa on the slopes of Fiesole's verdant hill is one of the most sought-after addresses.

The main route from the centre of Florence is the Via San Domenico (the No. 7 bus goes from Piazza Stazione or Piazza San Marco), which climbs up to Fiesole's centre. The views on the way up reveal a landscape of extraordinary beauty dotted with Renaissance villas perched on the slope of the hill.

Everything you will want to see in Fiesole lies a short distance from the Piazza Mino da Fiesole, the main square. A lane leads north to the **Teatro Romano**, where you can buy

Map on page 114

LEFT: olive trees and views over Florence.
BELOW: attractive villas' cling to the hillsides above the city.

The Teatro Romano, with its numbered seats, could originally accommodate an audience of up to 2,000 people. It is in a remarkable state of repair, and is still used for dances and shows during the summer festival season.

tickets for Fiesole's **Zona Archeologica** (open Wed–Mon 9.30am–5pm in winter, daily until 7pm in summer), entered from the ticket office and comprising the city's 1st-century BC Roman theatre, public baths of the same era, and an Etruscan temple, built in the 4th century BC and dedicated to Minerva, goddess of wisdom and healing. Also within the complex, the **Museo Archeologico**, built in the style of a Roman temple, is packed with finds from excavations in Fiesole. Included in the ticket is entry to the **Museo Bandini**, behind the cathedral on Via Duprè – a small art gallery with a fairly wide and representative selection of paintings from the early and middle Renaissance, as well as some school of della Robbia terracottas.

On the square, the huge **Cattedrale di San Romolo** (open daily) is almost completely unadorned except for four frescoes, which include a serene portrait of *St Sebastian* by

Perugino (early 16th century), and later 16th-century apsidal frescoes by Nicodemus Ferrucci of the *Life of St Romolo*. The Cathedral's jewel is the marble funerary monument to Bishop Leonardo Salutati, by Mino da Fiesole (1429–84), with a realistic portrait bust of the smiling bishop.

From the southwest corner of the square, Via Vecchia Fiesolana leads to the **Villa Medici ❷** *(see page 116)*.

Take any of the downhill paths from here to reach the hamlet of **San Domenico ❸**, about a 15-minute walk. The church of San Domenico dates from 1406 and contains a recently restored *Madonna with Angels and Saints* (1430), an early work of Fra Angelico, who began his monastic life here before transferring to San Marco.

Opposite the church, the Via della Badia dei Roccettini descends to the **Badia Fiesolana** (open Mon–Fri), once a monastery and now home to the European University. The un-

Around Florence

finished brick-and-stone façade of the huge church (dull inside, so don't worry if it is closed) incorporates the lovely green-and-white Romanesque façade of an earlier and smaller church. The No. 7 bus can be caught in San Domenico for the return journey to Florence.

The Mugello valley

Just a few kilometres north of Florence, the Apennine foothills and Sieve river basin form the Mugello region (www.mugellotoscana.it). Like Chianti, only less well trodden, it is characterised by gentle hills and fertile valleys, olive groves, vineyards, oak and chestnut woods. The landscape is at its most picturesque in the western Sieve valley.

The Mugello has great associations with the Medici, who originated from here and lavished a lot of attention on the region. In 1451 Cosimo il Vecchio had Michelozzo alter the old fortress of Cafaggiolo just west of **San Piero a Sieve ❹** to create a country retreat, where Lorenzo il Magnifico spent part of his childhood, and writers and artists were lavishly entertained.

The palace was modified by the Borghese family, who acquired it in the 19th century. The recently restored **Villa Cafaggiolo** (open to the public: Sat and Sun 10am–12.30pm and 2.30–6.30pm; from mid-Apr to mid-Oct also open Wed and Fri 2.30–6.30pm; at other times by appointment; tel: 055-847 9293; www.castellodicafaggiolo.it) is now privately owned and used for weddings, events and a cooking school.

A little further south, **Castello del Trebbio** (guided visits every morning Mon–Fri by appointment only; tel: 055-8456230), received similar treatment at the hands of Michelozzo, and, more than any other 15th-century Tuscan villa, retains the feudal atmosphere of a Medici villa.

Overlooking San Piero a Sieve, high on a thickly wooded outcrop, is the **San Martino** fortress built in 1569 by Lanci and Buontalenti to enable Cosimo I to defend the Florentine state. This massive pentagonal castle is currently being restored, though you can walk along its walls.

Just north of San Piero a Sieve is the town of **Scarperia ❺**. Its spot-

Map on page 114

Badia Fiesolana, former monastery and now home to the European University. From the terrace in front of the church there are views down the Mugnone river valley back to Florence.

BELOW: Villa Medici.

Villas and Gardens

The idea of a country retreat, so popular in Tuscany today, originated with the Romans. The villas were either working farms, which supplied the townhouses with produce, or were planned purely for pleasure. They would be visited for a day's outing and many did not even have bedrooms.

In the 15th century the idea of the country villa was revived by the Medici family, who commissioned magnificent residences and elaborate gardens, modelled on classical ideas. In 1452 Leon Battista Alberti laid down the essential ingredients for a truly well-appointed country retreat: it had to be on a slope, full of light and air, with rooms grouped round an inner hall. The villas and gardens described here are either on the city out-skirts, in the hills around Fiesole or Settig-nano, or are easily accessible from Florence.

The **Villa Medici** (Via Vecchia Fiesolana; by appointment only; tel: 055-59164) at Fiesole, which has been described as "the first true Renaissance villa", was designed by Michelozzo for Cosimo il Vecchio between 1458 and 1461. It commands a superb view of Florence.

On the outskirts of Florence, the 15th-century **Villa la Pietra** (guided tours of the villa Fri pm, tours of the garden Tues am; advance booking necessary; tel: 055-5007210; fax: 055-5007333; www.nyu.edu/global/lapietra) belonged to Sir Harold Acton, doyen of expatriate writers in Florence, who bequeathed it to New York University. The villa contains a fine collection of Renaissance art.

Another American-owned villa in the Florentine hills is the historic **Villa i Tatti** (by appointment; tel: 055-603251; www.itatti.it), by the pretty village of Settignano. Formerly the home of art collector Bernard Berenson (1865–1959), who landscaped the gardens and restored the villa to house a collection of Renaissance paintings, it is now the Harvard University Center for Renaissance Studies.

Near by, the **Villa Gamberaia** (gardens open daily 9am–7pm; villa by appointment only; tel: 055-697205; www.villagamberaia.com) is another fine Renaissance villa which survives with most of its original garden intact.

The **Villa Medicea Poggio a Caiano** (*see page 118*) is often dubbed the perfect villa. The façade was modelled on a Greek temple by Sangallo to satisfy the tastes of Lorenzo the Magnificent. In the 19th century the gardens were converted according to the fashionable English style, with romantic temples, fountains, an aviary and a mock Gothic ruin.

Set on a steeply sloping hill, the **Villa Medicea della Petraia** (loc. Castello; open daily 8.15–sunset; villa by guided tour only, every 45 mins from 8.30am; closed 2nd and 3rd Mon of the month; entrance fee) was designed by Buontalenti for Ferdinando de' Medici as an elegant villa suitable for sumptuous entertaining. The interior is marred by the pretentious taste of the house of Savoy, but the Italianate gardens are a delight.

Only the gardens of the **Villa Medicea di Castello** (open daily 8.15am–sunset; closed 2nd and 3rd Mon of the month; entrance fee) can be viewed. The original water features are no more, but grottoes and statuary abound.

Another villa with attractive surroundings is the **Villa Demidoff and Parco di Pratolino** (open Apr–Sept Thur–Sun, Mar and Oct Sun, 10am–sunset; entrance fee), whose Mannerist gardens were restructured in the English romantic style. ❏

LEFT: cypress avenue leading to Villa la Pietra.

less monuments are rarely visited, yet there is much to see. **Palazzo de Vicari** in the main street is one of the finest examples of 13th-century civil architecture in Tuscany, similar in style to Florence's Palazzo Vecchio. The outer façade, decorated with the coats of arms of local notables, carved in stone or worked in della Robbia terracotta, faces the **Oratorio della Madonna della Piazza** in the small square, which has a *Madonna and Child* by Taddeo Gaddi. At the bottom of the main street, near the entrance to the town, is the **Oratorio della Madonna dei Terremoti**, dedicated to Our Lady of Earthquakes, which contains another fresco of the *Madonna and Child*, said to be by Filippo Lippi.

Scarperia is famous as a centre of knife-making. In local workshops traditional methods are still used to fashion knives by hand. There is even a museum dedicated to the craft, the **Museo dei Ferri Taglienti** (Museum of Cutting Tools) in the Palazzo dei Vicari (open June–Sept Sat and Sun 10am–1pm, 3.30–6.30pm, Wed–Fri 3.30–7.30pm; entrance fee), and in September the town hosts an international knife exhibition.

Scarperia is also known for the racetrack on its outskirts. The scenic "Mugello" circuit is used as a Ferrari F1 test centre and hosts the Italian motorbike grand prix in June.

A turning on the left of the southern approach to Scarperia wends its way through dense woodlands to the remote **Bosco ai Frati** convent (open daily; ring the bell and one of the monks will usually be happy to let you in; tel: 055-848111). This Franciscan retreat retains the peace and solitude of the Franciscan ideal that places like Assisi lack; no touring hordes, no postcard-sellers, only the peace and quiet offered by a church and its convent in a clearing in the woods. The monastic buildings were restructured by Miche-lozzo around 1440 for Cosimo il Vecchio. They house a little-known, large wooden *Crucifix*, attributed to Donatello, one of the greatest masters of the Italian Renaissance.

Prato

Prato , to the northwest of Florence, is the third-largest city in Tuscany, and long-time rival of Florence. It is renowned for its textile manufacturing industries, with numerous factory outlets selling fine fabrics, cashmere and designer clothes. Although the trade has made contemporary Prato a rich city, it was already an important centre for textiles in the 12th century and its magnificent monuments are evidence of its former wealth. Amid the industrial estates lies a compact *centro storico*, contained within medieval walls.

The city possesses an extraordinary relic: in the delightful green and white **Duomo** (open July–Sept daily 7.30am–12.30pm, 4–7.30pm, Oct–June daily 7am–12.30pm, 3–6.30pm, until 8pm Sun) is what is believed to be the girdle of the Virgin Mary. The legends surrounding this relic have

While painting the fresco cycles in Prato's Cathedral, Fra Filippo Lippi famously seduced a nun, Lucrezia Buti, who was modelling for his Madonna. The nun and friar ran away together and had a son, Filippino Lippi, who became an important fresco painter in his own right. It is said that the face and figure of Salome dancing at Herod's feast in the John the Baptist cycle are those of Lucrezia.

BELOW: a Henry Moore sculpture in Prato's Piazza San Marco.

The Pulpit of the Holy Girdle on Prato's Duomo.

been celebrated by Agnolo Gaddi, whose frescoes cover the walls of the Chapel of the Holy Girdle. Above the high altar are fresco cycles of *The Life of St Stephen* and *The Martyrdom of St John the Baptist* by Filippo Lippi. Outside the Duomo is the Pulpit of the Holy Girdle, decorated with dancing cherubs by Donatello, where on Christmas Day and several other holy days in the year the girdle is displayed. The **Museo dell' Opera del Duomo** (Wed–Mon 9.30am–12.30pm, 3–6.30pm, Sun am only; entrance fee) in the cloister contains paintings, sculptures and reliefs by Donatello, Fra Lippi and others.

Other notable monuments in Prato's small historic centre include the church of **Santa Maria delle Carcere** (open daily 7am–noon, 4–7pm), built by Giuliano Sangallo in typical no-frills Brunelleschian style. In front of the church is the **Castello dell' Imperatore** (open daily 10am–sunset; entrance fee), built by Frederick II Hohenstaufen in the first half of the 13th century, and unique in Tuscany, taking as its model the Norman castles of

Puglia. A walk along its ramparts offers a good view of Prato.

In Via Rinaldesca is the mid-14th-century frescoed **Palazzo Datini** (open Mon–Sat 9am–noon, Wed–Fri 9am–noon, 4–6pm; entrance fee), former home of Francesco Datini (1330–1410), better-known as the Merchant of Prato, the title and subject of Iris Origo's historical biography. Datini, a successful wool merchant, died one of the richest men in Europe, leaving his money to city charities, and is commemorated in statues around the town.

Further north in the Piazza Comune is the **Palazzo Pretorio**, once Prato's seat of government, now housing the Museo Civico (temporarily closed for restoration – its main works have been transferred to Il Chiostro di San Domenico).

For a break from Renaissance art, the **Centro per l'Arte Contemporanea Luigi Pecci** (open Wed–Sun 10am–7pm; entrance fee; www.centropecci.it) lies on the edge of town. It exhibits a modest collection of contemporary works by internationally renowned artists.

Outside the historic centre is the excellent **Museo del Tessuto** (Via Santa Chiara 24; open Mon–Fri 10am–6pm, Sat 10am–2pm, Sun 4–7pm; entrance fee), dedicated to the fine textiles that made Prato's fortune. Gorgeous masterpieces of antique cloth are on display, and the skills that led to their production are not lost, as the section on contemporary textiles clearly demonstrates.

Leonardo country

A gentle meander into the countryside due west of Florence takes in some lovely views, a few small towns and Leonardo's birthplace at Vinci.

Head west out of Florence on the SP66 (in the direction of Pistoia), and turn south at **Poggio a Caiano** ❼, site of Lorenzo the Magnificent's favourite retreat, built by Sangallo

BELOW: Prato as depicted in a 15th-century fresco.

(1480–85). It is one of the most magnificent and best-preserved of Florentine rural retreats (open daily 8.15am–sunset; villa by guided tour only, hourly from 8.30am; closed 2nd and 3rd Mon of the month).

The walled village of **Artimino** , about 11 km (7 miles) from Poggio a Caiano, is the setting for another huge Medicean villa (open by appointment only; tel: 055-8751427), this one built by Bernardo Buontalenti as a hunting lodge for Ferdinando I in 1594 and curious for the number of tall chimneys stuck on the roof. It has been beautifully restored, and converted into a distinguished hotel and conference centre, complete with a restaurant specialising in dishes with Medici origins. Part of the villa is open to visitors, including a small Etruscan museum.

A tortuous road leads through olive groves and vines from Artimino to **Vinci** ❾, alleged birthplace of Leonardo. Here, the 13th-century castle in the centre of town houses the **Museo Leonardiano** (open daily 9.30am–7pm in summer, 9.30am–6pm in winter; entrance fee), which

has a vast selection of mechanical models built to the exact measurements of Leonardo's drawings. He is said to have been christened in the 14th-century Santa Croce church next door. In **Anchiano**, near his rustic birthplace, another museum features more prosaic mementoes of his life.

Five km (3 miles) southwest of Vinci is the hill town of **Cerreto Guidi** ❿. Once owned by the Guidi counts, it now produces a good Chianti Putto wine and boasts yet another Medici villa, the **Villa di Cerreto Guidi** (open daily 8.15am–7pm; closed 2nd and 3rd Mon of the month; entrance fee), built in 1564 for Cosimo I as a hunting lodge. An austere building, it contains some fine portraits of the Medici family. Isabella, daughter of Cosimo I, is said to have been murdered here by her husband for her infidelities.

West of Florence

To the west of Florence, the first major stop along the *superstrada* is **Empoli** ⓫, a prosperous, modern market town with a small *centro storico* and a superb Romanesque

Map on page 114

TIP

San Miniato is famous for the highly prized white truffle *(tuber magnatum pico)*. The Association of Trufflers of the San Miniato Hills issues a map showing where to find the aromatic plant, which is dug out of the ground with a type of pole called a *vangheggia*. Truffling season runs from mid-September to Christmas. On weekends in November a huge market and exhibition display the best of the season.

BELOW LEFT: San Miniato.

San Miniato

The ancient town of San Miniato, whose origins go back to Etruscan and Roman times, is set on the top of three hills and gazes out upon magnificent views. The nature and history of the town have always been closely linked to its geographical position, equidistant from the important cities that played a decisive historical role: Pisa, Florence, Lucca, Pistoia, Siena and Volterra. High on the hillside are the two towers of the **Rocca** (open Apr–Sept daily 10am–7pm, Oct Tues–Sun 10am–6pm, Nov–Mar 10am–5pm), which was rebuilt in the 12th century by Frederick II. The oldest tower of the fortress, the Torre di Matilde, was converted into a bell-tower when the **Duomo** (open daily 8am–12.30pm, 3–6.30pm) was added, with its Romanesque brick façade and later restructuring. The **Museo Diocesano d'Arte Sacra** (open Apr–Sept Tues–Sun 10am–1pm, 3–7pm, Oct–Mar Sat–Sun 10am–1pm, 3–6pm; entrance fee), in the old sacristy of the Duomo, exhibits art and sculpture, including works by Lippi, Verrocchio and Tiepolo. Built by the Lombards in the 8th century, the magnificent church of **San Francesco** (same opening hours as the Duomo) is the oldest building in San Miniato.

Map on page 114

The Padule di Fucecchio is the largest inland marsh in Italy and the habitat for a variety of rare birds and wetland flora.

BELOW: Impruneta, just south of Florence, is an important centre of terracotta production.

church, the **Collegiata Sant'Andrea**. The green-and-white-striped façade is reminiscent of Florence's San Miniato, and the small **museum** (open Tues–Sun 9am–noon 4–6pm; entrance fee) contains a surprising amount of precious 13th- and 14th-century Florentine art.

A few kilometres west of Empoli is **Fucecchio** , the ancient core of which is surrounded by more modern outskirts. A variety of its buildings, including Castruccio's Tower, are worth visiting.

The **Padule di Fucecchio**, to the north of the town, is Italy's biggest inland marsh, covering 1,460 hectares (3,600 acres). The area was a Medicean fishing ground in the 16th century, and Cosimo I had a bridge and weirs built to facilitate the sport. It is now home to rare birds and a variety of flora. The land is privately owned, but the wetland centre in **Castelmartini di Larciano** (tel: 0573-84540) organises guided tours.

Valdarno

East of Florence, off the SS70, a narrow pass climbs up the western slope of the Pratomagno hills to the monastery of **Vallombrosa** ⓭, founded in the 11th century, but remodelled over the centuries. The reward for making the journey is not so much the monastery itself as the splendid beech wood that surrounds it. Romanesque churches worth visiting in the vicinity include **San Pietro** in **Cascia** and **Sant'Agata** in **Arfoli**. Near by, the tiny village of **Saltino** is handy in the winter for the ski runs of **Monte Secchieta**.

Towards Chianti

Not far south of Florence, towards Chianti, is the town of **Impruneta** ⓮, an important sanctuary in the early medieval period when a shrine was erected here to house an image of the Virgin Mary, thought to have been the work of St Luke and believed to be capable of performing miracles. This shrine, the **Basilica di Santa Maria**, with its terracotta tabernacle by Luca della Robbia in Michelozzo's Chapel of the Cross, underwent numerous alterations over the centuries, and was bomb-damaged in World War II. Subsequent restoration and repair to this and to other pre-17th century buildings has meant that Impruneta has retained a great deal of its early character, though without the patina of age. Brunelleschi insisted that the tiles for the roof of the Duomo in Florence be supplied by Impruneta, which is still important as a centre for terracotta production.

West of Impruneta, **San Casciano in Val di Pesa** ⓯ is a quiet old Chianti town, enlivened every February by a carnival. The town's reputation today rests solely on the great quantity of art held by the Collegiata church, the convent, the church of St Francis and the church of the Misericordia – paintings by Simone Martini, Ugolino di Neri, Taddeo Gaddi and Fra Bartolomeo.

We are now in the Chianti region covered on pages 197–200. ❑

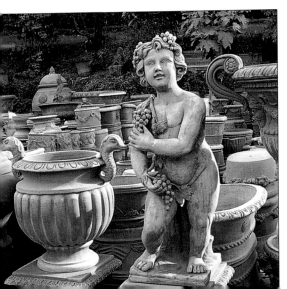

RESTAURANTS

Artimino

Biagio Pignatta
Paggeria Medicea,
Viale Papa Giovanni XXIII
Tel: 055-875406
www.artimino.it
This restaurant is part of a four-star hotel, Paggeria Medicea, which occupies the former stables of a Medici villa. Dishes with historical origins a speciality. Closed Wed evening and Thur lunch. €€–€€€

Da Delfina
Via della Chiesa 1
Tel: 055-8718074
www.dadelfina.it
Seasonal ingredients of high quality are served in this elegant setting, overlooking the Medici villa. Tuscan food, often with a twist. Closed Sun evening and Mon. €€–€€€

Barberino di Mugello

Cosimo de' Medici
Via del Lago 19
Tel: 055-8420370
A well-respected restaurant, serving Tuscan and international food of a consistently high standard. Closed Sun evening and Mon. €€

Cerbaia, Val di Pesa

La Tenda Rossa
Piazza del Monumento 9/14
Tel: 055-826132
www.latendarossa.it
One of the best restaurants in the Florence area, serving elegant and creative food in modern, refined surroundings. Excellent wine list. Worth the trek for a special treat. Closed Mon lunch, Sun and Aug. €€€€

Fiesole

La Reggia degli Etruschi
Via San Francesco 18
Tel: 055-59385
www.lareggia.org
The patio of this restaurant has a wonderful view over the city of Florence spread out below. The food, if not quite as breathtaking as the view, is nonetheless good, solid Italian fare. Closed all day Tues, and lunchtime Mon and Wed. €€

Pizzeria Etrusca
Piazza Mino 2
Tel: 055-599484
Set in the small main piazza near the bus stop, this small pizzeria is a good place to grab a quick slice of pizza before heading back into Florence. Closed Thur in winter. €

Pizzeria San Domenico
Piazza San Domenico 11
Tel: 055-59182
This is a simple restaurant with a huge selection of pizzas and pastas and friendly service. If you don't fancy a carbohydrate blow-out, try the big salads followed by a *coppa della casa* (the house sweet) for dessert. Closed Mon. €–€€

Galluzzo

Bibe
Via delle Bagnese 1r
Tel: 055-2049085
Above-average rustic trattoria with a delightful garden for alfresco meals. Magnificent puddings. Closed Thur lunch and all day Wed. €€

Da Stefano
Via Senese 271
Tel: 055-2049105
www.ristorantedastefano.it
Seafood restaurant in the unremarkable Florentine suburb of Galluzzo, serving the freshest fish. Dinner only; closed Sun and Aug. €€€

Prato

Il Baghino
Via dell'Accademia 9
Tel: 0574-27920
This traditional establishment in the historic heart of Prato serves local specialities to a faithful clientele. Closed Aug, Sun, and Mon lunchtime. €–€€

Osvaldo Baroncelli
Via Fra Bartolomeo 13
Tel: 0574-23810
Acclaimed restaurant which mixes traditional and innovative choices. Good wine list. Booking advised. Closed Sun. €€€

San Casciano in Val di Pesa

Trattoria Mamma Rosa
Loc. Calzaiolo
Tel: 055-8249454
Off the beaten track, this unpretentious but elegant trattoria serves some of the best Tuscan food in the region, using locally sourced and seasonal ingredients. Excellent wines. The proprietor-chef also runs a cooking school in the nearby Il Borghetto hotel. Closed Mon. €–€€

San Miniato

Il Convio – San Maiano
Via San Maiano 2
Tel: 0571 408114
A pleasant, rustic country-house restaurant with views over the hills and alfresco service in summer. Traditional Tuscan fare with the emphasis on meat. Closed Wed. €€

Sesto Fiorentino

Dulcamara
Via Dante Castiglione 2
Tel: 055-4255021
www.ristorantedulcamara.it
Restaurant set in a shady garden. Good, imaginative food in a truly relaxed atmosphere. Vegetarian options. Open for dinner only, closed Mon. €–€€

PRICE CATEGORIES

Average cost of a three-course meal per person with a half-bottle of wine:
€ = under €25
€€ = €25–€40
€€€ = €40–€60
€€€€ = more than €60

PISTOIA PROVINCE

The smallest Tuscan province, Pistoia is sandwiched
between Lucca and Florence and was fought over
for centuries by both. Today it enjoys a more
peaceful existence

Pistoia province is part fertile
plain and part mountains, bordered in the north by the Apennines where Abetone, a popular ski
resort, is little more than an hour's
drive from the city of Pistoia. The
other major town in the province is
Pescia, cradled in the plain of the
Valdinievole and famous for its
flower production. The province is
also important for railway construction, embroidery, furniture-making
and shoe manufacture. Here, too, is
Montecatini Terme, an elegant international spa town.

Pistoia ❶ (pop. 83,700) is only 37
km (22 miles) from Florence and
rather unfairly neglected as a result.
Its historic heart is a delight, and it has
enough good hotels tucked away in
the medieval streets, as well as excellent restaurants and elegant shops, to
make it an attractive alternative base.

The citizens of Pistoia take great
pride in their many historic monuments and churches. There are shops
as glamorous as in Florence or
Lucca, and when dusk falls, the
lamp-lit shadowy streets of Pistoia
still have an authentic medieval
atmosphere. Church bells peal, Franciscan monks stride along in their
unmistakable brown habits and rope
belts, and the stone slabs outside the
shops are laid out with goods for sale
just as they were in the Middle Ages.

A rich history

Pistoia was originally a Roman
town, founded as a staging post on
the Via Cassia, but it was razed to
the ground in AD 400 by the invading
Lombards. It flourished as a banking
centre during the Middle Ages when
most of its important buildings were
constructed, but it suffered during
the wars between Florence and
Lucca, eventually falling under the
dominion of Florence.

The impressive trapeze-shaped
walls with bastions and four gates

**Maps
City: 124
Area: 126**

LEFT: Pistoia's 12th-
century Cathedral of
San Zeno and cam-
panile. **BELOW:** detail
of the Duomo's façade.

that still encompass the centre of the city were built by the Medici during the 15th century. A number of streets around the central **Piazza del Duomo Ⓐ** have been pedestrianised, and when not full of bustling market stalls (Sat and Wed), the piazza is a good quiet place to take stock of Pistoia's riches.

The **Cattedrale di San Zeno Ⓑ** (open daily 7.15am–7pm) originated in the 5th century, but was rebuilt in the Romanesque style in the 12th century with a splendid façade of green-and-white marble stripes. A marble porch was added later and decorated with an exquisite blue-and-white Andrea della Robbia bas-relief.

Inside are many medieval frescoes, an impressive *Crucifix* (1274), Renaissance paintings and – most glorious of all – the massive, ornate silver altar in the **Chapel of Saint James** (Dossale di San Jacopo; open 10am–noon, 4–7.30pm; entrance fee),

decorated with bas-reliefs and statues over a period of two centuries by many different artists, including Brunelleschi. Next door in the Palazzo dei Vescovi (Bishops' Palace) and above the helpful tourist office (tel: 0573-21622) is the **Museo della Cattedrale Ⓒ** (open Tues, Thur and Fri; guided tours only at 10am, 11.30am and 3pm; entrance fee).

Beside the Duomo is the soaring **Campanile**, originally a watchtower, to which have been added three tiers of green-and-white Pisan arches, reflecting the Duomo façade. You can climb the bell-tower for magnificent views over the town (guided tours on the hour in summer, 10am–noon, 4–6pm; by reservation only at the tourist office). Opposite is the 14th-century octagonal **Baptistery** of San Giovanni in Corte, designed by Andrea Pisano (open daily, in summer 8am–6pm, Oct–Mar 9.30am–12.30pm, 3–6pm).

Majolica plaque on the Ospedale del Ceppo, which was named after the offertory boxes in which alms for the poor were collected.

Pistoia

The piazza is lined with a number of fine Renaissance palaces, including the **Palazzo del Podestà**, still the city's law court, with a finely decorated inner courtyard. Opposite is the **Palazzo del Comune** (Town Hall), with a harmonious façade of arches and delicately pointed windows, decorated with the ubiquitous Medici crest and a grim black marble head. Inside is a courtyard and sweeping stairway, and sculptures by local artist Marino Marini, many of them based on his favourite theme of riders and horses. Upstairs in the first- and second-floor rooms is the impressive art collection of the **Museo Civico** (open Tues–Sat summer 10am–7pm, winter 10am–5pm, Sun 9am–12.30pm; entrance fee), which includes a rare 13th-century painting of St Francis and many delightful polychrome wooden sculptures.

To the north of the Piazza del Duomo in Piazza Giovanni XII is the **Ospedale del Ceppo** . It was founded in 1287 and still functions as a hospital. Above the external loggia, added in 1514, is a brilliantly coloured majolica frieze by Giovanni

della Robbia. In rich colours it depicts the *Seven Works of Mercy (Sette Opere di Misericordia)*: worthy citizens handing out food to the poor, comforting prisoners and the sick and washing the feet of dusty travellers. The figures are realistic, and sometimes even humorous, despite the gravity of their occupations.

A congregation of churches

Pistoia has a large quantity of churches, many of great architectural interest, some with notable artworks – in particular the Pisano pulpits, which are the great pride of the town.

Due to a recent spate of thefts, some of the city's churches may not be open during winter. However, the local bishop and Associazione Fede e Arte are organising teams of volunteers to watch over the churches and help keep them open for visitors.

Sant'Andrea (open 7.30am–6pm), in the Via Sant'Andrea, has an arcaded façade and reliefs above the central door. Inside is a richly painted wooden ceiling and narrow nave, well lit from the upper clerestory. Here is one of the famous

Maps
City: 124
Area: 126

TIP

On one corner of the Piazza del Duomo is the newly opened Café Guardingo. Set in an old building with a beautiful vaulted ceiling, this is good place for an *aperitivo* and to nibble on the tasty savouries provided.

BELOW: Della Robbia's majolica frieze above the Ospedale del Ceppo loggia.

A single ticket is available which covers all Pistoia's museums; it costs €6.50 and is valid for three days.

pulpits by Giovanni Pisano, created between 1298 and 1301, modelled on the Nicola Pisano pulpit in the Pisa Duomo. The sharply carved marble reliefs border on the melodramatic in their depiction of *The Life of Jesus* and *The Last Judgement*.

San Bartolomeo in Pantano (St Bartholomew in the Swamp; open 9am–7pm), in the Piazza San Bartolomeo, is one of Pistoia's oldest churches, built in the 12th century with a five-bay façade and rich in marble carvings and reliefs. Inside there is a pulpit by Guido da Como (1250) with marble reliefs showing *Christ's Nativity*, the whole construction resting on the backs of men and lions carved out of marble.

In the pedestrianised Via Cavour is the 12th-century church of **San Giovanni Fuorcivitas** (open 7.30am–6pm), thus named because it was built outside the city walls. It has an elaborate green-and-white-striped marble façade and walls in

BELOW: Pistoia's market is set up on the pretty Piazza della Sala.

the Pisan style. The fine works of art inside include the pulpit created in 1270 by Fra Guglielmo da Pisa, a pupil of Nicola Pisano, a water stoup by Giovanni Pisano and a touchingly beautiful white-glazed terracotta of *The Visitation,* by Luca della Robbia.

The church and monastery of **San Domenico** (the permanent exhibition is open Mon–Fri 10am–noon, 4–6pm, Sat and Sun 9am–noon; for guided tours tel: 0573-32046), in Piazza Garibaldi, is a good illustration of what not to do to a church (due to rebuilding after damage in World War II). Its original windows have been filled in and new ones inserted, but there are a number of colourful original frescoes and works claimed to be by Rossellino and Bernini.

Opposite San Domenico is **Cappella del Tau** (open Mon–Sat 9am–1.30pm). This former chapel is now an artistic monument, with darkly dramatic Gothic frescoes on its walls and vaulted ceilings, including a fine fresco of *The Fall*. The Palazzo del Tau is now home to the **Museo Marino Marini** (open Mon–Sat 10am–6pm; entrance fee), named after Pistoia's most famous 20th-century son. Marino Marini (1901–80) left an important bequest to the city of his sculptures, etchings, prints and drawings based on the recurring themes of horses and riders. He later diversified into a series of portraits of famous people including Stravinsky, Marc Chagall, Thomas Mann and Henry Miller, which are also on view here. In the courtyard next door is the museum's lovely café.

Other churches worth including in a visit to Pistoia are the **Basilica della Madonna dell'Umiltà**, with its dome by Vasari, **San Francesco**, with a wooden ceiling reminiscent of early Florentine churches, **San Paolo**, on via Silvano Fedi and with a large impressive façade, and the baroque Jesuit church of **Spirito Santa**, whose altar was designed by Bernini.

Pistoia is famous for its tradition of embroidery, fine examples of which can be seen in the **Museo del Ricamo**, set in the Palazzo Rospigliosi (via Ripa del Sale 3; open Tues–Thur 10am–1pm, Fri, Sat and 2nd Sun of the month 10am–1pm, 3–6pm; entrance fee).

The main shopping streets, with high-quality clothes, shoes, leather and jewellery stores, are the Via Cavour, Via Cino, Via Ateo Vannucci and Via Orafi. At what was the centre of the Lombard town is the Piazza della Sala, a very attractive square. The town fruit-and-vegetable market is here, set out around an old well. At night the piazza is home to a number of lively bars.

About 5 km (3 miles) outside the town, in Via Pieve a Celle, is **Pistoia Zoo** (open daily; entrance fee; www.zoodipistoia.it), set in a large pine forest.

The spa towns

West of Pistoia, and most easily accessible via the A11 autostrada, are the spa towns, the grandest of which is **Montecatini Terme ❷**, famed throughout Europe for its elegance and luxury. It was rebuilt by Grand Duke Leopold of Tuscany in the 18th

Maps
City: 124
Area: 126

Decorative stained glass at the Terme Tettuccio, one of nine spa establishments in Montecatini.

BELOW: the funicular to Montecatini Alta.

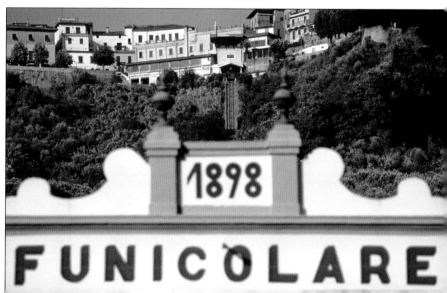

1898

FUNICOLARE

Taking the Waters

Spa treatment in Italy is available on the country's National Health Service, and many Italians are firm believers in the benefits of taking the waters. The spa cure has remained virtually unchanged for hundreds of years, since papal couriers used to carry the waters to Rome, and Ugolini di Montecatini wrote his treatise on mineral waters in the 14th century.

Tuscany is the location of a large number of different spas, ranging from open-air hot springs used by local people to luxuriously equipped and medically regulated residential establishments. Most can be visited for a few hours or a day and make a very pleasant diversion during a holiday, but less dilettante practitioners would recommend taking a full cure, which can last for a week or 10 days. You don't really need to have anything wrong with you to take a cure, and it is an excellent restorative way to spend a holiday.

There is plenty of medical evidence for the physical benefits of mineral waters taken externally and internally, but it is the concept of the complete cure that is so attractive. All the spas are in the middle of beautiful countryside, surrounded by mountains and lakes.

At Saturnia, near Grosseto, is a newly developed spa on an original Roman site. Now modern Romans come over from the Italian capital for the day to take the waters. In summer it can be an enervating experience, since the water here is very warm; perhaps the best time to go to Saturnia is in winter, when it is quieter and the pools steam gently in the frosty air.

Montecatini Terme is by far the most splendid of all the spas, famed throughout Europe and frequented since the 18th century by the grand and leisured. It comprises whole avenues of huge spa buildings dispensing waters to drink and treatments, from baths and inhalation to the famous mudbaths.

The Leopoldina pavilion is the most magnificent, a baroque 1920s edifice of rose marble, with fountains gushing the healing waters and an orchestra playing. Glamorous women sip coffee and eat pastries served by formally attired waiters. The different waters, prescribed for varying ailments, are dispensed from brass taps over marble basins worn smooth with use. It is recommended to drink the waters in the morning on an empty stomach, preferably while walking.

The most bizarre spa treatment of all, however, must be the Grotta Giusti, not far from Monsummano Terme. This spa offers a complete range of treatments, from thermal baths to hydro-massage, but the hot thermal springs themselves are deep underground, fed by an eerie green thermal lake. People swathed in white robes shuffle down a winding rocky passage into a dimly lit cave where shrouded sweating figures present what looks like a scene from a Fellini movie. The further you descend, the hotter it gets: the levels are appropriately named Paradiso, Purgatorio and Inferno. The water temperature is a constant 36°C (97°F), while the air temperature varies from 31–34°C (88–93°F). The humidity is 100 percent.

No wonder the composer Giuseppe Verdi called this place the eighth wonder of the world when it was discovered in 1849.

For a full list of spas offering health and beauty treatments, see page 287. ❑

LEFT: wallowing in the sulphurous hot springs of Saturnia.

century and has since become a company town, with whole avenues of huge spa buildings dispensing waters to drink and treatments ranging from baths and inhalation to the famous mudbaths. You can stroll through the magnificent parks, or sip the waters in marble pavilions – or, of course, you could commit yourself to a complete cure *(see page 128)*.

Montecatini Alto is the original medieval fortified town above the thermal springs, and can be reached by funicular railway or by road. Although full of wealthy tourists in high season, it is still a charming and restful place to visit, with a shady walk of chestnut trees around the lower terrace of the village and panoramic views over the plain of the Valdinievole.

The main square, **Piazza Giuseppe Giusti**, has large open cafés. Little remains of the original fortress, although its walls and towers are being restored. The adjacent church of St Peter has Romanesque origins, but has been hideously restored with its columns and exquisitely carved capitals barely visible.

Monsummano Terme ❸ is the birthplace of the poet Giuseppe Giusti (1809–50) and the site of a particularly extraordinary spa – a thermal grotto, Grotta Giusti (open daily mid-Mar–mid-Jan; entrance fee) – where the steam treatments are taken deep in underground caves.

Driving north of Montecatini along the N633, you arrive at **Marliana** ❹ via a stunning mountain road. Marliana has the remains of a castle, and a campanile from which there are magnificent views.

A little further on, **Vellano** is well worth exploring. Still a working village, little changed since medieval times, it's a handy place for lunch, as it has a number of good family restaurants overlooking the valley slopes and olive terraces.

Floral town

Pescia ❺ has the largest flower market outside Holland. The market itself can be visited, but you have to get there early because it is all over by 8am. Pescia is a prosperous town, surrounded by nurseries, greenhouses and olive groves.

Maps
City: 124
Area: 126

In the spring, the peach blossoms of Pescia are outstanding; every September in even-numbered years, Pescia hosts the colourful Biennale del Fiore – Festival of Flowers.

BELOW: cheeky decorative tiles at Tettuccio Terme Montecatini.

Elegant villas sheltered by cypresses are visible in the hills beyond Pescia, many of which can now be visited or rented. The town itself, most of which is 13th-century in origin, is divided by the river Pescia, and at its centre is the Piazza Mazzini, dominated at one end by the Oratory of the Madonna di Pie di Piazza, which dates from the 17th century. It has a finely carved wooden ceiling, embellished with gold leaf, by Giovanni Zeti, and there is a delightful little painting beneath the altar illustrating 17th-century Pescia.

At the opposite end of the piazza is the Palazzo Comunale, with its fortified tower, still used as the town hall. On the other side of the river the 17th-century baroque Cathedral retains its 14th-century bell-tower.

Pescia's most prized works of art are the earliest known paintings of St Francis in the church of San Francesco (Via Battisti). In the church of Sant' Antonio are frescoes by Bicci di Lorenzo. In the hills above Pescia is the Convento di Colleviti, a peaceful Renaissance monastery, accessible by footpath from Pescia.

The grand Palazzo Pretorio in Cutigliano.

BELOW: Ski runs from Monte Gomito, Abetone.

Contrasting villages

Just south of Pescia are two villages worth visiting, though they are in dramatically different states of repair. **Uzzano ❻** is a pretty hill village with winding streets, but it is not in good shape, and many of the houses are in danger of collapse. However, it has an interesting gateway and a curious church right at the crest of the hill which has a rose window and an elaborate Pisan doorway.

Buggiano ❼, by contrast, has been carefully restored. If you head towards the church and campanile you will find a very fine *palazzo*, where a proud caretaker will appear and show you round for a small consideration. The building has massive oak beams and lovingly preserved frescoes on the walls, and houses a store of documents from the town which date back to 1377.

Mountain pursuits

The drive up into the mountains to the north of Pistoia is stunningly beautiful, especially in autumn, when the colours of the trees rival those of New England. But winter-sports enthusiasts will prefer it with a good covering of crisp snow.

The main town here is **San Marcello Pistoiese ❽**. It is traditionally known for the *Mongolfiera*, or hot-air balloon, which is launched every year on 8 September to mark the end of the summer. Near to San Marcello, at Mammiano, is a spectacular foot suspension bridge, 220 metres (720 ft) long, connecting the village with the road across the river Lima.

Cutigliano ❾, further down the valley, is a typical mountain village, surrounded by fir trees, with limited skiing on 13 km (8 miles) of pistes and nine ski lifts (the more dedicated skier will probably prefer Abetone). Cutigliano has a surprisingly grand 14th-century Palazzo Pretorio, with numerous shields emblazoned on the façade, including a Medici coat of arms. Opposite is a quiet loggia, with arcading and stone seats.

Abetone ❿, about 90 minutes' drive from Pistoia, is 1,400 metres (4,660 ft) above sea level and is the most popular ski resort in the Apennines. It offers a wide range of pistes served by 25 ski lifts, has three ski schools and a wide variety of accommodation. In the absence of good snow, the recently installed artificial snow machines can cover 40 km (25 miles) of slopes. In the summer this is a good centre for climbing and walking expeditions in the surrounding pine and chestnut woods. *Rifugi*, or mountain shelters, are dotted around the area, supplying basic shelter and sometimes restaurants as well. ❏

Maps
City: 124
Area: 126

TIP

Abetone is well supplied with mountain restaurants, which command wonderful views of the dramatic landscape and supply hearty food and restorative drinks. A local speciality is *Grappa di mirtilli*, a strong spirit made from mountain bilberries.

RESTAURANTS

Abetone

Da Pierone
Via Brennero 556
Tel: 0573-60068
Rustic restaurant. Good cooking based on traditional mountain fare. Closed 15–30 June, 10–30 Oct and Thur (except Christmas period and mid-July–Sept). €€

Montecatini Terme

Enoteca Da Giovanni
Via Garibaldi 25
Tel: 0572-73080
The wine list is extensive, but the food is the main attraction. Excellent meat and fish. The annexe, known as the Cucina da Giovanni, serves more traditional Tuscan fare and is cheaper. Closed Mon. €€€–€€€€

Locanda Narciso
Via Marruota 79
Tel: 0572-72765
Trattoria offering variations on the Tuscan theme. Excellent game and truffles on offer in the autumn. Closed Thur. €€

Pescia

Cecco
Via Forti 96
Tel: 0572-477955
Mushrooms, asparagus and truffles feature highly here, and the fish is also good in this historic and welcoming trattoria. Closed Mon. €€

Monte a Pescia
Località Monte a Pescia
Tel: 0572-478887
This trattoria specialises in meats grilled over an open fire. Lovely terrace overlooking olive trees and hills. Closed Wed. €

Pistoia

La Limonaia
Via di Gello 9a
Tel: 0573-400453
Appealing, rustic trattoria a little way from the centre of town. Unusual herbs and flavourings pep up the Tuscan food. Closed Mon evening and Tues. €

Lo Storno
Via del Lastrone 8
Tel: 0573-26193
A tiny eatery, with a few tables on the street, just off Piazza della Sala. Local Pistoian dishes are the speciality here. €

Osteria Boccon di Vino
Corso Gramsci 83
Tel: 0573-358765
A central, pleasant restaurant serving simple but tasty food. Closed Mon. €

Ristorante San Jacopo
Via Crispi 15
Tel: 0573-27786
www.ristorantesanjacopo.it
One of the best restaurants in Pistoia, set in the *centro storico*. It serves dishes from Pistoia and elsewhere in Tuscany, with particularly good seafood and juicy *bistecca alla fiorentina*. Closed Sun evening and Mon. €€

Trattoria dell'Abbonda
Via dell'Abbondanza 10/14
Tel: 0573-368037
Friendly, traditional restaurant with recipes from the surrounding region such as *farinato* (a hearty Tuscan soup). Closed Wed. €€

● ● ● ● ● ● ● ● ● ● ● ● ●

Average cost of a 3-course dinner and half-bottle of wine:
€€€€ *over €60,* **€€€**
€40–60, **€€** *€25–40,*
€ *under €25.*

LUCCA AND THE VERSILIA

Take some mountains and spas, add a few grand
villas and beaches, blend in an underrated city
full of character, and you begin to paint a picture
of Lucca province

O ften bypassed by those intent on visiting Pisa, nearby Lucca is one of the least appreciated Italian cities. Its pinky-gold buildings, tree-topped walls, enchanting churches, and its renowned olive oil and wine production, are all good reasons to spend time here. To the west of the walled city is the Tuscan Riviera, known as the Versilia, a broad strip of land between the sea and the Apennines which contains a rich playground of villas and hotels. To the north is the steeply mountainous Garfagnana region *(covered in the next chapter)*. In 1996, the province was hit hard by floods and subsequent landslides. Although many areas were affected to some extent, worst hit were the small villages high up in the hills, where people lost homes, businesses, even families. Scars are still clearly visible around the province today.

The provincial capital

Lucca ❶ sits on a marshy plain between the Apennines and Monte Pisano, which has been inhabited since ancient times. Little remains of the Etruscan city of Luk, but evidence of the thriving Roman colony of Luca is seen in the grid layout of streets and more obviously in the elliptical Piazza Anfiteatro, around which houses were subsequently

built. Under the Lombards, Luca became a ducal residence and the capital of Tuscia. In the 11th century it became the commune of Lucca and spent the next 400 years defending itself against an ever more belligerent Florence. Even though the Florentines won the title of capital of the region, Lucca never ceded its political and economic autonomy. It remained an independent republic, apart from a brief period of Pisan rule, until the Napoleonic invasion of 1796.

Maps
City: 134
Area: 144

LEFT: smart bathing huts at Forte dei Marmi.
BELOW: Piazza Anfiteatro, Lucca.

The Palio di San Paolino – a medieval celebration of Lucca's patron saint, with costume parades, flag-throwing and crossbow-shooting competitions.

This graceful and prosperous provincial capital, 77 km (47 miles) west of Florence on the A11, is a city of many seductive charms, not least the walls encircling the city. They were built after 1500 to keep Lucca's enemies at bay. In 1817, the massive ramparts were planted with a double row of plane trees, which now shade the broad avenue running along the top of the walls, used by Lucca's citizens as a playground, a jogging and cycle track and a promenade.

The Cathedral square

A path from the walls takes you to the front of the **Duomo di San Martino** Ⓐ (open Mon–Fri 9.30am–5.45pm, until 6.45pm Sat, Sun 9–9.50am, 11.30–11.50am, 1–5.45pm; free). The Cathedral's striking façade is decorated with a sculpture of St Martin dividing his cloak (the original sculpture is now just inside the church), and with the inlaid marble designs that typify the Tuscan Romanesque style: hunting scenes figure large, with dogs, boars, and huntsmen on horseback. Flanking the central portal are scenes of the Labours of the Months and the Miracles of St Martin.

Inside is the domed *tempietto* that contains a larger-than-life *Crucifixion* in carved and painted wood. Known as the *Volto Santo* (Holy Face), the Romanesque carving was once believed to be a true and accurate portrait of Christ, carved by Nicodemus, who witnessed the Crucifixion (in fact, the highly stylised figure is probably a 13th-century copy of an 11th-century copy of an 8th-century original). Each year, on 13 September, this greatly revered relic is paraded through the streets at dusk. Off the south aisle is the **Sacristy** (open Mon–Sat 9.30am–5.45pm, until 4.45pm in winter, Sun open between services; entrance fee). This contains another celebrated image: the tomb of Ilaria del

Lucca

Carretto, who died in 1405, a masterpiece of realistic carving by Jacopo della Quercia. Ilaria was the wife of the then ruler of Lucca, Paolo Guinigi; she died two years after their marriage, at the age of 24, following the birth of their second child. It's a tender portrayal, and the little dog at her feet is a touching symbol of fidelity.

Across the Cathedral square is the church of **Santi Giovanni e Reperata** ❸ (open daily 10am–6pm; entrance fee). The now-redundant church has been comprehensively excavated, and beneath the modern floor there is a wealth of Roman and medieval structures. The earliest is a 1st-century BC mosaic floor, part of a house that was superseded by a 2nd-century AD Roman bathhouse, which itself gave way to a 5th-century baptistery, later joined by a series of churches, culminating in the present 12th-century building.

Via del Duomo leads west of the Cathedral to Piazza del Giglio, home to the city's theatre and opera house. Adjoining the square is the far larger Piazza Napoleone, where you'll find a choice of outdoor restaurants, shaded by tall plane trees.

Pisan Romanesque to Puccini

Heading north out of the square takes you to Piazza San Michele, ringed by Renaissance arcades. At the centre of the square, the church of **San Michele in Foro** ❸ (open daily 7.40am–noon, 3–6pm; free) built on the site of the old Roman forum, has one of the most spectacular Pisan Romanesque façades in Italy. The four storeys of arcades are decorated with delicate motifs and allegories; hunting scenes carved in green and white marble, with animals both exotic (bears, dragons and elephants) and domestic (a rabbit, a duck and a crow eating grapes). The church is topped by a huge gilded

statue of Archangel Michael slaying the dragon, flanked by two angels.

Turning your back on the façade, take Via di Poggio, which leads past the **Casa Museo Puccini** ❸ (closed for restoration until April 2006; normal opening hours June–Sept daily 10am–6pm, mid-Mar–May, Oct–Dec Tues–Sun 10am–1pm, 3–6pm; entrance fee), the birthplace of Lucca's celebrated composer, Giacomo Puccini (1858–1924).

Decorative art

Heading west, feel your way through Lucca's maze of medieval alleys to Palazzo Mansi, in Via Galli Tassi, which houses the **Museo e Pinacoteca Nazionale** ❸ (open Tues–Sat 8.30am–7pm, Sun 8.30am–1.30pm; entrance fee). Deities and allegorical figures romp across the ceilings of the splendidly furnished 17th-century home of Cardinal Spada (1659–1724). Upstairs, at the end of a sequence of rooms decorated around the theme of the Four Elements is a sumptuous bedchamber dedicated to Fire. This fire is not a destructive one, but the flame that

Maps
City: 134
Area: 144

Lucca is full of lanes too narrow for cars, so people get about by bicycle. This, combined with Lucca's reputation for culture and intellectual pursuits, has earned the city the nickname of "Cambridge in Tuscany".

BELOW: Pisan Romanesque façade of San Michele, Lucca.

TIP

The Bar San Michele on Piazza San Michele is a great place to stop for a drink and admire San Michele in Foro, Lucca's chief attraction. Alternatively, head for Via Fillungo, Lucca's main shopping street and evening strolling ground, for an ice cream or traditional pastry at the *belle époque* Antico Caffè di Simo (no. 58, closed Mon). Try the local speciality, *buccelato* – a sweet bread with raisins and aniseed – either with a coffee or sweet Vin Santo wine.

BELOW: bird's eye view of Lucca and the Apuan Alps beyond.

burns when Eros strikes with his arrow. The room features a gorgeous double bed, its lovely hangings decorated with birds and flowers.

Wealth and splendour

The wealth of Lucca, like that of Florence, was based on banking and its silk industry. As early as the 12th century, bankers were plying the waters of the Mediterranean or travelling north to Bruges, Antwerp and London, buying and selling silk and woollen cloth. Successful bankers, like the Guinigi family, built substantial city homes. To demonstrate their prosperity some of them erected towers, although only one of these, the 14th-century **Torre Guinigi** (open daily Mar–Sept 9am–8pm, Oct 10am–6pm, Nov–Feb 9am–5.30pm; entrance fee), remains. This is a rare example of the kind of defensive tower that was once commonplace in medieval Tuscany, built as a status symbol and place of retreat in times of trouble. If you climb the tower you will see, as well as views of the nearby countryside, the outline of Lucca's Roman Amphitheatre (Anfi-

teatro), perfectly preserved in the buildings that were constructed against it in the Middle Ages.

For a closer look at what is now a remarkable egg-shaped **piazza**, turn right out of the tower, and first right in Via delle Chiavi d'Oro. Passing the Art Deco baths (now a cultural centre), keep going until you reach the curving wall of the **Amphitheatre**. Ringed by pavement cafés, restaurants and souvenir shops, the Amphitheatre is an atmospheric place to put your feet up and enjoy an ice cream or linger on for dinner.

Exit through the opposite archway, and follow the curve of the Amphitheatre to Via Fillungo, Lucca's main shopping street *(see left)* and the church of **San Frediano** (open daily 8.30am–noon, 3–5pm), with its huge gold-and-blue façade mosaic of Christ in Majesty. The treasure of this church is its Romanesque font, as big as a fountain and carved with scenes showing Moses and his entourage of camels, leading his people (dressed in medieval armour) through the divided Red Sea.

To the rear and left of the church is

the **Palazzo Pfanner** ❶ (open daily Mar–mid-Nov 10am–6pm; entrance fee), a delightful 17th-century residence used as the location for the filming of *The Portrait of a Lady*. Without paying, you can get a sneak view of the wonderful garden and exterior staircase at the rear of the palace by climbing onto the city walls at the rear of San Frediano church and walking left for a short distance. Highlights inside include examples of exquisite 17th-century Lucchese silk in the bedrooms and beer-making equipment in the cellar – the palace was used as a brewery until 1929.

The Guinigi were not the only ones to display their wealth by creating towers. A picture hanging in the **Museo Nazionale Guinigi** ❼ (open Tues–Sat 9am–7pm, Sun and holidays 9am–2pm; entrance fee) shows that the city was once, like San Gimignano, a forest of towers, and illustrates just how wealthy late medieval Lucca was. Among the artistic treasures here is a pious *Madonna and Child* in bas-relief by Matteo Civitalli, a contemporary of Donatello and Lucca's most renowned sculptor.

Lucchesi villas

The area surrounding Lucca is rich in villas: the patrician Villa Torrigiani, the baroque Villa Mansi and the Villa Reale at Marlia are all surrounded by beautiful parks. Most of these villas are still in appreciative private hands, and often the gardens can be visited even if the house is not open to the public. Wandering through fragrant shrubbery and cool grottoes, past whimsical statuary and fountains, is a delightful diversion on a hot summer's afternoon.

Leave Lucca on the SS12 in the direction of the Garfagnana, and after passing through Marlia, turn off at **Villa Reale** ❷ (gardens open to the public with guided tours every hour on the hour Tues–Sun Mar–Nov 10am–noon, 3–6pm; entrance fee). It

was built in the 17th century by the noble Orsetti family, and substantially remodelled by Elisa Bacciocchi, Napoleon's sister. There is a lush park with a lake, which surrounds the formal Italian gardens. Most wonderful of its many fine features is the *teatro verde*, an outdoor theatre surrounded by clipped yew hedges, the setting for concerts during Lucca's summer festival.

Continue on through a fairly built-up area to Segromigno in Monte and the charming **Villa Mansi** ❸ (open Tues–Sun 10am–12.30pm, 3–7pm, until 5pm Nov–Mar; entrance fee), with beautifully landscaped gardens. Just 2 km away in Camigliano, **Villa Torrigiani** (open Mar–Oct Wed– Mon 10am–12.30pm, 3pm– 1 hour before dusk; entrance fee) is one of the best examples of baroque architecture in Tuscany.

Equally splendid is the **Villa Garzoni** (villa closed for renovations; gardens open: mid-Mar–mid-Nov daily 9am–sunset, rest of year Sat–Sun 9am–sunset; entrance fee) in the village of **Collodi** ❹, with a glorious baroque garden full of

Maps
City: 134
Area: 144

Christ in Majesty mosaic on the façade of San Frediano. Every year on 27 April, a flower market is held outside the church to honour St Zita, patron saint of maidens, whose mummifed body lies within.

BELOW: ornamental gardens of the Villa Reale.

TIP

In Viareggio, a newly opened carnival museum, the Museo della Cittadella (Via Santa Maria Gorretti 16; by appointment only; tel: 0584-51176), on the site where the floats are made, tells the story of the origins and characters of the famous *carnevale*.

BELOW: Villa Garzoni gardens at Collodi.

mythical monsters modelled in terracotta, fountains and topiaried animals. The steep terraces of the 17th-century garden lead to some memorable viewing points.

If you were entranced as a child by the adventures of a wooden puppet with a remarkable nose, you may recognise the name of this town as being that of the author of *The Adventures of Pinocchio* (1881). Carlo Lorenzini adopted Collodi as his penname because he had fond memories of staying here as a child. The town now has a **Children's Park** (open daily 8.30am–sunset) devoted to Pinocchio, consisting of mosaics, mazes and statues based on scenes from the story. Contemporary children, accustomed to virtual reality and snazzy theme parks, may find it rather tame, but there are plans to revamp the park, and to enhance the attractions at the nearby Villa Garzoni.

The Versilia

This coastal region of Italy has always attracted the attention of scholars, poets, writers and artists. It is the area west of Lucca, squeezed between the Apuan Alps in the east, the sea and the mouth of the Cinquale river in the north, and Lake Massaciuccoli in the south. The flat, pine-covered landscape has lost a lot of its earlier rustic and remote appeal now that it has been developed and built on so heavily. The sea can be reached only if you pay an entrance fee and want to lie on a sunbed among rows of others, on sand carefully raked and flattened for your added comfort.

Viareggio ⑤ is the oldest of the coastal towns in the Versilia. Its origins are Roman, and in the Middle Ages it was an important sea landing. In the 19th century it was reputed to build some of the best boats ever launched on the Tyrrhenian Sea, and the boatyards are still very much active. Today, Viareggio is more famous for its February Carnival. Floats are built to a specified theme and are usually spiced up with political satire and irony. The whole town joins in the football matches, masked balls and fireworks.

Viareggio reached its heyday at the beginning of the 20th century; there are a number of buildings of this period remaining in the town, such as the **Bagni Margherita** on the seashore, as well as a great many Art Nouveau hotels on the seafront boulevard, the **Passeggiata Margherita**. Look out for the Liberty-style Gran Caffè Margherita (Viale Margherita 30) – Puccini's favourite. During the summer months there is a very lively atmosphere here; the town attracts foreigners and Italians alike, and the stretch of coastline going towards Forte dei Marmi is well known as a playground for the Milanese.

Lakeside retreats

Just south of Viareggio, along the Viale dei Tigli, is **Torre del Lago Puccini ⑥**. The approach to this lakeside resort passes through one of Viareggio's two pine forests, of which the **Macchia Lucchese** is the more beautiful. On **Lake Massaciuccoli ⑦** at Torre del Lago Puccini is Giacomo Puccini's villa, in which were written all his operas except *Turandot*. The area has been rather over-popularised, but when Puccini first came here it was a peaceful back-water where he was able to indulge not only in composing but in his other favourite pastime, which was shooting birds and animals.

Puccini's **villa** (open Tues–Sun 10am–12.30pm, 3–6.30pm, until 5.30pm in winter; guided tours every 30 minutes; entrance fee) displays his musical instruments as well as his guns. Puccini, his wife and his son are all buried in the nearby chapel. Each August, in his memory, Torre del Lago holds a festival of his operas here in a very atmospheric setting – a stage is built by the lake near his house.

The lake and some of the neighbouring wetlands form a nature reserve and haven for birdlife – the **Parco Regionale di Migliarino-San Rossore** (tel: 050-525500; www.parcosanrossore.it). You can take a pleasant boat trip around the lagoon.

Seaside resorts

Continuing north from Viareggio, the resorts fall into line in quick succession. **Lido di Camaiore ⑧** is slightly more downmarket than the other places further north, but then access to the beach is easier – being virtually free of pay-as-you-enter stretches of sand. From this part of the shore it is easy to reach **Camaiore ⑨** (to the Romans, *Campus Maior*), which is about 7 km (4 miles) to the east. The town has an interesting range of architecture, of which the 8th-century **Badia dei Santi Benedetti**, with a monumental 14th-century portal, and the Romanesque church of **Santa Maria Assunta** are the most important.

From Lido di Camaiore the subsequent pockets of watering holes are collectively known as Marina di Pietrasanta. **Pietrasanta ⑩** itself is about 8 km (5 miles) inland from the sea; its name, "Holy Stone", refers to the town's chief product, marble. Not much happens in Pietrasanta today except for the celebration of the town's main product. It is the Tuscan centre for stone sculptors, who come

Maps
City: 134
Area: 144

Giacomo Puccini, composer of La Bohème, Tosca *and* Madame Butterfly, *lived and died at Torre del Lago, where his villa is now a museum dedicated to his life and work.*

BELOW: Lake Massaciuccoli at Torre del Lago.

Maps
City: 134
Area: 144

Fresco by the 20th-century Colombian artist, Botero, in Pietrasanta's church of Sant'Antonio.

BELOW: luxury villa at Forte Dei Marmi.

here in droves to work the marble in the privacy of rented studios. It has long been a magnet for famous sculptors and painters, including Henry Moore and Joan Miró. A fine white dust covers everything in Pietrasanta, even the wineglasses in the bars of the Piazza Carducci.

While this town has some of the loveliest monuments in the Versilia, including the 13th-century marble **Duomo** and the church of **San Biagio and Sant'Antonio**, the **marina** down on the shore is unexceptional. The two are joined by a tree-lined avenue which reaches the marina at Fiumetto. The marina is really a series of former villages – **Fiumetto**, **Tonfano**, **Montrone** and **le Fucette**. Each offers something different. Fiumetto has a pretty park.

Luxurious villas

The gem of the Versilia is **Forte dei Marmi ⓫**, still further to the north. Here the rich old villas of the late 19th century are still occupied as private residences, some Art Nouveau, some ornate and ugly, all forming a suitable backdrop to lives of the utmost luxury. The Agnellis, owners of Fiat, have houses here. So do holidaying industrialists from Turin and fashion magnates from Milan, and the number of expensive sports cars seen cruising the streets in the early evening is directly proportional to the number of bulletproof vests required by the drivers and their bodyguards.

Forte dei Marmi grew up around a fort built in 1788 by Leopold I of Tuscany, the remains of which survive in the main square of the town. The shops and cafés around the square somehow still manage to retain something of a small-town atmosphere, even if they do sell some of the most expensive items money can buy.

There are no high-rise buildings, unlike Lido di Camaiore. The highest things are the pine trees in the gardens of the villas, and in the backstreets there is still the quiet that artists and writers found here in the late 19th century. Patches of beach are freely accessible, while the remainder is made up of smart bathing huts and tropical-style bars, perched on the fine pale-grey sand. The gently sloping shore means bathing is safe. ❑

RESTAURANTS

Bagni di Lucca

Corona
Frazione Ponte a Serraglio
Tel: 0583-805151
Overlooking the Lima river, this charming restaurant specialises in local cuisine and seafood dishes. Pleasant terrace for alfresco dining. Closed mid-Jan–mid-Feb. €€–€€€

Forte dei Marmi

Lorenzo
Via Carducci 61
Tel: 0584-89671
Expensive, chic Michelin-starred restaurant where the speciality is fish. Popular with well-heeled Milanese. Must book. Closed Mon and lunchtime July–Aug. €€€€

Lucca

Agli Orti di Via Elisa
Via Elisa 17
Tel: 0583-491241
Good choice for a quick lunch: a busy trattoria with a wide choice of pasta and pizzas, plus a self-service salad bar. Closed Wed and lunch. €

Buca di Sant'Antonio
Via della Cervia 1/3
Tel: 0583-55881
Renowned restaurant serving Lucchese and Garfagnana classic dishes (try the fettuccine with pigeon sauce), alongside dishes with a more modern slant. Closed Sun evening, Mon and periods in Jan and July. €€€

Giglio
Piazza del Giglio 2
Tel: 0583-494058
Charming restaurant specialising in fish and Tuscan meat dishes, Tables spill out onto the piazza. One of Lucca's best restaurants, and very popular with locals. Closed Tues evening, Wed and Feb. €€

La Mora
Via Sesta di Moriano 1748
Località Ponte a Moriano
Tel: 0583-406402
www.ristorantelamora.it
The 15-minute drive north of Lucca (on the Barga road) is worth the effort for the superb food. Seasonal local ingredients are inventively prepared and beautifully presented. Closed Wed. €€€

Puccini
Corte San Lorenzo1
Tel: 0583-316116
Warm and welcoming restaurant with excellent, creative dishes. One of Lucca's best. Closed Tues and Wed lunch and Feb. Must book. €€€

San Colombano Ristorante/Caffeteria
Baluardo San Colombano 10
Tel: 0583-464641
www.caffetteriasancolombano.it
Excellent restaurant on the city walls with superb views over the city. Typical Lucchese dishes change with the season. The café serves good snacks throughout the day and is a lovely spot for an *aperitivo*. Closed

Mon. Reservations recommended. €€€

Solferino
Via delle Gavine 50
San Macario in Piano
Tel: 0583-59118
Six km (4 miles) from Lucca, this is rated among the best restaurants in rural Tuscany. There are two sections: one serves more sophisticated dishes; the other is an *osteria* with cheaper, simpler fare. Closed Thur lunch, Wed and two weeks in Aug. €€€

Pietrasanta

Enoteca Marcucci
Via Garibaldi 40
Tel: 0584-791962
This fashionable wine bar has a vast choice of wines. The food is simple but good and freshly prepared. Must book. Closed Mon and lunchtime (except July–Aug) and Nov. €€–€€€

Torre del Lago

Butterfly
Belvedere Puccini 24/26
Tel: 0584-341024
A restaurant with rooms overlooking the lake. Sardinian dishes feature alongside Tuscan and fish specialities. Good value. Closed 5–20 Nov. €€

Viareggio

Cabreo
Via Firenze 14
Tel: 0584-54643
Pleasant family-run restaurant specialising

in traditional cuisine with the emphasis on the "catch of the day". Closed Mon and Nov. €€

Il Puntodivino
Via Mazzini 229
Tel: 0584-31046
Young and buzzing atmosphere; serves full meals as well as snacks and wine tastings in the *enoteca* (wine bar). Closed lunchtime July–Aug, and Mon Sept–June. €€–€€€

L'Oca Bianca
Via Coppino 409
Tel: 0584-388477
Possibly Viareggio's finest restaurant, with a creative and original seafood menu. Exquisite service; exceptional wine list. Near the port. Closed Tues (except July–Aug) and lunchtime. €€€–€€€€

Ristorante al Porto
Via Coppino 118
Tel: 0584-383878
www.alporto.it
Cheaper than many of the other good fish restaurants in town and famous for its visually spectacular steamed crustaceans. Closed Sun evening and Mon, June and end Dec–mid-Jan. €€€

PRICE CATEGORIES

Average cost of a three-course meal per person with a half-bottle of wine:
€ = under €25
€€ = €25–€40
€€€ = €40–€60
€€€€ = more than €60

THE GARFAGNANA AND LUNIGIANA

The northern corner of Tuscany is one of its wildest,
most beautiful, yet least explored areas – a dramatic
landscape of pine-covered mountains, craggy ravines,
remote castellated villages and marble peaks.
This is excellent walking country

Firenze

he coastal lowlands of the Versilia give way to a dramatic hinterland of snowcapped mountains, terraced hillsides, deep gorges and mountain streams, populated by deer, wild boar, mouflons, badgers, stone martens and wolves, not to mention the flocks of walkers, rock climbers, cavers and canoeists. Tuscany's northernmost tip is an untamed rocky region known as the Lunigiana, bordered by the Apuan Alps in the south and sharing frontiers with Liguria in the west and Emilia to the east. Bordering it to the south is the Garfagnana, cut through by the Serchio river that flows between the Apuan Alps and the Apennines. Together they make up one of the wildest, most beautiful, yet least explored parts of Tuscany.

An ideal base for exploring the Garfagnana is the lively town of **Castelnuovo di Garfagnana ⑫**, about 64 km (40 miles) north of Lucca. This fortress town once controlled the route from Genoa to Lucca and Pisa, and was ruled by the Este dukes of Ferrara until Italian unification. The town was also of strategic importance during World War II, when a great deal of its town centre was destroyed. However, the Duomo survived, and so did the town walls surrounding the church of San Michele, which contains a 14th-century *Madonna* by Giuliano di Simone da Lucca. The **Rocca**, or governor's palace, which dates from the 12th century, is now the town hall. In the 16th century, it was the home of Ludovico Ariosto, the quintessential Renaissance man who combined his talents as a poet with the functions of soldier and statesman. The 14th-century Monte Alfonso fortress at the top of the hill offers magnificent views. The tourist office provides maps and information on local excursions.

Map on page 144

LEFT: the Devil's Bridge spanning the river Serchio.
BELOW: Montefegatesi.

Scenic routes

Northwest of Castelnuovo di Garfagnana, a scenic road runs from Poggio to Vaglia alongside the river Edron and **Lago di Vagli** . It leads first to **Vagli di Sotto** and then on to **Vagli di Sopra**. The old stone houses and parish church in Vagli di Sotto are worth seeing, but the main attraction is the artificial lake. In the 1940s the river Edron was dammed up, submerging the medieval village of Fabbrica di Careggine, parts of which can be seen peeking through the surface, depending on the water level. Every 10 years the village is entirely exposed when the lake is drained to service the dam. The next emptying is scheduled for 2014.

Just north of Castelnuovo, at the foot of the pass which leads up through the rugged heart of the Garfagnana, are the thermal springs of **Pieve Fosciana** . Among the treasures displayed in Fosciana's church is a terracotta *Annunciation* by Luca della Robbia.

From here the road winds its tortuous way through mountain scenery for about 18 km (11 miles) to **San Pellegrino in Alpe** , an ancient monastery housing the

Museo Etnografico Provinciale (open Tues–Sun, Apr–May 9am–noon, 2–5pm, June–Sept 9.30am–1pm, 2.30–7pm, Oct–Mar Tues–Sat 9am–1pm, Sun 9am–noon, 2–5pm; entrance fee), an interesting museum documenting peasant life in the Garfagnana. Views from its mountainside perch are magnificent.

San Romano in Garfagnana is an interesting town with a large medieval castle and stunning views across the Alta Garfagnana, whose barren beauty is best appreciated with a visit to the **Parco Naturale dell' Orecchiella** *(see page 64)*, now part of the newly created Parco Nazionale Tosco Emiliano (www.appennino park.it). This nature park, laced with waymarked trails and cycling paths, is the preserve of rare flowers, wild boar and deer, in the embrace of the grandiose peaks of the Apennines.

Other places worth keeping an eye out for in the vicinity include **Sassorosso** (an atmospheric red-stone village), **Castiglione di Garfagnana** (an impressive medieval fortress), **Villa Collemandina** (a Romanesque church) and **Corfino** (a small resort

at the foot of Pania di Cor fabulous views from the the Apennine Alps).

A scenic route to the Castelnuovo di Garfa along the spectacular **T** through the Parco N Alpi Apuane, via the **Giganti** ("Giants' Cooking ru. – 23 huge hollows (20 metres/65 ft in diameter) made by Ice Age glaciers – and through the Galleria del Cipollaio, a long tunnel carved out of the marble. From here the road winds down to Seravezza and Forte dei Marmi on the Versilia coast *(see page 140)*.

Barga

Pretty, fashionable **Barga** to the south is by far the most interesting town in the district. Leave your car outside the old city walls and head through the gate to explore the old town, with its narrow, winding streets lined with Florentine-style *palazzi* overlooked by the Romanesque **Duomo**, which commands fine views of the Garfagnana from its hilltop position. Inside is an

Barga's best บar . historic Caffè Capretz (Piazza Salvo Salvi), a favourite meeting place for poets and politicians at the end of the 19th century. It has a terrace with a view at the back and tables laid out under the loggia at the front.

BELOW: colourful façades of Barga's backstreets.

Ruins of an aqueduct near Barga.

extraordinary marble pulpit, carved in the 13th century by Guido Bigarelli, a highly original sculptor from Como, and a Lombardic polychrome figure of St Christopher. The annual opera festival brings the old town to life in July and August.

The Apuan Alps

From Barga, cross the Serchio valley to Gallicano. Just after the village, look out for signs to the 13th-century **Eremo di Calomini**, a gleaming white hermitage clinging to a rocky slope between the trees. Another 9 km (5½ miles) of steep and winding road brings you to the village of Fornovalasco and the **Grotta del Vento** ⑱ (Cave of the Wind; open daily; guided tours only, departing on the hour; entrance fee), in the Apuan Alps, a labyrinthine system of tunnels, caves and secret passages full of dramatic stalactites and stalagmites, underground lakes and echoing chambers. There are guided tours of one, two and three hours. The three-hour itinerary (departing at 10am and 2pm) is the most dramatic (and strenuous). The caves are consistently chilly, even in summer, so be sure to take some warm clothing.

There are more than 1,300 caves in the Apuan Alps, most of which lie within the boundaries of the **Parco Apuane**, a regional park founded in 1985. The largest and most important cave system in Italy is here: the **Antro del Corchia** (open daily July–Aug, 9am–6pm, guided tours on the hour, including night tours in Aug; reduced opening hours in spring and autumn; tel: 0584-778405; www.antrocorchia.it) at Levigliana di Stazzema, just west of the Grotta del Vento, only recently opened to the public, is over 1,200 metres (3,900 ft) deep and extends over 50 km (31 miles).

The Serchio valley

Nestled in a valley at the confluence of the Lima and Serchio rivers is **Bagni di Lucca** ⑲, a fashionable spa town in the 19th century. Shelley, Byron and the Brownings all bathed in its warm, sulphurous waters. There are 19 springs in the town, as well as two steam-vapour grottoes which easily sustain temperatures of up to 47°C (118°F). The open season for the springs lasts from May to September, and they are said to be particularly good for anyone suffering from arthritis and rheumatism. The tourist office is full of useful information on the local thermal baths and all the treks, trails and natural highlights of the surrounding area.

An upward detour from Bagni di Lucca takes you to the picturesque, high-lying village of **Montefegatesi**. From here a roughish road leads to the white-water gorge of **Orrido di Botri**, an authentic wilderness with a rich variety of flora and fauna. The canyon can be explored on a gentle two-hour trek or more arduous four-hour trek.

The road continues to **Coréglia Antelminelli**, a small town surrounded by chestnut woods with a small crafts museum and a couple of Romanesque churches.

From Bagni di Lucca the road continues along the banks of the river Serchio to **Borgo a Mozzano** ㉒ and the 14th-century Ponte della Maddalena, also known as the Ponte del Diavolo – Devil's Bridge *(see page 142)*. The splendid five-arched bridge was built by Countess Matilda of Tuscany (1046–1115), who also financed the building of the Romanesque churches of Diecimo and San Giorgio di Brancoli.

Massa Carrara

Bordering on Liguria, the province of Massa Carrara has been part of Tuscany only since the middle of the 19th century, and is very different from the archetypal image of the Tuscan landscape. Inland, Lunigiana is a little-known region of pine-covered mountains, craggy ravines and remote castelled villages. The coast is a predictable, overdeveloped continuation of the Versilian Riviera, but overshadowed by the marble industry. The beaches are dominated by the majestic marble peaks of the Apuan Alps glittering deceptively like snow in bright sunshine.

The towns of Massa and Carrara have both prospered as a result of the still thriving marble trade, although the resulting industrial development has blighted great swathes of the surrounding area. **Marina di Massa** ㉑ is a popular resort, with fine wide sandy beaches interspersed with groves of pine trees and a promenade of pretty pastel-shaded holiday villas. The ribbon of development extends up to and beyond **Marina di Carrara**, where the beach is divided by the sight and sound of the mighty port out of which ships carry marble all over the world.

Massa ㉒ is a busy modern town but has a well-preserved medieval centre, built by the dukes of Malaspina who ruled Massa for three centuries, holding sway over the entire region. The core is the Piazza degli Aranci, edged with orange trees and presided over by the elegant 17th-century Palazzo Cybo Malaspina, with airy courtyard loggias where cultural events are staged in summer. Beyond a cluster of narrow winding streets

The impressive Ponte della Maddalena that spans the Serchio just south of Bagni di Lucca is also known as the Ponte del Diavolo, or Devil's Bridge. Legend has it that the bridge-builder appealed to the devil for assistance. The devil agreed, but in return demanded the soul of the first to cross the bridge. The shrewd builder kept his promise by sending a dog across.

BELOW: the Serchio river at Bagni di Lucca.

stands the Duomo. It was begun in the 13th century, but now has a baroque interior and a modern marble façade. The crypt, where the Malaspinas were entombed, is a museum.

Massa is dominated by its magnificent Renaissance **Castello** (open mid–June–mid-Sept Tues–Sun 9.30am–12.30pm, 5.30–8pm, mid–end Sept Sat–Sun 9.30am–noon, 4–7pm; entrance fee). Beyond the narrow old streets of the town, walk on up through leafy lanes past decaying villas dotted over the mountainside. The walls of the old fortress provide marvellous views, and welded onto it is a graceful Renaissance palace, its delicate marble pillars and frescoes providing a powerful contrast to the grim towers of the original castle.

The main evidence of the famous marble quarries in **Carrara** ㉓ is the river of white mud that flows through the town, which has a dusty, disaffected air about it. It is a working town, not a monument to marble; there are few fine marble statues to be seen. Even the **Duomo** – with distinctive features like its 14th-century rose window, Pisan-style façade and,

inside, the 14th-century statue of the *Annunciation* – is in need of cleaning.

The interesting sights are within a few streets of one another. Worth visiting is the **Accademia delle Belle Arti** (open Tues–Sat 9am–1pm; free), a 16th-century Malaspina residence built around an older medieval castle. To view the galleries you need permission from the director, but a brief reconnaissance will reveal splendid marble bas-reliefs on the walls and sculptures from the Roman site of Luni, as well as a Roman altar found in the marble quarries.

In nearby Piazza Alberica are two imposing 17th-century *palazzi,* and here every July there is a massive symposium of work in marble. Carrara also holds a biennial sculpture exhibition and an annual International Marble and Machinery Fair.

Finally, in a scruffy area off the Via Aurelia north of Carrara, is **Luni,** the original Roman settlement from which marble was shipped**.** There is an amphitheatre and museum, and excavations have revealed columns, capitals, mosaic floors and tomb fragments.

Marble Mountains

The fine-grained pure white marble for which Carrara is renowned has been quarried here since Roman times. Italian medieval churches are decorated with marble from Carrara, and it has supplied artists from Michelangelo to Henry Moore with raw material. Formed from limestone, hardened by great pressure and heat, Carrara marble is still the world's single largest and most important source of the stone. About 200 quarries are still functioning, while over a thousand have been worked out or abandoned. They are scattered across three steep valleys: the Colonnata, Fantiscritti and Ravaccione. Here the villages cling to the mountainside that has been sliced away like chunks of cheese. There are extraordinary views down into the quarries, where precarious-looking staircases are strung across the sides, and massive trucks trundle across the marble surface far below. Since the Parco Apuane has been given national park status, opposition by environmentalists to the speed of extraction has heightened. However, the quarry owners continue to fight back in protection of their tough and fearless employees.

Just on the border of Tuscany before heading inland is **Sarzana** , a bustling market town which has been colonised by artists and is being carefully restored. There is a large market in the Piazza Matteotti, which is surrounded by arcades of Romanesque arches sheltering smart little cafés.

Lunigiana

Luni gave its name to **Lunigiana**, "the land of the moon", an almost undiscovered part of Tuscany which sees few tourists and makes little provision for them. It has always been a main trading route, however, and its many castles were built to extract tolls from pilgrims and merchants by the powerful Malaspina family who controlled the region.

Lunigiana was in the front line of fighting at the end of World War II, and this has left its mark. Since then there has been inevitable rural depopulation, with many people emigrating to the United States. Now, an enlightened attitude to tourism promises new hope for the area, villages and castles are being

restored and the roads are in good repair. There are enough hotels, pensions and local restaurants to make a visit comfortable, but the area's attractions are unlikely ever to generate mass tourism; this will probably help preserve its charm.

It is a mountainous region of steep winding roads, deep wooded valleys and unpolluted, rushing streams. On the lower slopes of the hills vines and olives grow. Narrow valleys are dotted with tiny villages; higher up are forests of oak and the chestnut trees which have provided a staple of the local diet for centuries, and there are deer and wild boar *(cinghiale)* in abundance. The terrain ranges from the busy, productive flat valley of the river Magra to the profound silence of deep river gorges.

The region is famous for its Romanesque churches and intact medieval villages, as well as its castles, many of which are in the process of being restored through government grants. A number have been taken over by artists and sculptors, and are used both as private homes and cultural centres.

Map on page 144

TIP

In August, one of the most important Italian antique markets, *"La soffitta nelle strade"* (the open-air attic), is held in Sarzana, and in August the Cittadella hosts the National Antique Exhibition.

BELOW: a Carrara marble quarry in the Garfagnana.

The fortress at Fosdinovo is one of the region's best-preserved castles.

BELOW: Lunigiana landscape.

The inhabitants of Lunigiana are proud and insular, in rural areas still growing most of their own food, wine and olives, and regarding all other produce with some suspicion. They will buy in grapes from Chianti, making the wine themselves rather than buy an unknown finished product from foreigners.

Fortified villages

Fosdinovo ㉕ is the first fortified village you arrive at as you drive towards Aulla on the winding road from Sarzana. Its little piazzas are shaded by huge chestnut trees, and the steep twisting streets are dominated by the magnificent castle. It is one of the best-preserved castles in the region, despite the fact that it was damaged by Allied fire during World War II. The Germans had a command post there, exploiting its superb strategic position with views from all sides. It was constructed by the Malaspina family between the 13th and 14th centuries with a complicated network of corridors and loggias. Beautiful frescoed walls and ceilings and furniture have been restored; it is sometimes used for cultural events and is one of the few castles with an interior open to the public on a regular basis (open for guided tours Wed–Mon: summer 9am–11am, 3–5pm, winter 10am–noon 4–6pm; entrance fee).

Aulla ㉖ itself is the gateway to the Lunigiana region, where the rivers Magra and Taverone meet, but much of it is war-damaged. Of the 10th-century abbey of San Caprasio only the original apse survives. **Brunella**, the *fortezza* of Aulla, broods over the town. It was originally built in the late 15th century as a defensive rather than a residential castle, with walls 3 metres (10 ft) thick, narrow windows and vaulted ceilings. It was restored earlier last century by Montagu Brown, the British consul in Genoa, and now houses a small **Natural History Museum** (open daily 9am–noon, 4–7pm summer, 9am–noon, 3–6pm winter; entrance fee). It is accessible up a steep driveway off the main Via Nazionale from Aulla, and surrounded by a large park of holm oaks and heather.

Map on page 144

Fivizzano , a few kilometres east of Aulla along the 63 road, is an attractive market town full of elegant Renaissance palaces. The young people of Fivizzano are prominent in the movement to revive folk traditions, and they participate in colourful flag-waving performances, dancing and mock duels, and travel all over Tuscany giving demonstrations.

Near by is the enchanting castle of **Verrucola**, a completely fortified settlement on the banks of the river which has been superbly restored. Little red-roofed houses and narrow medieval streets cluster around the fortified square keep, with geraniums spilling from window boxes and gardens full of zucchini, beans and tomatoes crammed right down to the river's edge.

The castle is thought to date back as far as the 11th century and is distinguished by its two separate fortified towers, erected when the town was divided between two rulers. The 15th-century church, with its peaceful arched loggia, is open to the public on Friday afternoons, but the privately owned castle can only be visited by appointment (tel: 0585-992466).

To the northwest of Fivizzano is **Licciana Nardi** , an 11th-century fortified town. Much of the town wall is still visible, with narrow passageways running through immensely thick walls into the village. In the Piazza del Municipio, the imposing 16th-century castle dominates the square, and is joined to the graceful baroque church by a small bridge spanning the narrow street. There is a small market held once a week in the leafy main square.

Above the nearby Taverone river are the hill villages of **Bastia** and **Cisigliana**, good bases for walking, with high meadows and wonderful views out to sea, perfect for picnics and mushrooming. Bastia has a 15th-century square-bodied fortress with cylindrical corner turrets, built by the Malaspinas and now privately owned.

Along the valley from Licciana is **Crespiano**, with a Romanesque church, Santa Maria Assunta di Crespiano, so old that it was restored in 1079.

Comano is an important base for walking and riding, and near by is the Castello of Comano, a ruined, malevolent-looking tower surrounded by a tiny farming community, with ducks and chickens wandering the streets, and steep steps up to the tower.

Remote villages

At the end of the valley is **Camporaghena** , the last outpost before the Apennines, where there is a sad war memorial in the church. When German soldiers came hunting escaped prisoners of war and partisans, the priest rang the church bell as a warning and was summarily shot for his brave deed.

Monti is a tiny village with a particularly charming domesticated castle, complete with geraniums,

Lunigiana is a popular area for property hunters, although the locals still find it hard to understand the appeal of a ruined farmhouse. One English purchaser, deciding that the farmer's cowshed spoilt his view, offered to buy it along with the farm. But the farmer wanted more money for the shed than for the farm; the house was his grandparents', falling down and no use to him, but the cowshed was his livelihood!

BELOW: cooling off in the river near Pontrémoli.

The church of Pieve di Sorano, near Filattiera.

BELOW: Bagnone.

lace curtains and even a street number on the door. It is well restored, with its original gateway, keep and towers, and is apparently still used as a summer residence by a surviving member of the Malaspina family. The church of Santa Maria Assunta di Venelia has an apse in *pietra serena* (the local grey "sacred stone") dating from the 12th century.

Pallerone is famous for its crib, which can be seen in the church on request. It is an extraordinary clockwork nativity scene which changes from night to day and has a huge cast of busy clockwork characters, the Holy Family, angels, millers, blacksmiths and fishermen.

A 16-km (10-mile) drive south of Fivizzano brings you to **Equi Terme,** a popular spa resort smelling strongly of sulphur, with restorative waters that are claimed to have radioactive properties. If you follow the path through the old village tucked into the mountain gorge, you reach a bridge and a waterfall and the high-roofed caves called **Buca del Cane** (guided tours daily June–Sept, Sun only Oct–May or by appointment;

tel: 0585-948269), where the remains of palaeolithic men, dogs and even lions and leopards were found.

Close to Aulla is another fine castle, **Podenzana** (private; closed to the public), a well-proportioned, triangular white building, massively restored in the 18th century after an explosion in the powder room. The castle is at the top of a steep hill, and near by is an excellent local restaurant which specialises in the regional dish of *panigacci*, chestnut-flour pancakes cooked over an open wood fire and served with creamy cheese and home-cured meats. Every year, from 5–15 August, the Sagra del Panigaccio (Festival of the Panigaccio) is celebrated in Podenzana.

The Magra valley

Along the main road (SS62) up the Magra valley between Aulla and Pontrémoli are many fascinating villages and castles, all within just a few kilometres. The small villages tend not to have facilities such as shops, restaurants or even bars, so if in need of refreshment try Villafranca or Bagnone.

Villafranca in Lunigiana 31 lies in a strategic position near a ford over the River Magra and has some remaining medieval streets. But its 12th-century castle is in ruins, destroyed during World War II, and only parts of the keep and outer walls remain. The church of San Francesco has a terracotta of the school of della Robbia, and there is an interesting **Ethnographic Museum** (open Tues–Sat 9am–noon, 4–7pm summer, 10am–noon, 3–5pm winter; entrance fee) in an old watermill near the river, which specialises in exhibits of typical local rural activities such as weaving, crafts and woodwork.

Bagnone 32 is a large, attractive town of Renaissance palaces, wide streets and cool shady arcades with a number of little bars and cafés. A

Map on page 144

honeycomb of houses, arches and passageways leads down to the river bank and tiny gardens. The 15th-century village of Bagnone is clustered on the hillside above, surrounding the cylindrical tower of the Castello and a fine 15th-century campanile. There is an exquisitely carved wooden pulpit in the church of San Nicolò a Bagnone.

Nearby **Filetto** is a delightful, totally symmetrical, square-walled village with a tower at each corner. Almost every street is linked by covered overhead passages or bridges. Originally a defensive structure, it is now quite cosy, with cats snoozing in corners and village women passing the time of day.

Malgrate and **Filattiera 33** are also worth a detour, and near by, next to the main highway, is a magnificent Romanesque church, **Pieve di Sorano**. The nave is ruinous and has been turned into a cemetery, but in the main apse is a very simple and beautiful little chapel.

Mulazzo 34 was the headquarters of a branch of the Malaspina family which had territories to the west of the river Magra; their arms are emblazoned over a fine arched doorway which guards the steep steps up to the town. Fragments of the original walls are left, and in the upper part of the town the narrow streets widen into charming little squares which are overlooked by elegant loggias and their inhabitants.

The town of **Pontrémoli 35** was once divided in two to separate the warring factions of the Guelfs and Ghibellines, and the Castruccio fortress, built in 1332, similarly divides the town. There are rich medieval townhouses, and the church of the Annunziata has a 16th-century octagonal marble temple by Sansovino.

The **Castello del Piagnaro** houses the fascinating **Museo delle Statue-Stele** (open Tues–Sun 9.50am–12.30pm, 3–6.30pm in summer, 9.30am–12.30pm, 2.30–5.30pm in winter; entrance fee). Some 20 prehistoric statues or menhirs found in the area are on display, the oldest of which date from 3000 BC. Pontrémoli is also famous for its travelling booksellers, and awards the Bancarella literary prize each July. ❏

TIP

At almost every turn there are more medieval villages, more castles, more breathtaking views. One of the best ways to see this rich and varied region is to take the little train between Aulla and Lucca on its slow journey through the mountains.

RESTAURANTS

Carrara

Il Trillo
Via Bergiola Vecchia 3
Località Castegnetola
Tel: 0585-46755
A restaurant in the hills above industrial Massa, 7 km (4 miles) south of Carrara, Il Trillo is set in a lemon grove with sea views. The food is traditional and plentiful. €€

Ninan
Via Lorenzo Bartolini 3
Tel: 0585-74741
Sophisticated gourmet dining, where the young chef, Marco Garfagnini, has won a Michelin star for his excellent Tuscan cuisine. Must book. Closed Sun. €€€€

Bagni di Lucca

Corona
Frazione Ponte a Serraglio
Tel: 0583-805151
Overlooking the Lima river, this charming restaurant specialises in local cuisine and seafood dishes. In warm weather there is a pleasant terrace for alfresco dining. Closed mid-Jan–mid Feb. €€–€€€

Marina di Massa

Blue Inn
Via Fortino di San Francesco 9
Loc. Partaccia (4 km from Massa)
Modern creative cuisine from a young chef whose speciality is fish. The extensive wine list includes regional offerings, as well as the great Tuscan reds. Closed Sun in winter, Mon in summer, 2–15 Jan and 1–15 Nov. €€€

Pontrémoli

Cà del Moro
Via Casa Corvi 9
Tel: 0187-830588
Charming restaurant with rooms. Very popular with golfers as well as those looking for regional Tuscan specialities. Closed Sun evening and Mon, two weeks Jan, one week July, two weeks Nov. €€–€€€

●●●●●●●●●●●●●
Average cost of a 3-course dinner and half-bottle of wine.
€€€€ *over €60,* **€€€**
€40–60, **€€** *€25–40,*
€ *under €25*

PISA AND ENVIRONS

Beyond the iconic Leaning Tower and
"Field of Miracles", this ancient city and its
province have much to offer

The Leaning Tower draws tourists to Pisa like a magnet, many of them pausing to appreciate the religious architecture, others to enjoy the glorious art and history of this Tuscan city. Once a thriving Roman port, Pisa's harbour had silted up in the 15th century, and it now stands on the Arno river, 10 km (6 miles) from the coast. Great sea battles were fought during the Middle Ages, with the city-state of Pisa becoming first an ally then a rival of a number of other states, including Genoa, Lucca, Venice and Florence. At its height, Pisa's power extended to Sardinia, Corsica and the Balearic Islands. Trade with Muslim Spain, North Africa and the Lebanon proved a rich source of money and ideas. Arabic numerals were introduced to Europe through Pisa, and the city's major architectural monuments – the Leaning Tower, the Duomo and Baptistery – show the clear influence of Islamic architecture.

Pisa ❶ is split in two by the gently curving river Arno, its steep stone banks coloured by floating green algae. Elegant 16th-century *palazzi* along the banks hide the less imposing buildings and general decay in the narrow streets and alleys behind. Crossing the original city bridge, Ponte della Citadella, the Via Nicola Pisano leads to the

Campo dei Miracoli (Field of Miracles), a green swathe of manicured grass in the northwestern corner of the city walls with probably the most perfect assemblage of religious buildings anywhere. The Campo dei Miracoli information office (open daily 9.30am–6.30pm) to the right of the Leaning Tower sells tickets to all the sites.

The Leaning Tower

Visitors flock from all over the world to marvel at the phenomenon of the

Maps
City: 156
Area: 160

LEFT: Italy's icon.
BELOW: Pisa's eventful Regatta di San Ranieri, held in June.

Pisa

| 0 | 150 m |
| 0 | 150 yds |

Torre Pendente (open daily Apr–Sept 8am–8pm, Mar, Oct 9am–6pm, Nov–Feb 9am–5pm; advance bookings www.opapisa.it/boxoffice; it may be possible to buy tickets on the day from the Campo dei Miracoli information office to the right of the Tower, open daily 9.30am–6.30pm; no entry to children under eight, and children between eight and twelve must be held by the hand; *see right*). The best place to catch your first sight of the 12th-century Campanile is through the archway of the Porta Santa Maria, otherwise known as the Porta Nuova. When the sun is shining, the whiteness dazzles; when raining, it glistens.

The Cathedral

The **Duomo** (open Nov–Feb Mon–Sat 10am–1pm, 3–5pm, Sun and hols 3–5pm; Mar Mon–Sat 10am–6pm, until 8pm from 21 Mar, Sun and hols from 1pm; Apr–Sept Mon–Sat 10am–8pm, Sun and hols from 1pm; Oct Mon–Sat 10am–7pm, Sun and hols from 1pm; entrance fee – free on Sun and hols), built between 1068 and 1118, is one of the major monuments in Italy. The beautiful white-marble façade, the model for the Pisan Romanesque style, is set with mosaics, inlaid marble and glass stones.

The tomb of Buscheto, the architect of the building, is set above eye level on the left of the façade, designed by Rainaldo and built in the early 12th century. The 16th-century bronze doors are surrounded by frames enlivened by animals. The main entrance to the Duomo was intended to be through the bronze transept doors of the Porta di San Ranieri, near the Tower. The work of Bonanno Pisano, dating from 1180, they are decorated with 24 New Testament vignettes, including such delightful scenes as shepherds in their conical caps playing their pipes to soothe the new-born child, and the figures of the Apostles under swaying palm trees.

The rich complexity of the Cathedral interior is created by the forest of pillars rising to arches of banded white-and-grey stone, and the colourful mix of altar paintings and Cimabue's apsidal mosaic, from

Maps
City: 156
Area: 160

TIP

The number of visitors to the Leaning Tower is strictly controlled, and each tour is restricted to 30 minutes. There are 181 steps to the first observation gallery, 36 steps to the second, 35 very narrow steps to the third, and the final flight of 37 steps is up a very narrow spiral staircase to the top balcony.

BELOW LEFT: climb to the top of the Tower for fabulous views.

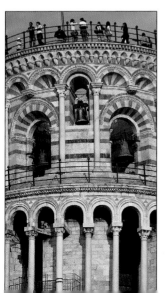

Halting the Tilt

Pisa's landmark building, the Torre Pendente, really does lean to a frightening degree. Detractors have often accused Pisa of deliberately building the tower on a slant to attract attention. In reality, the unstable subsoil that underlies the Piazza dei Miracoli has caused all the buildings to tilt and subside to dizzying effect. Just to the right of the entrance to the Tower is a date stone inscribed ANDMI MCLXXIII (standing for Anno Domini 1173), the year in which building work started on the Campanile. But work stopped at the third stage because the building was already collapsing. A century later, three more stages were added, deliberately constructed to tilt in the opposite direction, so the Tower has a decided kink as well as a tilt.

By 1989 the Tower was leaning to such a perilous degree that it was in danger of collapse. It was promptly closed to the public, and an international team of engineers spent the next decade in a battle to save it. In 2001, work to stabilise the Leaning Tower was pronounced a success, and, after more than a decade under wraps, the Tower reopened to the public.

TIP

Pisa's annual Anima Mundi festival is a celebration of sacred music, with concerts by world-class musicians staged in the Duomo. This acclaimed event runs from mid-Sept to the end of Oct. For information and bookings tel: 050-3872229/210, or visit www.opapisa.it

BELOW: the pink glow of sunset on the Campo dei Miracoli.

1302. The beautiful **marble pulpit** by Giovanni Pisano (1301–11) is a masterpiece. Supported by figures representing prophets, Sibyls and allegorical figures, its crowded and dramatic marble panels depict scenes from the *Life of Christ*.

Hanging from the westernmost arch of the great dome is Galileo's Lamp, so called because its pendulum movement is said to have inspired Galileo to discover the rotation of the earth (in reality, the lamp wasn't here in Galileo's time).

The Baptistery

Across from the Rainaldo façade is the third building of the Duomo complex: the **Battistero** ⊙ (open daily, Nov–Feb 9am–4.30pm, Mar, Oct 9am–6pm, Apr–Sept 8am–8pm; entrance fee), the largest baptistery in Italy, with richly decorated exterior niches and statues of saints. The interior is far plainer, but it has one great treasure: Nicola Pisano's **pulpit** of 1260, carved with scenes from the *Life of Christ*, clearly influenced by ancient Roman art (the source for which we shall see next,

in the Camposanto). Mary, for example, has the long neck, veil and ringlets typical of middle-aged matrons in Roman portraiture. You may be lucky enough during your visit to hear one of the attendants demonstrate the Baptistery's remarkable acoustics – they tend to do it when groups of visitors are present. As four or more individual notes are sung, the long echo allows them to build up to a complete chord that rings eerily round the dome.

Camposanto

The fourth element of the Duomo group is the **Camposanto** ⊙ (opening hours same as the Baptistery; entrance fee), one of the world's most beautiful cemeteries. The graceful white-marble cloister is paved with the grave slabs of medieval Pisans, carved with coats of arms or tools of their trade. Roman sarcophagi, imported from the Holy Land and reused as coffins for wealthy Pisans, line the walls, carved with the mythological scenes that inspired the pulpits of Nicola and Giovanni Pisano. Frescoes damaged by incendiary bombs during World War II have been restored to their original positions. They include a grim series of images (1360–80) inspired by the Black Death, on the themes of the *Last Judgement* and the *Triumph of Death*.

On the opposite side of the Piazza dei Miracoli is the **Museo delle Sinopie** Ⓔ (open daily Nov–Feb 9am–4.30pm, Mar, Oct 9am–5.30pm, Apr–Sept 8am–7.30pm; entrance fee), where you can learn more about the Camposanto frescoes and how they were created by laying down a sketch on the plaster undercoat using red paint (called *sinopia* because the pigment came from Sinope on the Black Sea). When the final thin layer of white plaster was applied, the *sinopia* sketch showed through and guided the artists as they completed the fresco in full colour.

The fire which followed the bombing of the Camposanto destroyed some of the frescoes and left the others in so precarious a condition that it was necessary to remove them – but that was how the immense *sinopie* lying beneath the frescoes came to light and were salvaged, and now carefully restored.

The Cathedral Works Museum

Last on the itinerary of the piazza is the **Museo dell'Opera del Duomo** Ⓕ (open daily Nov–Feb 9am–4.30pm, Mar, Oct 9am–5.30pm, Apr–Sept 8am–7.30pm; entrance fee) – the Cathedral Works Museum. Room 1 contains casts of the foundation stones of each of the buildings and a chronology, which begins in 1064 with the start of work on the Cathedral, followed by the Baptistery in 1154, the Campanile in 1173, and the Camposanto a century later, in 1277. This short burst of fireworks was followed by swift decline as the city's harbour silted up. (Recent excavations have revealed Roman and medieval boats, complete with cargoes, preserved in the water-logged silt, now exhibited in the maritime museum; *see page 161*). By 1406, the city had been conquered by Florence and was about to be eclipsed culturally by that city's

Maps
City: 156
Area: 160

TIP

A couple of minutes' walk from the Campo dei Miracoli is the Orto Botanico di Pisa (Botanical Gardens; Via L. Ghini 5; tel: 050-561795; open Mon–Fri 8am–1pm, 2–5.30pm, Sat 8am–1pm; entrance fee). Founded in the 1540s, these are the oldest botanical gardens in Europe. Now part of Pisa University, they offer a tranquil place to relax, right in the heart of Pisa.

BELOW: souvenir-hunting nuns.

Around Pisa, Livorno and the Maremma Pisana

determination to build even bigger and bolder monuments.

The museum is packed with 12th–15th-century sculptures and paintings: Giovanni Pisano's ivory *Virgin and Child* (1299) is one of the highlights, using the natural shape of the ivory tusk to give the Virgin her naturalistic stance. There are models to show the construction techniques used to build the domed Baptistery, and to explain the marble-inlay technique used to give all the buildings their intricate exterior decoration. Best of all, the rooms of the museum open out onto a quiet shady cloister, with a spectacular view of the Leaning Tower and the Cathedral.

Piazza dei Cavalieri

Students often congregate on the **Piazza dei Cavalieri**, one of the most attractive squares in the city. This was the centre of activity of the Pisan Republic. It was in one of the towers of the Palazzo dell'Orologio (the building with the clock to the north of the square) – so we learn from Dante's *Inferno* – that Count Ugolino, wrongly convicted of treason in 1284, was left to starve to death with his sons. The square is named after the order of knights *(cavalieri)* founded by Cosimo I (1561), to fight the Turks in the Mediterranean. The duke gave its members the **Palazzo della Carovana**, the former council chambers of the Pisan Commune. The magnificent sgraffito decoration (floral patterns, coats of arms, symbols) and the next-door church of **Santo Stefano dei Cavalieri** Ⓖ (open summer daily 10am–7pm, winter Mon–Sat 11am–4.30pm, Sun 11.30am–5.30pm; entrance fee) were based on plans by Vasari (1511–74). In 1606 Giovanni de' Medici added the marble façade and placed the knights' emblem above the great doorway. Displayed inside are trophies and spoils of war from Pisan naval victories against the Ottomans.

To the Arno

The lively area of alleyways and shopping streets between the square and the Arno is known as the **Borgo Stretto quarter** . The arcaded Borgo Stretto opens out at Piazza Garibaldi and the Ponte di Mezzo.

To the west, some distance along the river, the **Museo della Navigazione** ❶ (Lungarno Simonelli; open Tues–Sun 10am– 1pm, 2–6pm, until 9pm in summer; entrance fee) in the Medici Arsenale, the old Medici shipyards , houses the finds from the ongoing excavation of Pisa's ancient port, buried by silt in the 15th century. In 1998, workers expanding the railway station stumbled on the site where the remains of 10 ancient Roman ships and their contents (including the skeleton of a sailor) have been unearthed. These docklands where the sea met the Arno were probably composed of marshy flatlands and lagoon, very similar to Venice. Proclaimed a "marine Pompeii", excavations and restorations continue so this remarkable archaeological site is called an "exhibition in progress".

On the opposite bank of the Arno, across the Ponte Solferino, stands the church of **Santa Maria della Spina** ❶ (open Mar–Oct Tues–Sun 10am– 1.30pm, 2.30–6pm, Sat and Sun until 7pm, Nov–Feb Tues–Sun 10am– 2pm, every 2nd Sun until 7pm). Don't worry if it is closed when you visit: it is the vivacious exterior that is the most important feature, a tour de force of Gothic pinnacles and niches, crowded with statues of saints carved by members of the Pisano family from 1230. Back in the days when Pisa was a port, before its harbour silted up, seafarers came to pray before setting sail.

The chapel once guarded what was believed to be a thorn *(spina)* from the crown of Jesus, but that relic, plus the original statues, are now housed in the **Museo Nazionale di San Matteo** ❶ (Lungarno Mediceo; open daily Tues–Sat 9am–7pm, Sun 9am–2pm; entrance fee), downriver. Set in rooms around the cloister of a medieval church, the museum contains such treasures as Masaccio's *St Paul* (1426), a contemplative man with a high brow, hooked nose

Borgo Stretto is an elegant street in the old town, lined with shops and cafés. Off its southern end, the arcaded Piazza delle Vettovaglie, is the site of a daily produce market. In the evening the reasonably priced bars and cafés are the haunt of students from Pisa University.

BELOW: Piazza dei Cavalieri.

BELOW: the Arno cuts
Pisa in two.

and patriarchal beard; Donatello's
bust reliquary for San Rossore; and a
whole room of glowing Renaissance
paintings by such artists as Gozzoli
and Ghirlandaio. There is a collection
of antique armour used in the *Gioco
del Ponte* (a medieval tug-of-war
held annually on the last Sunday in
June), which comprises breastplates,
helmets and other pieces dating from
the 15th and 16th centuries.

The Pisan coast

The pretty road from Pisa to the
coast pauses here and there at railway crossings as it follows the Arno
to the sea. About 6 km (4 miles)
southwest of Pisa, it passes **San
Piero a Grado**, a magnificent basilica which would once have overlooked the sea. Legend has it that
this is the spot where St Peter first
set foot on Italian soil. The fresco
cycle in the nave shows scenes from
the Apostle's life.

The road reaches the sea at **Bocca
d'Arno ❷**, where hanging trawl nets
and the rods of silent fishermen
evoke the atmosphere captured by
artists like Nino Costa and Gabriele

d'Annunzio. To the south, the pleasant old-fashioned bathing resort of
Marina di Pisa is a fascinatingly
run-down place. There's not much
beach left, and swimming isn't recommended these days because of
pollution from the Arno estuary. But
a stroll along the beach promenade or
a cappuccino in one of the many
cafés can be quite enjoyable. On a
clear day the two offshore islands of
Gorgona and Capraia can be made
out in the distance.

Five kilometres south down the
coast at **Tirrenia ❸** is a stretch of
Mediterranean pine forest – the one
place where building has been prohibited. The trees act as a natural bar-
rier against the *libeccio*, a strong
southwesterly wind, reducing it to a
light, scented breeze of pine and
juniper which cools the air on hot
summer days. As a much larger
resort than Marina di Pisa, Tirrenia
offers luxury hotels, boarding houses
and campsites. Nightclubs, restaurants and sporting facilities for golf,
tennis, horse riding, fishing, wind-
surfing, sailing and rowing are
enjoyed by Tuscans, but few for-

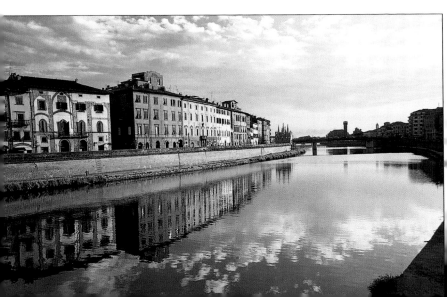

eigners take holidays along this coast. Each year colourful regattas and boat races are held, and the training centre for the Italian National Olympics is based in Tirrenia.

Inland retreats

Midway between Pisa and Lucca, at the foot of the Pisan mountains, is the spa town of **San Giuliano Terme ❹**. The Palazzo Termale, set in private grounds, is run by Italy's National Health Service. Olives, chestnuts and pines grow in the surrounding fertile countryside, and wild horses roam the hills. A number of ruins are dotted among the valleys, and at Capoluogo in the Caldaccoli region are eight stone arches remaining from the aqueduct built by Mediceo di Asciano in 1592.

Set in lush green countryside, near Calci 10 km (6 miles) east of Pisa, is **Certosa di Pisa ❺** (open Tues–Sat 8.30am–6.30pm, Sun 8.30am–12.30pm; entrance fee), the Charterhouse of Pisa, founded in 1366. From the end of that century modifications and additions were continually made to the Carthusian monastery, until

the final touches were finished in the early 18th century.

The Carthusians were one of the new strict orders who believed the increasing prosperity of the Cluniac orders was accompanied by a decline in religious observance. Their architecture reflected this; the monks lived in separate cells within a main enclosure. The centre of monastic life was the Great Cloister, of which the Certosa di Pisa has a particularly fine example. Work on the frescoes of the church walls began in 1701; Angelo Maria Somazzi from Livorno added fine stucco work, and in 1718 workmen from Carrara carved the marble and renovated the church façade. In 1981 a part of the Charterhouse was allotted to the University of Pisa to house the **Museum of Natural and Regional History** (open mid-June–mid-Sept Tues–Fri 10am–6pm, Sat and Sun until 7pm, mid-Sept–mid-June Tues–Sat 9am–6pm, Sun until 7pm; entrance fee).

Entering **Cascina ❻** past fields of sunflowers, grapevines and maize, the roads are lined with plane trees. Cascina is proud of its solid

Maps
City: 156
Area: 160

The spa waters of San Giuliano Terme have been famous since Roman times, and are supposed to be especially good for the treatment of rheumatism and arthritis. Montaigne, Byron and Shelley were among famous visitors of the past.

BELOW: trawl nets at sunset.

Maps
City: 156
Area: 160

*The original spa
building at Casciana
Terme was designed
in 1870 by Poggi, but
a direct hit from a
bomb in World War II
left only the façade
and the hall intact.
In 1968 the spa
(pictured below)
was completely
rebuilt around the
remains of the
original structure.*

BELOW: Casciana
Terme's modern spa.

stone walls, dating from 1142, which
are depicted in Vasari's energetic
painting of the *Battle of Cascina*,
now hanging in the Palazzo Vecchio
in Florence. The town is centred
round the production of wooden furniture. At the end of the arcaded
main street, Corso Matteotti, there
is a large factory with *MOSTRA DEI
MOBILI* displayed in huge letters and
containing a permanent furniture
exhibition. Yet most of the workshops are tucked away in the pretty
side streets, which are usually festooned with seasonal flowers. To
find out more about the town's tradition of wood craftsmanship, visit
the **Museo dei Mestieri e Arti del
Legno** (Via Tosco Romagnolo, 238;
tel: 050-701530; open Mon–Sat
8.30am–8pm, Sun 10am–12.30pm,
2.30–8pm; free).

Leaving the Mostra and walking
up Corso Matteotti, the tiny chapel of
**Suore di Carmelitane di Santa
Teresa** on the left has beautifully
detailed frescoes. The nearby church
of the Saints Casciano and Giovanni,
*c.*970, is a graceful building with a
simple interior.

Casciana Terme ❼, less than 40
km (25 miles) from Pisa, is surrounded by flourishing vineyards,
olive groves and peach orchards. The
beautiful hillsides and the mild climate provide a relaxing atmosphere.
The town exists solely for the **spa**
(www.termedicasciana.it; tel: 0587-
644608), and the pace of life is
leisurely. The thermal waters attract
people seeking a break, as well as
those "taking the cure".

The country around Casciana
Terme is good for walking, especially
in the nearby pine woods of Pineta
della Farnia. The village of **Colle
Montanino di Ceppato**, which has a
1,000-year-old tower, and **Pariascia,**
which has a fortress, are both within
easy reach, and a visit to the **Sanctuary of the Madonnina Dei Monti**
might serve to restore the spirit.

At **Crespina ❽** and **Fauglia ❾**
are several magnificent 19th-century
villas, as well as the church of **Chi-
anni** and the nearby **Lari Castle**
(opening times vary; tel: 0587-
684085; www.castellodilari.it), which
is heavily adorned with medieval
coats of arms and family crests. ❑

RESTAURANTS

Marina di Pisa

Da Gino
Via delle Curzolari 2
Tel: 050-35408
Excellent fish restaurant
near the sea; dishes
simply prepared and deli-
cious. Popular with both
locals and tourists.
Closed Mon and Tues
and Sept. €€–€€€

Foresta
Via Litoreano 2
Tel: 050-311116
Overlooking the sea, this
little family-run restaurant
serves gourmet cuisine.
The specialities are fish
and seafood. Must book
as covers are limited.
Closed Sun evening
(except June–Sept),
Thur and Nov. €€€

Pisa

A Casa Mia
Via Provinciale Vicarese 10
Ghezzano (just outside Pisa)
Tel: 050-879265
Very pleasant, family-run
restaurant set in a little
villa. Freshest ingredi-
ents form the basis of
the traditional Tuscan
cuisine, but with creative
flourishes. Closed Sat
lunch and Sun, 1–7 Jan
and Aug. €€

**Al Ristoro dei Vecchi
Macelli**
Via Volturno 49
Tel: 050-20424
Famous restaurant with
a cosy ambience. Try the
Menu di Primi, which
involves a succession of

pasta dishes. Must
book. Closed Sun lunch
and Wed. €€€

Da Bruno
Via Bianchi 12
Tel: 050-560818
Tuscan and Pisan
flavours are the hall-
marks of the cuisine in
this atmospheric and
popular restaurant.
Closed Mon evening
and Tues. €€–€€€

Il Campano
Via Cavalca 44
Tel: 050-580585
Set in a quiet spot by
the marketplace, this
restaurant dating back
to medieval times spe-
cialises in fish, seafood
and pasta. In summer its
terrace is a pleasant setting for dining alfresco.
Good wine list. Closed
Wed. €

La Clessidra
Via Santa Cecilia 34
Tel: 050-540160
Typical Tuscan flavours
feature at this pleasing
and popular restaurant
in an elegant part of
town. Booking advised.
Closed Sat lunch, Sun,
Christmas–early Jan and
Aug. €€

Osteria dei Cavalieri
Via San Frediano 16
Tel: 050-580858
Modern restaurant near
Piazza dei Cavalieri
where fish is the special-
ity. A simpler menu is
offered at lunchtimes.
Excellent value. Booking

essential. Closed Sat
lunch, Sun and Aug. €€

Osteria del Porton Rosso
Via Porton Rosso 11
Tel: 050-580566
A brother-and-sister
team create excellent
fish dishes in the centre
of Pisa. Booking recom-
mended for this rustic
and gastronomic find.
Closed Sun and Mon and
1–18 Aug. €€

Sergio
Via Aurelia, Località
Madonna dell' Acqua
(4 km/2 miles out of town
on the SS1)
Tel: 050-894068
One of the old glories of
Italian restaurants and
one of the best in Tus-
cany. Impeccable service
is matched by excellent
dining with specialities
from both land and sea.

Reservation advised.
Closed Sun, Mon
lunchtime and 22 Dec–
mid-Jan. €€€–€€€€

Tirrenia

Dante e Ivana
Via del Tirreno 207c
Tel/fax: 050-32549
Pleasant fish restaurant
with an open kitchen and
a tank from which to
choose the ingredients
of your meal. Closed Sun
and Mon, 20 Dec–end
Jan. €€€

PRICE CATEGORIES

Average cost of a three-
course meal per person
with a half-bottle of wine:
€ = under €25
€€ = €25–€40
€€€ = €40–€60
€€€€ = more than €60

RIGHT: fresh pasta, fresh pesto – the simpler the better.

LIVORNO AND THE MAREMMA PISANA

There's more to the unsung province of Livorno than the grimy ports that mar its reputation. Scratch beneath the surface and you'll find Etruscan ruins, scenic coastal stretches, forgotten hill towns and great fish restaurants. Even the industrial landscapes have their own fascination

he central coastal area of Tuscany is dominated by the busy comings and goings at the port of Livorno, just south of Pisa. This is the Tuscan gateway to the sea and a city crossed by canals. South of here is the area known as the Maremma Pisana – once a mosquito-infested swampland but now transformed – and the Etruscan coast, the "Costa degli Etruschi". Over 60 miles of coastline, Etruscan sites, medieval villages, hills, valleys and wild woods make this lesser-known part of Tuscany unique.

With barely enough Renaissance art to enliven an overcast beach holiday, Livorno should be on the defensive. In fact, the province is as varied as its famed fish soup, *cacciucco*. The fishy ingredients, a little of everything in the right proportions, apply to Livorno's seascapes. Captured in moody canvases by the Tuscan Impressionists, the rocky northern coast is as dramatic as the southern coast is soothing. The mainland stretches from wild, marshy Maremma to the rugged, hilly interior, or the Elban mountains. It was from Livorno that Shelley set sail on his fatal journey of 8 July 1822.

Livorno province is no architectural desert: a coastline of Pisan watchtowers and Medicean fortresses hides the occasional Roman

villa or Etruscan necropolis. Inland, the neglected hilltop villages inspired equally romantic verse from Carducci, Livorno's greatest poet. Livorno is rich in Romanesque and baroque architecture, but the lone sanctuary or homely red-painted farmhouse are truer to the province's individuality.

Livorno city

Livorno , now Italy's second-largest port after Genoa, owes its existence to the silting up of Pisa in the

Map on page 160

LEFT: the old port of Livorno. **BELOW:** a Livornese fisherman inspecting his nets.

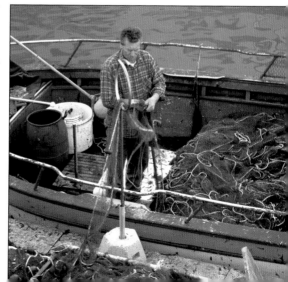

Livorno is the birthplace of painters and composers: Amedeo Modigliani, Pietro Mascagni and Giovanni Fattori and the Macchiaioli school, who influenced the development of art all over the world. It was also popular with British expatriates, such as Byron and Shelley, who anglicised the city's name to Leghorn.

15th century; the Livornese joke that, unlike their rivals, the Pisans, they will never be so careless as to let the sea slip away from them. The rivalry between Pisans and Livornese is legendary and very much alive today. There is a saying in Livorno: *"Meglio un morto in casa che un Pisano all'uscio"* – "It is better to have a dead body in your house than a Pisan on the doorstep."

In 1421 the Florentines paid the Genoese 100,000 florins for Livorno, a vast sum for such a malaria-infested and mosquito-ridden village. It was the enlightened Cosimo I who, in 1575, transformed Livorno into the greatest Medicean port. Cosimo was aided by Buontalenti, whose plan for the "ideal city" envisaged the present star-shaped port with its five bastions. Grand Duke Ferdinando employed Robert Dudley, the great naval engineer, to build the harbour walls and administer the port. Dudley benefited from Livorno's status as an "open city", with free trade, tax exemption and shelter from persecution. As late as the 19th century it was an enterpris-

BELOW: ship-painting, Livorno.

ing yet patrician city. Cosmopolitan salons, elegant avenues, Renaissance and baroque villas made it a fashionable port of call for the Grand Tourists. But after 80 bombing raids in World War II, Livorno resembles a modern necropolis.

The port

Visitors soon realise that the city lives on commerce, not tourism. A baffling one-way street system and gruff hotel and restaurant service do not encourage you to linger, and most tourists who choose to spend the night here are en route to the islands, the hills or to Florence. Livorno is often described as a *città particolare*, an unusual city, and it is hard to visualise it as a medieval town or an attractive seaside resort.

Except for the oyster beds laid down by Cosimo, the Medicean port is unchanged. The crumbling red-brick **Fortezza Vecchia** is a patchwork of Livornese history: Antonio da Sangallo and Buontalenti's masterpiece has Roman remains in its vast Medicean dungeons; 14th-century Pisan walls enclose a small

Medicean house and are topped by a Romanesque tower. The **Fortezza Nuova** (open daily 8am–7pm; free), built in 1590, completed the Medicis' ambitious fortifications. The murky canals encircling it once led to Pisa. Now restored, the New Fortress hosts conferences, festivals and children's romps through the gardens.

"New Venice"

Between the fortresses is the **Quartiere di Venezia Nuova**, an ill-lit, seedy area not unlike working-class Venice. The canals are lined with 17th-century *palazzi*, crumbling warehouses, fish stands and workshops. The area is not without its charm, however: the Effetto Venezia festival is held here in late July/August with performances, concerts and films. Restaurants serve *cacciucco* all day and are open until late. The area also comes alive in July with the Carnevale Marinaro, more of a water pageant than a race. Escorted by swimmers in carnival masks, bedecked boats follow the maze of canals between the two fortresses and sail under the main square, Piazza Repubblica.

Livorno's museums

South of the centre (1 km/⅔ mile), the Villa Mimbelli houses the **Museo Civico Giovanni Fattori** (Via San Jacopo in Acquaviva 65; open Tues–Sun 10am–1pm, 4–7pm; entrance fee), near the naval college, a gallery dedicated to the "Macchiaioli Movement", Italy's Impressionist counterpart, led by the artist Giovanni Fattori. While Florence's Pitti Palace has a fuller collection Signorini, Lega and Fattori are well represented here.

The **Centro di Documentazione di Cultura Ebraica** (Via Micali 21; open Mon and Tues 2.30–5pm, other days on request, closed Sat; entrance fee) also deserves a mention. The museum dedicated to Tuscany's most important Jewish community

has a varied collection of sacred objects, furniture, books, and documents and fragments of the synagogue, destroyed in World War II.

The rocky west coast

Most of the city's artistic and literary pretensions lie in **Ardenza** ⓫ and **Antignano** ⓬. These elegant coastal resorts are part of the Etruscan coast south of Livorno, and merge into their bigger, uglier sister. Most of the beaches are private and fee-paying, and are extremely popular during the summer months. This area was home to much of what the Livornese called "Leghorn's British Factory". The sea views and the dramatic summer storms revived Shelley enough to enable him to work on his blank-verse drama, *The Cenci,* and write his famous "Ode to a Skylark". Byron, living in Ardenza, was a frequent visitor. Ardenza is now a fashionable coastal resort flanked by palms, box hedges and Liberty villas.

From prosperous Antignano, once a mere creek at the foot of the Montenero hills, a road or solar-powered funicular railway climbs to

Map on page 160

TIP

Trips to the sleepy volcanic island of Capraia are worth looking into if you want to discover somewhere new. It's 64 km (40 miles) off the coast of Livorno – a two-hour boat-ride from the port. Ferry services are run by Toremar (www.toremar.it). For more information on the seven islands of the Tuscan Archipelago, *see box on page 182.*

BELOW: the rocky coast south of Livorno.

For a fabulous fish lunch with a sea view, this truck stop on the coast road a few kilometres north of Quercianella is worth knowing about.

BELOW: Castiglioncello beach.

the **Sanctuary of Madonna di Montenero** (open daily; closed 12.30–2.30pm; tel: 0586-579033; free), the patron saint of Tuscany. For those who dare to look, there are spectacular views of Livorno, Elba and even Corsica. Between 1345 and 1774 the original shrine was transformed into a church, which is always full of votive offerings from relics to crutches and gold hearts to handwritten promises. Beside the sanctuary is a deep series of watery grottoes. Outside, elixirs are on sale to gullible visitors who hail from beyond the Madonna's parish.

The high coastal road from Ardenza to Castiglioncello offers some delightful scenic stretches as it hugs the cliffs' edge and dips in and out of tunnels. The coast becomes progressively more rugged, and the road winds past Medici castles, watchtowers and follies. **Castello del Boccale**, encircled by gulls and rocky paths to the shore, is a Medicean fort converted into a private villa. At **Calafuria** ⑬, an isolated Medicean tower and distorted rock formations provided the Macchiaioli painters

with a dramatic setting. But their favourite spot was **Romito**, a grand ducal castle later occupied by the French in 1799. It looks like a whimsical folly, a miniature bandstand perched over the sea, but is not open to visitors.

After exposed Romito, the coastline becomes wild and wooded. As the small bathing resort of **Quercianella** ⑭ comes into view, pine woods run down to the water's edge; small coves, shingle beaches and a narrow harbour struggle for space.

Flat sands

Quercianella is followed by the popular rocky resort of **Castiglioncello** ⑮, which the Livornese seem to favour above the long but monotonous stretches of sand below **Cecina**. The Livornese also know that there are sandy bays tucked into the rocks. Cosimo's fort, built on the pine-clad promontory, was designed to keep the pirates at bay, but since the 19th century has drawn to it all the great Italian Impressionists. In the 1930s, Castiglioncello was very popular with film stars. It may not have the same cachet today, but it's nice enough for a dip and a cheap lunch at one of the dockside bars.

Rural Maremma

Ignoring Cecina and the vast **California** beach, take the inland road to see the real Maremma. Quiet lanes trace through marshy countryside dotted with red farmhouses and occasional herds of placid white Maremman cattle, and spiral up into the hills. The sun-baked hill town of **Casale Marittimo** ⑯ offers views back across the Livorno coast and out to Elba. **Bibbona** ⑰ is a higgledy-piggledy medieval village traditionally linked to Volterra *(see page 185)*. One of its simple churches, Santa Maria della Pietà, has the odd inscription, *Terribilis Est Locus Iste* (Terrible Is This Place) – either written after a touch of Livornese fever or because the church is built on a precarious slope.

From Bibbona it is a short drive to medieval **Bolgheri** ⑱, the land beloved by Giusè Carducci, one of Italy's finest poets. So potent is his work that Tuscans still tend to see the intensely green valley through Carducci's brooding eyes. The landscape is a shrine to a poet loved as much for his revolutionary fervour and commitment to national unity as for his melancholic verse.

The gateway to the village is the ancient door to the Gherardesca castle. The poet's home was in the village, as was the home of his first love, Maria Banchini. A square called Piazza Bionda Maria recalls his poem, "If Only I'd Married You, Blonde Maria", a lament which sounds marginally more poetic in Italian. Lines of Carducci's verse in Bolgheri are as common as Dante inscriptions are in Florence. Busts of Carducci are available, sold alongside bottles of Sassicaia, one of Italy's most costly wines, which comes from the Marchesi Incisi estate.

Bolgheri and **San Guido**, at the crossroads with the Via Aurelia, are linked by a magnificent avenue of cypresses, almost 5 km (3 miles) long, planted in 1801 by Camillo della Gherardesca. In Carducci's celebrated poem the tall trees are *quasi in corsa giganti giovinetti*, "galloping young giants" or ranks of upstanding Tuscan soldiers waiting in double file for inspection. The flatness beyond the trees is broken by low farmhouses, olive trees and the village vineyards. San Guido lies on the Strada del Vino, a wine trail linking the vineyards of the Etruscan coast *(see tip on page 173)*.

Near by is the **Oasi di Bolgheri** (open Oct–Mar; tours Fri and Sat 9am, 11am and 2pm, Apr–May additional tour at 4pm; by appointment only; tel (cell.): 329-8315712), a nature reserve and bird colony. It is a place apart, neither sea nor land. The "Oasis", part of the San Guido estate, is home to moorhens, wild ducks, herons, egrets and migratory birds.

Castagneto Carducci ⑲ was once a Gherardesca stronghold and a scene of more childhood misery for

Map on page 160

The church of Santa Maria della Pietà in the pretty inland village of Bibbona.

BELOW: open country in the Maremma.

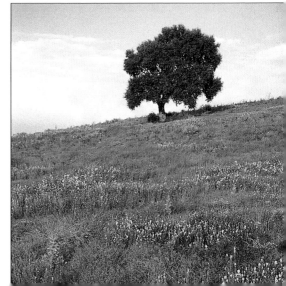

*October in Sassetta is
a month of celebra-
tions. A costumed
Palio is held on the
first Sunday of the
month. The second
sees a giant polenta
cooked in the main
square. The third Sun-
day is the sagra del
tordo, a celebration of
the thrush – this is a
place where hunting
is both a religious cult
and a hobby, carried
out in all seasons,
legally or otherwise.
A torchlit procession
is followed by a ban-
quet of roast thrush
served with chestnut-
flavoured polenta.*

BELOW: good wines
are on offer at the
Enoteca Savio, a cosy
wine bar in Bibbona.

the young Carducci, but is an attractive hilltop village in its own right.
Superficially, little has changed since
the Gherardesca lords drained the
land, planted the vines and encircled
the castle with high stone walls. From
its rocky balcony, the town surveys
pine forests, plains, golden beaches
and two castles. On summer evenings
the town is popular with *bourgeois*
families tempted by the views – and
the aromas of sizzling sausages,
roast pigeon and hare. Olive oil from
this town is among Italy's best.

Mountain villages

Sassetta ⓴, a bird's nest of a village, was once accessible only to
local warriors who thrived on feuds
and a diet of game. The area was
damned in Dante's *Inferno* as "an
impenetrable thicket without paths,
leafy patches or apple trees". Since
then, Sassetta has sat on its mass of
red marble and waited for visitors to
penetrate the deep chestnut woods.

Despite the serenity, few have visited its medieval Castello, parish
church and alleyways. The locals are
no longer ferocious except towards

their traditional enemy, Monteverdi
Marittima, with whom they share a
patron saint, Sant' Andrea, but nothing else. It is a hardy, self-sufficient
community, with a tradition of weaving, embroidery and pipe-making.

From Sassetta a winding road
through olives, oleanders and woodland leads to **Suvereto ㉑**, another
well-preserved village which adver-
tises itself under the banner: *La
Mattina al Mare, il Pomeriggio ai
Monti* ("Mornings at the Sea, Afternoons in the Mountains"). Suvereto
was the first "free commune" in
Maremma, and is proud of its fine
13th-century Palazzo Comunale,
with its intact loggia and crenellated
tower. The early Romanesque
church of San Giusto combines decorated Byzantine portals with a
Pisan façade. Many churches and
houses are vividly decorated with
the local red, brown or grey varie-
gated marble, which has been quarried since medieval times.

Suvereto's urban design, based
on rising concentric circles, is simple but effective: each level corre-
sponds to a street, from San Giusto

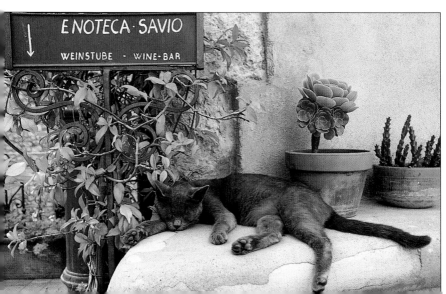

to the towering Rocca above. The steep ascent winds through a rabbit warren of covered passageways. The sedate village pours onto the streets for the evening *passeggiata* and, in season, for the *sagra del cinghiale*, a wild-boar feast combining food, folklore and spectacle.

This area is **Val di Cornia**, an enchanted region of gently wooded hills, hot springs, lush valleys and old quarries. Orchids and anemones grow on the rocky outcrops, while a mix of myrtle, broom and yellow saxifrage covers the slopes. Up towards **Monte Calvi**, the "Macchiaioli" artists liked to paint the cork trees: the contrast of the fragile leaves and gnarled branches occupied them for days. Wildlife often trotted into the picture, particularly white Maremman oxen and sad-eyed Chianina cows.

At **Montioni** ㉒, a village and spa southeast of Suvereto, Elisa Bacciocchi, Napoleon's sister, used to bathe nude in the hot springs. Pauline, his favourite sister, similarly scandalised the Elban natives *(see page 179)*. The ancient baths at **Terme di Caldana** are even more impressive than those at Montioni. Both the lake and pool contain ferrous sulphates and natural radioactivity which is apparently "guaranteed to restore youthful vigour in one session".

Mining town

In spite of its name, **Campiglia Marittima** ㉓ is a small market and mining town set in the hills. As a "free commune" it was fought over by the Florentines, Pisans and Sienese, all of whom have left heraldic traces on the town walls, four gateways and imposing Rocca. Coats of arms surmount the Gothic arches of Palazzo Pretorio. The Romanesque church of San Giovanni has an equally turbulent past. When San Fiorenzo's relics were found near by, Piombino and Campiglia disputed ownership. A test

was devised to establish the saint's posthumous sense of home: the relics were put on a cart and the oxen, left to decide where to go, trudged uphill to the saint's present resting place. Naturally the oxen were Campigliese.

Campiglia's mineral past is never far from the surface. In the quarry area of **Madonna di Fucinaia** and **Rocco San Silvestro** an archaeological mining museum park has been built (open 9.30am–sunset, June–Sept Tues–Sun, Oct–May Sat and Sun only; entrance fee). Recent excavations have revealed traces of copper, lead, silver and tin, proving that this site has been quarried since Etruscan times. The Campigliese boast that their marble contributed to Florence's Duomo is to be taken lightly: claiming ownership of national monuments is a regional habit.

Although mining is an important cultural tradition, food plays a bigger role in the local economy. The simple peasant dishes reflect Campiglia's traditional poverty and dignity. Many dishes – probably the most famous being the *zuppa Lombarda*, a soup of bread and beans – were imported by

Map
on page
160

TIP

Sassicaia, Ornellaia, Grattamacco and Le Macchiole are among the best of the Costa degli Etruschi's DOC wines. Many estates in the area welcome visitors for wine-tasting and vineyard tours (except during the grape harvest). For more information, visit the Strada del Vino office in San Guido or go to www.lastradadelvino.com.

BELOW: Suvereto.

Most of the contents of the Etruscan tombs in Populonia are now kept in Florentine Museums, but a tiny Etruscan Museum (erratic opening hours; entrance fee) in Populonia contains some of the sacred objects found here.

BELOW: windswept Baratti Bay.

the so-called Lombardi, seasonal workers from the Emilian or Pistoian hills. These shepherds and woodcutters lived in tenements near the swamps, but came inland in the evenings to mix with the locals. In exchange for kindness and dinner, the Lombardi introduced those in the Val di Cornia to their regional favourites, such as chestnut polenta, rice soups and *raviolini*. Local game, sausages and *funghi porcini* were easily incorporated, and Campigliese cuisine has never looked back. The dynamic Suvereto and Campigliese tourist offices will suggest restaurants and *agriturismo* farm stays where these delights can be sampled.

The Etruscan coast

For sightings of flamingos sheltering under umbrella pines, the **Rimigliano Nature Reserve ㉔**, hugging the coast between San Vincenzo and Populonia, is where to head. If the coast beckons, San Vicenzo's metallic sands and monotonous strip of bungalows can be sacrificed to Populonia's Etruscan city. The Etruscans very considerately had themselves buried by a pine-fringed beach, reason enough to visit the only Etruscan city built on the coast.

Behind the sweep of **Baratti Bay** lie the substantial remains of **Populonia ㉕**, the last of the 12 Etruscan cities to be founded. The ancient city was divided into two parts: the "acropolis" – the religious centre clustered high around the village – and the maritime and industrial centre around the bay. The necropolises cover the slopes between the two centres.

Thanks to its proximity to Elba and to the metal-bearing Campigliese hills, Populonia became a rich industrial city. While Elban iron ore was smelted and then traded within the Etruscan League, minerals from Campiglia were shipped to Corsica, Sardinia and France. In the ancient "industrial zone", excavations have uncovered a blast furnace and sophisticated metalworking equipment dating back to the 6th century BC. Foreign slave labour was used to dig water channels, operate the furnace and mint coins. In the 6th century BC Populonia was the first Etruscan city to mint gold, silver and bronze coins, often featuring a lion's head. Sadly, many tombs lie buried or collapsed under the weight of ancient slag heaps. Others have been looted.

From Populonia there are smoky views of **Piombino ㉖**, which has been ruled by the Pisans, the noble Appiani family, the ignoble Cesare Borgia and, most effectively, by Elisa Bacciocchi, Princess of Piombino and Lucca and Napoleon's sister. Today, it's a grimy, relentlessly urban city, and the only reason most visitors come here is to catch a ferry to Elba, but it's not to be dismissed entirely. Vestiges of grand old Piombino remain in Piazza Verdi's town walls and in the heavily restored Palazzo Comunale and fortress. Best seen on foot, the city's genteel, dilapidated charm lingers on in quiet squares and Art Deco bars. ❏

Map on page 160

RESTAURANTS

Antignano

Il Romito
Via del Littorale 274
3 km from Antignano
Tel/fax: 0586-580520
Roadside restaurant suspended above the sea, with fabulous views from its spacious semicircular terrace. Service is brisk, but the dishes, predominantly fish-based, are presented with pride. €€

Trattoria In Caciaia
Via dei Bagni 38
Tel: 0586-580403
Set on a quiet piazza, this pleasing trattoria offers a great selection of typical Livornese fish dishes, including an excellent *cacciucco*. Service is swift. Closed Mon and Tues and weekday lunchtimes; also closed 20 days in Sept. €–€€

Ardenza

Ciglieri
Via Ravizza 43
Tel: 0586-508194
This elegant, well-established restaurant has recently relocated. The warm, inviting decor is matched with excellent cuisine using only seasonal specialities. Must book as covers are limited. Closed Wed and three weeks in Jan. €€€€

Oscar
Via Oreste Franchini 78
Tel: 0586-501258
Historic restaurant with modern designer ambi-

ence and a pleasant garden for alfresco dining. Fish predominates, with *cacciucco* a speciality (must be ordered in advance). Extensive wine list. Closed Mon and 20 days from 27 Dec. €€€

Castagneto Carducci

Da Ugo
Via Pari 3/A
Tel: 0565-763746
Family-run restaurant that lives up to its well-earned reputation. Robust dishes feature wild boar, wood pigeon, rabbit and *porcini*, and there's an excellent choice of local wines from their well-stocked cellar. Go with a good appetite. €€

Livorno

Da Galileo
Via della Campana 20
Tel: 0586-889009
Trattoria specialising in fish and authentic Livornese cuisine at very reasonable prices. Popular with locals, so booking recommended. Closed Sun evening and Wed and last two weeks in July. €€

Gennarino
Via Santa Fortunata 11
Tel: 0586-888093
Classic fish restaurant serving local specialities such as *triglia* (red mullet) *alla livornese* (with garlic and mushrooms), and an excellent *cacciucco* (fish soup). Closed

Wed, Feb and two weeks in June. €€

Osteria del Mare
Borgo dei Cappuccini 5
Tel: 0586-881027
Characterful tavern in the port area. Two small but welcoming dining rooms offer a good selection of seafood at prices that won't melt the plastic. Closed Thur and 25 Aug–10 Sept. €€–€€€

Ristorante Albergo Bar Montallegro
Piazza Montenero 3
Tel: 0586-579030
Set in a panoramic spot near the Sanctuary of Madonna di Montenero, this restaurant has been in the Orlandi family since 1889. *Cacciucco* features every day of the year, with other traditional specialities. There is a

very pleasant frescoed dining room and a terrace for warmer weather. €€–€€€

San Vincenzo

Gambero Rosso
Piazza della Vittoria
Tel: 0565-701021
Elegant restaurant overlooking the sea; one of Tuscany's best. Fish features prominently. The wine list is around 100 pages long. Closed Mon–Tues. €€€€

PRICE CATEGORIES

Average cost of a three-course meal per person with a half-bottle of wine:
€ = under €25
€€ = €25–40
€€€ = €40–60
€€€€ = over €60

RIGHT: *cacciucco* – Livornese fish soup.

ISOLA D'ELBA

Every August the beaches of "Tuscany's island" are invaded by sun-worshipping Italians. For the rest of the year, its rocky roads, wooded slopes and sandy bays belong to intrepid tourists who make the short sea crossing in search of unspoilt nature, crystal waters, Napoleonic landmarks and good food and wine

Known to the Etruscans as *Ilva* ("Iron") and to the Greeks as *Aethalia* ("Soot Island"), Elba has exploited its mineral wealth for more than 3,000 years. As the European powers occasionally took an interest in the island's attractive strategic position, waves of Romans, Pisans and Genoese were followed by Spanish, Turkish and French invasions. In 1548, the powerful and vainglorious Medici duke, Cosimo I, fortified the capital and named it Cosmopolis, after himself. His great military architect, Giovanni Camerini, designed the star-shaped defensive system and the two Medicean forts, Forte della Stella and Forte Falcone, to keep the Saracens at bay. Today, Portoferraio's horseshoe harbour, backed by a cluster of sun-baked pastel houses, is more welcoming than forbidding, as ferries, fishing boats, yachts and pleasure cruisers glide in and out of its embrace.

Napoleon's Elba

Portoferraio ❶ is inextricably linked to that other great imperialist, Napoleon Bonaparte. He made his official home in two converted windmills above the charming Forte della Stella. Under the terms of the Congress of Vienna in 1814, Elba became a principality of the fallen sovereign. Napoleon's great empire

shrank to his faithful "old guard", pragmatic mother and libertine sister Pauline. Most Elbans were proud to have him improve the administration, build new roads, develop the mines and expand the island's fleet. The foreign commissioners, however, rightly feared that the "Eagle" might spread its wings: after nine months Napoleon flew, with the connivance of the Elbans. He escaped with no less than 1,000 troops, the Elbans' affection, his sister's diamond necklace and his mother's

Map
on page
178

LEFT: Portoferraio.
BELOW: an Elban fishing boat.

The emblem of Elba's most famous resident seen at San Martino villa, Napoleon's country residence during his 10-month exile on the island. A requiem Mass is said for him here on 5 May each year, and an empty black coffin is carried in a solemn procession down to the waterfront.

curt blessing, "Go and fulfil your destiny." His **Palazzina dei Mulini** (open Mon, Wed–Sat 9am–7pm, Sun 9am–1pm; entrance fee) was lined with silver and books from Fontainebleau and furniture from his sister Elisa's house in Piombino. Most of its charm lies in the period furnishings and Italianate gardens.

The 17th-century **Misericordia** church on the Via Napoleone, a broad stairway near by, displays one of Napoleon's bronze death-masks.

A few kilometres inland from Portoferraio is the emperor's country residence, **San Martino** (open Tues–Sat 9am–7pm, Sun 9am–1pm; entrance fee), purchased with one of Pauline's handy diamond necklaces. The villa's classical façade was installed in 1851 by the Russian emigré Prince Demidoff. But after the grand cypress-lined avenue and grandiose façade, the house itself seems a spartan affair, and is quickly visited. In one room, Napoleon's Nile campaigns of 1798–9 are recalled in the Egyptian-style frescoes, painted in 1814. In another, his tiny bed is a reminder of just how short he was. Information on the emperor's life and times is thin on the ground here (though souvenir stands are not), but the fine garden, shaded by evergreen oaks and terraced vineyards, is pleasant to stroll through.

Portoferraio to Marciana

The scenic drive westward from Portoferraio to Marciana Marina passes a number of popular beaches. Le Ghiaie, the nearest beach to the town, is noted for its multicoloured pebbles, but it's worth going the extra distance to **Capo d'Enfola ❷**. The road to the cape ends at Porto di Sansone, a tiny isthmus flanked by two small pebble beaches and a couple of restaurants. Formerly restricted for military use, the cape itself remains closed to traffic, but is popular among walkers. **Viticcio** is another pretty cove, but sand-seekers head for **La Biodola** ❸, considered the chic-est beach on Elba, dominated by expensive resort complexes filled with rich bronzed Florentines in Valentino swimwear. At La Biodola and **Procchio** ❹, a more egalitarian paradise, the rocky ocean bottom means clear, sediment-free water.

Between Procchio and Marciana Marina is "La Paolina", an islet named after Napoleon's sister, whose passion for nude sunbathing would scandalise the natives.

Marciana Marina ❺ has evolved smoothly from fishing village to elegant resort, set amidst magnolias, palms and oleanders at the end of a long valley. The thin, pastel-coloured houses in the old quarter are reminiscent of those on the Ligurian coast. On 12 August the port explodes in a firework display to honour Santa Chiara, the patron saint.

Marciana Alta ❻, perched above, is the island's best-preserved medieval town. Chestnut woods frame the red-tiled rooftops, narrow alleys and the crumbling Pisan fortress. The local "Antiquarium" displays Etruscan sacred objects, as well as Roman oil lamps and ivory statues found in shipwrecks.

Twin peaks

From the foot of Marciana, a cable car, the Cabinovia del Monte Capanne (Mar–Oct 10am–12.15pm, last descent from the peak 12.45pm, 2.30–6pm, last descent 6.30pm) lurches over crags and chasms up to the summit of **Monte Capanne** ❼. On a clear day (when the peak is free from the clouds that frequently shroud it), the views from up here are all-encompassing. Even in high summer, this wooded mountain area is wonderfully quiet and breezy. Depending on the season, patches of orchids, snapdragons and helianthemums are as common as the cedars and chestnuts. Even the coastal vegetation is more exotic than in the east: eucalyptus and magnolia rather than vines or rough maquis.

The high road from Marciana to the south side of the island winds past the quiet, neglected village of **Poggio** ❽ to **Monte Perone** nature

Heading up to the heights of Monte Capanne in the cable car.

BELOW: a cloud-covered Poggio.

BELOW: smooth rocky platforms attract sunbathers.

reserve (for a scenic walk on the mountain, stop off at Poggio and follow the waymarked trail), vineyards and the plains behind Marina di Campo, the only part of the island flat enough for an airport.

The "Other Elba"

The northwestern corner of Elba is a protected area of wild, natural beauty. Granite cliffs, thick holm oak and chestnut woods, and dense *maquis* make it a property developer's nightmare and a nature-lover's dream. Tagged by the tourist board as the "Other Elba", this craggy corner attracts the active and eco-conscious. The sea here is ideal for snorkelling, diving and kayaking, while the surrounding mountains are exploited by mountain bikers, birdwatchers, trekkers and climbers. A long, winding road leads down past houses and hotels to **Capo Sant'Andrea ❾**, a tight bay with a small port protected from westerly winds by the surrounding cliffs. This is an ideal base for exploring the area, starting with the walk from Capo Sant'Andrea to the next bay at Cotoncello.

The coast road from Sant'Andrea to Marina di Campo clings to the edge of the island, an exhilarating and occasionally heart-stopping drive. Wherever you see a cluster of parked cars, chances are there's a rocky cove below, where those in the know gather to swim and sunbathe. This section of the coast is good for diving and snorkelling; most of the diving schools can be found in and around **Pomonte**.

As you round the southwestern corner, the first visible stretch of sand at **Fetovaia ❿** comes into view – a pretty, child-friendly sweep of beach, edged by trees, that gets very crowded in summer. Between Fetovaia and **Cavoli**, another small, pleasant enough resort, the low rocks make perfect sunbathing platforms.

The south

With its expanse of golden sand, **Marina di Campo ⓫**, in the south, is the largest resort on the island, full of bars and buzzing with nightlife. Often overlooked are two dusty medieval villages nestling in the hills behind. Fortified by the Pisans in the

12th century, **San Piero in Campo** and **San Ilario** conceal Romanesque churches and hermitages.

Capoliveri ⑫ is a traditional inland village, with a Roman and medieval past as dramatic as its location high on the southern promontory. Carved into the iron mountain of **Monte Calamita**, Capoliveri is also an old mining village. The black, iron-bearing lodestone still plays havoc with the compasses of passing ships, but is ideal for the production of sweet red Aleatico, said to be the favourite wine of Napoleon Bonaparte. Often independent, Capoliveri was the only village to reject Napoleon in 1814. The story is that only the intercession of a local beauty saved the village. It soon became part of Napoleon's hunting estate, and to this day is noted for its dishes of woodcock, pheasant and hare.

The hills are covered with heath, fern and juniper; the scent of thyme and rosemary are never far away. Roads from the hills to the sea often turn into cart tracks but are worth pursuing unless specifically marked *strada privata*; this is often the only access to the loveliest beaches, as most of this southeastern headland is privately owned. **Innamorata** is a sandy inlet linked to the romance between a nymph and a fisherman. Believing her lover drowned in a shipwreck, the nymph drowned herself; he survived and asked the gods to turn him into a seagull so he could seek her out.

The east

Capoliveri also surveys fashionable **Porto Azzurro** ⑬, the main town on the east coast of Elba and once part of the Spanish protectorate. The vast Forte Longone, constructed in 1603 as a Spanish naval base, is now a top-security prison. Visitors can purchase crafts from the prison shop, the scene of a mass breakout in 1987. Forte Focardo, its sister fortress across the bay, has uninviting ramparts running down a sheer cliff. By day, Porto Azzurro has a rather uninspiring seafront. In the evening, however, it is a favoured place for a leisurely promenade (the famous *passeggiata*), designer shopping and people-watching. It is also a top place for

Map
on page
178

Elban wine is known for its distinct flavour, due to the mineral-rich and fertile soil. The dry whites, Chianti-like reds and Aleatico and Anson-ica dessert wines are all excellent accompaniments to traditional Elban dishes.

BELOW: the pretty resort of Marciana Marina *(see page 179).*

Map on page 178

The island of Elba was long known as a mineralogical paradise. Semi-precious stones such as green quartz, black onyx and pink or pale-green beryl, can all be found here. The proper mineral name for most gem tourmalines, in fact, is "Elbaite".

sampling some of the local seafood specialities, such as a *cacciucco* (soup) of octopus, scorpion fish, dogfish and prawns; *riso nero* or "black rice" (risotto made with the dark ink of cuttlefish or squid), perhaps followed by *schiaccia briaca* ("drunken cake"), made with hazelnuts and Aleatico wine. After enough Elban wine, one's impressions of Porto Azzurro are of harbour lights, cheerful bustle and gently bobbing boats.

Behind Porto Azzurro is the most mystical spot on the island, the remote sanctuary of **Madonna di Monserrato ⓮** (open daily mid-July–mid-Sept). It was built in the Toledan style by a Spanish governor, Ponce de León, in 1606. A steep, rocky track leads high up the mountain to the tiny red-domed church precariously balanced among the crags. Despite mountain goats cavorting on impossible ledges, the place has great solemnity and few visitors, and is the most important shrine on Elba. The Spanish façade and bell-tower find echoes in the Black Madonna inside, which is a copy of an early Spanish painting. Every September,

an Elban pilgrimage celebrates the *Festa della Madonna* with a walk past ravines and isolated grottoes to the church. At the foot of the hills is a rustic restaurant with service as leisurely as an Elban Sunday.

Elba's iron heart

To the east of Portoferraio is Elba's iron heart. The island's mineral wealth has been exploited since Etruscan times; the swords of Roman legionaries were famously made of Elban iron. But the last mine was closed in 1984, and the island's economic mainstays are now tourism, agriculture and fishing.

The workaday town of **Rio Marina ⓯** was once the centre of the mining activity. Surrounded by hills rich in ferrous oxide, the whole port has a pinkish hue, including the 16th-century tower of San Rocco overlooking the harbour. More than 700 mineral exhibits are on display in the **Museo Mineralogico** (open May–Sept; closed Mon–Sat 9am–12pm 3–6pm, Sun 9am–12pm; in winter by request; tel: 0565-962168; entrance fee).

Inland, **Rio nell'Elba ⓰** is a strange, rather wild village perched on a couple of ledges among desolate mountain slopes and scattered remains of mines. A few kilometres west, on the road to Portoferraio, a steep road leads uphill to **Volterraio** and the ruins of an 11th-century Pisan fortress, perched on a rock.

From Rio nell'Elba to the small beach resort of **Cavo ⓱** in the northeast, the picturesque road cuts through woods and moorland. Paths trail through gorse, heather and the wild flowers of the maquis. Like the northwestern corner of the island, Elba's northeastern tip has unspoilt stretches of natural beauty, and is less crowded in summer than most of the island. Just north of Cavo, the remains of a Roman villa can be seen at **Capo Castello**. ❑

The Tuscan Archipelago

Elba is the largest island in a chain of seven islands between the Ligurian and Tyrrhenian seas, all protected as part of the Arcipelago Toscano national marine park. On a clear day, Pianosa, Gorgona, Montecristo and Capraia are visible from the island's highest reaches. Pianosa, just 14 km (9 miles) from Elba, was a maximum-security prison until 1997. It is now a marine nature reserve. Montecristo, 34 km (21 miles) away, is also a nature reserve, uninhabited but for its four guardians. So as not to disturb the fragile environments, the number of visitors is restricted (to enqu ire about organising a trip tel: 0565-914671). Gorgona, the smallest and northernmost island in the archipelago, is still a prison. Capraia is a miniature Elba without its history or architecture. It is a two-hour ferry ride from Livorno *(see page 167)*.

Giglio, the second-largest island in the archipelago after Elba, and its sister Giannutri, are the southernmost islands in the chain. Giglio is popular with weekending Romans and daytrippers. Both can be reached from Porto Santo Stefano *(see page 239)*. For further information, visit www.arcipelago.turismo.toscana.it or www.parks.it

RESTAURANTS

Capo d'Enfola

Da Giacomino
Loc. Viticcio
Tel/fax: 0565-915381
www.ristorantedagiacomino.it
A small, family-run trattoria, a short drive from the island capital. Sunsets from the terrace across the bay are memorable. Pizzas served in the evening. Closed Oct–Easter. €–€€

Ristorante Emanuel
Porto di Sansone,
Tel: 0565-939003
The road to Capo d'Enfola promontary ends at a pebble beach with a couple of restaurants. Emanuel is a good option for a snack lunch, and one of few places to offer a vegetarian menu. Open daily Easter–Oct €–€€

Marciana Marina

Affrichella
Piazza Santa Chiara
Tel: 0565-996844
Intimate restaurant, tucked down a backstreet away from the seafront bustle, offering an inventive fish-based menu. Closed Weds. €–€€€

Borgo al Cotone
Via del Cotone 23
Tel: 0565-904390
Romantic harbourside restaurant where fish and seafood come grilled and gratinated, or in

more adventurous concoctions such as lasagne with chickpeas and clams. Closed Mon. €€–€€€

Ristorante Capo Nord
Loc. La Fenicia
Tel: 0565-996983
The island's top restaurant, where you will be fed exquisite Tuscan food by impeccably dressed and deferential waiters. Dress up and book. Ask for table 5 or 6. Open daily in high season. Closed Mon rest of year. €€€–€€€€

Marina di Campo

La Lucciola
Viale degli Eroi
Tel: 0565-976395
www.lalucciola.it
Brush the sand off your feet and step onto the wooden-decked terrace of this relaxed beach bar/restaurant, where you can enjoy a drink, a big summer salad or go for the full works including the catch of the day. Home-made pastries too. Daily in summer. €–€€

Poggio/Marciana Alta

Publius
Piazza XX Settembre
Tel: 0565-99208
Nestled on the mountainside, Publius has a well-established reputation on the island, and offers fine views from the ter-

race. Elban wines and fish and game dishes. Closed Mon. €€–€€€

Porto Azzurro

I Quattro Gatti
Piazza del Mercato 4
Tel: 0565-95240
A cosy and convivial restaurant decorated with copper pots, beaded lamps, old wirelesses and other knick-knacks. The menu is equally eclectic with offerings like herrings with apple, carpaccio of cod and fish ravioli. In a resort town full of bright and brash restaurants, this is a real find. Closed Mon. €€–€€€

Portoferraio

Da Lido
Salita Falcone 2
Tel: 0565-914650

Set back from the port area, this consistently good and constantly bustling trattoria is one of Portoferraio's best. Closed mid-Dec–mid-Feb. €€

Osteria Libertaria
Calata Matteotti 12
Tel: 0565-914978
Traditional hostelry overlooking the marina. Grab one of the two outdoor bench tables and watch the boating bustle over a pasta or fish dish. Open daily April–Nov. €–€€

PRICE CATEGORIES

Average cost of a three-course meal per person with a half-bottle of wine:
€ = under €25
€€ = €25–€40
€€€ = €40–€60
€€€€ = more than €60

RIGHT: the traditional Osteria Libertaria overlooks Portoferraio's marina.

VOLTERRA AND THE COLLINE METALLIFERE

Perched on a windy plateau overlooking the Sienese hills, Volterra has some of the best Etruscan art outside Rome. The terrain south of Volterra goes from the dry and desolate crags of Le Balze to the dense, eerie forests of the "Metal-Bearing Mountains"

One of the most important towns in Tuscany is **Volterra ❶**, which has a richly layered history with abundant evidence of its 3,000 years of civilisation. It commands a beautiful, windswept and majestic position on a steep ridge 545 metres (1,780 ft) above sea level between the valleys of the Era and Cecina rivers. Walking round the ancient defensive walls is an excellent way to view the town, the Roman remains and the wide sweep of countryside below.

Volterra was the Etruscan city-state of Velathri, one of the confederation of 12 city-states which made up Etruria. It became an important Roman municipality (Volterrae) when Rome annexed Etruria in 351 BC. It followed the new faith of Christianity, and at the fall of the Roman Empire in AD 476 it was already the centre of a vast diocese.

The modern city of Volterra sits within the walls of a much larger Etruscan predecessor. Wherever archaeologists dig in the city, they turn up new treasures. Sometimes they do not even need to dig, since parts of the city, built on soft tufa and undermined by subterranean springs, have been slipping slowly down the hillside for centuries, revealing the remains of an extensive necropolis.

Exploring Volterra

The **Porta all'Arco** (the Arch Gate) is the best-preserved Etruscan gateway in Italy, dating from the 4th century BC (though partly rebuilt by the Romans in the 1st century BC), with sides of huge rectangular stone blocks and three mysterious carved basalt heads above the gateway, thought to represent Etruscan gods.

From the arch, a pretty road winds its way uphill to the **Piazza dei Priori**. Evidence of the Middle Ages is demonstrated not only in Volterra's

Map on page 186

LEFT: Volterra sits majestically on a steep ridge. **BELOW:** the Palazzo dei Priori.

TIP

Traditional craftsman-
ship in alabaster
is a legacy from the
Etruscans, who made
great use of it from the
5th century BC
onwards, primarily for
their beautifully sculp-
tured urns. Alabaster is
sold at many of the
local workshops, as
well as being exported.

BELOW:
a 13th-century lion
stands guard outside
the Palazzo dei Priori.

urban structure but also in its buildings, the most important of which
are clustered around the main
square. It is dominated by the tall
Palazzo dei Priori (1208) the oldest
town hall in Tuscany, and said to be
the model for Florence's Palazzo
Vecchio. Across the square is the
13th-century **Palazzo Pretorio**, with
its crenellated Torre del Porcellino
(Tower of the Little Pig), so named
due to the decorative relief of a boar.

To the south of the square, Via
Turrazza leads to the 12th-century
Duomo (Piazza San Giovanni; open
daily 7am–12.30pm, 2–6pm in winter, 7am–7pm in summer; free),
which houses works of art from the
Middle Ages to the Renaissance. The
sculpture of the *Deposition* is an
extremely rare and unusual Romanesque woodcarving, simple in execution but full of dramatic pathos.

The bishop's palace next door
houses the **Museo d'Arte Sacra** (Via

Roma; open daily 9am–1pm, 3–6pm,
Nov–mid-Mar 9am–1pm; entrance
fee), a collection of gold reliquaries,
church bells, illuminated manuscripts
and some 13th-century sculptures of
the Sienese school. The octagonal
Baptistery opposite has an elegant
marble doorway with a fine baptismal font sculpted by Sansovino.

Heading back towards the square,
Via Roma leads into Via Buonparenti and the Pisan-style **Casa Torre
Buonparenti**, a pair of so-called
house-towers (13th-century).

At the top of Via Buonparenti, the
Pinacoteca e Museo Civico in the
Palazzo Minucci-Solaini (open daily
9am–7pm, until 2pm in winter;
entrance fee) houses valuable paintings of the Sienese and Florentine
schools, including an *Annunciation*
by Signorelli and *Christ in Glory* by
Ghirlandaio. The most famous painting in the collection is the *Deposition
from the Cross* by Rosso Fiorentino

(1495–1540), considered by many to be his greatest masterpiece.

The **Palazzo Incontri-Viti** on Via dei Sarti (open Apr–Oct 10am–1pm, 2.30–6pm, winter by appointment only; tel: 0588-84047; entrance fee) is another impressive building whose façade is attributed to Ammannati, who worked on the Palazzo Pitti in Florence. This and other Renaissance buildings, such as the Palazzo Minucci-Solaini, blend gracefully with the medieval Volterran houses.

The Etruscan museum and Roman theatre

The best of the city's ancient treasures are displayed in the **Museo Etrusco Guarnacci** (Via Don Minzoni; open daily 9am–7pm, until 2pm Nov–mid-Mar; entrance fee). This is packed with ancient Etruscan funerary urns. The *Married Couple* urn is a masterpiece of realistic portraiture, and even more stunning is the bronze statuette known as *L'Ombra della Sera* (Evening Shadow), resembling a Giacometti sculpture but cast in the 5th century BC. The mysterious elongated figure does indeed resemble the shadow of a human being thrown by the low beams of the setting sun.

Volterra is dominated at its highest point by the **Fortezza Medicea**, a magnificent example of Renaissance military architecture – today it serves as a prison. Near by, on the site of the former Etruscan acropolis, the **Parco Archeologico** (open daily 10am–5.30pm in summer, weekends and bank holidays only 10am–4pm in winter; entrance fee) is an ideal spot for a picnic.

On the north side of town, just below the city walls, is the excavated **Roman Theatre** (open daily 10.30am–5pm, until 4pm in winter), the impressive remains of a complex built during the reign of Augustus, behind which lie the ruins of a 3rd-century Roman bathhouse.

Le Balze

The countryside around Volterra is one of gentle, undulating hills, interrupted in the west by the wild and awe-inspiring spectacle of abrupt crevasses known as **Le Balze** (the Crags). Over the centuries, these deep gullies, created by the continual erosion of layers of sand and clay, have swallowed up churches and settlements along with Etruscan and early Christian remains. Today an 11th-century abbey, the Badia, sits on a precipice, awaiting its inevitable fate. For the perfect view of this dramatic landscape, exit through the western San Francesco Gate, passing the Borgo San Giusto and its remains until you reach the Le Balze campsite (a 20-minute walk).

Metal mountains

The wide vistas of the dry, desolate terrain just south of Volterra seem a world away from the cosy green hills of Chianti. At Saline di Volterra, an industrial suburb that has developed around its railway terminus and salt mine, the SS439 leads south to Massa Marittima and the coast, cutting

Map on page 186

TIP

Walk along the remains of Volterra's Etruscan walls at the northwestern edge of town, for lovely views at sunset.

BELOW: Larderello, at the centre of geothermic activity.

TIP

There are some excellent walks in the Forestali Berignone-Tatti, near Pomarance, especially in the autumn, when the leaves of the sweet chestnut turn golden-yellow and the forest becomes carpeted with bright pink cyclamen. Bicycle tours and horse-riding excursions can be booked through Pomarance's tourist office (in the car park on the SS439).

BELOW:
Massa Marittima.

through the Colline Metallifere, or Metal-Bearing Mountains. Beyond the Upper Cecina valley the landscape transforms into one of dense forests of chestnut, beech and oak, punctuated at intervals by fumaroles, cooling towers and gleaming silver pipelines, making for a strange and distinctly un-Tuscan picture.

The first noteworthy town on this surreal route is **Pomarance** ❷, which retains vestiges of its prosperous medieval past, including two 14th-century town gates. La Piazza della Pretura is dominated by the church of San Giovanni, with a Romanesque façade, and a short walk away the Via Roncalli is lined with *palazzi*, one of which houses the **Bicocchi Museum** (open daily 9am–1pm; entrance fee), a well preserved early 19th-century home, whose lavish decorations evoke the lifestyle of the rich, upper-class families whose fortunes were mostly made exploiting the region's mineral wealth. Pomarance makes a good base for exploring the local countryside.

A little further along the road is the small settlement of **San Dalmazio**

❸. From here, a short but steep walk (2 km/1¼ miles) takes you to the impressive ruins of the 11th-century castle **Rocca Sillana**. This site, 530 metres (1,700ft) above sea level, offers commanding views over the surrounding provinces of Grosseto, Siena and Pisa.

Across the valley, the medieval hamlet of **Montecastelli Pisano** ❹ is dominated by the Torre dei Pannocchieschi. Like the Rocca Sillana, this settlement was the object of many an inter-city-state battle, the Florentines finally winning out in the 16th century. Follow the signs to Castelnuovo Val di Cecina and the "Buca delle Fate", a small but well-preserved 6th-century BC Etruscan tomb, just outside the village.

The road south from Montecastelli Pisano offers the best views of the medieval village of **Castelnuovo Val di Cecina** ❺, which is built on the side of a steep ridge and surrounded by woodland. A short walk east of the village leads through chestnut woods and down to the river Pavone, where you can swim in the rock pools, overlooked by two medieval bridges.

Geothermic activity

At the heart of this vast geothermic area, the industrial village of **Larderello** ❻ has been valued for its healing spring waters for centuries. In the Middle Ages the bubbling lakes brought wealth to local merchants, who bottled the sulphur, vitrio and alum and sold them as healing balms throughout Italy. Larderello was named after the French industrialist François de Larderel, who set up a factory here to produce boric acid. The village was built to house the factory workers. There is a public swimming pool fed by the thermal waters, and the **Geothermal Museum** (open Sun–Fri 9am–4.30pm; free) is dedicated to the history of the community and its important resource. There's an impressive view of the power plant from the SS439 as it crosses the hill towards Castelnuovo Val di Cecina.

Heading south along a back road from Larderello, two small villages worth a look are **Leccia** and **Sasso Pisano**, linked by a narrow, winding road that cuts through a landscape of steaming fumaroles. Just outside the hamlet of Leccia are the ancient baths of Bagnone, a vast Etruscan-Roman bathing complex from the 3rd century BC. The medieval village of Sasso Pisano is built on a rocky outcrop above the Cornia river. This strangely appealing place is often shrouded in clouds of steam from the surrounding fumaroles and the air is heavy with the smell of sulphur. The road through the village leads back to the SS439.

As the main road continues to wind south towards Massa Marittima it passes through steep wooded hillsides and up to the summits of the Colline Metallifere. It is an area of outstanding natural beauty, with dense forest and large open views across to Maremma and the Gulf of Follonica; on a clear day, the islands of Elba and Corsica are visible.

Massa Marittima

Massa Marittima ❼ is about 24 km (15 miles) inland, despite its maritime name. It is one of the most astounding Tuscan cities, perched on top of a high hill on the edge of the Colline Metallifere. It was the most important town in the Maremma until the 17th century, when the land silted up.

Massa Marittima was built around the 10th century, after the decline of ancient Populonia *(see page 174)*, which was too exposed to coastal malaria and plundering by pirates. It was known for its copper and silver mines even in Etruscan times, and the rich variety of metals available was a major factor in its economic development. The affluence of medieval Massa Marittima, and pride in its republican status (in 1225 the city overthrew its feudal lord, declaring itself a free commune), are reflected in the concentration of public buildings around the Duomo.

In the main square – the spectacular **Piazza Garibaldi**, one of the finest squares in Tuscany – are Palazzo Vescovile (seat of the

Map on page 186

The mountains south of Volterra are rich in metal ores, and for centuries provided Tuscany with the precious commodities of silver, copper, lead and zinc. However, by the end of the 19th century mining and related industries had fallen into decline, and now these hills are a remote and lonely region. The ruins of mines and factories engulfed in thick forest littered with heaps of coloured metals present a surreal picture.

BELOW: a classic Tuscan snapshot.

Map
on page
186

TIP

A memorable experience – and a lot easier to see than Siena's *Palio* – is the traditional Balestro del Girifalco, every last Sunday in May and every second Sunday in August. The three *terzieri* of Massa (old city, new city and the outer Borgo) hold a shooting contest using mechanical falcons with ancient crossbows.

BELOW RIGHT: the Gothic ruins of San Galgano.

bishop), Palazzo del Podestà (seat of the governor, now an archaeological museum), Palazzo del Comune (town hall), Zecca Cittadina (the mint), Fonte Pubblica (public fountain) and Palazzo dell' Abbondanza (the public granary).

The **Duomo** is an example of Pisan Romanesque architecture, with marvellous reliefs of the *Madonna delle Grazie*, ascribed to Duccio di Buoninsegna (1316) and the *Arca di San Cerbone* (St Cerbone's Ark), a masterpiece of the Sienese school of sculpture (1324).

There are two mining-related museums in Massa Marittima: the **Museum of Mining Art and History** in Piazza Mateotti (open Apr–Oct Tues–Sun 10–11.30am, 3.30–5pm; entrance fee) and the **Mine Museum** in Via Corridoni (open Apr–Oct Tues–Sun 10.15am–5.45pm; guided tours; entrance fee), with exhibits from the Stone and Bronze ages. The **Torre del Candeliere**, a clock tower dating to 1443 (open daily 10am–1pm, 3–6pm; entrance fee) in Piazza Mateotti, offers great views across the city.

Gothic ruin

Heading east from Massa Marittima along the SS441 towards Siena takes you to what some have claimed as Italy's most impressive Gothic ruin. Located in a field, with the panorama of sky and fields to match its majesty, is the ruined **Abbazia di San Galgano** ❽. This roofless abbey, with grass for a nave and the sparsest of frescoes still clinging to its crumbling walls is definitely worth a visit. The best time to come is towards evening, when the coach tours have gone and the setting sun sends shafts of light through its windows. Concerts and operas are staged here in the summer (tourist office in the abbey).

On a nearby hill overlooking the abbey is the Romanesque church of Monte Siepi, built on the spot where St Galgano had a vision of Saint Michael and renounced his profession as a soldier to become a hermit, thrusting his sword into a rock. The event is illustrated by the frescoes of Ambrogio Lorenzetti that can be found in the adjacent, rectangular chapel. Siena is about 35 km (22 miles) from here on the SS73. ❑

The Abbey of San Galgano

Consecrated in 1288, the abbey of San Galgano was originally the main centre for the Cistercian Order that dominated this area in the 12th and 13th centuries, exerting influence across the whole of central Italy. Its abbot had the power of arbitration in the disputes between city-states, and its monks oversaw the building of Siena's Duomo as well as the accounts of Massa Marittima's free republic. But this period of power for the Cistercian Order was short-lived. In the mid-14th century, the abbey was ransacked by the English mercenary Sir John Hawkwood – an attack sanctioned by the pope, who was fearful of the Order's influence. Now in the hands of the papacy, the abbey's income was diverted to Rome, and slowly the building began to fall into disrepair.

Bouts of plague across the decades weakened the order further and by 1576 it is said that San Galgano was occupied by one solitary monk "who didn't even wear a robe". A lightning strike during a village Mass in 1778 saw the collapse of the campanile and marked the last service at San Galgano and the beginning of its final ruination.

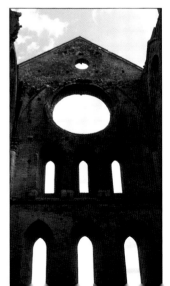

RESTAURANTS

Massa Marittima

Il Brillo Parlante
Vicolo del Ciambellano 4
Tel: 0566-901274
The best way to approach
a meal in this tiny restaurant – there are just four
tables – is to ask what's
available. The dishes are
lovingly prepared and
seasonal, and there's a
good selection of fine
wines. Booking essential.
Closed Mon. €€€

Le Mura
Via Norma Parenti 7
Tel: 0566-940055
This large and busy
restaurant has
panoramic views
towards Follonica and
Elba, from both inside
and out. The extensive
menu incorporates typi-
cal Tuscan ingredients
from the nearby wooded
hills and fresh seafood
from the coast beyond.
Closed Tues. €€€

Osteria Da Tronca
Vicolo Porte 5
Tel: 0566-901991
A reasonably priced and
popular family-run
restaurant offering sim-
ple, well-prepared dishes
cooked to traditional
recipes by both *mamma*
and her daughter. Book-
ing recommended.
Closed Wed. €€

Trattoria Dei Cavalieri
Via Norma Parenti 35
Te: 0566-902093
Well lit, friendly and
with a pleasant atmos-

phere, this restaurant is
both value for money
and a joy to be in. Local
dishes such as *tortelli
maremmani* and *aqua-
cotta* predominate.
Booking essential.
Closed Thur. €€

Volterra

Da Badò
Borgo San Lazzaro 9
Tel: 0588-86477
Restaurant just outside
the city, serving Volterran
specialities. Features
prominently in guide-
books, so it is advisable
to book. Closed Wed. €€

Don Beta
Via Matteotti 39
Tel: 0588-86730
Ignore the yellow table-
cloths, this is a great
restaurant specialising
in the traditional cuisine
of the local huntsmen;
try the *cinghiale* (wild
boar) or *lepre* (hare).
Closed Mon. €

Il Pozzo Degli Etruschi
Via delle Prigioni 28-30
Tel: 0588-80608
The simple medieval
backdrop of this recently
renovated eatery is
echoed in the unpreten-
tious and delicious Tus-
can fare. In summer the
shady inner courtyard is
also open for dining.
Closed Fri. €

Il Sacco Fiorentino
Piazza XX Settembre 18
Tel: 0588-88537
Pleasant and welcoming

eatery in two parts: one
side is a trattoria serving
interesting Tuscan fare;
the other is a wine bar
with a shorter, cheaper,
more traditional menu
and snacks. Closed
Wed and mid-Jan–end
Feb. €–€€

Ombra della Sera
Via Gramsci 70
Tel: 0588-85274
Families and young
Volterrans flock to this
brightly lit, no-frills pizzeria, attracted by the
buzzy atmosphere and
excellent, reasonably
priced pizza. The restau-
rant next door offers a
quieter, more intimate
atmosphere, and spe-
cialises in dishes based
on truffles, mushrooms
and local game. Closed
Mon. €

Osteria San Lorenzo
Via Massetana, San Lorenzo
(5 km southwest of Volterra)
Tel: 0588-44160
Good, traditional home
cooking in this welcoming
osteria which also serves
snacks. Closed Tues. €

**Vecchia Osteria
dei Poeti**
Via Matteotti 55
Tel: 0588-86029
Central restaurant, popu-
lar with residents and
tourists alike. Closed
Thur. €€

RIGHT: hearty bean dishes are a Tuscan staple.

SAN GIMIGNANO AND CHIANTI COUNTRY

An exploration of the ordered and harmonious landscape spanning the fertile hills between Florence and Siena, taking in the medieval skyscrapers of San Gimignano, the red-brick hill town of Certaldo, and the vineyards and villas along the Chianti trail

Perhaps the most spectacular sight anywhere in Tuscany is the town of **San Gimignano** ❶, famous for the sculptural quality of its skyline and richly rewarding – despite the huge number of visitors. It may be a cliché to call it a "Medieval Manhattan", but the famous towers thrusting up from the hill town do resemble miniature skyscrapers. This view is best appreciated from the approach roads to the town. Once you are there, it is the unspoilt townscape that bowls you over: almost nothing seems to have changed since the Middle Ages.

In its heyday the city had a total of 76 towers, only 14 of which remain. The towers were built in the 12th and 13th centuries by the *magnati*, or nobles, during the Guelf-Ghibelline conflicts. As well as defending the city, they served as status symbols: the higher the tower, the more rich and powerful its owner. The local 14th-century poet Folgore, who wrote during this period of relative wealth, described the "earthly pleasures" he encountered in the city, including "silk sheets, sugared nuts, sweets and sparkling wine". The arrival of the Black Death in 1348, however, put an end to silk sheets in San Gimignano until the 20th century. The diminished population fell under Florentine control, and this once important city became an economic backwater, bypassed by the Renaissance. While more civilised cities were exchanging towers for *palazzi*, San Gimignano destroyed nothing and built nothing. The city's misfortune has made it the best-preserved medieval city in Tuscany.

Exploring San Gimignano

The towers are concentrated around the **Piazza del Duomo** and **Piazza della Cisterna**, teeming with tourists all year round. They alone make a

Map on page 194

LEFT: view from a San Gimignano tower.
BELOW: a bountiful harvest.

TIP

To see San Gimignano at its best, it's worth considering an overnight stay in one of the characteristic hotels. Then you can savour the peaceful beauty of the town in the evening and early morning, after the coach trippers have gone.

visit here worthwhile, but the town possesses many other sights worth seeing. The Romanesque **Collegiata** (open Mon–Fri 9.30am– 7.30pm, Sat 9.30am–5pm, Sun 1–5pm, Nov–mid-Jan and Mar Mon–Sat 9.30am–5pm, Sun 1–5pm; closed late Jan, Feb; entrance fee) will detain you longest, as every inch of wall space is covered in frescoes. The north aisle has Bartolo di Fredi's dramatic scenes from the *Old Testament* (1367), while the opposite aisle has Lippo Memmi's *Life of Christ* (1333–41) and the nave the *Last Judgement* by Taddeo di Bartolo (1393–6). Contrast these Gothic-style narrative paintings with Ghirlandaio's lyrical Renaissance frescoes (1475) on the life of a local saint, in the chapel of Santa Fina.

Four museums

Next to the Collegiata, the **Museo d'Arte Sacra** (open daily mid-Mar–Oct 9.30am–7.30pm, Nov–mid-Mar 9.30am–5pm; closed late Jan and Feb; entrance fee) contains a variety of sacred art from the 13th to the 15th centuries.

Alongside is the **Museo Civico** (open daily Mar–Oct 9.30am–7.20pm, Nov–Feb 10am– 5.50pm; entrance fee), housed in the Palazzo del Popolo, a forbidding fortress that served as the town hall. Completed in 1311, its tower, the **Torre Grassa**, is the tallest in the town (54 metres/ 175 ft) and the only one you can climb; the views of the Val d'Elsa from the top are spectacular. Among the museum's many good paintings is a set of early 14th-century frescoes by Memmo di Filippucci – rare in that they depict secular rather than religious scenes. Known as the *Wedding Frescoes*, they show a young bride and groom sharing a bath and climbing into their nuptial bed – an intimate glimpse into the private life of medieval Italy.

The former convent of Santa

Chiara is now home to the **Museo Archeologico** (open daily 11am–6pm, mid-Jan–Feb Fri–Mon only, Nov–mid-Jan closed Fri; entrance fee). Fascinating exhibits range from ceramic-and-glass vessels containing herbal remedies and healing lotions and potions, to Etruscan finds.

The nearby **Piazza della Cisterna** is a lovely triangular square with a 13th-century well and medieval *palazzi*. East of the square, on Via di Castello, is the **Museo della Tortura** (open Mon–Fri 10am–midnight, Sat and Sun 10am–6pm; entrance fee), with a gruesome collection of medieval instruments of torture.

Every church in San Gimignano offers some reward, but perhaps the best is **Sant' Agostino** (open daily 7am–noon, 3–7pm, Oct–Apr until 6pm) to the north of the town (near Porta San Matteo). Here, in Gozzoli's frescoes on the *Life of St Augustine* (1465), you will find the same love of colour, rich clothing and exact portraiture as in Gozzoli's other frescoes such as *The Journey of the Magi* in the Palazzo Medici Riccardi in Florence (*see page 90*).

A short walk along the city walls to the 14th-century fortress before leaving is worthwhile. This semi-derelict **Rocca** has views over tiered gardens and olive groves winding down to the "Vernaccia" vineyards.

The Val d'Elsa

A few kilometres north of San Gimignano, the medieval hill town of **Certaldo ❷** straddles the summit of a steep hill. To reach it, park in the lower town, Certaldo Basso, and take the *funicolare* up the steep slope to the upper town (closed to traffic). Certaldo Alto is a literary landmark as it was the home of Giovanni Boccaccio (1313–75), author of *The Decameron*, who died here in 1375. What is thought to have been his home was restored in 1823, bombed during World War II, and has now been rebuilt as the **Casa di Boccaccio** (closed for restoration at time of writing). The differences between Certaldo Alto and Certaldo Basso are marked by the silence of the former, where, on summer afternoons, the only sounds are footsteps and the distant music of a radio. The red-brick

Map on page 194

One of five circular towers in San Gimignano's city walls.

BELOW: San Gimignano newsagent.

Nectar of the Gods

The vine – along with olives and grain – became an integral part of Tuscany's agriculture very early in the region's history. The Etruscans were certainly enamoured with the fruits of the vine, as is evidenced by the wine cup found in an Etruscan tomb at Castellina in Chianti, and surviving Etruscan frescoes that depict scenes relating to Bacchus, the Roman god of wine. Monasteries played a large part in establishing a successful viticulture in the area – as they did through much of medieval Europe. Several old monastic sites – such as Badia a Coltibuono and Badia a Passignano – are still important wine estates today.

The wicker-covered Chianti flask, called a *fiascho*, is rarer these days in Italian restaurants than red-and-white check tablecloths. This emblem of the early days of Tuscan vine culture – now considered impractical, expensive to produce and a bit too "rustic" – has been superseded by an elegant square-shouldered bottle, reflecting the upgrading in quality of one of Italy's best-known wines.

If you order wine without referring to a wine list in a bar or restaurant in Tuscany, you will almost certainly be served the local *vino da tavola* (table wine) in a jug or carafe. It is always drinkable and often rather good. Now, however, Tuscany is much more conscious of its standing as a producer of higher-quality wines, and increasingly you will find a sophisticated list of superior Tuscan vintages.

Nevertheless, in wine terms, Tuscany is still synonymous with Chianti – to the chagrin of producers of the region's other fine wines. The heart of the Chianti district stretches in a large oval between Florence and Siena, with branches extending west towards Lucca and Pisa, south to Montalcino, southeast to Montepulciano, east to Arezzo and past Pontassieve, and north past Pistoia. The heartland is called Chianti Classico, covering the communes of Barberino Val d'Elsa, Castellina, Greve, Gaiole, San Casciano and Tavarnelle Val de Pesa.

The concern for the quality of wine has been evident in the Chianti Classico area since the 1700s, when grapes and wines began to be classified, and recommended methods of production were developed. The real mover in this area was Barone Bettino Ricasoli, who, in the mid-19th century, conducted experiments that led to a specific formula for making the wine. In 1924 a consortium, the Consorzio Chianti Classico, was founded to control production. To signify that a bottle was "Consorzio approved", a special sticker was placed around its neck carrying the symbol of the Consorzio, a black cockerel *(gallo nero)*.

Once in the European Union, Italy had to develop a countrywide wine law. In line with EU regulations, "quality" wines were designated *Denominazione di Origine Controllata* (DOC), distinguishing them from their "lesser" brethren, called just *vino da tavola*. In 1984 Chianti joined the élite (including Brunello di Montalcino and Vino Nobile di Montepulciano) that were entitled to call their wines DOCG, the G standing for *e garantita*, "and guaranteed".

A few basics to keep in mind when shopping for wine in Tuscany: make sure it has the DOC designation; go for wines with family names or farm titles (avoid acronyms such as CA.VI.T) and look for the black cockerel label on the neck if you want a good Chianti. ❏

LEFT: the Sangiovese grape.

town is crowned by the 15th-century **Palazzo Pretorio**, the front façade of which is studded with terracotta coats of arms. Exploration around the back of the town will reveal the early gateways, the portals of which are still intact and which lead down to steep, narrow approach lanes. The frescoed rooms of the **Palazzo del Vicario** (open summer daily 10am–7pm, winter Tues–Sun 10.30am–4pm; entrance fee) are worth visiting. The Palazzo also houses a delightful hotel and a Michelin-starred restaurant *(see page 201)*.

South of San Gimignano, **Colle di Val d'Elsa ❸** is split between two sites. The lower "new" town is a busy, haphazard sprawl, whose centre of activity is the crystal factory – Colle is Italy's largest producer of crystal and fine glass, and there are plenty of shops selling it. The recent Museo del Cristallo (Via dei Fossi; Apr–Oct Tues–Sun 10am–noon 4–7pm, Nov–Mar Tues–Fri 3–7pm, Sat–Sun 10am–noon 3–7pm; entrance fee) tells its story. Follow the signs up to the ancient upper town. Here the main street is lined with 16th-century *palazzi* of unusual refinement, and, at one point, the stately procession of buildings is interrupted by a viaduct from which there are splendid views of the surrounding landscape.

More spectacular sights await in nearby **Monteriggioni ❹**, just off the N2 to Siena. The fortified town, encircled by walls and 14 towers, was built in 1213 to guard the northern borders of Sienese territory. Like Montepulciano, this little hill village is emblematic of the Tuscan landscape, and merits a short visit. It is seen at its best first thing in the morning, when you can enjoy a coffee on the main square before the coach parties arrive.

The Chiantigiana

The Chianti is a spiritual rather than a geographical location. Its shifting borders reflect the fluctuations in Florentine and Sienese power, but, although it lies in Siena province, its soul remains where it has always been: on Florentine soil. Unlike the southern part of Siena province, the Chianti is not an area for artistic or architectural set-pieces. Instead, it is

Map on page 194

In 1716 a decree issued by the Grand Duke of Tuscany defined the boundaries of the Chianti area and established the laws governing the production and sale of wine. Today this region is the world's oldest wine-producing league. The Chianti Classico area includes the communes of Barberino Val d'Elsa, Castellina, Greve, Gaiole, San Casciano and Tavernelle Val di Pesa.

BELOW: all the elements of a classic Tuscan landscape.

a place whose turbulent history has shaped a scene of utter tranquillity, a harmony of tame hills and gentle people. In a place where nothing is essential viewing, everywhere is a glorious detour.

The SS222, known as the Chiantigiana, or Chianti Way, winds its picturesque way from Florence to Siena, through the heart of the region, offering archetypal scenes of cypress trees, olive groves and vineyards. First stop is the market town of **Greve ❺** with an impressive arcaded square, Piazza Matteotti, topped with wrought-iron balconies dripping with geraniums. The shops under the arcades are crammed with the usual assortment of local foods (such as extra virgin olive oil and traditional boar sausages), crafts and wines. The annual September Mostra Mercato del Chianti draws a large crowd.

An oft-missed jewel just five minutes' drive west of Greve is the ancient, tiny medieval walled town of **Montefioralle**, which was built as a feudal castle. Its narrow streets, stone houses and underpassages are beautifully preserved, and splendid views are to be had from the various *trattorie* in the town.

Next on the SS222 is **Castellina in Chianti ❻**. Castellina surveys symmetrical vineyards and wooded groves, a landscape dotted with low stone houses and Renaissance villas. New wine estates have been built from the remains of medieval castles. Villas have lazily domesticated the original castle or tower, but names like "La Rocca" or "La Torre" reveal the original function.

Castellina's name also reveals its medieval function as a Florentine outpost. In the late 13th century it was the first site of the Chianti League, a group of three Florentine feudal castles, each responsible for a third of the territory. The castle is now a fortified town hall hiding a small Etruscan museum and a warren of atmospheric backstreets with half-glimpsed views of the Chianti hills.

The other attraction is the **Enoteca La Bottega del Vino** (Via della Rocca 13; tel: 0577-741110; www.enobottega.it), the wine-tasting centre which gives advice on wine tours and *vendita diretta*, direct sales.

TIP

Cycling is an immensely popular way of touring Chianti country, and countless companies organise group or family holidays for people of all ages and abilities. You can also organise bike rental by the day or week through the Castellina in Chianti tourist office on Via Ferruccio (tel: 0577-741392; open daily 10am–1pm, 2–6pm).

BELOW: cyclists stop for souvenirs in Castellina.

Chianti's capital

East of Castellina, **Radda in Chianti** ❼ retains its medieval street plan and imposing town hall. As in Castellina, the spontaneous rural architecture is more rewarding. Classical Medici villas with 16th-century windows and wells compete with romantic villas, constructed magpie-fashion from castles or Etruscan ruins. One 17th-century masterpiece is Villa Vistarenni, a white beacon of sophistication. The elegant loggias and the openness of the architecture symbolise the increasing wealth of the countryside and its proximity to urban Florence. In the tranquil Chianti, the country is richer and more civilised than the town.

From Radda a tortuous road climbs to **Volpaia** ❽, a pretty medieval village, with a ruined castle and Brunelleschi-style church. If Chianti villages and towns have little sense of identity and few artistic treasures, it is because they came into being with fully-fledged Florentine and Sienese identities, while military outposts like Radda had no time to develop artistically. Only the Chianti abbeys, endowed separately, had the independence to shape their own culture.

Abbey of the Good Harvest

Between Radda and Gaiole is the aptly named **Badia a Coltibuono** ❾ (Abbey of the Good Harvest; open May–Oct; closed am, Sun and Aug; tel: 0577-744832; www.coltibuono. com), set among pines, oaks, chestnuts and vines. Since the Dissolution of the Monasteries in 1810, this medieval abbey has belonged to one family. The lovely 15th-century cloisters, chapel and frescoed ceilings can be viewed as a guest of the Tuscan cookery school or bed and breakfast, while the 12th-century walls and bell-tower are open to all. Below the abbey are cellars filled with Chianti Classico, the abbey's traditional living. No less famous are the aromatic chestnut honey and olive oil. Much of the produce can be bought on the premises or savoured in the excellent abbey restaurant.

Chianti castles

Gaiole in Chianti ❿ is a newer riverside development in a wooded

Map on page 194

A winemaker promotes his produce at the Chianti wine festival held in Greve every September.

BELOW: café on Piazza Matteotti, Greve.

Map on page 194

The famous Chianti flask is no longer mass-produced for export. However, the nostalgic will be pleased to find rustic wicker fiaschi *for sale throughout the region.*

BELOW: San Gimignano through the early morning mist.

valley. It is a popular *villeggiatura*, a summer escape for hot Florentines in search of family-run hotels, home cooking and the familiar *gallo nero* (black cockerel) wine symbol. History lies in wait at Meleto and Vertine, unusual castles, and Barbischio, a medieval village, is a short walk away. Tempting footpaths marked *Sentieri del Chianti* lead all the way to Siena. With vineyards rising up gentle slopes, tranquil Gaiole and sleepy Greve are traditional Chianti.

The countryside from Gaiole south to Siena and east to Arezzo is higher, wilder and wetter. The wooded peaks are green and fresh with scents of thyme, rosemary and pine. Deep chestnut woods provide ideal cover for wild boar, recently reintroduced.

Of the many Florentine castles in the woods, **Castello di Brolio ⓫** (open daily summer 9am–noon, 3–6pm, winter Sat–Thur 9am–noon, 2.30–5pm; entrance fee) is the most impressive – not least because of its views over the original Chianti vineyards stretching as far as Siena and Monte Amiata. On the medieval chessboard, every Florentine castle

faced its Sienese shadow. If the surviving castles are Florentine, it is because Siena lost the match and all its pieces. While Sienese Cereto and Cettamura are small heaps, Florentine Brolio and Meleto are resplendent. As a Florentine outpost, Castello di Brolio's past spans Guelf-Ghibelline conflicts, sacking by the Sienese in 1529 and German occupation and Allied bombing during World War II. The medieval walls are the castle's most striking feature, along with the 14th-century chapel, set in lush grounds. Brolio has long been controlled by the Ricasoli, Chianti landowners since the eighth century. Baron Bettino Ricasoli, Italian premier in 1861, founded the modern Chianti wine industry, a business continued by the present family (to visit the cellars and taste the wines, tel: 0577-730220; www.ricasoli.it).

The Chianti is a place for pottering and chance encounters, one of which is tiny **Campi di San Gusmé ⓬**, just south of Brolio. A short climb leads to a small tower, Romanesque church and views of tumbledown castles, villas and vineyards. ❏

RESTAURANTS

Castellina In Chianti

Albergaccio
Via Fiorentina 63
Tel: 0577-741042
www.albergacciocast.com
The dishes change,
but the quality of the
food – which is Tuscan
with flair – remains the
same. Booking advisable
– this can be done on
the website. €€

La Torre
Piazza del Comune
Tel: 0577-740236
Restaurant with terrace
outside the fortress.
Extensive menu of
predictable Tuscan fare,
but reasonable. Closed
Fri. €€

Le Tre Porte
Via Trento e Trieste
Tel: 0577-741163
This pizzeria by the
Cathedral does a brisk
trade and is big enough
to cater for the hungry
tourist hordes with a
craving for good pizza.
Closed Tues. €€

Certaldo Alto

L'Antica Fonte
Via Valdracca 25
Tel: 0571-652225
Small, simple restaurant
offering Tuscan speciali-
ties in a friendly and
relaxed atmosphere. In
summer there's addi-
tional seating in the garden opposite, with views
across the Val d'Elsa.
Booking essential.
Closed Jan and Feb. €€

Osteria del Vicario
Via Rivellino 3

Tel: 0571-668228
www.osteriadelvicario.it
Pleasantly set in
Romanesque cloisters,
this Michelin-starred
restaurant serves inven-
tive variations on Tuscan
and international dishes.
Closed Mon–Wed. €€€

Gaiole In Chianti

Badia a Coltibuono
Loc. Badia a Coltibuono
Tel/fax: 0577-749424
www.coltibuono.com
Set on a glorious rural
wine estate 5 km (3
miles) from Gaiole, com-
plete with 11th-century
abbey. Specialities
include home-made
pasta with wild duck
sauce and *antipasto
della Badia*. Wine and oil
from the estate is for
sale. Popular with
tourists on the Chianti
trail. Closed Mon except
May–Oct. €€€

Il Carlino d'Oro
Località San Regolo
Tel: 0577-747136
Family-run trattoria, far
removed from the
tourists that swarm
around this part of the
Chianti. Lunch only. €

**Ristorante della Pieve
(Castello di Spaltenna)**
Località Spaltenna 13
Tel: 0577-749483
www.spaltenna.it
Magnificent restaurant
in a hotel converted from
a fortified monastery.
Dishes use fresh local
ingredients, and food
is cooked in a wood-

burning stove. Closed 7
Jan–1 April. €€€€

Greve in Chianti

Bottega del Moro
Piazza Trieste 14r
Tel: 055-853753
Restaurant serving good-
quality traditional Tuscan
fare. Try the *coniglio*
(rabbit) or *trippa alla
Fiorentina* (tripe) after a
fresh pasta dish. Closed
Wed. €€

Monterrigioni

Il Pozzo
Piazza Roma 20
Tel: 0577-304127
Famous restaurant full
of foreigners in summer,
but deservedly popular,
in a gem of a tiny walled
town. Dishes from
Tuscany and further
afield. Closed Sun
evening, Mon, most of
Jan and period in Aug. €€

Radda In Chianti

Le Vigne
Podere le Vigne Est
(1 km outside town)
Tel: 0577-738640
Beautifully located
among vineyards, and
serving great food, this is
a real treat. Simple, reasonably priced rooms to
rent above the restau-
rant. Closed Tues in win-
ter, Jan and Feb. €€–€€€

Vignale
Via XX Settembre 23
Tel: 0577-738094
Restaurant housed in a
converted farm building,
serving refined and

imaginative Tuscan cui-
sine. However, prices
are high and tourists
abound. Must book.
Closed Thur. €€€–€€€€

San Gimignano

Dorandò
Vicolo dell'Oro 2
Tel: 0577-941862
www.ristorantedorando.it
Stylish restaurant
specialising in recipes
with ancient origins.
Closed Mon (except
Easter–Oct). €€€€

Osteria delle Cantene
Via Mainardi 18
Tel: 0577-941966
New-wave trattoria where
traditional and contem-
porary ideas success-
fully coexist. Try the local
Vernaccia wine. Closed
Wed and Jan. €€

Volpaia

La Bottega
Piazza della Torre 2
Tel: 0577-738001
A gorgeous spot for
lunch on a maple-shaded
terrace with views over
the valley. The quality
can vary, but the friendly
service and prime loca-
tion make up for any
shortcomings. €€

PRICE CATEGORIES

Average cost of a three-
course meal per person
with a half-bottle of wine:

€ = under €25
€€ = €25–€40
€€€ = €40–€60
€€€€ = more than €60

THE CHIANTI WINE TRAIL

A trip to Tuscany, home of the famous Chianti Classico and other fine Italian wines, is not complete without exploring some wine estates

What has become known as the Chianti area of Tuscany covers an enormous region, spanning seven different wine "zones". At its heart, in the hills between Florence and Siena, is Chianti Classico, while the remainder – the Colli Fiorentini, Colli Senesi, Colline Pisane, Colli Aretini, Rufina and Montalbano – spread out over central Tuscany.

The main centres in Chianti Classico are Greve, Panzano, Castellina, Gaiole, Fonterutoli and Radda – the official seat of the vintners' association known as the Consorzio del Marchio Storico. Scattered in and among these towns, many of them accessible off the picturesque route SS222, are innumerable vineyards and estates. Most of the estates welcome visitors. Treasure troves of art and history as well as wine, they are well worth exploring. *Chianti News* (www.chiantinews.it), available at local hotels and restaurants, lists estates open for wine-tasting. Estate owners are usually proud to show off their wines and explain their particular methods of wine-making. They will discuss the astounding number of factors, from soil conditions to pruning and grafting, which come into play in order to produce the region's distinctive wines, as well as the science behind processes such as fermentation to ageing. Experimentation is constant, and the different schools of thought encountered along the way are fascinating. Any given winemaker could discuss for hours the pros and cons of various types of wood used in the barrels and casks for ageing and storage. But the best reason for visiting the vineyards is without question… the tasting. Sip, savour and enjoy.

ABOVE: Although chestnut was the traditional wood of the region, Chianti *normale* is now usually kept in oak barrels for several months. The smaller barrels are known as *barriques*; the larger are *botti*.

BELOW: The hills of Chianti are blanketed with vineyards; many of the wine estates are hundreds of years old.

ABOVE: Trebbiani and Malvasia grapes hang up to dry for Vin Santo, made in Chianti and other parts of Tuscany. The wine is fermented and aged for up to six years in small barrels, *orcaratelli*. This strong dessert wine is comparable to a good medium sherry.

LEFT: Hard-earned DOCG labels on bottles of Chianti Classico at Riecine estate near Gaiole. The wine here is made using both meticulous and classic methods.

THE ESTATES

Below are a selection of recommended wine estates in the Chianti region. The majority have shops where you can taste the wine before purchasing, but for a more memorable experience call the estate in advance to arrange a tasting *(degustazione)* combined with a tour of the vineyards and cellars. Good websites for up-to-date information on wine in the area are www.florencewine.it and www.chianticlassico.com.

Badia a Coltibuono
Gaiole in Chianti; tel: 0577-744832; www.coltibuono.com
This wine estate, run by the Stucchi Prinetti family, markets itself as a "wine resort" – visitors can eat, sleep and take courses within the former abbey. Tastings are available to pre-formed groups of six or more people.

Castello di Brolio
Gaiole in Chianti; tel: 0577-730220; www.ricasoli.it
Baron Ricasoli, whose descendants now run the Castello di Brolio, first designated the grape mixes to be used in Chianti wine. Today the famous estate can be visited by appointment.

Castello di Fonterutoli
Castellina in Chianti; tel: 0577-73571; www.fonterutoli.it
Owned by the family since the 15th century, Fonterutoli's wines have won several awards.

Castello di Gabbiano
Mecatale Val di Pesa; tel: 055-821053; www.gabbiano.com
The estate shop offers an opportunity to taste and purchase wine produced at Castello di Gabbiano. Tours can be organised on request.

Montevertine
Radda in Chianti; tel: 0577-738009; www.montevertine.it
The Manetti family only founded this small estate in 1967, but its quality wines are already famous. Call for details on tastings.

Vignamaggio
Greve; tel: 055-854661; www.vignamaggio.it
This *tenuta* is a wine estate and an *agriturismo*. Wine-tasting can be done at the shop, or combined with a pre-arranged guided visit.

SIENA

Siena's tumultuous history as arch-rival of Florence is written in the streets and squares, and resonates in the passionate souls of the Sienese. It is a magical Gothic city, full of pleasant surprises, but the glorious main square alone makes it worth a visit

From its striped marble Cathedral to its tunnelled alleys, brilliant Campo and black-and-white city emblem, Siena is a chiaroscuro city. In its surging towers it is truly Gothic. Where Florence is boldly horizontal, Siena is soaringly vertical; where Florence has large squares and masculine statues, Siena has hidden gardens and romantic wells. Florentine art is perspective and innovation, while Sienese art is sensitivity and conservatism. Siena is often considered the feminine foil to Florentine masculinity.

For such a feminine and beautiful city, Siena has a decidedly warlike reputation, nourished by sieges, city-state rivalry and *Palio* battles. The pale theatricality in Sienese painting is not representative of the city or its inhabitants: the average Sienese is no ethereal Botticelli nymph, but dark, stocky and swarthy.

A brief history

In keeping with Sienese mystique, the city's origins are shrouded in myths of wolves and martyred saints. According to legend, the city was founded by Senius, son of Remus, hence the she-wolf symbols in the city. St Ansano brought Christianity to Roman Siena and, although he was promptly tossed into a vat of hot tar and beheaded, he has left a legacy of mysticism traced through Sts Catherine and Bernardino to the present-day cult of the Madonna. The power of the Church came to an end when the populace rose up against the Ecclesiastical Council and established an independent republic in 1147. The 12th century was marked by rivalry in which the Florentine Guelfs usually triumphed over the Sienese Ghibellines.

In 1260 the battle of Montaperti routed the Florentines and won the Sienese ten years of cultural

Map on page 206

LEFT: Siena's Town Hall and Torre del Mangia, in the Campo.
BELOW: the glow of the rosy brick warms Siena's narrow passageways and arches.

The city is divided into three districts or terzi *(thirds) – The Terzo di San Martino, Terzo di Città and Terzo di Camollia. But this is purely an administrative division; Siena's true identity is inextricably linked to the* contrade*, the 17 medieval districts from which its social fabric is woven (see "Contrade* Passions*" box opposite).*

supremacy which saw the foundation of the University and the charitable "fraternities". The Council of the Twenty-Four – a form of power-sharing between nobles and the working class – was followed by the Council of Nine, an oligarchy of merchants which ruled until 1335. Modern historians judge the Nine self-seeking and profligate, but under their rule the finest works of art were either commissioned or completed, including the famous Campo, the Palazzo Pubblico and Duccio's *Maestà*.

The ancient republic survived until 1529, when the reconciliation between the pope and the emperor ended the Guelf-Ghibelline feud. The occupying Spanish demolished the city towers, symbols of freedom and fratricide, and used the masonry to build the present fortress. The final blow to the republic was the long siege of Siena by Emperor Charles V and Cosimo I in 1554.

After the Sienese defeat, the city of Siena became absorbed into the Tuscan dukedom. As an untrusted member of the Tuscan Empire, impoverished Siena turned in on itself until the 20th century. Today, change is anathema to the

Map on page 206

city: traditional landowning, financial speculation, trade and tourism are more appealing than new technology or industry. Siena has made a virtue of conservatism; stringent medieval building regulations protect the fabric of the city; tourism is decidedly low-key; old family firms such as the *Nannini* cake shop – Siena's most famous café – do a roaring trade with locals (and also produced Gianna Nannini, one of Italy's best-known female singers). It is a city with the psychology of a village and the grandeur of a nation.

Il Campo

All roads lead to **Il Campo** , the huge main central square, shaped like an amphitheatre – the Sienese say that it is shaped like the protecting cloak of the Virgin, who, with St Catherine of Siena, is the city's patron saint. From the comfort of a pavement café on the curved side of the Campo you can note the division of the paved surface into nine segments, commemorating the beneficent rule of the "Noveschi" – the Council of Nine which governed Siena from

the mid-13th century to the early 14th, a period of stability and prosperity when most of the city's main public monuments were built.

The Campo is tipped with the Renaissance **Fonte Gaia** (Fountain of Joy). The marble carvings are copies of the original sculptures by Iacopo della Quercia, which are on display in Santa Maria della Scala *(see page 210)*. Beneath the fountain lies one of Siena's best-kept secrets – a labyrinth of medieval tunnels extending for 25 km (15½ miles), constructed to channel water from the surrounding hills into the city. The underground aqueduct has two main tunnels: one leads to the Fonte Gaia and the other to the Fonte Branda, the best-preserved of Siena's many fountains, northwest of here. Parts of this subterranean system can be visited on a guided tour (ask at the tourist office).

At the square's base is the **Palazzo Pubblico** , the dignified Town Hall with its crenellated façade and waving banners, surmounted by the tall and slender tower. The Town Hall, which has

TIP

As an introduction to the city, a visit to the State Archives in the 15th-century Palazzo Piccolomini (Banchi di Sotto; open Mon–Sat, guided tours at 9.30am, 10.30am and 11.30am) provides a pictorial history of Siena through illuminated manuscripts and paintings.

BELOW LEFT:
Romulus, Remus and the she-wolf: Remus' son is said to have founded Siena.

Contrade Passions

Siena's cultural aloofness owes much to the *contrade*, the 17 city wards designated for now defunct administrative and military functions during the Middle Ages, which continue to act as individual entities within the city. To outsiders, the only real significance of the *contrade* appears to be in connection with the *Palio (see page 214)*, but their existence pervades every aspect of everyday life. Despite its public grandeur, much of Siena is resolutely working-class and attaches great weight to belonging to a community. Events such as baptisms and deaths are celebrated together, while the traditional Sienese will only marry within his or her *contrada*.

All over the city, the importance of the various *contrade* is evident. Little plaques set into the wall testify to which *contrada* you are in (dolphin, caterpillar, goose and so on). Each neighbourhood has its own fountain and font, as well as a motto, symbol and colours. The latter are combined in a flag, worn with pride and patriotism by the inhabitants and seen hanging and draped around buildings for important *contrada* events, most notably a *Palio* triumph.

The interior of the Duomo, a magnificent Gothic structure of banded black-and-white stone, with a superb floor of inlaid marble depicting themes not only from the Bible, but also from pagan myth and magic.

BELOW: Siena's spectacular Cathedral.

been the home of the commune since it was completed in 1310, is a Gothic masterpiece of rose-coloured brick and silver-grey travertine. Each ogival arch is crowned by the *balzana*, Siena's black-and-white emblem representing the mystery and purity of the Madonna's life.

The distinctive **Torre del Mangia** (open daily 10am–7pm, until 4pm Nov–mid-Mar; entrance fee) – named after the first bellringer, Mangiaguadagni, the "spendthrift" – is 87 metres high, and it's a 500-step climb to the top to enjoy glorious views of the pink piazza and Siena's rooftops. At the bottom of the tower, the **Cappella in Piazza** (Chapel in the Square) was erected in 1378 in thanksgiving for the end of the plague.

The city museum

Although bureaucrats still toil in parts of the Palazzo Pubblico, as they have for some seven centuries, much of the complex is now devoted to the **Museo Civico** (open daily Mar–Oct 10am–7pm, until 5.30pm or 6.30pm Nov–mid-Mar;

entrance fee; www.comune.siena.it/museocivico), which houses some of the city's greatest treasures. Siena's city council once met in the vast Sala del Mappamondo, although the huge globe that then graced the walls has disappeared. What remains are two frescoes attributed to the medieval master Simone Martini: the majestic mounted figure of Guidoriccio da Fogliano and the *Maestà*. Martini's *Maestà*, a poetic evocation of the Madonna on a filigree throne, has a rich, tapestry-like quality. The muted blues, reds and ivory add a gauzy softness. Martini echoes Giotto's conception of perspective, yet clothes his Madonna in diaphanous robes, concealing her spirituality in dazzling decoration.

Opposite is the iconic *Guidoriccio*, the haughty diamond-spangled *condottiero* (mercenary) reproduced on calendars and *panforte* boxes. But in recent years, despite Sienese denials, doubts have been cast on the authenticity of the fresco. Art historians maintain that a smaller painting uncovered below the huge panel is Martini's original, and the Guidoriccio we see was executed long after the artist's death.

In the next room is a genuine civic masterpiece, Ambrogio Lorenzetti's *Effects of Good and Bad Government*, painted in 1338 as an idealised tribute to the Council of the Nine. The narrative realism and vivid facial expressions give the allegory emotional resonance. A wise old man symbolises the common good, while a patchwork of neat fields, tame boar and busy hoers suggests order and prosperity. Bad Government is a desolate place, razed to the ground by a diabolical tyrant, the Sienese she-wolf at his feet.

The Cathedral

Exiting the Campo, turn left and head up the hill via one of the winding streets to the Piazza del Duomo. The **Duomo** (open June–Aug Mon–Sat 10.30am–8pm, Sun 1.30–6.30pm, Mar–May and Sept–Oct Mon–Sat 10.30am–7.30pm, Sun 1.30–5.30pm, Nov–Feb Mon–Sat 10.30am–6.30pm, Sun 1.30–5.30pm; entrance fee) is Siena's most controversial monument, either a symphony in black-and-white marble or a tasteless iced cake, depending on your point of view. It began in 1220 as a round-arched Romanesque church, but soon acquired a Gothic façade festooned with pinnacles. Bands of black, white and green marble were inlaid with pink stone and topped by Giovanni Pisano's naturalistic statues.

The Cathedral interior is creativity run riot – oriental abstraction, Byzantine formality, Gothic flight and Romanesque austerity. A giddy chiaroscuro effect is created by the black-and-white walls reaching up to the starry blue vaults. The floor is even more inspiring: major Sienese craftsmen worked on the marble *pavimentazione* between 1372 and 1562. The finest are Matteo di Giovanni's pensive Sibyls and marble mosaics by Beccafumi. In order to preserve the floors, many of the most interesting scenes are covered by hardboard for most of the year and only revealed to the public for two months at the start of autumn (www.operaduomo.siena.it).

Nicola Pisano's octagonal marble pulpit is a Gothic masterpiece: built in 1226, it is a dramatic and fluid progression from his solemn **pulpit** in Pisa Cathedral. Off the north aisle is the decorative **Libreria Piccolomini**, built in 1495 to house the personal papers and books of Pope Pius II. The frescoes by Pinturicchio (1509) show scenes from the life of the influential Renaissance pope, a member of the noble Sienese Piccolomini family and founder of Pienza *(see page 219)*.

In the unfinished eastern section of the Cathedral is the **Museo dell' Opera Metropolitana** (open daily mid-Mar–May and Sept–Oct 9.30am–7pm, June–Aug until 8pm; Nov–Feb until 1.30pm; entrance fee) and Pisano's original statues for the façade. In a dramatically lit room above is Duccio's *Maestà*, Siena's

Map on page 206

TIP

The Duomo's museum allows access to the parapets, which offer dazzling views of Siena – a more accessible alternative to the Torre del Mangia's panorama.

BELOW: The figure of Peace from the *Allegory of Good Government*, by Lorenzetti (1338).

BELOW: Siena's unmistakable Campo.

best-loved work, which was escorted from the artist's workshop to the Duomo in a torchlit procession; the largest known medieval panel painting graced the High Altar until 1506. The biggest panel depicts the Madonna enthroned among saints and angels, and, since the separation of the painting, facing scenes from the Passion. Although Byzantine Gothic in style, the *Maestà* is suffused with melancholy charm. The delicate gold and red colouring is matched by Duccio's grace of line, which influenced Sienese painting for the next two centuries. The Sienese believe that Giotto copied Duccio but sacrificed beauty to naturalism. The small panels do reveal some of Giotto's truthfulness and sense of perspective.

Opposite the Duomo on the piazza is the **Ospedale Santa Maria della Scala ⊖** (open daily mid-Mar–Oct 10am–6.30pm, Nov–Mar 10.30am–4.30pm; entrance fee). This former pilgrims' hospital, believed to have been founded in the 9th century, was in its day one of the most important hospitals in the world; it is now being turned into a major arts centre and

exhibition space with restoration facilities. Used as a practising hospital until 1995, its main ward is adorned with frescoes by Domenico di Bartolo. The city's **Museo Archeologico** (open mid-Mar–Oct Mon–Sat 10.30am–6.30pm, Nov–mid-Mar until 4.30pm; entrance fee), with its significant collection of Etruscan and Roman remains, is housed here; other rooms host temporary exhibitions.

A set of steps behind the Duomo leads down to Piazza San Giovanni, a small square dominated by the **Battistero di San Giovanni ⊖** (open mid–Mar-Sept 9am–7.30pm, Oct until 6pm, Nov–mid-Mar 10am–5pm; entrance fee), built beneath part of the Cathedral. Inside are frescoes and a beautiful baptismal font by Jacopo della Quercia.

Two art museums

There are two art museums in the vicinity of the Cathedral complex, at opposite ends of the scale of their content. The **Pinacoteca Nazionale ⊖** (Via San Pietro 29; open Tues–Sat 8.15am–7.15pm, Sun and Mon until 1.15pm and 1.30pm respectively; entrance fee) contains the finest collection of Sienese "Primitives" in the suitably Gothic Palazzo Buonsignori. The early rooms are full of Madonnas, apple-cheeked, pale, remote or warmly human. Matteo di Giovanni's stylised Madonnas shift to Lorenzetti's affectionate *Annunciation* and Ugolino di Neri's radiant *Madonna*. Neroccio di Bartolomeo's *Madonna* is as truthful as a Masaccio.

As a variant, the grisly deaths of obscure saints compete with a huge medieval crucifix with a naturalistic spurt of blood. The famous landscapes and surreal Persian city attributed to Lorenzetti were probably painted by Sassetta a century later. But his *Madonna dei Carmelitani* is a sweeping cavalcade of Sienese life.

Those suffering from a surfeit of medieval sacred art can visit the **Palazzo delle Papesse** (Via di Città 126; open Tues–Sun noon–7pm; entrance fee), a contemporary art gallery with changing exhibitions, which also offers a 360-degree view of Siena from its loggia.

For some outdoor space and greenery, turn left out of the gallery and head south to the **Orto Botanico** ❶ (open daily 8.30am–12.30pm, 2.30–5.30pm), a small botanical garden just inside the city walls. Opposite the Orto Tolomei is another little garden, with a view over the countryside and a sculpture which – although not obvious at first glance – outlines the shape of the city.

St Catherine trail

Slightly outside the historic centre, on Vicolo del Tiratoio, is the **Casa di Santa Caterina da Siena** ❶ (Costa di Sant' Antonio; open daily 9am–12.30pm, 3–6pm), the home of Catherine Benincase (1347–80), canonised in the 15th century by Pope Pius II and proclaimed Italy's Patron Saint in 1939. The house, garden and her father's dye-works now form the "Sanctuary of St Catherine".

Inside the nearby **Basilica di San Domenico** ❶ (open Apr–Oct 7am–1pm, 3–6.30pm, Nov–Mar 9am–1pm, 3–6pm) – a huge fortress-like church founded by the Dominicans – a reliquary containing the saint's head is kept in the Cappella Santa Caterina.

St Catherine, the daughter of a Sienese dyer, devoted her early life to the needs of the poor and sick. She then turned to politics and dedicated herself to reconciling anti-papal and papal forces; she was instrumental in the return of Pope Gregory XI, exiled in Avignon, to Rome. All the places she visited, from the day of her birth, have been consecrated.

BELOW:
contrada procession in the Campo, by Vincenzo Rustici.

Map
on page
206

*Statue of Sallustio
Bandini, founder of
Siena's library, on
Piazza Salimbeni.*

BELOW: a more
unusual view of Siena.

The chapel is decorated with frescoes depicting events in the saint's life, the majority completed by Sodoma in the early 16th century. The view from outside the Basilica across to the Duomo is spectacular.

The Fortress

From here it's a short walk to the Forte di Santa Barbara, also known as the **Fortezza Medicea ◐**, built by Cosimo I after his defeat of Siena in 1560. The red-brick fortress now houses an open-air theatre, provides glorious views of the countryside and contains the **Enoteca Italiana** (open Tues–Sat noon–1am, Mon noon–8pm; closed 10 days in Jan; tel: 0577-288497). The latter, a wine exhibition and shop, offers visitors the chance to sample and buy from a wide range of Tuscan wines and have any questions answered about the winemaking process.

Via Banchi di Sopra, lined with fine medieval *palazzi*, is one of the three main arteries of the city centre (the other two being Via Banchi di Sotto and Via di Città). It links the Campo with the splendid **Piazza Sal-**

imbeni ◍ at its northern end. The grand *palazzi* flanking the square are the head office of the Monte dei Paschi di Siena, one of the oldest banks in the world. Founded in 1472 and still an important employer, it is known as "the city father".

Basilica of St Francis

From the square, Via dei Rossi leads east to the **Basilica di San Francesco ◎** (open 7am–noon, 3.30–7pm). Now housing part of the University, the vast church exhibits fragments of frescoes by Pietro and Ambrogio Lorenzetti. Next door, the 15th-century **Oratorio di San Bernardino** (open mid-Mar–Oct 10.30am–1.30pm, 3–5.30pm; entrance fee), dedicated to Siena's great preacher, contains frescoes by Il Sodoma and Beccafumi.

At this extremity, as well as elsewhere, the city has well-preserved walls and gateways. Siena's compactness makes these easy to reach, offering the opportunity to wind through the narrow streets and stumble across hidden buildings and fountains on the way. ❑

RESTAURANTS & BARS

Restaurants

Al Mangia
Piazza del Campo 42
Tel: 0577-281121
www.almangia.it
In a wonderful position on the Campo, this restaurant serves good, classic Tuscan cuisine, and is popular with tourists and locals alike. Outside tables in summer. Closed Wed, except Mar–Oct. €€€–€€€€

Al Marsili
Via del Castoro 3
Tel: 0577-47154
www.ristorantealmarsili.it
Elegant restaurant in an ancient building with wine cellars cut deep into the limestone. Sophisticated cuisine, including gnocchi in duck sauce. Closed Mon. €€–€€€

Antica Trattoria Botteganova
Via Chiantigiana 29
Tel: 0577-284230
This refined restaurant serves some of the finest cuisine in Siena. Specialities include local Tuscan delicacies, fish and delicious puddings. Closed Sun, period in Jan, early Aug. €€€–€€€€

Certosa di Maggiano
Strada di Certosa 82
Tel: 0577-288180
www.certosadimaggiano.com
This converted Carthusian monastery, now a hotel, serves gourmet food in a magical setting: a cloistered courtyard overlooking Siena. €€€€

Da Guido
Vicolo del Pettinaio 7
Tel: 0577-280042
Veritable Sienese institution, set in medieval premises and popular with visiting VIPs. Traditional Sienese cuisine. Closed Wed and Jan. €€–€€€

Osteria del Castelvecchio
Via Castelvecchio 65
Tel: 0577-49586
Converted from ancient stables, this hostelry creates contemporary dishes with traditional flavours. Interesting wine list. Closed Tues. €€

Osteria Il Carroccio
Via Casato di Sotto 32
Tel: 0577-41165
Well-run quaint and tiny trattoria serving simple local dishes. Closed Wed and Feb. €

Osteria La Chiacchiera
Costa di S. Antonio 4
Tel: 0577-280631
Small, rustic *osteria* offering typical Sienese fare (try the thick *pici*), on a steep street leading down to Santa Caterina. Closed Tues. €

Osteria La Taverna di San Giuseppe
Via G. Dupré 132
Tel: 0577-42286
www.tavernasangiuseppe.it
Delicious Tuscan fare in an atmospheric cavern with wooden furnishings. An antipasto is a must; delicious dishes using pecorino. Closed Sun. €–€€

Osteria Le Logge
Via del Porrione 33
Tel: 0577-48013
Restaurant set in a 19th-century grocer's shop, with an authentic dark-wood and marble interior. On the menu are duck and fennel, chicken and lemon, and such exotic dishes as stuffed guinea fowl *(faraona)*. Closed Sun and Jan. €€–€€€

Pizzeria di Nonno Mede
Via Camporegio 21
Tel: 0577-247966
Serves a good pizza and great desserts. Splendid view across to the Duomo, which is well lit in the evenings. €

Trattoria Papei
Piazza del Mercato 6
Tel: 0577-280894
Ideal place for sampling genuine Sienese home cooking in generous helpings. There's a variety of grilled meats, too. Closed Mon (except public holidays) and end July. €€

Tre Cristi
Vicolo di Provenzano 1–7
Tel: 0577-280608
www.trecristi.com
Elegant restaurant with a contemporary Mediterranean menu. Frescoed walls add to the atmosphere. Booking advised. Closed Tues. €€–€€€

Bars

Nannini (Banchi di Sopra) is an obligatory coffee stop on Siena's main shopping street. Opposite is **Caffè del Corso** – chic by day, boisterous by night. **Bar le Logge** (Via Rinaldini, at the end of Banchi di Sotto) is a non-touristy place to drink cappuccino. Once into Il Campo, numerous bars have food and drink to suit all tastes; the prices are elevated but the vantage point superb. To the left of the Palazzo Pubblico, **Gelateria Caribia** (Via Rinaldini) offers creamy ice cream in a multitude of flavours. **The Tea Room** (Via Porta Giustizia; closed Mon) is a cosy place for tea and cake, or a cocktail to accompany the live jazz. **American Bar** (Via di Città) is a good refreshment stop between visiting the Duomo and the Pinacoteca. For the sweet-toothed, **Fonte delle Delizie** (Costa di San Antonio, near the Casa di Santa Caterina) makes delicious pastries. Further from the centre, **Il Masgalano** (Via del Camporegio, next to San Domenico) is a friendly place for coffees, light lunches or an *aperitivo*.

PRICE CATEGORIES
Average cost of a three-course meal per person with a half-bottle of wine:
€ = under €25
€€ = €25–40
€€€ = €40–60
€€€€ = over €60

THE PASSION OF THE *PALIO*

In little more than a minute, the Campo is filled with unbearable happiness and irrational despair as centuries-old loyalties are put to the test

It is strange how a race that lasts just 90 seconds can require 12 months' planning, a lifetime's patience and the involvement of an entire city. But Siena's famous *Palio* does just that, as it has done since the 13th century, when an August *Palio* made its debut. At that time, the contest took the form of a bareback race the length of the city. The bareback race run around the Siena's main square, the Piazza del Campo, was introduced in the 17th century. Today the *Palio* is held twice a year, in early July and mid-August. The *Palio*, which has been run in times of war, famine and plague, stops for nothing. In the 1300s, criminals were released from jail to celebrate the festival. When the Fascists were gaining ground in 1919, Siena postponed council elections until after the *Palio*. In 1943, British soldiers in a Tunisian prisoner-of-war camp feared a riot when they banned Sienese prisoners from staging a *Palio*; Sienese fervour triumphed.

Although, as the Sienese say, *"Il Palio corre tutto l'anno"* ("The Palio runs all year"), the final preparations boil down to three days, during which there is the drawing by lots of the horse for each competing ward *(contrada)*, the choice of the jockeys and then the six trial races – the last of which is held on the morning of the *Palio* itself. Although many do pack into the Campo for the actual race, other citizens cannot bear to watch it and cluster around the TV set in the *contrada* square or go to church to pray.

ABOVE: On the day of the *Palio*, the horses are taken to each *contrada* church for a blessing. The priest holds the horse's head and commands it, *"Vai e torni vincitore!"* ("Go and return victorious!").

LEFT: The words *"C'è terra in piazza"* ("There's earth in the Campo") are the signal to remove the colourful costumes from Siena's museums to feature in the great Historical Parade.

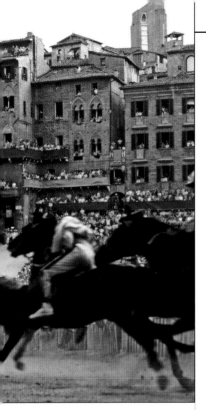

THE POWER OF THE *CONTRADE*

In Siena the *contrada* rules: ask a Sienese where he is from and he will say, *"Ma sono della Lupa"* ("But I'm from the Wolf *contrada*"). The first loyalty is to the city in the head, not to the city on the map.

Ten out of Siena's 17 *contrade* take part in each *Palio*: the seven who did not run in the previous race and three selected by lot. Each *contrada* appoints a captain and two lieutenants to run the campaign. In the *Palio*, the illegal becomes legal: bribery, kidnapping, plots and the doping of horses are all common.

Each of the *contrade* in the city has its own standard, many of which are displayed around the city during the *Palio* and play an important role in the ceremonial aspect of the event.

Flags, or standards, are a central theme of the *Palio* event. In fact, the *Palio* itself – the trophy of victory for which everyone is striving – is a standard: a silk flag emblazoned with the image of the Madonna and the coats of arms of the city, ironically referred to by the Sienese as the *cencio*, or rag. The *contrada* which wins the event retains possession of the *palio* standard until the next race.

ABOVE: The ruthless race lurches around the Campo three times. If a riderless horse wins, the animal is almost deified: it is given the place of honour in the victory banquet and has its hooves painted gold.

RIGHT: The Historical Parade, which is staged in the run-up to the main race, retraces Siena's centuries of struggle against Florence, from the glorious victory against its rival in 1260 to the ghastly defeat in 1560.

BELOW: A highlight of the *Palio* pageantry is the spectacular display of the flag-wavers, famous throughout Italy for their elaborate manoeuvres of twirling and hurling the huge standards dozens of feet in the air.

SOUTH OF SIENA

The route through the dramatic Crete region delivers you to the heart and soul of Tuscany. Pienza, Montalcino and Montepulciano are must-sees, but countless other lesser-known towns await discovery, while the hidden beauty of the Val d'Orcia river valley and the tortuous roads of Monte Amiata beckon the intrepid

The area just south of Siena is a primeval landscape of stark beauty. Appropriately called **Le Crete**, it is a moonscape of interlocking pale-clay hummocks and treeless gullies. In winter it is cold, bleak and even more crater-like. In summer the curvaceous terrain is softened by a deep green blanket. Sienese city dwellers love this barren landscape and are successfully discouraging local farmers from accepting European Union funds to flatten the land and grow wheat.

There is an extraordinary range of wildlife in the area: by day, wild deer roam by the Ombrone river; by night, porcupines and foxes are about in the woods. If intrepid walkers venture out in the late autumn evening they may meet a strange character with a couple of dogs, a torch and a harness. He is a truffle hunter, sniffing out truffles in the dampest ditches. More legal are the Sardinian peasants selling cheese. Unlike many Tuscans, Sardinians are prepared to live in remote, infertile places.

The best route through the Crete is the SS438 to Asciano, and the SP451 to Monte Oliveto Maggiore – empty roads through a barren landscape, dotted with striking hilltop farmhouses and lone cypresses. Known as the Accona desert in medieval times, it retains its spiritual remoteness.

Monte Oliveto Maggiore

After so much pale, undulating land, the red abbey of **Monte Oliveto Maggiore ❶** (open daily 9am–noon, 3.15–6pm, until 5pm in winter) is glimpsed through a wood of pines, oaks and olive trees. If the land appears to fall away from the abbey, it is not far from the truth: land erosion and frequent landslides provide a natural defence to the abbey's mystical centre. In 1313 Tolomei, a wealthy Sienese, abandoned the law for a life of prayer in the wilderness,

Map on page 218

LEFT: a timeless Tuscan landscape.
BELOW: church of San Biagio, Montepulciano.

TIP

The pretty walled village of Monticchiello offers fine views of Pienza, just 4km away. It is also renowned for the Teatro Povero – an annual play written and starring the villagers about life in rural Tuscany *(see page 39)*.

taking with him two fellow hermits. After a vision of white-robed monks, Tolomei established an Olivetan Order under Benedictine rule. The monks followed St Benedict's precept that "a real monk is one who lives by his own labour". Fortunately, a meagre diet, fervent prayer and lack of conversation stimulated the monks to artistic endeavour in the form of woodcarving, sculpture and manuscript design. As a noted artistic centre, the abbey invited Luca Signorelli and Il Sodoma to decorate the cloisters with scenes from St Benedict's life *(see box right)*.

The excitement of Sodoma aside, Monte Oliveto is a spiritual retreat. The austere refectory, the library cluttered with ancient manuscripts and books, the exquisite marquetry work of the choir stalls are as peaceful as the hidden walks deep into the woods. There is a restaurant, and former monastic cells are also available for overnight visitors (tel: 0577-707652; closed in winter).

Situated on a plain in the heart of the Crete, **Buonconvento** is worth a brief stop, if only to admire the imposing red 14th-century walls and massive medieval city gates of iron-bound wood. In 1366 Siena rebuilt the walls because, as a Sienese outpost, Buonconvento had been devastated. Today, the town is essentially a place for a leisurely introduction to truffles or game, or for a summer picnic in the peaceful gardens beside the town walls.

Utopian town

Pienza ② is an exquisite Renaissance doll's house. Although created by a humanist pope, Pius II, Pienza is almost too perfect to be human and too precious to be spiritual. Every fountain, piazza and painting is harmonious. Model citizens walk through streets as romantic as their names – Via dell'Amore, Via del Bacio, Via della Fortuna – streets of "love", "kiss" and "fortune".

Pienza's origins date back to 1458. When E.S. Piccolomini was elected pope, he could not resist playing God in his home village, Corsignano. He chose the noted Florentine architect, Bernardo Rossellino, to ennoble the hamlet in accordance with humanist principles. When the first masterpiece in modern town planning

emerged late and over budget, the Pope reduced his fraudulent architect to tears with his words, "You did well, Bernardo, in lying to us about the expense involved in the work… Your deceit has built these glorious structures; which are praised by all except the few consumed with envy."

Bernardo Rossellino was rewarded with a scarlet robe, 100 ducats and some new commissions. The decision to build a cathedral enabled the pope to rechristen Corsignano the village as Pienza the city – named, modestly, after himself. The result is what locals call a *città d'autore*, a city inspired by one vision. After Pienza, other cities in Tuscany or elsewhere are liable to look chaotic.

Much of the symmetry lies in the cathedral square, **Piazza Pio II**, and the slightly listing Duomo adds to the charm. Despite a Renaissance façade, the interior is late Gothic and decorated with mystical paintings from the Sienese school. In one central alcove is a chilling *Assumption* by Vecchietta, in which St Agatha holds a cup containing her breasts, torn off by the executioner.

Map on page 218

Pienza is famous for its homemade cheeses, especially pecorino and ricotta.

BELOW LEFT: one of the more spiritual. aspects of the St Benedict frescoes.

Il Sodoma's Frescoes

The main cloister of Monte Oliveto Maggiore *(see page 217)* is covered in frescoes on the *Life of St Benedict*, begun by Luca Signorelli in 1495 and completed by Sodoma from 1505. Of the two contemporaries, Signorelli had the more spiritual approach, but his loveliest work is a domestic scene portraying two monks being served by girls at an inn. In 1497, after only nine frescoes were completed, Signorelli left the rest for Il Sodoma to execute. Vasari adored Signorelli's spirituality as much as he loathed Il Sodoma's exuberance, hedonistic lifestyle and "licentious" fondness for "boys and beardless youths" which earned him his name. Il Sodoma's love of what Vasari called his Noah's Ark of "badgers, squirrels, apes, dwarf asses and Elba ponies" is often present, but his landscapes only come to life with the temptations of the flesh. His gaze rarely focuses on the main subject, but is deflected by the turn of an attractive leg, a mischievous smile, a perky badger or a soldier's buttocks. Needless to say, the inhibited monks preferred Signorelli's work to that of the man they labelled "Il Mataccio", imbecile or madman.

The Duomo's façade, the gracious arches, the well and the Palazzo Piccolomini, the pope's home, are just as Pius left them when he set off to fight the crusades, never to return. **Palazzo Piccolomini** (open Tues–Sun 10am–12.30pm, 3–6pm; guided tours only; entrance fee), now a museum, is lined with grand and homely treasures, including a library and arms collection. In the pope's bedroom, the intriguing book-holder, as cumbersome as a church lectern, is proof that the pope did not read in bed. The library opens onto a tranquil loggia with Etruscan urns, hanging gardens and a panorama stretching across the Orcia valley as far as Monte Amiata.

On the opposite side of the square, the **Museo Diocesano** (open Wed–Mon 10am–1pm 3–6pm; entrance fee) has a rich collection of medieval paintings, tapestries, and ornate gold- and silverware.

Just outside Pienza is the **Pieve di Corsignano**, a simple but coherent Romanesque church where Pope Pius II was baptised. You can ask for the key at the Pienza tourist office.

Cinquecento pearl

The winding road from Pienza up to **Montepulciano** ❸ – visible for miles around, with houses clustered on the sides of the hump of a hill on which it is built – is lined with *vendita diretta* signs, offering pecorino and wine. After Pienza, Montepulciano's asymmetrical design and spontaneous development give it the architectural tension that the earlier city lacks. If Pienza belongs to Rossellino, Montepulciano is Antonio da Sangallo's masterpiece.

Just outside and below the city walls, at the end of a long line of cypresses, lies Sangallo's church of **San Biagio**, the Renaissance building most at ease with its setting. The isolation focuses attention on the honey-coloured travertine, the Greek Cross design, the dome and the purity of the line. Sangallo's design skills rival Bramante's, not just in the church, the elegant well and the porticoed Canon's House, but elsewhere in the city. The airy interior has a deeply classical feel, more akin to the Roman Pantheon than to a small Tuscan church.

TIP

Take a stroll around Pienza's city walls for splendid views of Monte Amiata and the Val d'Orcia. If overwhelmed by beauty or hunger, retreat to the restaurants behind the main square.

BELOW: Piazza Pio II, Pienza.

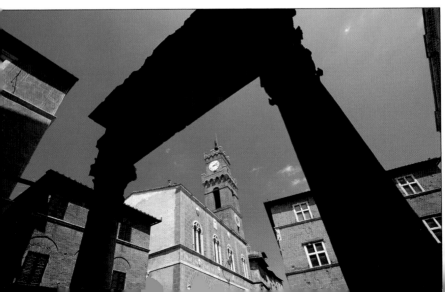

Traffic is banned inside the city walls, but you can park outside San Biagio. It's a short but steepish walk from here into town. Alternatively, you can park in one of the many car parks at Montepulciano's eastern end and enter the town through the Porta al Prato, into Piazza Savonarola guarded by a statue of the Marzocco lion (symbol of Florentine power) on a column. From here the principal shopping street, Via di Gracciano nel Corso, leads up to the main square. Its lower end is lined with noble palaces. The Renaissance **Palazzo Bucelli**, at no. 73, is decorated with a mosaic of Etruscan urns and pots, a reminder of the city's ancient origins. The road continues upwards to **Piazza Grande**, the highest part of town and the highest spot culturally.

Florentine design has shaped the grand façades on Piazza Grande, but earlier Sienese Gothic touches are present in the interiors, double arches and doorways. Both styles reflect the city's buffeting between the two city-states and the eventual supremacy of Florence. On one side, the 15th-century **Palazzo Comunale** (Town Hall) has a Florentine Michelozzo façade adorning Sienese turrets. The **Tower** (open Mon–Sat 10am–6pm; entrance fee), modelled on that of Florence's Palazzo Vecchio, surveys the whole province: from Monte Amiata to Siena and even Lake Trasimeno. Once in the Palazzo, do not be deterred by the presence of a police station: the view, albeit restricted by iron railings, is legally yours.

Sangallo's **Palazzo Contucci** (open Mon–Sat 8.30am–1.30pm), on the other side of the square, still belongs to the aristocratic Contucci family, who produce Vino Nobile. Part of the building has been converted into small apartments which are available for rent (www.contucci.it). In the **Cantine Contucci** (wine cellars; open Mon–Fri 8.30am–12.30pm, 2.30–6.30pm), Adamo, the wine master, will be delighted to expand on the entire noble history of the Contucci family and on his essential role on the Vino Nobile Wine-Tasting Committee. Vino Nobile, a smooth red wine with a hint of violets, was "ennobled" in 1549 when Pope Paul III's

Map on page 218

Pienza's reverence of Pope Pius is surpassed by Montepulciano's devotion to Poliziano. The renowned scholar, poet and resident tutor to Lorenzo de' Medici's children was named after the Latin term for the town – inhabitants of Montepulciano are called Poliziani. Poliziano eulogised the Montepulciano countryside in his Stanzas, *which are thought to have inspired Botticelli's* La Primavera.

BELOW:
Montepulciano's Etruscan origins are evident everywhere.

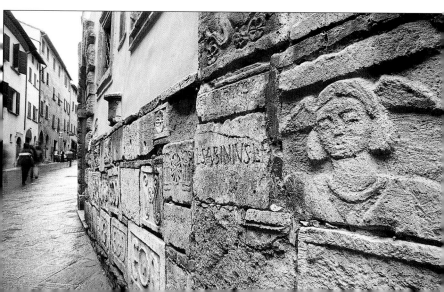

sommelier proclaimed it "a most perfect wine, a wine for lords".

Between the two grand *palazzi*, at the top of wide steps, stands the **Duomo** (open daily 9am–noon, 4–6pm), which contains a masterpiece of the Siena school: the huge *Assumption* triptych by Taddeo di Bartolo (1401) shines out above the high altar in the vast, gloomy nave.

A circular tour

Scattered among the rolling landscape of Siena province are some beautiful villages, each with a separate identity and artistic treasures espied almost incidentally over the brow of a hill. A circular itinerary from Montepulciano unites a group of tiny villages once ruled by the Cacciaconti barons. **Montefollonico** ❹, 8 km (5 miles) northwest of Montepulciano, has a 13th-century frescoed church and one of the best restaurants in Italy, La Chiusa *(see page 231)*.

Petroio ❺, set on a rocky, wooded promontory, is a grand fortified village on an old pilgrim route. In recent years it has been undergoing a revival thanks to its terracotta

– examples of which adorn the city walls, Palazzo Pretorio and the medieval towers. Look out for the Canon's House, which contains a remarkable *Madonna and Child* by Taddio di Bartolo. Near the village is the intact **Abbadia a Sicille**, built by the Knights Templar as a refuge for knights on the way to the Holy Land. The adjoining Romanesque church is decorated with two Maltese crosses, but an Olivetan coat of arms marks the abolition of the Templars.

Set among farmland and woods, **Castelmuzio** ❻ is a medieval village wrapped up in itself, its Museum of Sacred Art and its direct line to San Bernardo. Narrow shops in winding streets sell honey, salami and cheese made by an ageing population of churchgoers.

Once a Cacciaconti fortress, aristocratic **Montisi** ❼ commands a view over two valleys. Although the "low town" has a few young families and newer attitudes, the "high town" is a relic of medieval Italy. The village offers intriguing alleys, views, restaurants and two tiny Romanesque churches, one decorated with a

TIP

Vino Nobile is excellent with two local peasant dishes: *bruschetta*, a toasted garlic bread drenched in olive oil, or *panzanella*, a bread salad with herbs.

BELOW: Montepulciano is bathed in a russet glow at sunset.

Scuola di Duccio crucifix. A few apparently stark, uninviting farmhouses conceal the occasional private chapel. conceal wonderful frescoes and the occasional private chapel.

One can return to Montepulciano via **Sinalunga** ❽, a schizophrenic Tuscan town with a hideous "low town" but a pleasant "old town". The town's original name, Asinalunga, echoes its shape, "the long donkey". But in the lively market, pigs, not donkeys, are in evidence in the form of *porchetta*, the local speciality of roast pig flavoured with rosemary.

Val d'Orcia

The **Val d'Orcia** is a beautiful rural area at the southern border of Le Crete, but its villages have suffered from the desertion of the countryside in the 1950s and 1960s. **San Quirico d'Orcia** ❾ is a dignified valley town still waiting for its heyday. It survived an attack by Cesare Borgia's troops in 1502 and a World War II bombardment. The Romanesque **Collegiata**, made from sandstone and local travertine, has three remarkable portals. In the town, there are a couple of churches worth

seeing, and the frescoed rooms of the newly restored **Palazzo Chigi** are now open to the public (daily 8am–6.30pm; entrance fee).

Just south of San Quirico, off the SS2, **Bagno Vignoni** ❿ is a tiny but lively spa station, at its most evocative at dusk. The steam rises from the hot springs, and the yellowish light of the lanterns dimly illuminates the stone façades of the buildings lining the square, which is in fact a stone pool of sulphurous water, where both Lorenzo de' Medici and St Catherine once bathed. The hot springs were used by the Romans, and became public baths in medieval times. You are not allowed to bathe here now. However, the baths in Hotel Posta Marcucci are open to non-residents for a fee, and are also open at night on summer weekends.

From the pool, all senses are fulfilled at once: the imposing **Rocca d'Orcia** looms above; outside the pool of light, the sound of sheep and crickets reverberates; the softness of the hot, chalky water dissolves tiredness; and the smell of sulphur evaporates into the night air. After a swim, a

The Strada del Vino Nobile di Montepulciano is an association that promotes the local wines. As well as organising tours of the local vineyards and cellars they offer a range of cultural tours including visits to the Garden of Villa La Foce, the Montepulciano spa, and Siena's pottery workshops. Their office is on Piazza Grande (Mon–Sat 10am– 1pm, 3–6pm; tel: 0578-717484; www.stradadei vinonobile.it)

BELOW: chapel in a golden field outside Pienza.

Etruscan Art

Since there is no extant Etruscan literature, our knowledge of the living Etruscans is oddly dependent on a reading of their funerary art for clues. We know them as they would like to be known, these idealised aristocrats elevated by Greek myths. The women were depicted as pale while the men were uniformly reddish-brown, either suntanned or ritually painted. Friezes of serene married couples, tender lovers, absorbed wrestlers, erotic dancers or grieving warriors reflect the fullness of Etruscan life. Aristocratic Etruscan women had freedom and social status, as well as influence. They are frequently depicted attending banquets without their husbands, riding covered wagons to their landholdings and playing flutes or lyres at funerals. The men are rarely still: they charge through games, boar-hunts, processions, journeys, dances, banquets and diving competitions. The "ordinary" Etruscan is only glimpsed in passing: a prized blonde courtesan flits past dancing slaves; a serf mourns his dead master.

In keeping with primitive religions, natural forces were personified as gods of the sea, earth and rising sun. The Etruscans also reinvented Greek gods in their own image: Zeus, Hera and Athena were Tinia, Uni and Minerva. Oriental and Greek motifs coexisted: Egyptian sphinxes watched winged Etruscan demons pursue menacing Greek Furies.

But it is the tombs that remain as a cultural testimony to the power, wealth and beliefs of their owners. The tomb and mode of burial varied according to the local custom and period, but in general the rich were buried in decorated stone sarcophagi placed in chamber tombs, often decorated with lively frescoes, while the ashes of the poor were put in small urns in shallow graves. Tombs, in every shape and form, can be seen in the Etruscan necropolises: "temple" tombs at Saturnia; melon-shaped tombs at Cortona; oriental "trench" tombs at Vetulonia. At Sovana, "pigeon-hole" tombs are niches cut into the rock, while at Chiusi a mysterious labyrinth reputedly conceals the sarcophagus of Lars Porsenna, mythical king of the Etruscans.

In Etruscan funerary art, the man is often shown wearing his chains of office over his bare chest. He may hold an egg, container of the soul, or clutch the *patera*, a circular dish arguably symbolising the continuity of life. The bejewelled woman is surrounded by a mixture of feminine and sacred symbols: perfume boxes and earrings to beautify; a pomegranate or pine cone to symbolise either sexuality or death; a mirror to reflect her physical and spiritual perfection. In effect, these were portraits which were commissioned to show to the gods the noble patrons at their best.

Etruscan art is essentially regional; Arezzo had a reputation for *Arretino*, fine red pottery, and for its metalwork. The famous bronze Chimera remains a magical illusion: a goat's head springs from a lion's back and is seized by the lion's tail, suddenly transformed into a serpent's mouth. Chiusi boasts Canopic urns, cinerary urns with an idealised effigy of the deceased on the lid, while Cortona's bronze figurines represent Etruscan deities. Volterra's alabaster sarcophagi run the gamut of Etruscan demonology and Greek mythology, featuring sea monsters, Greek gods, beaked griffins and sirens. ❏

LEFT: the delicate eroticism of Etruscan dancers.

short *passeggiata* around the old baths shows the well-restored square at its most romantic.

In the vicinity are three medieval fortresses – Ripa d'Orcia, Rocca d'Orcia and Castiglione d'Orcia. After the turning to Bagno Vignoni, **Ripa d'Orcia** ⑪, an enchanted castle (now a hotel; tel: 0577-897376; www.castelloripadorcia.com) set among cypress groves, comes into view. Although goats and pheasants are the commonplace fauna here, the locals nevertheless make claims that wolves roam the area.

Rocca d'Orcia ⑫, a fortified village once owned by the warring Salimbeni clan, has an impressive castle open to visitors. **Castiglione d'Orcia** offers more of the same: an atmospheric, well-preserved village, a ruined fortress and wonderful views. The abbey of Sant' Antimo *(see page 230)* can be reached from here. The mountain roads in the area are tortuous but beautiful.

The Etruscan towns

Although set among attractive low hills, **Chiusi** ⑬ comes across as a rather unprepossessing town, devoid of Renaissance charm. The "low town" is a commercial centre and the shabby "high town" is endearing but overwhelmed by its glorious Etruscan past. Then, as now, the **Chiusini** were farmers, merchants and craftsmen, a spirit which predominates over artistry. Yet with a little Etruscan knowledge and much curiosity, the town is as fascinating as any in Tuscany. It boasts a complete underground city; an unrivalled collection of female cinerary urns; and the only tomb paintings in their original setting in Tuscany.

As one of the greatest city-states in the Etruscan League, Chiusi, or "Kamars", controlled the area from Lago di Trasimeno to Monte Amiata. After reaching its zenith as a trading centre in the 7th century BC,

Etruscan Kamars became submerged by Roman Clusium and then by medieval Chiusi. The old city survives on three levels of civilisation: the Etruscan necropolis beneath the city hills; the Roman street-grid system below the Cathedral; and the medieval city above.

The **Museo Archeologico Nazionale** (open daily 9am–8pm; tel: 0578-20177; entrance fee) has one of the finest collections of its kind in Italy, which attests to the vitality of Kamars and shows a distinctly female bias in the outstanding female Canopic jars, cinerary urns and rounded *cippi* tombstones. The containers have Egyptian-style lids resembling human or animal heads. The Etruscans borrowed freely from the Greeks and Egyptians; the imitation Greek vases are less rational but more vigorous than the originals. A speciality of Chiusi is *bucchero*, glossy black earthenware, often in the form of vases with figures in relief. This pottery has a sophisticated metallic finish which cannot be reproduced by modern craftsmen. Although much of the domestic pot-

Map on page 218

Chiusi's Cathedral, built from Etruscan and Roman fragments.

BELOW: the thermal pool in Bagno Vignoni.

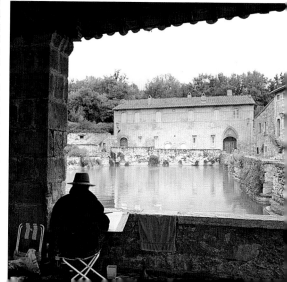

tery has a naturalness verging on the commonplace, the sarcophagi, the cinerary urns and the crouching sphinx reveal an underlying obsession with death and the appeasement of shadowy spirits.

A visit to the Etruscan tombs, 3 km (2 miles) outside town, can be arranged with the museum staff. The tombs contain sarcophagi, cinerary urns and, in the case of **Tomb of the Monkey**, rare wall-paintings of athletic games and domestic scenes.

In the Chiusi **Duomo**, three civilisations are visible at once: the "barbaric" Romanesque Cathedral is built from Etruscan and Roman fragments. The **Museo della Cattedrale** (open daily June–mid-Oct 9.45am–12.45pm, 4–7pm, mid-Oct–May 9.30am–12.45pm, 3–6pm; entrance fee) is of limited interest in itself, but your entrance ticket entitles you to a guided tour of a fascinating labyrinth beneath the Cathedral. The recently excavated tunnels are part of an Etruscan water system, cut into the rocks which provided natural filtration. The tour guide will lead you to a large Roman cistern dating from the 1st century BC, exiting at the bottom of the Cathedral bell-tower. Climb to the top for views of Monte Amiata, the Val d'Orcia and over to Lake Trasimeno in neighbouring Umbria.

Spa town

After underground Chiusi, **Chianciano Terme** is a breath of fresh air. It has the healthiest and wealthiest climate in Tuscany: hills, spas, pine forests, and more doctors and fur coats per square metre than anywhere else in Italy. "Chianciano for a Healthy Liver", the signs into town invite, exhort or cajole. The "high" spa town is where Italians have flocked since Roman times to enjoy the unique powers of *Acqua Santa*: as one of the world's top spas, Chianciano is a seriously rich town.

This southern part of Siena province is positively bursting with Etruscan remains, and digging produces a continual flow of exciting finds. In Chianciano, well-marked walks lead to several recently discovered tombs and temples, and an excellent **Etruscan Museum** (open Tues–Sun; closed 1–4pm; tel: 0578-

BELOW: 5th-century Tomb of the Monkey, Chiusi.

31384; entrance fee) contains many important and impressive finds, including an intact monumental tomb of a princess, lined with bronze and adorned with various gold and bronze artifacts. The large museum also features the remains from a spa complex dating from the 1st century BC, which was discovered in Chianciano and is thought to be the sacred magic spring that cured Emperor Augustus in 23 BC from a life-threatening stomach ailment.

An Anglo-Italian estate

Near the town are some of the loveliest walks and drives in Tuscany. Many walks start from **La Foce** , a 15th-century farmhouse which overlooks the fertile Val di Chiana and the desolate craters of the Val d'Orcia. The superb **gardens** here (open Wed 3–7pm; entrance fee) were designed by the famous landscape gardener Cecil Pinsent. There are views across an Etruscan site to Monte Amiata and Monte Cetona. Its excellent strategic position meant that its owners, the Anglo-Italian Origos, used it as the partisans' refuge during World War II. Ongoing excavations on the property have uncovered some 200 Etruscan tombs. From here, a rough track leads to Petraporciana, the partisans' hidden headquarters, and to a primeval forest full of giant oaks, cyclamens, wild orchids or snowdrops: a perfect short spring or autumn walk.

Beside La Foce is **Castelluccio**, a castle – and summer concert venue – which commands the best-loved view in the province: a sinuous line of cypresses plotting an Etruscan route across the craters. When Prince Charles stayed at Villa La Foce, proud locals were not surprised to see him painting this view.

A short walk leads to **Pocce Lattaie** and prehistoric caves with dripping stalactites shaped like teats or nipples. These pagan caves were used in fertility rites and propitiatory offerings made to the gods. Be prepared to hire a guide (and a torch) from Chianciano.

Around Monte Cetona

From Chianciano, an idyllic rural drive leads via La Foce to Sarteano and Cetona, two small medieval and Etruscan towns. These views of desolate *crete*, fortified farmhouses and hazy Monte Amiata are captured by Paolo Busato in his celebrated photographs. It is worth sacrificing a hired car to the dirt roads, but the nervous can take the more direct route to Sarteano.

Castiglioncello sul Trionoro is a tiny village with a *castello* and a church containing a Trecento Madonna. The village is set amid vast expanses of abandoned countryside in which Etruscan remains are uncovered by chance every few years.

Spilling over its double ring of city walls, **Sarteano** is a popular thermal centre which has retained its traditional identity. The town offers Etruscan remains, a grandiose 13th-century Rocca and crumbling

Map on page 218

TIP

Monte Cetona (1,148 metres/3,800 ft) is criss-crossed by woodland lanes and open tracks for walking, cycling and horse riding. A map of the network of mountain trails is available from the tourist offices of Cetona, San Casciano dei Bagni and Sarteano.

BELOW: the red earth of the Sienese landscape.

Radicofani is linked to the exploits of Ghino di Tacco, the "gentle outlaw" immortalised by Dante and Boccaccio. Exiled Ghino controlled the town from Radicofani Castle, built by Hadrian IV, the only English pope. A fierce basalt sculpture of Ghino stands in this forbidding town of low stone houses with external stairways, blind alleys and severe façades.

BELOW: Monte Amiata.

Renaissance *palazzi* built into the city walls. There is an interesting **Etruscan Museum** (open Tues–Sun; times vary; tel: 0578-269261 for information) but, contrary to rumours, the tomb of the Etruscan king Porsenna has never been discovered. In August each year, Sarteano holds a famous *Giostra* or tournament.

Cetona ⑱ clings to a richly wooded hill. The grand 18th-century houses on the plains are a relic of past prosperity, but Cetona is a refreshingly authentic Tuscan community. The broad traffic-free square is filled with locals going about their daily lives, free (as yet) of the wine, food and gift shops that are spreading like a rash over many of the better-known Tuscan towns. Although Cetona is noted for its textiles and copies of Etruscan vases, it now relies on *agriturismo* to keep its population from leaving. A short stay in a local farm with mountain walks, local cheeses and *bruschetti* drenched in olive oil is highly recommended.

A very scenic route, the Via della Montagna, goes from Cetona to the spa town of **San Casciano dei Bagni** ⑲ (take the high road north out of town and follow signs to Mondo "X"). En route, it's worth stopping at the beautifully restored **Convento di San Francesco**. It now houses a rehabilitation centre (Mondo "X"), but if you ring the bell, one of the occupants of the *comunità* will be happy to show you round. The restaurant and hotel here are well known throughout the area *(see page 231)*.

The recently opened Fonteverde Thermal Resort on the edge of San Casciano dei Bagni offers a wide range of thermal therapies and beauty treatments, though the atmosphere is rather sterile, and the Medici villa has been converted into a swanky hotel (www.fonteverdespa.com).

Routes up to Monte Amiata

The varied approaches to Monte Amiata, southern Tuscany's highest peak, are at least as good as what awaits you on arrival. The fast Pienza to Abbadia San Salvatore route allows for a detour to the thermal baths at **Bagni San Filippo**, a bit ragged round the edges compared to the Fonteverde resort above, but more authentic for it.

The alternative route via Sarteano and **Radicofani** ⑳ was the one taken by both Dickens and Montaigne to a location second only to Volterra for natural drama. While the mountain villages have sports and leisure industries to thank for their revival, the villages on the edge of Amiata seem to be in permanent limbo, trapped rather than enhanced by a medieval identity. Dickens found Radicofani "as barren, as stony, and as wild as Cornwall, in England". Perched on a craggy basalt rock, it is the only place in Italy to possess a triple Medicean wall. The town overlooks *"Il Mare di Sassi"*, the "Sea of Stones", suitable only for very hardy sheep. Although an 18th-century earthquake destroyed much of the town, enough atmosphere remains.

The drive from Radicofani up to **Abbadia San Salvatore** ㉑ is via Le Conie, a tortuous road known as "Amiata's sentry". For those not interested in skiing, mountain walks and disused mercury mines, Abbadia is best-known for its much overrated **Abbazia** and its medieval "high town". The Romanesque **San Salvatore** (open summer Mon–Sat 7am–6pm, Sun 10.30am–6pm; closes 5pm in winter) is all that remains of a once magnificent abbey. Unfortunately it has been heavily restored, once in 16th-century baroque and again in 1925. A 12th-century *Crucifix* and the crypt with 36 columns remain relatively unspoilt. Geometric symbols, grapes, palm leaves, animals and Gordian knots decorate the pillars.

From Abbadia, a winding road with sharp bends and sheer drops leads to the top of **Monte Amiata**, 1,738 metres (5,700 ft) high. The wooded area around the extinct volcano has attractive walks. The Fosso della Cocca, a leafy tunnel, is the best place to spot unusual wildlife and vegetation.

Although **Castel del Piano** in neighbouring Grosseto province, set among pine forests and wild raspberries, is the oldest settlement in the area, **Piancastagnaio** ㉒ is a better base. Perched among chestnut groves, the town has a newly restored Rocca and Franciscan monastery.

Arcidosso ㉓ was the birthplace of a man called David Lazzaretti, "The Prophet of the Amiata". In the 19th century Lazzaretti created a revolutionary social and religious movement with its headquarters on **Monte Labro**, a lonely peak which forms part of a nature reserve where deer, chamois and wolves roam, and protected trees and wild flowers grow. The best time is autumn, when the crowds have left and the wild mushrooms appear.

Santa Fiora ㉔ is particularly delightful, and has fine works of art in the 12th-century Santa Fiora and Santa Lucilla churches, including some della Robbia ceramics.

Quintessential Sienese

In both temperament and identity, **Montalcino** ㉕ is certainly the most

Sienese shepherd.

BELOW: Montalcino.

Map on page 218

Brunello di Montalcino is one of Italy's best wines. Opportunities abound to taste and buy Brunello and the younger Rosso di Montalcino.

BELOW: Romanesque abbey of Sant'Antimo.

Sienese town in the province. In essence, its history is a microcosm of all Sienese history. From a distance Montalcino even looks like a Sienese Trecento painting: the landscape could be a background to a saint's life; in the foreground would be the fortress and scenes of rejoicing and celebration after a historic victory.

Montalcino has been known as "the last rock of communal freedom" since its time as the Sienese capital in exile between 1555 and 1559. After the fall of Siena, exiles gathered around Piero Strozzi and the Sienese flag. As a reward, Montalcinesi standard bearers have the place of honour in the procession preceding the *Palio* in Siena.

The magnificent 14th-century **Rocca** (open Apr–Oct daily 9am– 8pm, Nov–Mar Tues–Sun 9am–6pm; free) is the key to Montalcino's pride. The approach is through olive groves and the slopes famous for Brunello wine. But the asymmetrical fortress, astride a spur of land, dominates the landscape. From its gardens there is a sense of boundless space and absolute freedom. In winter, the wind howls

over the massive walls and drives visitors to a different type of fortification in the **Enoteca** bar inside. This "National Wine Library" naturally serves Brunello, the first wine in Italy to be given the DOCG *denominazione* for excellence.

Architecturally, Montalcino offers a neoclassical Cathedral, a Gothic loggia, a Romanesque church and a myriad of intriguing alleys. The Duccio and della Robbia schools are well served by the Civic and Sacred museums. Most significant is the Palazzo Comunale, a mass of *Fiorentinità* finished off by a Sienese tower to prove that the Sienese always surpass the Florentines.

In spring, the area is very green, but yellow rape seed, poppies, sunflowers and grapes soon retaliate. Before leaving, try *pici*, home-made spaghetti, and sweet *sospiri* ("sighs") in a *fin de siècle* bar.

Sant'Antimo

Near by is **Sant'Antimo** ㉖, the remains of a Romanesque abbey founded by Charlemagne, set amidst cypresses in a peaceful valley. If the church is closed, try the sacristan in **Castelnuovo dell'Abate**, the village up the hill. Designed in the French and Lombard style, the abbey is built from local travertine, which resembles alabaster or onyx. The interior has a translucent quality and, as the light changes, turns luminously golden, white and brown.

Not far away, **Sant'Angelo in Colle** ㉗, a fortified hilltop village, once cast a dramatic shadow over Grosseto and other enemies. Until 1265 it was a Sienese outpost, but the tower is all that remains. Today it is a quiet medieval village.

Modern Siena province ends just there. As a frontier castle, Sant' Angelo looked down onto the plain which falls into Grosseto. After Siena province, Grosseto can look deceptively flat. ❏

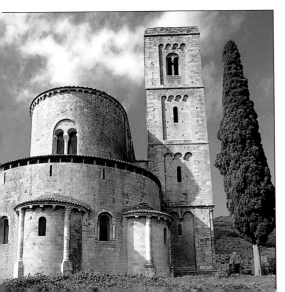

RESTAURANTS

Cetona

Frateria di Padre Egidio
Convento di San Francesco
Tel: 0578-238261
www.mondox.it
In the hills outside Cetona, this Franciscan monastery dating from 1212, is now an unusual setting for a top-class hotel and restaurant run by young members of the rehabilitation centre "Mondo X". The set menu (nine courses) is very original. Exceptional wine list. Worth the considerable expense. Closed Tues. €€€€

Montalcino

Taverna Il Grappolo Blu
Via Scale di Moglio
Tel: 0577-847150
Intimate, well-run inn with a rustic atmosphere. Typical dishes include filling soups, rabbit dishes and pasta with *porcini*. Excellent wine list. Reserve. Closed Fri. €€–€€€

Trattoria Sciame
Via Ricasoli, 9
Tel: 0577-848017
Among the over-priced restaurants of Montalcino, this well known trattoria remains a down-to-earth and fairly priced option. Good bean soup and home-made pasta. Closed Tues. €

Montefollonico

La Chiusa
Via Madonnina
Tel: 0577-669668
www.ristorantelachiusa.it
One of Tuscany's fanciest restaurants, set in an old oil mill on the outskirts of Montefollonico, with glorious views of the surrounding countryside. Come here for a special occasion. 15 rooms to rent. Closed Tues. €€€€

Monte Oliveto

La Torre
Monte Oliveto Maggiore
Tel: 0577-707022
Tourists fill every table on the lovely shaded terrace of this restaurant by the Benedictine abbey, but the food is surprisingly good. Service is brusque but efficient. Picnic tables nearby. Closed Tues. €

Montepulciano

Caffè Poliziano
Via di Voltaia nel Corso, 27
Tel: 0578-758615
Fax: 0578-752856
www.caffepoliziano.it
Lovingly restored Art Nouveau café–restaurant in the historic heart of Montepulciano. It's a landmark, so often full, but worth trying to get a table, even if it's just for coffee. Glorious panoramic balcony. €–€€

La Grotta
Località San Biagio 16
Tel: 0578-757607
Once the home of architect Sangallo, and right next to his stunningly positioned church of San Biagio. Rustic Tuscan dishes, with French influence from the owner.

Alfresco dining in summer. Closed Wed and Jan–Feb. €€€

Osteria Acquacheta
Via del Teatro
Tel: 0578-758443
Authentic *osteria* serving uncomplicated, but flavoursome dishes such as *pici* (the local pasta) with wild boar ragù and tagliatelle with white truffles. Wine is sloshed into glass tumblers and your bill will be scribbled on the tablecloth. Excellent value, but book or be prepared to wait. €–€€

Monticchiello

La Porta
Via del Piano, 1
Tel/Fax: 0578-755163
Pleasant little *osteria* just outside the walled town of Monticchiello. Stop here for a snack and glass of wine, or a full meal, choosing from both traditional and more inventive dishes. Panoramic terrace. €€

Pienza

La Buca delle Fate
Corso il Rossellino, 38/a
Tel: 0578-748448
Simple trattoria and bar in the lovely 16th-century Palazzo Gonzaga, on main thoroughfare through town. One of the best of Pienza's many eateries. Closed Mon. €

Proceno

La Fondue
Loc. Fosso Acquaviva

Tel/Fax: 0763-710163
After running restaurants in Atlantic City and Moscow, Neapolitan chef Francesco has chosen this scruffy hideaway by the border with Lazio as the unlikeliest of settings for a new venture. The food is simple but prepared with southern Italian flair. The decor needs work, but improvements are planned. Check out the photo gallery of celebrities he has fed. €€

Sinalunga

Le Coccole dell'Amorosa
Località l'Amorosa 2 km (1 mile) south.
Tel: 0577-679282
Fax: 0577-678216
www.amorosa.it
Superb restaurant in the hotel Locanda dell' Amorosa, romantically set in the stables of a medieval estate. The food is a mix of traditional and new, with a good choice. There is no better place to eat a *bistecca chianina* (farmed locally). Book well in advance. Closed Mon and Tues lunch.
€€€–€€€€

PRICE CATEGORIES

Average cost of a three-course meal per person with a half-bottle of wine:
€ = under €25
€€ = €25–40
€€€ = €40–60
€€€€ = over €60

GROSSETO AND THE MAREMMA

Grosseto province has some of the most beautiful stretches of coast and wilderness areas in the region. The Maremma, "the marsh by the sea", is Tuscany's wild west, where cowboys and long-horned cattle roam. Inland, the marshy plains give way to densely wooded hills, where little towns seem to grow out of the tufa

Tuscany's southwestern corner, the Grosseto province, offers a wonderfully varied landscape, ranging from the flat plains around the provincial capital, Grosseto, to the thickly wooded peak of Monte Amiata, capped with snow throughout the winter months, to the smooth hills bordering the neighbouring province of Siena. The coastline has an unrivalled mix of Mediterranean flora and fauna, but the region is dominated by the marshy plain of the Maremma, stretching from the Piombino headland to Tuscany's border with Lazio. This coastal stretch of flat marshland backed by remote hills, famous for its horse-breeding, wild-boar hunting, Etruscan sites and austere inland villages, not to mention its rich cuisine, remains one of the least developed areas on the Tuscan tourist itinerary.

Abundant remains reveal that the Etruscans thrived in this area, cultivating the land and exploiting the mineral wealth of the nearby island of Elba. However, while the Romans continued to mine Elba for the iron they needed to make swords, they allowed the drainage and irrigation systems the Etruscans had put in place on the mainland to decay. By the Middle Ages, with territorial wars raging and the additional threat of Saracen invasion, the area had become a near derelict malarial swamp where the average life expectancy was less than 20 years. Local populations migrated to the hills, where the air was sweeter and threat of invasion from the sea less imminent. It wasn't until the mid-19th century, with the draining of the swamps and land reclamation, that the revival of the Maremman lowlands began, spearheaded by the return of the *butteri* (Tuscany's tough cowboys) with their herds of long-horned cattle.

Map on page 234

LEFT: the tufa town of Sorano.
BELOW: a solitary spot in the Maremma.

The pink-and-white candy-stripe façade of Grosseto's Cathedral overlooks Piazza Dante, the main hub of the town.

Grosseto

The provincial capital, **Grosseto ❶**, is a commercial and administrative centre, with little to recommend it from a touristic point of view. The town began life as a fortified citadel around 950, following the Saracen looting of the former capital, Roselle, less than 12 km (8 miles) away. For centuries, the low-lying citadel remained a backwater in the mosquito-infested plain, overshadowed by the larger, more powerful neighbouring strongholds of Massa Marittima and Pitigliano in the hills. Flattened by bombs in World War II, Grosseto's post-war regeneration resulted in an unappealing sprawl of factories and modern housing blocks. It is not the most inviting of towns; graffiti is rife and the old buildings of the historic centre unloved. However, if you are passing and have an interest in things Roman and Etruscan, the museum is worth a visit.

The *centro storico* is contained within an ancient hexagonal wall, one of town's few intact monuments, erected by the Medici in the 16th century. The bombastic **post office** building on Piazza Fratelli Rosselli was Mussolini's gift to Grosseto, but the hub of the city and its evening *passeggiata* is the Corso Carducci, a street lined with shops and cafés leading to **Piazza Dante**, the main square, dominated by the pink-and-white **Duomo**. Dedicated to San Lorenzo, the original Cathedral was built towards the end of the 13th century over an existing church constructed about 100 years earlier, but the pink-and-white building is the product of a heavy-handed restoration in the 19th century.

Most of the Cathedral's artworks have been transferred to the nearby **Museo Archeologico e d'Arte della Maremma** (Piazza Baccarini 3; open Nov–Feb Tues–Fri 9am–1pm, Sat–Sun 9.30am–1pm, 4.30–7pm,

Mar–Apr Tues–Sun 9.30am–1pm, 4.30–7pm, May–Oct Tues–Sun 10am–1pm, 5–8pm; free), one of the richest museums in the area. It has a fine collection of pre-Etruscan, Etruscan and Roman artefacts from the archaeological sites of Roselle, Vetulonia, Talamone, Pitigliano and Saturnia to the south. The top floor is given over to sacred art, mostly by Sienese artists. Among the most notable works are the *Madonna delle Ciliege* (Madonna of the Cherries, *c.*1440–50), considered a Sassetta masterpiece, and a *Last Judgement* attributed to Guido da Siena (13th century), both from the Cathedral.

For Etruscan enthusiasts

The excavations at **Roselle ❷** (open daily 9am–sunset; entrance fee; follow signs to the ruins, not the town of Roselle), about 10 km (6 miles) northeast of Grosseto, reveal one of the most important Etruscan cities in northern Etruria. The paved streets, ruins of Etruscan taverns and workshops and the nearly intact circuit of Romano-Etruscan walls, as well as the outlines of the Roman forum and amphitheatre, are all very evocative. Most of the finds are on display in Grosseto's museum.

On the other side of the old Roman Via Aurelia (less romantically known as the N1), about 20 km (12 miles) north of Grosseto, the hilltop village of **Vetulonia ❸** lies above another ancient Etruscan city, Vetluna. The small excavated area (the *Scavi Città*) is more Roman than Etruscan. More interesting are the nearby tombs (museum open daily 10am–2pm, 4–8pm; 10am–4pm in winter; entrance fee; archaeological park open daily 9am–sunset; free).

The coast

Grosseto is in the middle of a flat plain formed by the Ombrone river and is about 17 km (10 miles) from the sea. Many Grossetans have a second home along the coast, either in congested **Marina di Grosseto ❹** or in the more snobbish and quieter **Principina a Mare ❺**, hidden in a pine forest.

Some prefer the old fishing village of **Castiglione della Pescaia ❻**, where they can keep a sailing boat,

Map on page 234

The Maremma's increasing reputation as a centre for wine-making and gastronomy has been endorsed by high profile French chef Alain Ducasse. He has transformed a former ducal residence near Castiglione della Pescaia into an elegant hotel with a superb restaurant (see page 276). Wine and olive oil are produced by the estate which is surrounded by ancient olive groves and vineyards.

BELOW: an early evening gathering on Grosseto's Piazza Dante.

TIP

The beaches within the Parco dell'Uccellina are among the most beautiful and unspoilt in Tuscany. To preserve this wilderness, the number of visitors is limited during the summer, and apart from the road to Marina di Alberese, cars are not permitted in the park. Transport from Alberese is arranged on buses. Visiting in the height of summer is ill-advised, as the weather becomes hot and humid, and there are tiny insects, *serafiche*, whose bite is painful.

BELOW: *butteri* rounding up horses.

ideally located at the foot of the mountains north of Grosseto. The harbour, crowded with fishermen's and tourists' boats, is believed to be the Etruscan Hasta, or Portus Traianus in Roman times. Overlooking the port is the Rocca Aragonese, with its walls and towers dating back to the 14th century. It's rather ordinary as beach resorts go, but has all the facilities you need.

The road connecting the resorts of Marina di Grosseto and Castiglione della Pescaia runs along the coast for a straight 10-km (6-mile) stretch separated from the sand and sea by a magnificent forest of umbrella pines known as the **Pineta del Tombolo**. You can leave your car by the roadside and take any of the footpaths through the umbrella pines to the lovely beach.

From here the road leads north to the Gulf of Follonica. The gulf's southern promontory is occupied by **Punta Ala ❼**, a semi-private resort with a flashy marina, upmarket hotels, golf clubs, horse riding and polo facilities. It's an attractive spot, but not really worth a detour, unless

you're into purpose-built resorts and want to hang out with moneyed Italians. Follonico, at the opposite extreme, is just plain ugly. If you are in the area and yearning for the seaside, **Cala Violino** is a quiet bay just before Follonico. Alternatively, there are some good beaches between Follonico and Piombino. Otherwise, at this point you're better off heading inland to **Massa Marittima** (*see page 189*) or back south to the beautiful Parco della Maremma.

"Park of the Little Bird"

The **Parco dell'Uccellina ❽**, also known as the **Parco Regionale della Maremma**, covers an area of around 60 sq. km (150 sq. miles), with about 20 km (12 miles) of coastline. The landscape is incredibly varied, ranging from salt marshes, sand dunes and open plains to rocky mountains, pine forests and Mediterranean maquis – dense scrubland characterised by rosemary, broom, sea lavender and holm oaks. Wild deer, boar and small mammals thrive in the undergrowth, while it is incredibly rich in birdlife – hence the name,

Map on page 234

which means "Park of the Little Bird". Wading birds flock to the marshes around the mouth of the Ombrone river, and birds of prey circle the hills. The park is also an important pit-stop for birds migrating between Europe and Africa.

Down on the open fields and low-lying olive groves, herds of long-horned cattle and horses graze. They are reared by *butteri*, the tough Tuscan cowboys who settled in the region in the 19th century, after the swamps were drained and the land could be used for cattle grazing.

Evidence of human settlement here can be seen in the remains of a castle, the Benedictine monastery of **San Rabano**, and lookout towers used for the unfortunate soldiers posted here to watch for Saracen pirates and Spanish galleons.

The main entrance to the park is at **Alberese ❾**, where you have to leave your car. The visitor centre (open daily Mar–June 8am–sunset, July–Sept 7.30am–sunset, Oct–Mar 8.30 am–sunset; tel: 0564-407098; www.parcomaremma.it; entrance fee to park), where you buy your entrance ticket, is full of information on the flora and fauna, and activities within the park. With your ticket you'll be given a map of the various way-marked trails you can follow, which range in levels of difficulty and duration, from gentle two-hour walks to day-long treks. Shuttle buses into the park leave from outside the visitor centre at regular intervals (times are posted outside the visitor centre), but be sure to check the time of the last bus back down.

Activities within the nature park include canoeing on the Ombrone river, sailing along the coast, riding across the mountains, birdwatching by the salt marshes and visiting the noble ruins of San Rabano and the many other towers strung out along the mountain tops, overlooking the sea, each with its story of marauding pirates and hidden treasures, going back to the times of the Saracens and Spanish galleons.

If time is limited or you'd rather not walk, you can take the one access road (you still need a ticket) from Alberese to **Marina di Alberese ❿**, a 6-km (4-mile) stretch of beach.

Umbrella pines line many of the long, straight roads through the Maremman plains.

BELOW: fishing at Castiglione della Pescaia.

TIP

An annual rodeo is held in August, which brings American cowboys to Alberese. Other local festivals include the Sagra del Cinghiale (Boar Fair) in Montepescali, a summer opera festival in Batignano, the Sagra della Gastronomia (Gastronomic Fair) in Manciano, and the Sagra della Trippa (Tripe Fair) in Montemerano.

BELOW: Porto Santo Stefano.

Just outside the southern boundaries of the park is the walled village of **Talamone** ⓫ (18km/11 miles from Alberese), a small, low-key resort with some decent hotels and restaurants to choose from. You can gain access to the trails in the southern sector from nearby Caprarecce.

Argentario

It's a short drive from Talamone along the Aurelia-Etrusca (Grosseto–Rome highway) to **Monte Argentario**, a craggy peninsula that was once an island, thought to have been occupied by Roman moneylenders in the 4th century – *argentarius* in Latin is money-lender. From 1556 until 1815, Argentario existed as a separate state from the Grand Duchy of Tuscany, under Spanish rule. This kingdom encompassed the whole promontory and the existing ports of Orbetello, Talamone and Porto Azzurro, on the island of Elba. The Spanish legacy remains in architectural structures dotted throughout the area.

Monte Argentario gradually became attached to the land by two long sandbanks which built up over the centuries: Tòmbolo della Giannella and Tòmbolo di Feniglia. Both have fine beaches, but while Giannella is backed by a main road linking Porto Santo Stefano to the mainland, Feniglia is traffic-free and backed by protected pine forest. It's a 7-km (4-mile) walk or bike ride to the mainland.

Like two outstretched arms holding onto the mainland, the sandbanks embrace a lagoon, an important wintering spot for migrating birds. The lagoon is cut in half by a central causeway which links Argentario to the town of **Orbetello** ⓬, sited on a peninsula which projects into the lagoon from the mainland. The town's baroque architecture reflects its history as a 16th-century Spanish garrison town. The sea laps right up to the stout city walls, and visitors come from afar for the excellent fish restaurants found here and on Monte Argentario.

The rugged peninsula rises to a height of 635 metres (2,000 ft) and is cloaked in Mediterranean maquis, olive groves and vineyards. Apart from **Porto Santo Stefano** , most of the mountain has been spared from the property developers, but the exclusive villas outside the port towns remain the preserve of the rich. The coastline is extremely varied, but most of it is inaccessible, unless, of course, you are the owner of a yacht. The best way to enjoy Argentario is to stay in a hotel with a private beach. Otherwise, of the few beaches with public access, the nicest are Le Cannelle (roughly opposite Isola Rossa) and the beach to the left of the luxury hotel Il Pellicano, near Porto Ercole.

Porto Santo Stefano's busy harbour is crowded with small fishing boats and large yachts. It is an atmospheric town, with many shops, bars and fish restaurants. For a breathtaking and often hair-raising drive, the scenic coastal road from here (follow signs to La Panoramica) takes you along the clifftops, with spectacular views at every turn. The road is blocked by a rock fall beyond Cala Piccola and you have to turn back.

Porto Ercole on the south side is Santo Stefano's smaller, supposedly more exclusive sister, but what was once a quiet fishing village is now overwhelmed by all the traffic that converges on it from sea and land. Its main attractions for landlubbers are the *centro storico* and the 16th-century Spanish fortress overlooking the harbour.

Island excursions

Santo Stefano has ferry connections with Giannutri and Giglio, two of the seven islands in the Archipelago Toscano *(see page 182)*. The entire archipelago was declared a nature reserve in 1996 – a move that, while obviously made to protect the environment, has created much controversy among both those involved with the tourist industry and local fishermen, whose rights have been restricted. Although swimming has not been affected, there are some areas where boats are not allowed to drop anchor.

Crescent-shaped **Giannutri** is a tiny, flat, virtually uninhabited island 22 km (14 miles) away, where day trippers go to visit the ruins of a Roman villa – columns, mosaics, baths and a private pier.

Giglio , an hour's sail from Porto Santo Stefano, has more to offer. It is a playground for sailors and divers, and its proximity to Rome makes it a very popular weekend destination. Giglio is the second-largest island in Tuscany after Elba and has an impenetrable coastline with only one easily accessible port, Giglio Porto. A rocky road uphill leads to Giglio Castello, which dominates the landscape. Set among vineyards (which produce grapes for the very strong, distinctive local wine, Ansonica), it is a picturesque fortified settlement, with archways, alleyways and stairs carved from the rock. Giglio has a number of sandy beaches on its western side and is covered in typical Mediterranean vegetation: aromatic herbs and plants, and orange and lemon groves.

Map
on page
234

It's always worth packing a pair of binoculars. Apart from being useful for close inspection of frescoes, in this area they will be handy for some rewarding birdwatching. The Orbetello lagoon and Parco dell'Uccellina are among the few places along the Italian coast which provide refuge for a wide variety of native and migratory birds.

BELOW: an old coastal watchtower on Giglio island.

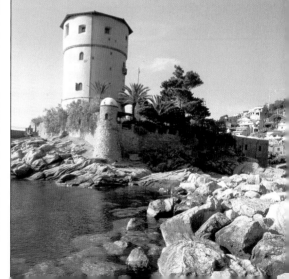

Cosa to Capalbio

Back on the mainland coast, across the Aurelia from the town of **Ansedonia** are the important Roman remains of **Cosa** built on top of what was originally an Etruscan settlement. Excavations have revealed a main street, a forum, a walled acropolis and *capitolium* with magnificent views out to sea; the site is somewhat overgrown and has a melancholy air.

Below the promontory is the silted-up Roman port and the Tagliata Etrusca, the Etruscan Cut – a canal in fact built by the Romans to drain the **Lago di Burano**. This protected lake is another favourite stopping place for thousands of migratory birds *(see page 284)*.

Inland lies **Capalbio**, one of the first towns on the hills bordering Lazio (Rome's province). Capalbio is a popular getaway among wealthy Italians, who have bought up every corner of the village and turned it into a fashionable summer refuge from the capital. It is famous for its food, and several excellent restaurants specialise in local dishes of wild boar and other game. The woodland around Capalbio is managed as a game reserve, and a game festival is held here every September.

Near by is the magical **Giardino dei Tarocchi**, or Tarot Garden (open daily 2.30–7.30pm in summer, 1st Sat of month 9am–1pm in winter; entrance fee), created by French sculptor Niki de Saint Phalle, who died in 2002, and inspired by the arcane symbolism of tarot. The park displays 22 fantastic, brightly coloured sculptures covered in mirror and mosaic, glinting in the sun among the flowers and fountains.

Fortified towns

Across the densely wooded hills north of Capalbio is the flat plain of the river Albegna, now completely drained, which leads to the castle of **Marsiliana**, once an Etruscan town and now the only property left belonging to the Corsini family, who originally owned the entire area. Most of these swamps were expropriated by the state, drained and then distributed to small landowners.

The Maremma is famous for its brigands. One notorious bandito, Domenico Tiburzi, a local Robin Hood, was executed in 1896. There was disagreement over whether he could be buried in consecrated ground, and eventually a typical Italian compromise was reached: he was buried at the edge of a cemetery with his head in sacred ground, and the rest of his body outside.

BELOW: bathing in the Cascate del Gorello.

North of here lies **Magliano in Toscana** ㉑, a fortified medieval village perched above olive groves. Both civil and religious architecture show a strong Romanesque influence, with Gothic and Renaissance additions. A perfect example of the blend of styles is San Giovanni Battista, a Romanesque church with Gothic side windows and a Renaissance façade.

A few kilometres further inland, **Scansano** ㉒, a breezy hill village with a separate fortified section *(oppido)*, was once the summer capital of the province, when all the administrative powers were moved from malarial Grosseto during the hot season. It is now famous for the fine DOC wine, Morellino di Scansano, and there are several *cantine* for wine-tasting.

Spa town

Travelling eastwards across hills and moors inhabited by *butteri* (cowboys) and Maremman cattle, you come to Montemerano, another typically Tuscan walled town, with 15th-century fortifications. From here you can take the road to the ancient Roman town of **Saturnia** ㉓. On the approach to the town, around a sharp curve, you will glimpse – and smell – the **Cascate del Gorello**, a steaming waterfall where you can bathe in hot sulphur springs. Alternatively, you can soak car-weary limbs in the thermal swimming pools of the nearby Terme di Saturnia, a modern spa and luxury hotel. Further on, Saturnia itself is a quiet little village, drowsy under the immense weight of its past. It was the Etruscan Aurinia, and then came under Roman control in 280 BC. The village is centred around a large oak-ringed piazza with one or two notable *trattorie*.

Tufa towns

Sorano, Sovana and Pitigliano are three southern Tuscan jewels situated above dramatic cliffs of soft, porous tufa covered in a thick jungle of fern, ivy and evergreen trees. The roads here, hewn out of the hills, are an experience in themselves. The winding stretch between Sovana and Pitigliano, which rises spectacularly above it, is particularly memorable.

Map on page 234

The Equinos Association (www.cavallo maremmano.it) organises horse-trekking and butteri *shows in the Maremma. The Via Equestre Grossetana is a 1,000-km (620-mile) network of bridlepaths, with 43 equestrian tourism centres (www.via equestregrossetana.it)*

BELOW: Pitigliano.

Map on page 234

Ciborium from the 8th or 9th century inside Sovana's exquisite Romanesque church of Santa Maria.

BELOW: farm outbuilding and view of the surrounding countryside, near Sovana.

In the mid-18th century **Pitigliano** ㉔ was one of the most important settlements in southern Tuscany. This majestic town is built on a hill of volcanic tufa and straddles a vast arched aqueduct with wine and olive-oil cellars carved out of the hillside below. It is laid out around two parallel streets that run along its length, crossed by 60 narrower streets which intersect with tiny alleys. Pitigliano used to be called "little Jerusalem", because it was a refuge for Jews fleeing from religious persecution in the Papal states. Even today the Jewish quarter of the city, which has the oldest Italian synagogue, remains distinct. It is one of the few places in Catholic Italy where you can find kosher wine or turkey "ham" *(billo)*, a Jewish speciality.

The town is centred around a magnificent citadel built by the Orsini in the 16th century. **Palazzo Orsini** (open Tues–Sun 10am–1pm, 3–7.30pm; entrance fee) houses an **Etruscan Museum** (open Tues–Sun 10am–1pm, 4–7pm; entrance fee), containing finds from the nearby Etruscan site of Poggio Buco.

Before leaving, dip into one of the bars and enjoy a glass of Bianco di Pitigliano from the tufa wine cellars.

Sovana ㉕, a few kilometres away, is a tiny one-street village with two outstanding proto-Romanesque churches. The surrounding area is scattered with Etruscan tombs, hidden in the surrounding woods. These are best seen with a guide.

Situated above a deep ravine with a roaring stream and waterfall is medieval **Sorano** ㉖, which is also built on a tufa outcrop. Unfortunately, some of the buildings have begun to collapse into the steep valleys around the city, but the great majority of Sorano can be seen without danger.

Visible from every corner of Grosseto province on a clear day, particularly in snowy winter, is **Monte Amiata** *(see page 228)*, the highest peak in Tuscany south of Florence. It is a dormant volcano, with hot geysers on its slopes and underground waters that supply the spa at Saturnia. Monte Amiata is a refreshing escape during the hot summer months and a popular local ski resort in winter. ❏

RESTAURANTS

Capalbio

Il Fontanile dei Caprai
7 km (4.5 miles) from Capalbio on the Marsiliana road
Tel: 0564-896526
This country restaurant and its jovial owner are full of rustic charm. Savour the delicious Maremman dishes, made from locally sourced ingredients. Open weekends for lunch and dinner and from mid-June–mid-Sept in the evenings too. €€

Grosseto

Il Canto del Gallo
Via Mazzini 29
Tel: 0564-414589
Tiny trattoria in the old town walls. Interesting cooking with, unusually, organic vegetables featuring strongly. Closed Sun and two weeks in Feb. €€

Montemerano

Da Caino
Via della Chiesa 4
Tel: 0564-602817
Pretty restaurant in Grosseto province, one of the best in Tuscany. Exquisite and creative food, specialising in wild mushrooms and truffles; complementary wine list. Must book. Closed Wed, Thur lunch and early-Jan–late Feb. €€€€

Orbetello

Osteria dell Lupacante
Corso Italia 103
Tel: 0564-867618

One of the best known of Orbetello's many good fish restaurants. Serves creative, fresh seafood dishes *alla siciliana*.

Osteria Il Nocchino
Via Lenzi 64
Tel: 0564-860329
Squeeze yourself into this tiny fish restaurant and tuck into such salty fresh dishes as grilled sword-fish, spaghetti with *cozze* and *vongole* (mussels and clams), salt cod and chick peas, or a sea food risotto. Evenings only. Closed Wed. €€

Pitigliano

Trattoria del Grillo
Via Cavour, 18
Tel: 0564-615202
Authentic trattoria, by the aqueduct, mixing Tuscan classics with local flourishes so you might follow good old *bruschetta* or *pici*, with escalopes in Pitigliano wine. Honestly priced and packed with locals. €

Porto Ercole

Bacco in Toscana
Via San Paolo delle Chiesa 6
Tel: 0564-833078
Good selection of seafood for a busy yachting community. The mixed *antipasti* and the lobster are both recommended. Only open for dinner – booking advised; closed Nov, Feb and Mon–Wed in winter. €€€

Porto Santo Stefano

Il Moletto
Via del Molo
Tel: 0564-813636
www.moletto.it
The last in a long line of fish restaurants along the marina's main drag. Go for lunch early to bag one of the quayside seats and share a seafood platter while watching the port activity. Closed Wed. €€

Saturnia

Due Cippi-da Michele
Piazza Vittorio Veneto 26/A
Tel: 0564-601074
Maremman dishes in a patrician *palazzo*. Closed Tues. €€–€€€

Sovana

Taverna Etrusca
Piazza del Pretorio
Tel: 0564-616183

Local specialities served in a medieval dining room and in the garden in fine weather. Closed Mon. €€

Scilla
Via del Duomo
Tel: 0564-616531
www.scillasovana.it
The bright and elegant hotel/restaurant has a more contemporary feel than the Taverna Etrusca down the road, with the added advantage of a vegetarian menu. Closed Tues. €€

PRICE CATEGORIES

Average cost of a three-course meal per person with a half-bottle of wine:
€ = under €25
€€ = €25–40
€€€ = €40–60
€€€€ = over €60

RIGHT: dining alfresco in Massa Marittima.

AREZZO AND EASTERN TUSCANY

Known for its gold, art and antiques, Arezzo city is one of the wealthiest in Tuscany, and the province is equally well-off in terms of prosperous farms and villages. The source of the Arno is here, too, in an area of great natural beauty known as the Casentino

The landscape of the province of Arezzo is rugged, with steep, thickly wooded valleys that shield its towns and villages from view. To the north, the Casentino is a remote area of chestnut woods, vineyards and monasteries; to the south are the prosperous farms of the fertile Val di Chiana. To the west, across the Pratomagno ridge, lies the Arno valley, which becomes more and more industrialised as you near Florence. At the heart of the province, its capital, Arezzo, was one of the most important towns in the Etruscan federation, thanks to its strategic position on a hill at the meeting point of three valleys. Today, it is one of Tuscany's wealthiest cities, known for its gold art and antiques, and boasts a large number of jewellers, antique shops and furniture restorers.

Arezzo city

Arezzo ❶ is rich in buildings, monuments and works of art of all eras. The old hilly part of the city is the most picturesque, with its massive main square, the **Piazza Grande ❹**, so far from being level that its numerous slopes and steps present a severe test even to the sober. On the first Sunday of every month, this square is the venue for an antiques market, the largest and oldest of its kind in Italy. Stalls cover the square, run around the base of the Duomo and spill into the cobbled **Corso Italia ❸**, the city's main shopping street.

Rising from the southern side of the square, sitting on the Corso, is the **Santa Maria della Pieve ❸** (open daily 8am–7pm in summer, 8am–noon, 3–6pm in winter) with its "tower of a hundred holes", so named because of the filigree pattern of arches piercing the belfry. This is one of the most beautiful Romanesque churches in all Tuscany.

Maps
City: 246
Area: 248

LEFT: view from Cortona.
BELOW: detail from the *Legend of the True Cross* fresco cycle by Piero della Francesca.

Some great intellectuals hailed from Arezzo – Maecenas, Roman patron of the arts who encouraged the work of Virgil and Horace; Petrarch, classical Italian poet; Guido d'Arezzo, the inventor of musical notation; and Giorgio Vasari, the 16th-century painter, architect and art historian.

A spiritual fresco

Two blocks west you will find the church of **San Francesco** ⓓ (open daily 8.30am–noon, 2.30–6.30pm) where you can see Piero della Francesca's restored *Legend of the True Cross* (1452–66) (30-minute guided tour Mon–Fri 9am–6pm, Sat 9am–5.30pm, Sun 1–5.30pm; advance booking necessary; tel: 0575-2400; entrance fee). This masterful fresco cycle weaves together a complex story in which the wood of the Tree of Knowledge (from which Adam and Eve ate the apple) becomes the wood of the cross on which Christ died, and which was later discovered by the Empress Helena, mother of the Emperor Constantine the Great, who converted to Christianity and made it the state religion of the Roman Empire in AD 313.

The Cathedral

Medieval monuments cluster together in the northern part of the city, where you will find the **Duomo** ⓔ (open daily 7am–12.30pm, 3–7pm), sheltered by the encircling walls of the Grand-Duke Cosimo's 16th-century Fortezza, now a public park with fine views of the town and the Casentino beyond. The Duomo's construction, mainly from the late 13th to the early 16th centuries, has been described as one of the most perfect expressions of Gothic architecture in Italy. The Gothic façade, however, is fake and dates from 1914.

The real highlight of the Cathedral are the 16th-century stained-glass windows by Guillaume de Marcillat, a French artist who made Arezzo his home. Other great works here are the 14th-century tomb of Guido Tarlati, which flanks the *St Mary Magdalene* fresco by Piero della Francesca. This work can be contemplated in comparative peace, unlike the frescoes in San Francesco. The **Museo Diocesano** ⓕ (open Thur–Sat 10am–noon; entrance fee), behind the

BELOW: browsing the antique stalls.

Cathedral, contains medieval crucifixes and Vasari frescoes.

Vasari trail

Further west is the **Casa del Vasari** Ⓖ (open Mon, Wed–Sat 9am–7pm, Sun 9am–1pm; entrance fee), the attractive house that Giorgio Vasari – painter, architect and author of *The Lives of the Artists* (1550) – built for himself and decorated with frescoes of the artists he most admired.

Close by is the **Museo Statale d'Arte Medioevale e Moderna** Ⓗ (open Tues–Sun 8.30am–7.30pm, Sat until 11pm July–Sept; entrance fee), housed in the 15th-century Palazzo Bruni. Spread across three floors, its varied collection includes an excellent display of majolica pottery, frescoes and examples of the Arezzo goldsmiths' work, alongside paintings by Vasari and modern works by local artists.

Roman Arezzo

Last but not least, in the flat southern part of the city you will find the **Anfiteatro Romano** Ⓘ (open daily 8.30am–7.30pm; entrance fee). The

Roman Arretium was originally an Etruscan city, but in 294 BC it became a Roman settlement, a convenient resting post on the Via Cassia between Rome and Florence. The site was later plundered to build the city walls and churches, and the perimeter wall is all that remains.

A section of the amphitheatre walls was incorporated into an Olivetan monastery (near the station), now occupied by the excellent **Museo Archeologico** Ⓙ (open daily 8.30am–7.30pm, more restricted hours in winter; entrance fee), which features some of the finest examples anywhere of the Aretine ware for which Arezzo has long been famous. This high-quality Roman pottery once competed with the more famous Samian ware as the crockery of choice on aristocratic Roman dinner tables.

Piero della Francesca trail

East of Arezzo, the Upper Tiber valley is tightly enclosed at its northern end by the Alpe di Catenaia and the Alpe della Luna. Two important towns for Piero della Francesca en-

Maps
City: 246
Area: 248

Piazza Grande is the scene of the Giostra del Saracino, a historic jousting tournament held twice a year, in June and September.

BELOW: the Corso.

Piero della Francesca's 1463 masterpiece, the Resurrection, *was hailed by Aldous Huxley as "the best picture in the world".*

thusiasts are here. **Sansepolcro ❷** is famous for two things: as the town where Buitoni pasta is produced and as the birthplace of the great Renaissance artist. The old town huddled behind crumbling ramparts is an important artistic centre. The quiet, narrow streets are linked by four ancient gates, the best-preserved of which is the Porta Fiorentina.

In the town centre, at the junction of Piazza Torre di Berta and Via Matteotti, is the **Duomo** (open daily 7.30am–noon, 3.30–6.30pm). Dedicated to St John the Evangelist, it began life in the 11th century as a monastic abbey. A wide range of excellent artworks cover the walls of the interior, including a tabernacle by the della Robbia school. Perugino's *Ascension of Jesus* is also here.

But the reason most people make the pilgrimage here is to see Piero della Francesca's greatest work, the *Resurrection*. The fresco was nearly destroyed by the Allies during World War II as they bombarded Sansepolcro, believing the Germans were still occupying the town. It was thankfully saved from destruction by the villagers, who surrounded it with sandbags. Today, this intense, brooding work is displayed in the **Museo Civico** (open daily June–Sept 9am–1.30pm, 2.30–7.30pm, Oct–May 9.30am–1pm, 2.30–6pm; entrance fee), in Via degli Aggiunti, alongside the **Madonna della Misericordia**, another della Francesca masterpiece.

Other key buildings to look out for are the 16th-century Palazzo delle Laudi (the Town Hall) and the Palazzo Gherardi, begun in 1300, both in Via Matteotti, and the Palazzo Pretorio opposite Piazza Garibaldi.

From Sansepolcro, the della Francesca trail leads south to **Monterchi ❸**, where a former schoolhouse displays his striking *Madonna del Parto* in the **Museo Madonna del Parto** (open Tues–Sun 9am–1pm, 2–7pm, until 5pm in winter; entrance fee). The Madonna, heavily pregnant and aching, has unbuttoned the front of her dress, while above, two angels hold up the entrance to the tent in which she stands.

Michelangelo's birthplace

Northwest of Sansepolcro, on a steep slope above the Tiber, is the hamlet of **Caprese Michelangelo ❹**, birthplace of Michelangelo. Protected by an almost complete set of walls, this cluster of rustic buildings – which includes the Buonarroti house, the old town hall where Michelangelo's father was the Florentine governor, and the tiny chapel in which Michelangelo was baptised – are interesting more for their connections than for their contents. The views over Alpine countryside explain why Michelangelo attributed his good brains to the mountain air he breathed as a child.

The Casentino

The Casentino is the name given to the little-known region of the Upper Arno valley that runs from the eastern side of the Consuma Pass down to the source of the river just north of Arezzo. It is an area of great

natural beauty, enclosed by high mountains, cloaked in fir, chestnut and beech woods, and concealing ancient monasteries and farming villages. You have no choice but to explore it at a leisurely pace. The narrow, winding, rural roads are slow going, and with views at every turn, the temptation to stop and admire them is hard to resist.

At its remoter edges this region cannot have changed much since the 13th century, when St Francis took to a lonely, desolate crag on the wooded slopes of **Monte Penna** at **La Verna ❺**, using a niche between two huge boulders as a hermitage. The mountain was given to the Franciscan Order as a free gift by a local devotee, Count Orlando da Chiusi di Casentino, who had been inspired by one of St Francis's sermons. On this spot in 1224 St Francis is supposed to have received the stigmata while he was praying. Today, in the middle of the ancient forest, a Franciscan sanctuary still occupies the rock. Assembled around a tiny piazza is a collection of monastic buildings, including one large church containing yet more fine

Portrait of a turbaned Michelangelo, by Giuliano Bugiardini, 1522.

BELOW: detail from the *Resurrection*, by Piero della Francesca.

TIP

The Parco Nazionale delle Foreste Casentinesi is one of Italy's newest national parks and is heavily promoted in the region. It lies along the Apennine ridge that forms the border between Tuscany and Emilia Romagna. There are waymarked trails through the park, and a number of *agriturismo* establishments if you want to spend a few days exploring the woods and mountains *(for more information, see page 64).*

BELOW: in Tuscany, shop decoration is an art form.

terracotta sculptures by the gifted della Robbia family.

Sixteen kilometres (10 miles) northeast of La Verna, high in the spectacular woodland, cut by mountain streams and waterfalls, is another more ancient monastery, **Camáldoli** 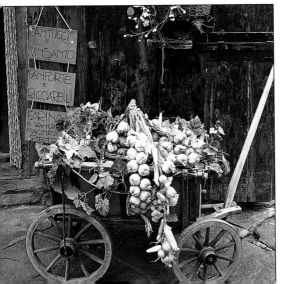 (open daily 9am–1pm, 2.30–7pm; until 7.30pm in summer; tel: 0575-556012). It was founded in 1012 by San Romualdo (St Rumbold), a former member of the Benedictine Order, who founded a strict community of hermits. The monastery is still inhabited, and the monks run a welcoming café here. The old cloister **pharmacy** (open 9am–12.30pm, 2.30–6pm), with its mortars and crucibles, is a pleasing relic of past times and now sells soaps and liqueurs made by the monks.

Another 300 metres (1,000 ft) up the mountain (a beautiful hour-long walk), above the monastery is the **Eremo**, a hermitage consisting of nothing more than a small baroque church and ten cells, each surrounded by a high wall and a tiny kitchen garden. Here the hermits still live in solitude and silent contemplation.

The church and St Rumbold's cell are open to visitors (daily 9am–noon, 3–5pm, until 6pm in summer; tel: 0575-556021), but access to the monks' quarters is closed.

After immersing yourself in the silence and isolation of Camáldoli, a visit to noisy **Bibbiena** 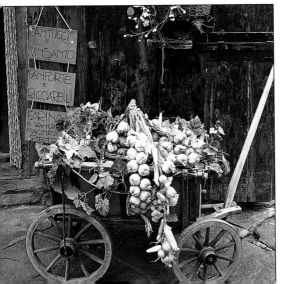 will bring you sharply back to the modern world. At its heart is a typical Tuscan hill town, but its inner charms are hidden by the modern sprawl around it. Bibbiena is the Casentino's main commercial centre, best-known for its own particular brand of salami and as a centre for industry related to tobacco production. Buildings of note in the historic centre include the church of **San Lorenzo**, which has some richly decorated della Robbia panels, and the church of **Santa Ipolito and San Donato** (open daily 7am–noon, 3–6pm) which has a fine triptych by Bicci di Lorenzo. Near by is the Renaissance **Palazzo Dovizi**, home of Cardinal Dovizi, who, as Cardinal Bibbiena, became the secretary of Pope Leo X. Bibbiena's central piazza offers distant views to Camáldoli and Poppi – the latter is the gateway to an interesting area of castles and fortified towns.

Casentino castles

This region was continually fought over by the Guelf Florentines and the Ghibelline Aretines. A decisive battle in 1289 which firmly established the dominance of the former over the latter is marked by a column on a site called **Campaldino**, just between Castel San Niccolò and Poppi.

Poppi 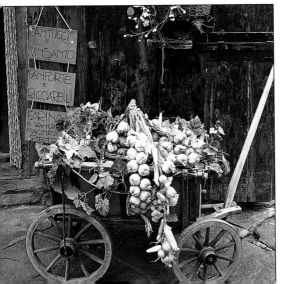 surveys the surrounding countryside from its hilltop perch, dominated by the brooding **Castello dei Conti Guidi** (open daily 10am–5pm Nov–mid-Mar, until 6pm mid-Mar–Oct, until 7pm July–Aug), the most important medieval monument in the Casentino. Built in the 13th century for the powerful Guidi counts who ruled most of the area,

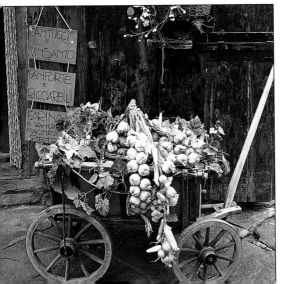

the castle's design was based on that of the Palazzo Vecchio in Florence, and it is thought likely that Arnolfo di Cambio was the architect. The courtyard and stairway are impressive, and the Florentine frescoes may be viewed on request. The ancient streets of this quiet town are lined with arcades linked by steep steps and decorated with finely carved capitals and stone seats. There's a Romanesque church and a few shops selling locally made copper pots.

Off in the distance, on a hill above the village of **Pratovecchio** ❾, birthplace of Paolo Uccello, is the 11th-century **Castello di Romena** (visits by appointment; tel: 0575-58633), another Guidi castle. The noble family gave refuge to Dante here after his expulsion from Florence at the beginning of the 14th century. Of the 14 towers that Dante would have seen at the castle, only three remain.

Standing on a lonely slope, a stone's throw from the castle, **Pieve di Romena** (visits by appointment with the custodian; tel: 0575-58725) is one of the most important Roman-

esque churches in Tuscany. Beneath its apse, which dates from 1152, excavations have revealed the remains of an Etruscan building as well as two earlier churches. The finely carved capitals atop the gigantic granite columns in the nave make reference to the four Evangelists and to St Peter.

Back down in Pratovecchio, you'll find the headquarters of the Casentino national park (Via G. Brocchi 7; tel: 0575-50301; *see tip opposite*).

To the north and guarding the source of the Arno (Monte Falterona) is the medieval town of **Stia** ❿, with a pretty porticoed piazza. Here stand the ruins of the **Castello di Porciano** (open mid-May–mid-Oct Sun 10am–noon, 4–7pm, or by appointment; tel: 0575-582626), another Guidi stronghold which stood guard over the Arno valley.

The Castello di Romena is visible from up here. Whereas these monuments are all easily accessible, the fortified remains at Castel Castagnaia, with the nearby ruined Roman temple, both to the west of Stia, are harder to reach. The road peters out,

Maps
City: 246
Area: 248

Fiat's classic Cinquecento "Bambino" is still a much-loved runaround, perfect for the narrow streets of small towns like Poppi.

BELOW: view across Poppi from the Palazzo Pretorio.

TIP

East of the Arno and
skirting the western
edge of the high
Pratomagno ridge is
the panoramic road
known as the Strada
dei Sette Ponti, or
Road of the Seven
Bridges. The winding
route passes through
several medieval
towns, including
Castelfranco di Sopra,
Loro Ciuffena to the
south and the abbey
at Vallombrosa *(see
page 120)* to the north.

BELOW RIGHT: the
white Chianina cattle
are highly prized for
their beef.

and they can only be reached on foot
through rough, stony countryside.

Remains of yet another Guidi
castle can be seen in the tiny village
of **Montemignaio**. There's not
much left to see, but the village
church has Ghirlandaio's *Virgin and
Child with the Four Church Elders*.

On the slope of the forested Pratomagno ridge, south of Bibbiena, is
the restored castle at **Chitignano ⓫**.
The medieval remains were rebuilt
in the 18th century. There are other
ruined castles at Talla and Subbiano.

The Valdarno

There are two possible routes through
the Arno valley between Florence
and Arezzo. The SS69 runs parallel
to the river and provides the quickest access to the Valdarno's sights,
though traffic here can be heavy.
More scenic is the road that skirts the
Pratomagno ridge on the eastern side
of the Arno. It's full of twists and
turns, but the views are rewarding.

In the Middle Ages, the Valdarno,
like the Casentino, was bitterly
fought over by the Ghibellines and
the Guelfs. At the close of the 13th

century pressure was exerted on the
Florentines by the warlike Aretine
bishops, who controlled powerful
strongholds in the Arno valley. In an
effort to resist them, the Florentines
built three fortresses, which were
really fortified towns, at San Giovanni Valdarno, Terranuova and
Castelfranco di Sopra.

Halfway between Florence and
Arezzo, **San Giovanni Valdarno ⓬**
was fortified as a bulwark against the
Aretines, but little evidence remains
of its former military function. Today
it is a lively industrial centre with a
prominent display of architectural
and artistic wealth. The central
piazza and arcaded Palazzo Comunale were designed by Arnolfo di
Cambio. The nearby church of **Santa
Maria della Grazia** (open Tues–Sat
10am–12.30pm, 4–7pm, Sun 4–
7pm; free) contains a *Virgin and
Child with the Four Saints* by Masaccio, who was born here in 1401. Just
outside the town, the Renaissance
monastery of Montecarlo houses an
Annunciation by Fra Angelico.

In prehistoric times the Arno basin
was one big lake, and farmers today

Val di Chiana and Its Cattle

The Val di Chiana is the most extensive valley in the Apennine
range. In prehistoric times, the area between Monte San Savino
and Cortona was submerged in water. It was drained by the Etruscans, but by the late Middle Ages the whole valley had become
a swamp, and for refuge from malaria, as well as from marauding,
hostile armies, the people took to the hills, barricading themselves
behind high defensive walls on precipitous outcrops of rock.

Today Val di Chiana is a prosperous, malaria-free zone of rich
farmland which is mainly used to rear one of Italy's two prized
breeds of cattle for meat – Chianina, which is native to Tuscany.
(The other is Razza Piemontese from Piedmont.) The Chianina
cow grows quickly to a large size, so that it is butchered when
the steer is a grown calf. The meat is firm and tasty, with a distinctive flavour. For any beef- loving Italian, *bistecca alla
Fiorentina* – a huge, tender Val di Chiana T-bone steak, grilled
over an open fire seasoned with nothing more than crushed
peppercorns, salt, and a hint of garlic and olive oil, served very
rare – is the ultimate steak.

frequently dig up fossil remains and bones of long extinct animals. At **Montevarchi** , south of San Giovanni Valdarno, is the **Accademia Valdarnese** (open Tues–Sat 9am–12.30pm, 4–6pm, Sun 10am–noon; entrance fee), an important museum of prehistory, which houses an impressive collection of fossilised remains from the Pliocene period discovered in this stretch of the Arno valley. Apart from the museum and the church, there is not much to detain the traveller here, though in the hills to the south of the town, above **Bucine** ⓮, there is a beautiful hexagonal font in the church of tiny **Galatrona**, covered with reliefs of the *Life of St John the Baptist*.

Unlike San Giovanni Valdarno, **Castelfranco di Sopra** ⓯, across the Arno (also fortified for the Florentines by Arnolfo di Cambio), retains its military character; the Porta Fiorentina gate is as forbidding as it ever was, and many of the 14th-century streets and buildings have survived.

About 10 km (6 miles) south of Castelfranco on the scenic Strada dei Sette Ponti (Road of the Seven Bridges) is **Loro Ciuffenna** ⓰, a medieval village positioned on a chasm cut by the Ciuffenna river. A couple of kilometres away is the rural Romanesque church of **Gropina**, dating from the early 13th century, noted for the carvings of animals, figures and geometrical patterns on the pulpit and columns. From here the picturesque route to **Talla**, where you'll find another ruined castle, crosses into the Casentino.

Val di Chiana

The broad flat valley south of Arezzo is known as the Val di Chiana, a fertile plain surrounded by hills and picturesque towns, where cattle are bred to supply the restaurants of Florence with the raw ingredient of *bistecca alla Fiorentina* (steak Florentine). **Monte San Savino** ⓱, on the edge of the Val di Chiana, has been a citadel since Etruscan times, although the fortifications that survive date from the Middle Ages. In 1325 the inhabitants were unable to fend off a ruthless Aretine mob who razed the town as

Colourful contemporary ceramics can be found in and around Cortona.

BELOW: Castiglion Fiorentino.

Church and square in Lucignano, famous for its unique concentric street plan.

punishment for their Guelf sympathies. It was subsequently rebuilt. Its once large Jewish community was wiped out – many were burned at the stake – for resisting the French army in 1799. Progress has hardly touched Monte San Savino; it retains medieval and Renaissance houses, of which the **Palazzo Comunale**, with a façade by Antonio da Sangallo the Elder and a fine **museum** (open Sat–Sun 9am–noon, 3–6pm, other days by appointment; tel: 0575-843098), is the most important.

Other important landmarks here include the **Loggia del Mercato** by Sansovino and the churches of Santa Chiara and Sant' Agostino.

The wild hills northwest of the town shelter a feudal retreat, the **Castello di Gargonza** ⓲. This 13th-century *borgo* or walled village, on the western slope of Monte Palazzuolo, dominates the Chiana valley and is the centre of a vast wooded estate producing oil and wine. The walled settlement has been converted into a hotel and restaurant complex (www.gargonza.it). The converted cottages, tiny cobbled streets, a

chapel, a baronial tower, attractive gardens and a magnificent view down to the Chiana all make Gargonza a very pleasant retreat.

South of Monte San Savino is **Lucignano** ⓳. Originally an Etruscan stronghold, the concentric arrangement of streets around a fortress make it unique among Tuscan hill towns. With a few exceptions Lucignano's buildings (13th–18th-century) are perfectly preserved, as is the Gothic church of San Francesco. The 14th-century **Palazzo Comunale** (open Tues–Sun 10am–12.30pm, 3.30–7pm, until 5.30pm in winter; entrance fee) contains frescoes from the Sienese and Aretine schools, as well as some examples of finely worked gold ornaments for which the province of Arezzo has long been famous, including the beautiful 14th-century *Tree of Lucignano*, richly embellished with jewels.

Fortified villages

Marciano della Chiana ⓴, 6 km (4 miles) northeast, another tiny village of great character, was also fortified in the Middle Ages. Much of the cas-

Maps
City: 246
Area: 248

tle remains intact, as do the walls and a gateway with a clock tower built into it. Three km (2 miles) to the southeast is the octagonal chapel of **Santa Vittoria**, designed by Ammannati to mark the spot where the Florentines defeated the Sienese in 1554.

Foiano della Chiana ㉑ clings prettily to the side of the hill. Much of it dates from the 15th–16th centuries, though traces of medieval defences can be seen around the edge of the town. At Cisternella, about 3 km (2 miles) to the northeast of the centre, are the remains of what is believed to have been a Roman bathhouse.

From here, looming large in the distance, is the fortified village of **Castiglion Fiorentino ㉒**, bounded by thick walls and dominated by the **Cassero Fortress** (open Tues–Sun 10am–12.30pm, 3.30–6pm; entrance fee). This well-preserved medieval settlement has an unusually high number of churches. The oldest of these, the Pieve Vecchia (the oldest church), has a Signorelli fresco of the *Deposition of Christ* (1451), and the 13th-century church of San Francesco contains a sculpted version.

Other sacred works and gold and silverware from the surrounding churches can be seen in the **Pinacoteca Comunale** (open Tues–Sun 10am–12.30pm, 4–6.30pm, until 7pm Sat–Sun; entrance fee). On the old market square are Vasari's famous **loggias**. The stone arches frame a fine vista of the rooftops and surrounding countryside.

Just outside the village is the fine octagonal temple of **Santa Maria della Consolazione**.

Cortona

Close to the Umbrian border, 30 km (18 miles) south of Arezzo, **Cortona ㉓** is one of the oldest and and most enchanting hill towns in Tuscany. It was founded by the Etruscans, who were among the first to appreciate its lofty heights. The Romans colonised it, the Aretines sacked it in 1258, and in 1409 it was sold to the Florentines, which linked it from then onwards to the fortunes of the Grand Duchy of Tuscany. By the 15th century, Cortona had become a major centre of power.

Cortona is perched majestically on a ridge of Monte Sant'Egidio, 650 metres (2130 ft) above the Val di Chiana. The road from the valley floor to the city winds its way through terraced olive groves and vineyards, past villas, farms, monasteries and churches surrounded with ilexes and cypresses. But Cortona's main attraction lies in the steepness of its crooked streets, linked by stone staircases, which work their way painfully to the Medici fortress at the top.

The town is entered from the relatively flat Piazza Garibaldi and Via Nazionale, which lead to Piazza Signorelli, with its 13th-century **Palazzo Comunale** (Town Hall) and the **Museo dell'Accademia Etrusca** (open daily 10am–7pm in summer, Tues–Sun until 5pm in winter; entrance fee). This rewarding museum has two star exhibits: the

Frances Mayes's books Bella Tuscany *and* Under the Tuscan Sun *(now a lavishly shot film) have elevated Cortona, site of her home, to celebrity status.*

BELOW: the lofty heights of Cortona.

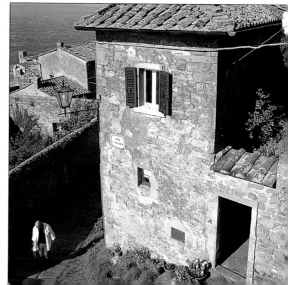

Maps
City: 246
Area: 248

One of a number of celebrated artists from Cortona, Luca Signorelli (1450–1523) produced frescoes for Orvieto Cathedral, and was summoned to the Vatican to complete frescoes in the Sistine Chapel. In a tiny courtyard below the Medici Fortress, the church of San Nicolò houses his wonderful standard of the Deposition.

BELOW: the domed church of Santa Maria della Grazia, below Cortona.

lovely fresco of *Polymnia*, generally considered to be a fine Roman painting of the Muse of Song until recent research proved it to be an 18th-century forgery; and a genuine Etruscan chandelier dating from 300 BC, consisting of 16 bronze oil lamps set around a wheel.

West of the piazza is the 16th-century Cathedral and its companion, the **Museo Diocesano** (open daily 10am–7pm in summer, Tues–Sun until 5pm in winter; entrance fee), which contains some rare masterpieces by Fra' Angelico, Lorenzetti and Luca Signorelli.

Returning to the town centre, it is worth seeking out Via Janelli for its row of brick buildings with overhanging upper storeys – some of Tuscany's oldest surviving medieval houses. Other picturesque streets to look out for include the Via Ghibellina and Via Guelfa.

It's a steep climb up to the **Basilica di Santa Margherita**, which contains the remains of Santa Margherita, the town's patron saint. She was a farmer's daughter who joined the Third Order of St Francis

and founded a convent and hospital. The citizens of Cortona still make pilgrimages up the winding stone-flagged streets to her tomb to offer her prayers during hard times.

The **Medici Fortress** above is overgrown and rarely open, but the views from up here are splendid, and it's a fine spot for a picnic.

Lake Trasimeno

One side of Cortona's public gardens opens to a belvedere with sweeping views. As you look south you will notice a glistening body of water. This is **Lago di Trasimeno**, Italy's fourth-largest lake, which lies in neighbouring Umbria. Its shallow waters are surprisingly clean and, in summer, full of swimmers, boaters and windsurfers. There was a day, though, in 217 BC when the lake waters ran red with the blood of the Roman legions, more than 16,000 of whom were slaughtered by Hannibal's troops. Today the scene is considerably more peaceful, especially on the southern shore, which is generally less crowded. A number of fine fish restaurants line the lake. ❑

RESTAURANTS

Arezzo

Antica Osteria L'Agania
Via Mazzini 10
Tel: 0575-295381
Very pleasant and hugely popular family-run trattoria serving good, homely Tuscan fare. Excellent value. Closed Mon, except June–Sept. €–€€

Buca di San Francesco
Via San Francesco 1
Tel/fax: 0575-23271
Fax: 0575-360588
www.bucadisanfrancesco.it
A famous cellar restaurant adjoining San Francesco church, with Trecento frescoes and a Roman-Etruscan pavement below. The lovely, medieval atmosphere is matched by straightforward, rustic, tasty cuisine. Closed Mon evening and Tues. €€

Il Cantuccio
Via Madonna del Prato 76
Tel/fax: 0575-26830
Vaulted basement restaurant run by the Volpi family who produce their own wine and olive oil. Try the *bistecca*, perhaps with deep-fried *porcini* mushrooms. Closed Wed. €€

Il Torrino
Strada dei Due Mari 1
Tel: 0575-360264
www.iltorrino.com
Eight km (5 miles) along the San Sepolcro road, this restaurant is worth seeking out for the good food and wonderful view. Truffles in season. Closed Mon. €€

La Lancia d'Oro
Piazza Grande 18/19
Tel: 0575-21033
Excellent Arezzo cuisine features here in this pleasing, central restaurant. In summer you can dine al fresco. Closed Sun evening, all day Mon and 5–25 Nov. €€–€€€

La Torre di Gnicche
Piaggia San Martino 8
Tel: 0575-352035
Just off the northern corner of the main square, this tiny little wine bar is an excellent choice for a cheap and simple meal – a hearty *ribollita*, or a platter of cheese – with a glass of wine from a long list of excellent selections. Popular with the antique dealing fraternity. Closed Wed. €

Cortona

Il Falconiere
Loc. San Martino 370
(4km/2½ miles north of Cortona)
Tel: 0575-612679
Fax: 0575-612616
www.ilfalconiere.it
In a lovely setting in the hills, this elegant hotel makes you feel as though time stands still. Good, imaginative cuisine includes both fish and meat dishes and service is excellent. Lovely panoramic terrace. Reserve in advance. €€€€

La Grotta
Piazzetta Baldelli 3
Tel: 0575-630271

A well-established family-run trattoria with local food and a warm welcome. Alfresco dining in summer. Popular with tourists. Closed Tues. €€

Osteria del Teatro
Via Maffei 2
Tel: 0575-630556
www.osteria-del-teatro.it
Simple, but delicious food, a fine location in a 15th-century *palazzo* and friendly service make this one of Cortona's nicest eateries. Closed Wed. €€–€€€

Lucignano

Osteria da Totò
Piazza del tribunale 6
Tel: 0575-836763
www.trattoriatoto.it
Run by well-known chef Lorenzo Totò, the cuisine takes its inspiration from traditional Italian cooking. Closed Tues. €–€€

Mercatale di Cortona

Mimmi
Tel: 0575-619029
www.tuscanydimimmi.it
A wonderful dining experience: arrive early to sit down to never-ending dishes of home made Tuscan cuisine, cooked in a wood fired oven. Vegetables from the kitchen garden and good local wines. €

PRICE CATEGORIES

Average cost of a three-course meal per person with a half-bottle of wine:
€ = under €25
€€ = €25–40
€€€ = €40–60
€€€€ = over €60

TRANSPORT

GETTING THERE AND GETTING AROUND

GETTING THERE

By Air

From the UK, low-cost airlines like Ryanair and Easyjet operate from many of Italy's smaller provincial airports, thus making travel between the UK and Italy easy as well as opening up Italian routes to greater competition. In addition to the national airline, Alitalia, many major scheduled airlines run direct flights to Italy, as well as charter flights which tend to offer lower fares and often fly to more convenient provincial airports than scheduled ones.

From the US, the main carriers are Alitalia, Delta and US Airways, which fly to Rome, Milan and Venice. European airlines such as British Airways and Air France also fly to Italy, with a stopover.

The country has two airports designed for intercontinental flights: **Roma Leonardo da Vinci** (known as Fiumicino) and **Milano Malpensa**.

Pisa's Galileo Galilei Airport is the usual airport for international visitors to Florence. Getting from Pisa to Florence is easy and cheap *(see page 259)*.

Florence's Peretola-Florence (also known as Amerigo Vespucci) is set 4 km (2 miles) northwest of the city centre. Some international flights land here, but these tend to be more expensive than flights to Pisa. Meridiana operates regular flights between Florence and the UK (www.meridiana.it).

Bologna Airport is a further alternative; it is conveniently located for Florence and Tuscany (there's a direct train to Florence and Arezzo).

By Rail

Rail travel is a slow and not particularly cheap option unless you are travelling as part of the Inter-Rail scheme (providing a month's unlimited rail travel in Europe for anyone under the age of 26 at a very reasonable price). When travelling from Great Britain via Paris (the usual route when travelling to Florence or Rome, for example), it is necessary to change in Paris (from Gare du Nord to Gare de Lyon).

ES (Eurostar), EC (EuroCity), IC (Inter City) and TEE (Trans Europe Express) trains are top-of-the-range trains running between the main Italian and European cities. A special supplement is charged and seat reservation is obligatory.

You can check routes on the official Italian railway website: www.trenitaliaplus.com.

In the UK, for information and train bookings, contact the Rail Europe call centre tel: 08705-848848; or visit the ticket office at 178 Piccadilly, London W1 open Mon–Fri 10am–6pm, Sat until 5pm; or log on to www.raileurope.co.uk.

Visitors from the US and Canada can also buy tickets and passes in advance through rail Europe. Visit www.raileurope.com or tel: 08708-302008. Another useful website is www.traintraveling.com

By Road

When calculating the cost of travelling to Italy by car, allow for the price of motorway tolls as well as accommodation en route and petrol. The quickest cross-Channel car ferries are from Dover to Calais. The Channel Tunnel transports cars on the train between Folkestone and Calais (Eurotunnel, tel: 08705-353535; www.eurotunnel.com). The usual route from France to Italy is via Paris and the Mont Blanc Tunnel (between Chamonix and Courmayeur) or from Switzerland through the Gran San Bernardo Tunnel (between Bourg St Pierre and Aosta). Some of the alpine passes are seasonal, so check the viability of your route with the tourist board or a motoring organisation before setting off.

To take your car into Italy, you will need your current driving licence, your vehicle registration document and insurance certificate. You are also required to carry a warning triangle in case of breakdown. Headlights should be illuminated at all times.Some petrol stations require payment in cash, not credit card. Keep cash handy for *autostrada* tolls too.

The AA and RAC in the UK give up-to-date advice on Channel crossings, with or without a car, and also driving on the continent.

In the US, the AAA provides information on travel in Italy.

By Coach

Travelling to Italy from the UK by coach is not much cheaper than going by air. National Express Eurolines runs coaches from London Victoria, via Paris and Mont Blanc, to Aosta, Turin, Genoa, Milan, Venice, Bologna, Florence and Rome. To book from London, contact: National Express, Victoria Coach Station, Buckingham Palace Road, London SW1, tel: 08705-5143219; www.nationalexpress.co.uk.

GETTING AROUND

On Arrival

Pisa Airport The international airport, Galileo Gallilei (tel: 050-849111) has its own railway station. Trains take five minutes into Pisa Centrale and one hour for the 80 km (50 miles) to Florence (www.trenitalia.com). Bus No. 5 also links the airport with Pisa Centrale rail station. There is a frequent coach service between the airport (departing from outside the Arrivals hall) and Florence's Santa Maria Novella train station (www.terravision.it). Car hire is available from the airport, and so are taxis. A toll-free *superstrada* links Pisa airport with Florence. **Peretola (Amerigo Vespucci) International Airport** (tel: 055-30615) in northwest Florence is connected by bus (Vola in Bus) to the SITA bus company depot not far from Santa

Maria Novella station; the journey time is about 20 minutes.

By Air

Alitalia offers a huge range of internal flights from both Florence and Pisa airports. These are supplemented by Meridiana's domestic services, which are usually a bit cheaper.

By Rail

For information 24 hours daily call 89 20 21 or visit www.trenitalia.it. The state-subsidised railway network is a relatively cheap and convenient form of transport for travelling between major cities in Tuscany. The principal Rome–Milan line is convenient for Bologna, Florence and Arezzo, while the Rome–Genoa line serves Pisa, Livorno and Grosseto. The Florence–Siena route is much faster by coach than by train.

Note that Pisa and Florence both have several train stations: **Pisa Centrale** station serves Pisa city while **Pisa Aeroporto** serves the airport. In Florence, **Santa Maria Novella** is the main station for the city, although the second station, **Rifredi**, is served by several *Eurostar* trains.

Categories of Trains

Eurocity: these trains link major Italian cities with other European cities – in Germany and Switzerland, for instance. A supplement is payable on top of the ordinary rail fare.
Eurostar Italia: these swish, high-speed trains have first- and second-class carriages; supplements payable on both.
Intercity: this fast service links major Italian cities. A supplement is payable; reservations required.
Interregionali: these inter-regional trains link cities within different regions (e.g. Tuscany and Umbria) and stop reasonably frequently.
Regionali: these regional trains link towns within the same region and stop at every station.

Tickets

Booking

Reservations are mandatory for superior trains (such as Eurostar and Eurocity) and tickets should be purchased in advance. Other tickets with compulsory supplements should be purchased at least three hours in advance. You must date-stamp *(convalidare)* your rail ticket before beginning the journey at one of the small machines at the head of the platforms. Failure to do so may result in a fine. If you board a train without a ticket, you can buy one from a conductor – for an extra 20 percent. You can also pay the conductor directly if you wish to upgrade to first class or a *couchette*.

Expect long lines for tickets at major stations, but, for a small fee, they can also be purchased from many travel agents. There are automatic ticket machines at major stations, although these are often out of order. Payment can be made either by cash or by credit card.

Wagons Lits/Carrozze Letto (sleeping cars) are found on long-distance trains within Italy, as well as on trains to France, Austria, Germany, and Switzerland. Reservations are essential.

Special Offers

There are a wide variety of train tickets and special offers available, which vary constantly and with the season. Some of the more established are:
The Trenitalia Pass: available for foreign visitors, it allows between 3 and 10 days unlimited travel on the Italian State Railway network, within a two-month period.
Group fares: groups of between 6 and 24 people can benefit from a 20 percent discount.
Youth fares: students aged between 12 and 26 can buy a yearly *Carta Verde* – "green card". This season ticket entitles them to a 10 percent discount on national trains and a 20 percent discount on international trips.
Children's fares: children under four travel free; children aged

between 4–12 are eligible for a 50 percent discount on all trains but must pay the full supplement for Intercity and Eurocity trains.

Pensioners' fares: the over-60s can buy a *Carta d'Argento*. Valid for a year, this "silver card" entitles them to a 20 percent discount on all train tickets.

Railway Stations

The main railway stations are open 24 hours a day and are integrated with road and sea transport. They provide numerous services, including telecommunications, left luggage, food and drink, tourist information and porters (luggage trolleys are hard to find).

Florence: The train information office at Santa Maria Novella station is next to the waiting room. The train reservation office is just inside the building (open daily 6am–10pm). There is a left luggage counter, where pieces of luggage are left at your own risk, and badly packed or awkwardly shaped packages are likely to be damaged by the uncooperative staff. There is an air terminal at Santa Maria Novella where you can check in for Pisa airport. There are bars and a pharmacy in the main hall, and shops and a supermarket on the lower level.

Siena: The railway station has an information office, counter for left luggage (and bicycles) and restaurant. Immediately outside the station is a bus ticket office and a tourist office. However, Siena's railway station is outside the town centre. More useful, and with faster services and a greater range of local destinations, is the coach service, with coaches leaving from Piazza San Domenico to Florence and various other Tuscan towns.

By Coach

Coaches are very comfortable and often quicker, though usually more expensive, than trains. Provincial bus companies include (websites in Italian only):

CPT, via A. Bellatalla 1, Ospedaletto Pisa; tel: 0508-84111 or free information line: 800-012773; www.cpt.pisa.it (for travel in Pisa Province).

CAP, Piazza Duomo 18, Prato; tel: 0574-6081; www.capautolinee.it (for travel in Tuscany and other parts of Italy).

Lazzi, Piazza Stazione 3r, Florence; tel: 055-215155; www.lazzi.it (for travel in Tuscany), and at Piazza V Emanuele II, Pisa; tel: 050-46288.

Rama, Via Topazio 12, Grosseto; tel: 0564-475111; www.griforama.it (for travel around Grosseto and Tuscany).

Sita, Via S. Caterina da Siena 15, Florence; tel: 800-001311; www.sita-on-line.it (for travel in Tuscany and Italy in general).

Tuscan Island Ferries

Numerous ferries ply the waters between the mainland and the islands of the Tuscan archipelago (Elba, Giglio, Capraia, Gorgona and Pianosa). Services from Piombino to Elba are regular throughout the day – every half hour in the summer – but during the peak months, especially August, you should book in advance. At other times you can turn up and buy your ticket direct from the harbour office. The journey time for the car ferry is just under an hour. Hydrofoil services for foot passengers only are less frequent but take around 35 minutes.

The biggest operator is **Toremar**, which connects Piombino to Portoferraio, Porto Azzurro, Rio Marina and Cavo. For information and bookings tel: 199 123 199, Portoferraio office tel: 0565-918080. For online bookings go to www.toremar.it or www.visitelba.com.

Moby Lines, the other main operator, runs a regular service between Piombino and Portoferraio. For information and bookings: tel: 199 30 30 40, Portoferraio office, tel: 0565-9361. Online bookings: www.mobylines.it.

Toremar also operates services from Livorno to Capraia and Gorgona, from Piombino to Pianosa, and from Santo Stefano on the Argentario peninsula to the island of Giglio.

Various boat companies, such as Acquavision, run day excursions and mini cruises to and between the Tuscan islands.

City Transport

Local Buses

Buses within each province are cheap and plentiful. Tickets can be bought at designated offices, tobacconist's, bars and newspaper stands. A set amount is payable for one journey, with each province setting its own fare level. Tickets are purchased in booklets or singly, and have to be stamped by a machine on the bus at the start of a journey. Failure to do so risks a fine payable either on the spot or within a month. All provincial bus services are routed past the railway station in every town.

In **Florence**, a range of tickets is available from the ATAF office (Piazza Stazione; tel: 800-424800): 60-minute; multiple (four singles); 3-hour; 24-hour; 3-day; 5-day; 7-day and monthly.

Rather confusingly for English-speakers, **Siena's** city/regional bus service is called TRA-IN.

Pisa province bus times are displayed on a board in Pisa's APT office on Piazza Garibaldi. Just outside Pisa Centrale Station, on the left, is a ticket window where bus tickets are sold.

Sightseeing Buses

Numerous sightseeing tours are offered in all the main cities. Florence: **City Sightseeing Italy** (Piazza Stazione 1; tel: 055-2645363; www.city-sightseeing.it) offer a tour to Fiesole and a tour to Piazzale Michelangelo, both with multi-lingual commentary. Tickets are valid for 24 hours, allowing you to hop on and off at numerous points around the city. Details of other tours are available locally.

Taxis

Taxis are plentiful in all towns and tourist resorts. They wait in special ranks at railway stations and main parts of the city but can always be called by telephone. If you call a taxi by phone, the cost of the journey begins then. (In Florence, tel: 4390 , 4242 or 4798 for Radio Taxi.) Meters display the fares: the fixed starting charge varies and extra charges are payable for night service, service on Sunday and public holidays, luggage and journeys outside the town area.

In Florence, there are taxi ranks in Via Pellicceria, Piazza di San Marco and Piazza Santa Trinità and outside Stazione di Santa Maria Novella.

Cycling and Mopeds

Mopeds and bicycles are the most efficient way to get around the narrow streets of Florence, Siena and Lucca. They can be hired in the main cities. Try to find one with good brakes and a stand. You may be asked to leave an identity card or passport as security. Below is a list of some outlets.

Florence: Florence by Bike, Via San Zanobi 91r; tel: 055-488992; www.florencebybike.it. Alinari, Via Guelfa 85r; tel: 055-280500; www.alinarirental.com.

Siena: Perozzi, Via del Romitorio 5 (near the Lizza park), tel: 0577-223157; www.perozzi.it. Amici della Bicicletta di Siena, Via Campansi 32, tel: 0577-45159; www.adbsiena.it.

Lucca: Barbetti, Via Anfiteatro 23; tel: 0583-954444; Cicli Bizzarri, Piazza S. Maria, 32; tel. 0583-496031.

Driving

To ease traffic congestion, many city centres are closed to most vehicles. Since cities like Florence, Montepulciano and Pistoia have introduced partial or complete city-centre driving bans (at least for non-residents), it makes sense to leave the car in the car parks on the edge of the historic centre.

State highways in Tuscany include the No. 1 "Aurelia", which runs north–south, to the west of Pisa. National motorways (autostrade): the A11, the "Firenze–mare", and the A12, the "Sestri Levante–Livorno". Both of these are toll roads. The two superstrade (Florence–Siena and the Florence–Pisa–Livorno) are toll-free.

Car Hire

The major rental companies (Hertz, Avis, Europcar, etc.) have representation in most cities and resorts. The smaller local firms offer cheaper rates but cars can only be booked on the spot. Booking in advance, often as part of a fly-drive package, is usually cheaper than hiring on arrival.

Rates normally allow unlimited mileage and include breakdown service. Basic insurance is included but additional cover is available at fixed rates. Most firms require a deposit and often take and hold a credit card payment until the return of the car. You will usually be asked to return the car with a full tank of petrol; do so, as if the rental company has to fill the tank, they charge a premium for the petrol.

Licences and Insurance

Licences: Drivers must have a driving licence issued by a nation with a reciprocal agreement with Italy. The pink EU licence does not need an Italian translation. All other licences do need a translation, obtainable (free) from motoring organisations and Italian tourist offices. It is a legal requirement in Italy that documents pertaining to the driver and the car are kept on one's person.

Insurance: if you are bringing your own vehicle, check that your insurance covers you in Italy. A Green Card, obtainable from your insurance company, is not obligatory within the EU and does not give any extra cover, but it is an internationally recognised document, which may be helpful if you have an accident.

Rules of the Road

Italy drives on the right. Road signs are international, with a few local differences:

Road signs: ALT is a stop line on the road for road junctions; STOP is for a pedestrian crossing.

Precedence: at crossroads, motorists must give precedence to vehicles on their right, except on recently built roundabouts, when those already on the roundabout have priority. If a motorist approaching a crossroads finds a precedence sign (a triangle with the point downwards) or a Stop sign, he/she must give precedence to all vehicles coming from both the right and left.

Parking: Outside cities and towns, parking on the right-hand side of the road is allowed, except on motorways, at crossroads, on curves and near hilly ground not having full visibility. To find a car park in an Italian town online, look on www.parcheggi.it; for Florence go to www.firenzeparcheggi.it. There is a "parcheggio scambiatore" in Viale Europa (south Florence) – drivers can park their cars here and get a bus, take a bike or take part in the car-sharing scheme to get into the centre. Illegally parked vehicles will be towed away, and you will have to pay a hefty fine.

Breakdowns and accidents: In case of a breakdown on an Italian road, dial 116 at the nearest telephone box. On motorways, telephones are 2 km (1 mile) apart, with special buttons to call for the police and medical assistance. Both have to be contacted if an accident involves an injury.

Motorway Tolls

Motorways tolls in Italy can be high. There is a charge on the A11 from Florence to Pisa and from Florence to Lucca. Access signs to the motorways, unlike those of other European countries, are in green, not blue. There is rarely a hard shoulder on Italian motorways, and often there are only two lanes. Accidents are frequent, so take extra care.

A CCOMMODATION

SOME THINGS TO CONSIDER BEFORE YOU BOOK THE ROOM

Choosing a Hotel

The quality and choice of accommodation in Tuscany is extremely varied. Visitors can choose between a city *palazzo*, grand country villa, or historic family-run hotel, a rented apartment or villa, a bucolic farm-stay holiday *(agriturismo)* or even, in the most popular cities, a private home stay. (This is not known as bed and breakfast since breakfast is not usually provided.)

Hotel rooms generally need to be booked well in advance in Florence and Siena. During local summer festivals, particularly the Sienese *Palio* and Arezzo's *Giostra*, rooms are very scarce. Attractive accommodation in the centre of Volterra and San Gimignano is popular, so early booking is advisable.

There is a huge variation in what you get for your money. A moderately priced hotel in Florence may be an adequate 3-star *pensione*, whereas the same money could buy you a luxurious 4-star room in a grand country house off the tourist track.

Generally speaking, "high season" in Tuscany is June or July to September. However, in towns, this does not necessarily include August. In Florence, for instance, many of the more expensive hotels reduce their prices during this month. It can sometimes pay to bargain.

Many hotels with restaurants insist on a half- or full-board arrangement, especially in the high season. This ploy is particularly prevalent on the islands (e.g. Elba), in seaside resorts (e.g. Forte dei Marmi), in spa resorts (e.g. Montecatini Terme and Chianciano Terme), and where accommodation is in short supply.

Hotel Listing

The hotel recommendations listed on pages 265–277 are grouped to correspond to the Places chapters. The towns and hotels within each section are listed alphabetically.

In the case of Florence and Siena, where so many hotels are available, the listing is subdivided into price categories. Other cities' hotels have price indicators at the end of their descriptions.

These refer to the cost of a standard double room for one night during high season, usually including breakfast; the ranges are as follows:

€ = below €100
€€ = €100–200
€€€ = €200–300
€€€€ = over €300

Private Home Stays

This is a fairly new development in Tuscany but is a good way of meeting the locals while paying modest prices. In Florence and Siena, the homes are carefully graded from simple to luxurious.

In Florence, contact AGAP (Associazione Gestori Alloggi Privati) at Via de' Neri 9, 50122 Florence, tel: 055-5051012. In Siena, request the Affittacamere (private lodgings) booklet of addresses from the tourist office (APT, Via di Città 43, Siena, tel: 0577-280551). The list includes private accommodation in the whole of Siena Province, including San Gimignano, Montalcino and the Sienese Chianti.

Agriturismo

Farm stays *(agriturismo)* are an excellent way of experiencing the Tuscan countryside while staying on a farm or a wine estate. Standards vary from simple, rustic accommodation at low prices to relatively luxurious surroundings, complete with swimming pool. Before booking, check the website if they have one or insist on a description or a photo, since many may be modern and fail to match up with the visitor's romantic image of Tuscany. Some farms, however, are genuine 16th-century wine and oil estates. There is usually the chance to buy local produce on site and meals are sometimes provided. For obvious reasons, you will normally need a car to make the most of a farm stay.

Reservations: during peak season, it is best to book in advance. Official accommodation tends to be booked for a minimum of one week, but individual arrangements for weekends and overnight stays are often possible, especially during mid- and low season.

Every local tourist authority produces farm-stay booklets. Or you can browse the following websites: www.agriturismo.com, www.agriturismo.net and www.agriturist.it (Italian only).

Rural Stays

These overlap with farm stays but can include country houses or even entire restored medieval villages (such as Sovicille, near Siena). In general, there is a working farm attached to the accommodation or at least the opportunity to sample or buy wine, oil and local products grown on the estate. As with farm stays, accommodation can be in simple rooms or self-contained apartments. The owners often use the profits from letting to reinvest in the restoration of the family estate or village. With rural stays, the emphasis is on country living in traditional buildings rather than in luxurious villa accommodation.

Many of the owners may speak basic English, French or German, but at least a smattering of Italian is appreciated. Always request detailed descriptions and directions.

Local tourist offices are a good source for recommendations (see pages 292–3). Extensive listings, supported by images, can also be found on www.agriturismo.com and www.agriturismo.net. The following are some typical examples of rural

stays, but are just a handful among countless options:

La Ripolina, Località Pieve di Piana, 53022 Buonconvento, Siena Province; tel/fax: 0577-282280; www.laripolina.it. Most of the holiday apartments are in converted farmhouses; one is in a fortified abbey with its 10th-century wall. Fresh farm produce available.

Green Farm, Località Albavola, Madonna dell'Acqua, Via Vecchia Pietrasantina 11, 56017 San Giuliano Terme, Pisa Province; tel: 050-890671/055-280539; www.pisaonline.it/GreenFarm. This traditional rural estate, in the Migliarino nature reserve near the Pisan coast, offers Tuscan dishes, organic farm produce, horse-riding, nature rambles, and sheep dog demonstrations.

San Savino, Val di Chio, Località Santa Lucia 89/a, 52043 Castiglion Fiorentino, Arezzo Province; tel/fax: 0575-651000; www.agriturismo-sansavino.it. This restored 11th-century monastery overlooks a lake, olive groves and woods and offers several apartments (plus pool and stables).

Villa Igea, Torre Alta, 55060 Ponte del Giglio, Lucca province; tel; 0583-353122; fax 0583-353235; www.villa-igea.biz. This charming traditional Tuscan villa and cottage is set among woodland and olive groves overlooking a valley. Home produced extra virgin olive oils and tastings.

La Parrina, km 146 Via Aurelia, Località Parrina, 58010 Albinia, Grosseto province; tel: 0564-862636; www.parrina.it. This long-established agricultural estate is set among vineyards, olive groves and orchards. The rooms and dining rooms are decorated with an unfussy elegance that makes you feel right at home. To prove you're on a working farm you may be woken early by the sound of tractors. Rooms and apartments; swimming pool, chapel, farm shop, restaurant and wine tasting, and bicycles.

Villa and Apartment Rentals

One of the most popular ways of visiting Tuscany is to stay in a rented villa or apartment. They do not come cheap, but you have the benefit of independence, and the freedom to cook for yourself using delicious fresh Tuscan produce. Prices vary enormously, depending on the season and the luxuriousness of the accommodation. The following agencies deal with rentals:

Hello Italy, tel: (0044) 0870-0272373/ 01483-419964; fax: 01483-414112; www.helloitaly.co.uk. A small company with a good selection of villas and houses, particularly recommended for the Lunigiana region.

At Home in Italy, tel: (212) 421-9165; fax: (212) 533-0095; www.athomeabroadinc.com. This US-based company sources quality hotels and apartments in Italy and around the world.

The Best in Italy, tel: (0039) 055-223064; fax: (0039) 055-2298912; www.thebestinitaly.com. A Florence-based lettings agency offering luxurious villas and palazzi with pools, tennis courts, stables, domestic staff and other such luxuries.

Caffelletto, tel: (0039) 02-3311814/3311820 fax: (0039) 02-3313009; www.caffelletto.it. This Milan-based company offers a selection of villas, castles, stylish country manors and city apartments, some on a bed and breakfast basis, others self-catering. They also produce an annual guide to Bed and Breakfasts in Italy (Italian Bed and Breakfasts, a Caffelletto guide, by Michele Ballarati, Margherita Piccolomini and Anne Marshall, pub. Rizzoli). The 2006 edition is also available in English.

Cottages to Castles, tel: (0044) 01622-775217; fax: (0044) 01622 775278; www.cottagestocastles.com. UK-based with agents in many countries.

Cuendet, tel: (0039) 0577-576330; fax: (0039) 0577-

TRANSPORT
ACCOMMODATION
ACTIVITIES
A – Z
LANGUAGE

301193; www.cuendet.com. Monterriggioni-based company with a good selection of Tuscan villas and apartments.
Invitation to Tuscany, tel: (0044) 020-8600 2522; fax (0044) 020-8600 2521; www.invitationto tuscany.com. UK-based but with agents in many countries.
Solemar, tel: (0044) 020-8891 1294; www.solemar.it. UK firm with a wide choice of castles, villas, farmhouses and apartments.

Castles and Monasteries

Accommodation is available in a variety of castles and palaces. Standards will vary from very simple to luxurious. A list of places can be obtained from the ENIT (Italian State Tourist Offices abroad, *see page 292*) or enquire at the local tourist office.

Many convents, monasteries and other religious institutions offer simple accommodation for tourists and pilgrims. Monte Oliveto Maggiore is just one example *(see page 217)*. Each provincial tourist office should be able to supply you with a full list for the area.

Youth Hostels

A list of youth hostels is available from ENIT (Italian National Tourist Offices, *see page 292*) and places can be booked through them or through local Tuscan tourist offices. Alternatively, contact the Associazione Italiana Alberghi per la Gioventù, Via Cavour 44, 00184 Rome, tel: 06-4871152, www.ostellionline.org. The main city youth hostels in Tuscany are:

Arezzo

Villa Severi, Via F. Redi 13; tel/fax: 0575-299047; www.peterpan.it

Cortona

San Marco, Via Maffei 57; tel/fax: 0575-601392; www.cortonahostel.com

Florence

Archi Rossi, Via Faenza 94r; tel: 055-290804; fax: 2302601; www.hostelarchirossi.com
Villa Camerata, Viale Augusto Righi 2–4; tel: 055-601451; fax: 055-610300
Santa Monaca Hostel, Via Santa Monaca 6; tel: 055-268338; fax: 055-280185; www.ostello.it
Sette Santi, Viale dei Mille 11 tel: 055-5048452; fax: 055-5057085; www.7santi.com
Youth Hostel Firenze 2000, Viale R. Sanzio 16; tel: 055-2335558; fax: 055-2306392

Lucca

Ostello "Il Sercio", Via del Brennero 673, Salicchi, tel: 0583-341811
Two km (1½ miles) north of Lucca, accessible on bus no. 6.

Pisa

Centro Turistico Madonna dell'Acqua, Via Pietrasanta 15; tel: 050-890622
Madonna dell'Acqua is a few kilometres out of town, so take bus no. 3 from the station.

Siena

Ostello della Gioventù "Guidoriccio", Via Fiorentina 89; tel: 0577-52212; fax: 0577-50277
Guidoriccio is appealing, but it lies 2 km (1 mile) outside the city: catch bus no. 10 or 15 from Piazza Matteotti and ask to be let off at Lo Stellino.

Camping

For a free list of campsites contact the Federazione Italiana Campeggiatore, Via Vittorio Emanuele II, 50041 Calenzano, Firenze; tel: 055-882391; fax 055-8825918; www.federcampeggio.it.

Florence

Michelangelo, Viale Michelangelo 80, tel: 055-6811977; fax: 055-689348
Open Apr–Oct, crowded in high season. No. 13 bus from station. Good facilities; 320 pitches.

Camping Panoramico, Via Peramonda 1, Fiesole; tel: 055-599069; fax: 055-59186; www.florencecamping.com
Terraced site in Fiesole, outside Florence. Open all year.
Ostello Via Camerata, Viale Augusto Righi 2–4; tel: 055-601451; fax: 055-610300
Next door to the hostel is a campsite, Villa Camerata, which is also open all year round. No. 17B bus from station.

Pisa

Campeggio Torre Pendente, Viale delle Cascine 86; tel: 050-561704; fax: 050-561734
Open mid-Mar–Sep. No. 5 bus from the station.
Camping Internazionale, Via Litorenea 7, Marina di Pisa; tel: 050-35211
Facilities include a private beach, bar and pizzeria.

Siena

Campeggio "Siena Colleverde", Strada di Scacciapensieri 47; tel: 0577-280044; fax: 0577-333298
Open end Mar–end Oct. Two km (1 mile) from the city; no. 8 bus.

There are also companies which organise camping holidays in Tuscany. In the UK these include:
Eurocamp Travel, Hartford Manor, Greenbank Lane, Northwich, Cheshire CW8 1HW, tel: 0870-9019 410; www.eurocamp.co.uk.
Keycamp, Hartford Manor, Greenbank Lane, Northwich, Cheshire CW8 1HW, tel: 0870-7000740; www.keycamp.co.uk.

Caravan and Camper Hire

In Tuscany, this is available from **Caravanmec**, Via Cupola 281, Peretola, Florence, tel: 055-315101; www.caravanmec.it, although there are other companies too.

ACCOMMODATION LISTINGS

FLORENCE

Deluxe (€€€€)

Grand Hotel
Piazza Ognissanti 1
Tel: 055-288781
Fax: 055-217400
www.westin.com
Smaller than its sister hotel (the Excelsior, across the square) but almost as grand. Recently refurbished.
Grand Hotel Villa Cora
Viale Machiavelli 18
Tel: 055-2298451
Fax: 055-229086
www.villacora.it
Quiet, elegant hotel in a huge park on a hill above Florence. Free limo service; pool.
Helvetia & Bristol
Via dei Pescioni 2
Tel: 055-26651
Fax: 055-288353
www.royaldemeure.com
Possibly the best of the luxury small hotels in the city, with many illustrious names numbered among its guests. Supremely comfortable rooms and suites; excellent restaurant. Delightful winter garden.
Kraft
Via Solferino 2
Tel: 055-284273
Fax: 055-2398267
www.krafthotel.it
Ideally placed for music lovers, a stone's throw from the opera house, and performers often stay here. It has the only rooftop pool in the city.
Plaza Hotel Lucchesi
Lungarno d. Zecca Vecchia 38
Tel: 055-26236
Fax: 055-2480921
www.plazalucchesi.it

Comfortable and very efficiently run hotel overlooking the river Arno, a little east of the Ponte Vecchio.
Regency
Piazza d'Azeglio 3
Tel: 055-245247
Fax: 055-2346735
www.regency-hotel.com
Five-star luxury in a small hotel situated in a quiet, leafy square, a short walk from the sights. Cool, shady garden. Good restaurant.
Savoy
Piazza della Repubblica 7
Tel: 055-27351
Fax: 055-2735888
www.hotelsavoy.it
Beautiful and elegant 5-star hotel in the heart of the city, close to the Duomo and main museums, galleries and fashion houses. A flagship of the Rocco Forte Hotels brand.
Torre di Bellosguardo
Via Roti Michelozzi 2
Tel: 055-2298145
Fax: 055-229008
www.torrebellosguardo.com
Bellosguardo ("beautiful view"), the hill on which this Renaissance villa was built, is only 15 minutes' walk up from Porta Romana, but a world away. Superb gardens; pool; frescoed reception rooms.
Villa la Vedetta
Viale Michelangiolo 78
Tel: 055-681631
Fax: 055-6582544
www.villalavedettahotel.com
Deluxe hotel in a panoramic position near Piazzale Michelangelo.

Rooms are elegant and well-equipped; Michelin-starred restaurant.
Villa Medici
Via Il Prato 42
Tel: 055-277171
Fax: 055-2381336
www.villamedicihotel.com
Convenient hotel near the train station with a pool, gym, gardens and large airy bedrooms.
Westin Excelsior
Piazza Ognissanti 3
Tel: 055-264201
Fax: 055-210278
www.westin.com
The grandest hotel in Florence – a lavishly furnished 19th-century building on the banks of the Arno. You can look forward to sumptuous bedrooms, many with grand marble bathrooms, and there is a panoramic rooftop restaurant.

Expensive (€€€)

Astoria
Via del Giglio 9
Tel: 055-2398095
Fax: 055-214632
www.boscolohotels.com
Completely refurbished hotel near the station, with grand dimensions and elaborate decor.
Beacci Tornabuoni
Via de' Tornabuoni 3
Tel: 055-212645
Fax: 055-283594
www.bthotel.it
Deluxe guest house, comfortable and very welcoming, although some rooms are on the small side. Flower-filled rooftop terrace for break-

fast and drinks. Half-board terms compulsory. Particularly popular with Americans.
Botticelli
Via Taddea 8
Tel: 055-290905
Fax: 055-294322
www.hotelbotticelli.it
Fairly new hotel close to the central market. It is both comfortable and appealing, with all the mod cons you could want but also well preserved 16th-century features, including frescoes.
Grand Hotel Baglioni
Piazza dell' Unità Italiana 6
Tel: 055-23580
Fax: 055-2358895
www.hotelbaglioni.it
Classic hotel retaining its air of discreet elegance while providing extremely comfortable rooms. Popular with the business community.

PRICE CATEGORIES

These refer to the cost of a standard double room during high season, usually including breakfast.
€ = under €100
€€ = €100–200
€€€ = €200–300
€€€€ = more than €300

Hermitage
Vic. Marzio 1, Piazza del Pesce
Tel: 055-287216
Fax: 055-212208
www.hermitagehotel.com
Delightful hotel behind
the Ponte Vecchio. Per-
sonal attention from
staff. Lovely roof garden
views.

J&J
Via di Mezzo 20
Tel: 055-26312
Fax: 055-240282
The setting of this small
hotel – in a modest
street near Santa Croce
– belies the luxury
within. All 19 rooms and
suites are highly individual, romantic and chic.
Lovely old cloister for
summer breakfasts.

Loggiato dei Serviti
Piazza della SS Annunziata 3
Tel: 055-289592
Fax: 055-289595
www.loggiatodeiservitihotel.it
Atmospheric hotel facing
the Innocenti hospital
across a traffic-free
piazza. Sangallo's 16th-
century *palazzo* houses
29 rooms and suites, all
tastefully furnished. One
of the city's best-loved
and most refined hotels.
No garden.

**Marignolle Relais &
Charme**
Via di San Quiricino 16
Tel: 055-2286910
Fax: 055-2047396
marignolle.hotel-firenze.net
A few minutes to the
south of Florence, this
charming hotel with pool
is comfortable and
handy for exploring the
surrounding area.

Monna Lisa
Borgo Pinti 27
Tel: 055-2479751
Fax: 055-2479755
www.monnalisa.it
This Renaissance
palazzo, furnished with
antiques, drawings and
sculpture, is a popular

choice. There is a
delightful garden and
private parking.

Morandi alla Crocetta
Via Laura 50
Tel: 055-2344747
Fax: 055-2480954
www.hotelmorandi.it
Tiny *pensione* tucked
away in a backstreet
near the university,
housed in a former con-
vent. Antiques, parquet
flooring and colourful
rugs; 10 bedrooms, two
with private terraces.
Book well in advance.

Porta Faenza
Via Faenza 77
Tel: 055-214287
Fax: 055-210101
www.hotelportafaenza.it
Comfortable, family-run
hotel, with all mod cons,
near the central market.
Private garage (rare in
this part of town).

Moderate (€€)

Alessandra
Borgo SS Apostoli 17
Tel: 055-283438
Fax: 055-210619
www.hotelalessandra.com
An old-fashioned, simple
pensione conveniently
situated near the Ponte
Vecchio. Many of the 25
spacious rooms are fur-
nished with antiques.

Annalena
Via Romana 34
Tel: 055-222402
Fax: 055-222403
www.hotelannalena.it
A discreet *pensione* in a
15th-century *palazzo*,
opposite the rear
entrance to the Boboli
Gardens. Some rooms
have balconies looking
onto the horticultural
centre.

Aprile
Via della Scala 6
Tel: 055-216237
Fax: 055-280947
www.hotelaprile.it

Much more appealing
than most hotels near
the station, this is an ex-
Medici palace complete
with frescoes, a pleas-
ant breakfast room and
garden. Rooms range
from simple to reason-
ably grand.

Casci
Via Cavour 13
Tel: 055-211686
Fax: 055-2396461
www.hotelcasci.com
Frescoed *quattrocento*
palazzo, family-run and
enjoying a welcoming
atmosphere. Five min-
utes' walk north of the
Duomo.

Classic Hotel
Viale Machiavelli 25
Tel: 055-229351
Fax: 055-229353
www.classichotel.it
Elegant, pinkwashed
villa with lovely rooms, a
conservatory and pretty
gardens, situated just
above the Porta
Romana. Excellent
value.

Fiorino
Via Osteria del Guanto 6
Tel: 055-210579
Fax: 055-268929
www.hotelfiorino.it
Located in the centre of
the city, this unpreten-
tious hotel has a pleas-
ant family atmosphere.

Firenze
Piazza dei Donati 4
Tel: 055-268301
Fax: 055-212370
www.albergofirenze.net
Refurbished *pensione*
with modern, if unexcit-
ing, rooms, all with
baths and TV. Just off
the central Via del
Corso. Good value for
money; at the lower end
of the price bracket.

Giada
Canto de'Nelli 2
Tel: 055-215317
Fax: 055-268615
www.hotelgiada.it

Friendly *pensione* near
San Lorenzo market.
Some rooms overlook
the Medici Chapels.

Liana
Via Alfieri 18
Tel: 055-245303
Fax: 055-2344596
www.hotelliana.com
Simple hotel some way
north of centre in the former British Embassy.
Quiet, pleasant, but
slightly faded. Rooms
vary from simple to ele-
gant. Fresh flowers and
private car park.

Mario's
Via Faenza 89
Tel: 055-216801
Fax: 055-212039
www.hotelmarios.com
One of the most attrac-
tive of the many *pensioni*
in Via Faenza, behind
the central market. Dec-
orated in rustic Tuscan
style, with comfortable
bedrooms (quieter at the
rear). Friendly.

Orto de'Medici
Via San Gallo 30
Tel: 055-483427
Fax: 055-461276
www.ortodeimedici.it
Attractive little neo-
classical *palazzo* near
Piazza San Marco, with
grand public rooms. Sim-
pler bedrooms, most
with private baths; lovely
breakfast room leading
onto a terrace.

Palazzo Benci
Piazza Madonna degli
Aldobrandini 3
Tel: 055-213848
Fax: 055-288308
www.palazzobenci.com
Patrician *palazzo*, tradi-
tionally the seat of the
Benci family, recently
restored but retaining
original features.

Pensione Bretagna
Lungarno Corsini 6
Tel: 055-289618
Fax: 055-289619
www.bretagna.it

Suitably, this is a favourite with British business travellers. Drops a price bracket in low season.

Silla
Via de'Renai 5
Tel: 055-2342888
Fax: 055-2341437
www.hotelsilla.it
An elegant arched courtyard leads to this first-floor hotel in a quiet, relatively leafy area south of and overlooking the Arno.

Torre Guelfa
Borgo SS Apostoli 8
Tel: 055-2396338
Fax: 055-2398577
www.hoteltorreguelfa.com
Elegant, recently refurbished hotel with a grand "salon", pastel-shaded bedrooms, a sunny breakfast room

and the tallest privately owned tower in the city.

Villa Azalee
Viale Fratelli Rosselli 44
Tel: 055-214242
Fax: 055-268264
www.villa-azalee.it
Pleasant, 19th-century villa near the station, with the feel of a private house, set in a garden full of azaleas and camelias. Private garage; bicycles for hire.

Villa Belvedere
Via Benedetto Castelli 3
Tel: 055-222501
Fax: 055-223163
www.villabelvedere.com
Exceptionally friendly and modern hotel; south of the city. Sunny rooms, a pretty garden and lovely views across Florence. Amenities include pool and tennis court.

Inexpensive (€)

Pensione Sorelle Bandini
Piazza Santo Spirito 9
Tel: 055-215308
Fax: 055-282761
Extremely popular, if rather shabby and eccentric, *pensione* with huge rooms; those overlooking the lively piazza are noisy. Great rooftop terrace. No credit cards.

Residenza Johanna 1
Via Bonifacio Lupi 14
Tel: 055-481896
Fax: 055-482721
www.johanna.it
Excellent-value residence (even though there are few mod cons and breakfasts are do-it-yourself) in an unmarked building in a quiet street near Piazza Libertà.

Residenze Johlea 1 & Johlea II
Via San Gallo 80/76
Tel: 055-4633293 & 055-461185
Fax: 055-4634552 & 055-461185
www.johanna.it
These two residences are set in a nice area around San Marco. They retain an authentic feel, but are equipped with more modern conveniences than their sister residence (above).

Soggiorno Bavaria
Borgo degli Albizi 26
Tel/fax: 055-2340313
www.hotelbavariafirenze.it
Hotel right by the Duomo, with 16th-century original wood-beamed ceilings in the lobby and breakfast rooms.

AROUND FLORENCE

Artimino
Paggeria Medicea
Viale Papa Giovanni XXIII 1
Tel: 055-875141
Fax: 055-8751470
www.artimino.com
Grand hotel in the former stables of a restored Medici villa, nestling between olive groves and vineyards near Carmignano, 24 km (15 miles) west of Florence. Hunting and fishing on site. Very good restaurant. €€€

Candeli
Villa La Massa
Via La Massa 24
Tel: 055-62611
Fax: 055-633102
www.villalamassa.com
Some 7 km (4 miles) north of Florence, this cluster of beautifully converted 17th-century villas radiates elegance.

Riverside restaurant; swimming and tennis. €€€€

Fiesole
Pensione Bencistà
Via Benedetto da Maiano 4
Tel/fax: 055-59163
www.bencista.com
Delightful 14th-century villa, decorated with antiques and rustic furnishings. Reliable restaurant; half-board is compulsory. Flower-decked terrace with panoramic views over Florence. €€–€€€

Villa Fiesole
Via Beato Angelico 35
Tel: 055-597252
Fax: 055-599133
www.villafiesole.it
Comfortable but chic hotel with frescoes, panoramic views and pool. Full wheelchair access. €€

Villa San Michele
Via Doccia 4
Tel: 055-5945112
Fax: 055-598734
www.villasanmichele.com
One of the finest and most expensive hotels in Tuscany. Supposedly designed by Michelangelo, this former Franciscan monastery enjoys harmonious lines and heavenly views of the city, particularly from the loggia and restaurant. Spacious grounds; pool; piano bar. The plush suites have jacuzzis. €€€€

Galluzzo
La Fattoressa
Via Volterrana 58
Tel: 055-2048418
Fax: 055-2840418
Old farmhouse converted into simple but

comfortable accommodation. Just southwest of Florence and very conveniently situated for the *autostrada*. €€

PRICE CATEGORIES
These refer to the cost of a standard double room during high season, usually including breakfast.
€ = under €100
€€ = €100–200
€€€ = €200–300
€€€€ = more than €300

Relais Certosa
Via Colle Romole 2
Tel: 055-2047171
Fax: 055-268575
www.florencehotelcertosa.it
Former hunting lodge
(once attached to the
14th-century Carthu-
sian monastery) near
Florence, now a wel-
coming residence, with
spacious grounds and
views of the medieval
charterhouse. Tennis
courts and swimming
pool. €€€

Impruneta

Villa Cesi
Via delle Terre Bianche
Tel: 055-231101
Fax: 055-2011377
www.villacesi.it
A stone's throw from
Impruneta's main
square, the 28 rooms of
this modern hotel profit
from a restaurant and
swimming pool. There
are prettier towns to
spend a night in but this
is a decent place to
stay if you're in the area
and needing a bed. €€

Molino del Piano

Hotel il Trebbiolo
Via del Trebbiolo 8
Località Olmo
Tel: 055-8300583
Fax: 055-8300098
www.iltrebbiolo.it
Delightful 3-star hotel
14 km (9 miles) from
Florence. The villa is set
amid olive groves, with
cosy little rooms and an
annexe with cooking
facilities. The hotel
restaurant offers solid
Tuscan cuisine. €€

Poggio a Caiano

Hotel Hermitage
Via Ginepraia 112
Tel: 055-877040
Fax: 055-8797057
www.hotelhermitageprato.it
Nice, if business-like
hotel set on a hill, close
to the Medici Villa;
handy for exploring the
surrounding area. Mem-
bers receive discount at
the Le Pavoniere golf
course near Prato.
Restaurant; swimming
pool in summer. Good
value. €

Prato

Villa Rucellai
Via di Canneto 16
Tel: 0574-460392
www.villarucellai.it
This mellow, medieval
villa northeast of the
town is an oasis in
Prato's industrial land-
scape. An informal but
elegant bed and break-
fast establishment with
a family house atmos-
phere. Swimming pool,
chapel and garden. Very
good value for money.
€€

Sesto Fiorentino

Villa Villoresi
Via Campi 2, Colonnata di
Sesto Fiorentino
Tel: 055-443212
Fax: 055-442063
www.villavilloresi.it
Gracious villa, a world
away from the ugly
industrial suburb of
Sesto which surrounds
it. Complete with chan-
deliers and frescoes,
plus the longest loggia
in Tuscany. Restaurant
and pool. €€

Trespiano

Villa Le Rondini
Via Bolognese Vecchia 224
Tel: 055-400081
Fax: 055-268212
www.villalerondini.it
Secluded villa in a won-
derful setting, overlook-
ing the Arno valley just
4 km (2 miles) from Flo-
rence. Lovely views over
the city from the swim-
ming pool, set in an
olive grove. Restaurant.
Bus link to the city. €€€

Vicchio

Villa Campestri
Via di Campestri 19
Tel: 055-8490107
Fax: 055-8490108
www.villacampestri.it
Imposing Renaissance
villa in a wonderful, rural
setting in the Mugello,
35 km (25 miles) north
of Florence. Impressive
public rooms, excellent
food and a relaxed
atmosphere. Bedrooms
in the main villa are
quite grand; those in the
annexe less so. Pool,
horse riding. €€–€€€

PISTOIA PROVINCE

Abetone

Bellavista
Via Brennero 383
Tel: 0573-60028
Fax: 0573-60245
www.bellavista-abetone.it
Typical wood and stone
mountain building with
panoramic views, close
to the centre and ski
lifts. Comfortable and
spacious rooms. Sea-
sonal opening. €
Regina
Via Uccelliera 5
Tel: 0573-60257
Fax: 0573-60007
Pleasant 19th-century
villa within an attractive
setting. 3-star. €–€€

Monsummano Terme

Grotta Giusti Spa Hotel
Via Grotta Giusti 1411
Tel: 0572-90771
Fax: 0572-9077200
www.grottagiustispa.com
Handsome villa in park-
land with its own ther-
mal spring, natural
caves and excellent spa
facilities. Also has a
swimming pool and golf
course. Open 1 Mar–30
Nov. Half-board. €€€€
La Speranza
Via Grotta Giusti 162
Tel: 0572-51313
Basic *pensione* with
well-maintained garden.

Good option if you're
passing through and all
you want is a bed for
the night.

Montecatini Alto

Casa Albertina e Mario
Via Fratelli Guermani,12
Tel: 0572-900238
Fax: 0572-904298
www.casaalbertina.it
Charming 13th-century
villa in the medieval
walled village. The indi-
vidually designed rooms
are cosy, and some
have balconies. Excel-
lent breakfast served in
the little garden sur-
rounded by orange and

lemon trees with great
views over Montecatini
Terme. €€

Montecatini Terme

Florio
Via Montebello 41
Tel: 0572-78343

Fax: 0572-910269
Montecatini Terme is overrun with hotels. This one with its own garden is a good moderately priced option. €

Grand Hotel Plaza e Locanda Maggiore
Piazza del Popolo 7
Tel: 0572-75831
Fax: 0572-767985
www.hotelplaza.it
Flashy 4-star hotel with good facilities including a pool. €€–€€€

Torretta
Viale Bustichini 63
Tel: 0572-70305
Fax: 0572-70307
www.hoteltorretta.it

A modern, family-run hotel with a pool; special diets catered for. €

Pescia

Azienda Agricola Marzalla
Via Collecchio 1
Tel: 0572-490751
Fax: 0572-478332
Unpretentious, family-run *agriturismo* in the hills. With a pool, and a pleasant *trattoria* nearby. Weekly basis only in high season.

Pistoia

Il Convento
Via San Quirico 33

Tel: 0573-452651/2
Fax: 0573-453578
www.ilconventohotel.com
Tranquil hotel, formerly a Franciscan monastery. The dining room was once the monks' refectory and the bedrooms their cells; some have a terrace. Breakfast is served in the cloister in fine weather. Includes a lovely garden, swimming pool, good restaurant and chapel. Five km (3 miles) from town. €€

Hotel Patria
Via Crispi 8
Tel: 0573-25187

Fax: 0573-368168
www.patriahotel.com
Welcoming small hotel in the city's historic centre. Parking permits available. €

Villa Vannini
Villa di Pitecchio
Tel: 0573-42031
Fax: 0573-42551
www.villavannini.it
Delightful villa some 6 km (4 miles) north of Pistoia, with the atmosphere of a private house. Elegant and comfortable bedrooms; fine food; wonderful walks in the woods. Good value. €–€€

LUCCA AND THE VERSILIA

Lucca

Alla Corte degli Angeli
Via Degli Angeli 23
Tel: 0583-469204
Fax: 0583-991989
www.allacortedegliangeli.com
A sister hotel to the San Martino *(see below)*, this delightful tiny hotel is also within the city walls, close to the Piazza dell'Anfiteatro. Each of the six rooms has a flower theme and provides splendid views over the city roofs. €€€

Antico Casale Toscano
Località Piaggia 10
Tel: 340-3600646
Fax: 0583-228224
www.anticocasaletoscano.com
This charming typical Tuscan farmhouse is set in the hills above Lucca among olive groves in a working farm. Rooms are available on a nightly basis from Nov–March and on a weekly basis Apr– Oct. Teresa organises special free cookery evenings including tast-

ings of her own extra virgin olive oil during the summer. €

Diana
Via del Molinetto 11
Tel: 0583-492202
Fax: 0583-467795
www.albergodiana.com
Centrally located hotel off Piazza San Martino; a pleasant budget option. €

San Martino
Via della Dogana 7
Tel: 0583-469181
Fax: 0583-991940
www.albergosanmartino.it
Warm, welcoming little hotel in a quiet location, within the city walls, a stone's throw from the Duomo. Nearby private carparking organised by the hotel. Excellent value. €€

Hotel Carignano
Via per Sant'Alessio,
3680 Carignano
(5 km/3 miles outside Lucca)
Tel: 0583 329618
Fax: 0583 329848
www.hotelcarignano.it
This family-run hotel is

set in a quiet, hilly location outside Lucca, within easy reach of the sea and mountains. Rooms are large and bright. €–€€

Hotel Ilaria e Residenza dell'Alba
Via del Fosso 26
Tel: 0583-47615
Fax: 0583-991961
www.CharmeRelax.com
Ideally located in the historic centre and set in splendid grounds, this very stylish hotel is dedicated to comfort and good service. The annexe, Residenza dell'Alba, is located in the former medieval church of the Annunziata. Large bedrooms offer every modern amenity coupled with a historic interior. €€€

La Luna
Via Fillungo Corte
Compagni 12
Tel: 0583-493634
Fax: 0583-490021
www.hotellaluna.com
Family-run hotel in the

historic centre just steps away from the Piazza dell'Anfiteatro. €€

La Romea (B&B)
Vicolo delle Ventaglie 2 (corner of Via S. Andrea)
Tel: 0583-464175
Fax: 0583-471280
www.laromea.com
Small, very pleasing establishment on the

PRICE CATEGORIES

These refer to the cost of a standard double room during high season, usually including breakfast.

€ = under €100
€€ = €100–200
€€€ = €200–300
€€€€ = more than €300

first floor of a medieval *palazzo* in the historic centre. The two young hosts Giulio and Gaia are most helpful. Five rooms all with private bathrooms and air-conditioning. **€€**

Piccolo Hotel Puccini
Via di Poggio 9
Tel: 0583-55421
Fax: 0583-53487
www.hotelpuccini.com
A small and very popular hotel just around the corner from Puccini's birthplace, crammed with mementos of the maestro. Excellent value. **€€**

Stipino
Via Romana 95
Tel: 0583-495077
Fax: 0583-490309
www.hotelstipino.com
Simply decorated,

2-star hotel graced with a personal touch. **€**

Villa La Principessa
Via Nuova per Pisa 1616,
Massa Pisana
Tel: 0583-370037
Fax: 0583-379136
www.hotelprincipessa.com
Gracious villa near Lucca with bright blue and white paintwork, now a luxury hotel. Precious antiques and expensive fabrics abound. Restaurant in a 19th-century conservatory. Swimming pool. **€€€–€€€€**

Villa Rinascimento
Loc. Santa Maria del Giudice
Tel: 0583-378292
Fax: 0583-370238
www.villarinascimento.it
Rustic villa with a lovely garden and pool, on a hillside 9 km

(5 miles) west of Lucca. **€€–€€€**

Torre del Lago

Butterfly
Belvedere Puccini 24/26
Tel: 0584-341024
Fax: 0584-352006
A restaurant with rooms on the central piazza, overlooking the Lake and very close to the theatre. **€**

Viareggio

London
Viale Manin16
Tel: 0584-49841
Fax: 0584-47522
Very pleasant family-run hotel in a former Liberty-style *palazzo*. Good sized public rooms and 33 very comfortable bed-rooms. **€€**

Locanda le Monache
Piazza XXIX Maggio 36
Camaiore (10 km/6 miles from Viareggio)
Tel: 0584-989258
Fax: 0584-984011
www.lemonache.com
A traditional Tuscan restaurant with 15 rooms housed in a former monastery. The rooms are of a good size, albeit simply furnished. **€–€€**

Plaza e de Russie
Piazza d'Azeglio 1
Tel: 0584-44449
Fax: 0584-44031
www.plazaederussie.com
Liberty-style hotel, one of the most luxurious in this seaside resort. Beautiful rooms and lovely view from the elegant roof restaurant. **€€–€€€**

GARFAGNANA AND LUNIGIANA

Bagni di Lucca

Azienda Agriturismo La Torre
La Torre, Fornoli
Tel: 0583-805297
www.latorreagriturismo.com
Set among olive and chestnut groves, this delightful farmhouse can accommodate up to 15 people in six apartments. Simply furnished in traditional Tuscan style with lovely views over the rolling countryside. Good home cooking and swimming pool. **€–€€**

Barga

Alpino
Via G. Pascoli 1
Tel: 0583-723336
Fax: 0583-723792
This 3-star hotel in the lower, busier half of town has been offering a warm welcome for

over 100 years. The seven rooms and two suites have all been recently refurbished. Restaurant. **€€**

Castelnuovo di Garfagnana

La Lanterna
(1km/half a mile east at Monache-Piano Pieve)
Tel: 0583-639364
Fax: 0583-641418
www.hotellalanterna.com
Set in a peaceful, green location, with 22 plain but comfortable rooms and a large restaurant. A good base for exploring the Garfagnana. **€**

Fivizzano

L'Albergo Ristorante Pieve San Paolo
Località Pieve San Paolo
Tel: 0585-949800
Fax: 0585-949800

A small, family-run *albergo* in the heart of magnificent mountain scenery. Very welcoming. **€–€€**

Hotel Terme
Via Noce Verde (Equi Terme)
Tel: 0585-97830
Fax: 0585-97831
A 3-star hotel set in the beautiful Parco Naturale delle Alpi Apuane. There are 60 bedrooms and two swimming pools with spa treatments. **€–€€**

Il Giardinetto
Via Roma 151
Tel: 0585-92060
Rather eccentric hotel, full of character and characters. Traditional Tuscan food. **€**

Licciana Nardi

Del Pino
Via Bastia 37, Lunigiana
Tel: 0187-475041

Quiet, comfortable modern *pensione* in a mountain village, surrounded by pines. **€**

Pontremoli

Hotel Napoleon
Piazza Italia, 2bis
Tel: 0187-830544
Fax: 0187-831592
www.hotelnapoleon.net
Set in the heart of Pontremoli, this family-run hotel has lovely views of the Apennines. Elegant restaurant. **€–€€**

PISA AND ENVIRONS

Cascina Sant'Anna

Hotel Villa Guelfi
Via Tosco Romagnola 1301
Località Santa Anna Cascina
Tel: 050-775268
Fax: 050-760888
www.pisaonline.it/hotelvillaguelfi
Villa built in typical
Pisan 19th-century
style. Just 8 km (5
miles) outside Pisa and
convenient for the
Pisa–Florence motor-
way. €€

Marina di Pisa

Albergo Manzi
Via Repubblica Pisana 25
Tel: 050-36626
Fax: 050-34159
www.hotelmanzi.it
Reasonable 3-star hotel
on the seafront. €

Massa Pisana

Villa La Principessa
Via Nuova per Pisa, 1616
Tel: 0583-370037
Fax: 0583-379136
Exclusive 4-star man-
sion open Apr–Oct. Old-
fashioned elegance;
modern comforts.
Swimming pool, lovely
garden. €€€

Pisa

Albergo Helvetia
Via Don Gaetano Boschi 31
Tel: 050-553084
This small budget hotel
is situated in a particu-
larly quiet area and yet
it's right on the Piazza
dei Miracoli's doorstep.
Only half of the 23
rooms, have private
bathrooms. Pleasant
courtyard garden. €

Ariston
Via Cardinale Maffi 42
Tel: 050-561834
Fax: 050-561891
A lovely hotel, literally in

the shadow of the
Leaning Tower. Recently
renovated to a high
standard, it feels more
like a 4-star hotel than
its mere three. Taste-
fully decorated rooms
and well equipped bath-
rooms. €€

California Park Hotel
Madonna dell'Acqua
Tel: 050-890726
Fax: 050-890727
Rooms are in the
numerous small villas
scattered throughout
the grounds. Swimming
pool. Located 3 km/1½
miles outside Pisa. €€

D'Azeglio
Piazza V Emanuele 18b
Tel: 050-500310
Fax: 050-28017
www.hoteldazeglio.it
Four-star hotel with
good facilities. €€€

Grand Hotel Duomo
Via Santa Maria 94
Tel: 050-561894
Fax: 050-560418
www.grandhotelduomo.it
Comfortable, business-
like hotel. Restaurant;
private garage. €€€

Hotel Locanda La Lanterna
Via S .Maria 113
Tel: 050-830305
Fax: 050-834651
www.locandalalanterna.com
Pleasant, no-frills bed
and breakfast hotel,
close to the Leaning
Tower. Very good value
for money. €–€€

Hotel Relais dell'Orologio
Via della Faggiola 12/14
Tel: 050-830361
Fax 050-551869
www.hotelrelaisorologio.com
Conveniently located
between the Campo dei
Miracoli and Piazza dei
Cavalieri, this gracious
14th-century manor

house has been trans-
formed into a stylish
and elegant boutique
hotel with just 21 indi-
vidually decorated
rooms. Romantic court-
yard garden. A luxurious
treat. €€€€

Pisa Hotel
Via Manzoni 22
Tel/fax: 050-44551
Hotel offering good ser-
vice and comfort. €

Royal Victoria
Lungarno Pacinotti 12
Tel: 050-940111
Fax: 050-940180
www.royalvictoriahotel.it
The most characterful
hotel in the city opened
in 1842 and played
host to Dickens and
other Grand Tourists.
Old-fashioned atmos-
phere. Rooms overlook-
ing the Arno are in great
demand, though they
can be noisy. Private
garage. €€

Touring
Via Puccini 24
Tel: 050-46374
Fax: 050-502148
www.benotel.com/italy/pisa/touring
Well run, if dowdy hotel
across the Arno from
the main sights, but
near the station. €€

Villa Kinzica
Piazza Arcivescovado 2
Tel: 050-560419
Fax: 050-551204
www.hotelvillakinzica.it
Remarkably positioned
hotel, right under the
Leaning Tower, but
some rooms need
attention. Own restau-
rant/pizzeria. €€

San Giuliano Terme

Villa Corliano
Via Statale 50, Rigoli
Tel: 050-818897
Fax: 050-818341

www.corliano.it
Faded villa of grand
dimensions, half way
between Pisa and Lucca.
Informal, with plenty of
atmosphere. Restaurant
attached. €€

Tirrenia

Atlantico Continental Hotel
Largo Belvedere 26
Tel: 050-37031
Fax: 050-37283
Four-star luxury hotel
with pool, private beach
and tennis court. €€€

Bristol
Via delle Felci 38
Tel: 050-37161
Fax: 050-37138
www.bristol.it
Three-star, unpreten-
tious and comfortable
hotel. €€

Grand Hotel Golf
Via dell'Edera 29
Tel: 050-957018
Fax: 050-32111
www.grandhotelgolf.it
Rather impersonal 4-
star hotel but it has its
own golf course and is
right by the sea. €€€

LIVORNO AND THE MAREMMA PISANA

Casale Marittimo

Il Poggio
Località Il Poggio
Tel: 0586-652308
www.ilpoggio.org
Agriturismo on the road from Bibbona offering small apartments. Ideal base for exploring the area, especially for families with children. €

Livorno

Gran Duca
Piazza Micheli 16
Tel: 0586-891024
Fax: 0586-891153
www.granduca.it
Attractive hotel (for Livorno) on the seafront with views over the old harbour. A good place to stay if you are catching an early ferry. Fitness centre with pool, spa and sauna. €€

Montenero

La Vedetta
Tel: 0586-579957
Fax: 0586-579969
www.hotellavedetta.it
Modern hotel in Livorno hills. Rooms are basic but views are expansive. Near the sanctuary. €

Sassetta

Campo di Carlo
Via Campagna Nord 62
Tel: 0565-794257
Fax: 0565-705612
www.campodicarlo.it
Child-friendly guest-house in the heart of the

country, not far from Sassetta and within easy reach of the sea. Six lovely rooms. €

ELBA

Capo d'Enfola

La Hermitage
Loc. Biodola, Portoferraio
Tel: 0565-936911
Fax: 0565-969984
www.hotelhermitage.it
Large and lively resort hotel, founded in the 1950s. €€€

Hotel Scoglio Bianco
Località Viticcio
Tel: 0565-939036
Fax: 0565-939031
E-mail: scogliob@elbalink.it
Low-key whitewashed hotel in one of Elba's quieter corners. Great sunset views from the terraces. Half-board obligatory, but still good value. €€

Capo Sant' Andrea

Hotel Ilio
Via Sant'Andrea 5
Tel: 0565-908018
Fax: 0565-908087
www.ilio.it
This welcoming 19-room hotel is a hidden gem among the many small establishments stacked up on the hillside around Capo Sant' Andrea. As with many Elban hotels, half-board is obligatory, but the restaurant is excellent and pre-dinner cocktails on the terrace a nice touch. Mountain bikes for rent. €€

Marciana

Bel Tramonto
Località Patresis
Tel: 0565-908027
Fax: 0565-908280
www.valverdehotel.it
Modern hotel with lovely swimming pool and grounds. Most rooms have balconies over-looking the sea. €

Portoferraio

Villa Ottone
Località Ottone
Tel: 0565-933042
Fax: 0565-933257
www.villaottone.com
Refined hotel in a gleaming white 19th-century villa just east of

Portoferraio. Beautifully tended grounds and a poolside restaurant. Go for one of the original villa rooms with its own frescoed ceiling and ter-race with sea views. Or opt for one of the five "cottages". Many activi-ties on offer. €€

VOLTERRA AND ENVIRONS

Massa Marittima

Albergo il Sole
Corso della Libertà 43
Tel/fax: 0566-901959
Simple hotel in an old *palazzo* in the medieval heart of the town. €

Villa il Tesoro
Piazza Dante Alighieri 1/2
Tel: 0566-902284
Fax: 0566-901905
www.villailtesoro.com
Romantic hamlet 7km (4 miles) outside Massa Marittima, surrounded by vineyards and olive groves, offering glorious views. Modern accom-modation in spacious suites. €€

Volterra

Nazionale
Via dei Marchesi 11
Tel: 0588-86284
Fax: 0588-84097
www.albergonazionalevolterra.it
Ancient palazzo, a hotel since 1890, just round the corner from the Piazza dei Priori. Rooms

are non-descript but comfortable. Balconies have fabulous views. €

San Lino
Via San Lino 26
Tel: 0588-85250
Fax: 0588-80620
www.hotelsanlino.com
Monastic building whose original austerity has been softened by a successful conversion into a 4-star hotel. €

Villa Nencini
Borgo Santo Stefano 55
Tel: 0588-86386
Fax: 0588-80601
www.villanencini.it
Pleasant stone villa just outside the town walls, with a garden and pool, as well as a restaurant and an *enoteca*. €€

Villa Palagione
Località Palagione
Tel: 0588-39014

Fax: 0588-39129
www.villa-palagione.com
Aristocratic villa, 7 km (4 miles) from Volterra, converted into a hotel and cultural centre specialising in group activities (cooking, painting, riding, walking, etc.), but individuals are welcome. Beautiful frescoed rooms. €–€€

Villa Rioddi
Località Rioddi
Tel: 0588-88053
Fax: 0588-88074
www.hotelvillarioddi.it
15th-century villa on a hillside, 2 km (1 mile) from the centre. The 15 rooms are simply furnished; garden and swimming pool with views over the Cecina valley. €

SAN GIMIGNANO AND CHIANTI COUNTRY

Castellina in Chianti

Belvedere di San Leonino
Località San Leonino
Tel: 0577-740887
Fax: 0577-740924
www.hotelsanleonino.com
Imposing 15th-century country house surrounded by olive trees and vineyards. Swimming pool. €€

Colle Etrusco Salivolpi
Via Fiorentina 89
Tel: 0577-740484
Fax: 0577-740998
www.hotelsalivolpi.com
Well-restored farmhouse with an appealing garden and uncontrived rustic decor – original beams, whitewashed walls, terracotta tiles and decorative ironwork. €

Collelungo
Tel: 0577-740489
Fax: 0577-741330
www.collelungo.com
Lovingly restored stone farmhouse divided into comfortable apartments (named after the Siena *contrade*) for 2–4 people. Barbecue and pool. Minimum stay: three nights. €€

Le Piazze
Località Le Piazze
Tel: 0577-743190

Fax: 0577-743191
www.locandalepiazze.com
Converted 17th-century farmhouse with terraces and gardens. Rustic furnishings and luxurious bathrooms. Meals on request. €€

Tenuta di Ricavo
Località Ricavo 4
Tel: 0577-740221
Fax: 0577-741014
www.ricavo.com
A highly rated hotel occupying a series of rustic houses in a medieval hamlet, 5 km (3 miles) from Castellina. Pool; good quality restaurant. Open Mar–Oct. €€€

Villa Casalecchi
Località Casalecchi
Tel: 0577-740240
Fax: 0577-741111
www.villacasalecchi.it
Three-star hotel, set in a 19th-century villa, surrounded by oak trees. Pool, tennis courts, restaurant. Open Mar–Oct. €€€

Certaldo Alto

Osteria del Vicario
Via Rivellino 3
Tel/fax: 0571-668228
www.osteriadelvicario.it
Well-known restaurant with five simple rooms in a pretty hilltop town. €

Colle di Val d'Elsa

Villa Belvedere
Via Senese
Tel: 0577-920966
Fax: 0577-924128
www.villabelvedere.com
Delightful 18th-century villa surrounded by a large park. Excellent restaurant. €€

Hotel Arnolfo
Via F. Campana 8
Tel: 0577-922020
Fax: 0577-922324
Occupies a 15th-century *palazzo* in a commanding position at the top of town. Basic rooms are basic. €

Gaiole in Chianti

Castello di Spaltenna
Tel: 0577-749483
Fax: 0577-749269
www.spaltenna.it
Formidable fortified monastery, now a luxurious hotel with an excellent restaurant, indoor and outdoor pools, gym, Turkish bath, sauna and tennis court. Supremely comfortable, individualistic rooms. €€€

L'Ultimo Mulino
Loc. La Ripresa di Vistarenni
Tel: 0577-738520
Fax: 0577-738659
www.ultimomulino.it
Atmospheric hotel in a converted mill. An ideal

setting for exploring Chianti; pool. €€–€€€

Greve In Chianti

Albergo del Chianti
Piazza Matteotti 86
Tel: 055-853763
Fax: 055-853764
www.albergodelchianti.it
Small, pleasant hotel with pool, garden and a friendly atmosphere. €€

Monteriggioni

Hotel Monteriggioni
Via 1 Maggio 4
Tel: 0577-305009
Fax: 0577-305011

PRICE CATEGORIES

The price categories refer to the cost of a double room during high season, usually including breakfast.
€ = under €100
€€ = €100–200
€€€ = €200–300
€€€€ = more than €300

www.hotelmonteriggioni.net
A couple of village
houses have been con-
verted into an elegant
hotel with a garden and
pool, in a pretty walled
town 10 km (6 miles)
north of Siena. **€€–€€€**

Panzano in Chianti

Villa Le Barone
Via San Leolino 19
Tel: 055-852621
Fax: 055-852277
www.villalebarone.it
Aristocratic villa filled
with family antiques,
giving the feel of a pri-
vate house. Facilities
include pool, tennis
court and a good
restaurant. Half-board
rates. **€€–€€€**

Villa San Giovese
Piazza Bucciarelli 5
Tel: 055-852461
Fax: 055-852463

Well restored villa in the
Florentine Chianti, with
rooms in a converted
traditional farmhouse.
Noted restaurant and
wines. **€€**

Radda in Chianti

Relais Fattoria Vignale
Via Pianigiani 9
Tel: 0577-738300
Fax: 0577-738592
www.vignale.it
Discreetly elegant old
manor house with a
relaxed atmosphere.
Excellent wine produced
on site; bar and restau-
rant in the old wine cel-
lars; pool. **€€€–€€€€**

San Casciano Val di Pesa

Il Borghetto
Via Collina 23, Montefiridolfi
Tel: 055-8244442
Fax: 055-8244247
www.ilborghetto.org

Very welcoming *agritur-
ismo* with homely rooms
and apartments, part of
a working wine and olive
oil estate. Pool; cookery
classes. **€€**

San Gimignano

L'Antico Pozzo
Via San Matteo 87
Tel: 0577-942014
Fax: 0577-942117
www.anticopozzo.com
Old townhouse, carefully
restored and simply but
tastefully furnished. **€€**

Hotel La Cisterna
Piazza della Cisterna 23
Tel: 0577-940328
Fax: 0577-942080
www.hotelcisterna.it
Medieval *palazzo* with a
fine restaurant. One of
the most atmospheric
and popular hotels in
town. **€€**

Hotel Pescille
Località Pescille

Tel: 0577-940186
Fax: 0577-943165
www.hotelpescille.it
Converted manor house
3 km (2 miles) south-
west of San Gimignano.
Pool; tennis. **€€**

Le Renaie
Località Pancole
Tel: 0577-955044
Fax: 0577-955126
www.hotellerenaie.com/renaie
Modern family-friendly
hotel in a peaceful set-
ting 5 km (3 miles) from
San Gimignano. Pool;
restaurant. **€€**

Villa San Paolo
Strada per Certaldo
Tel: 0577-955100
Fax: 0577-955113
www.hotelvillasanpaolo.com
19th-century hillside
villa, 5 km (3 miles) from
San Gimignano, with
attractive rooms, ter-
raced grounds and a
fitness centre. **€€€**

SIENA

Certosa di Maggiano
Strada di Certosa 82
Tel: 0577-288180
Fax: 0577-288189
www.certosadimaggiano.com
This 14th-century
Carthusian monastery –
the oldest in Tuscany –
has been converted into
a 5-star hotel adorned
with antiques. Set in
olive groves with an out-
door pool, prestigious
restaurant and original
features.

**Grand Hotel
Continental**
Banchi di Sopra 85
Tel: 0577-44204
Fax: 0577-49020
www.ghc.royaldemeure.com
Majestic hotel, recently
restored, set in the
heart of Siena. Covered

courtyard, restaurant
and wine bar.

Park Hotel
Via Marciano 18
Tel: 0577-290290
Fax: 0577-49020
www.parkhotelsiena.it
Splendid 16th-century
Tuscan villa with an
exclusive, 5-star atmos-
phere and a famous
restaurant, L'Olivo.
Booking recommended.

Garden
Via Custoza 2
Tel: 0577-47056
Fax: 0577-46050
www.gardenhotel.it
16th-century patrician
villa, now a 3-star hotel
with a formal, Italian garden and a pool. Four-star
rooms available too.

Villa Scacciapensieri
Via Scacciapensieri 10
Tel: 0577-41441
Fax: 0577-270854
www.villascacciapensieri.it
Supremely elegant villa
hotel in lovely grounds
3 km (1½ miles) north
of the city. Sophisti-
cated interior, bed-
rooms with rural views,
and a panoramic city
view from the restau-
rant terrace.

Antica Torre
Via Fieravecchia 7
Tel/fax: 0577-222255
www.tuscany.net/anticatorresiena
A tiny, atmospheric
hotel, essentially a
conversion of a
17th-century tower.
Book early.

Duomo
Via Stalloreggi 38
Tel: 0577-289088
Fax: 0577-43043
www.hotelduomo.it
Situated right in the
heart of the historic
centre, close to Siena's
magnificent cathedral,
this 18th-century
palazzo has a clois-
tered, intimate atmos-
phere. Some rooms
have views of the cathe-
dral and Sienese hills.

Santa Caterina
Via Enea Silvio Piccolomini 7
Tel: 0577-221105
Fax: 0577-271087
www.hscsiena.it
Friendly hotel set in a garden just outside the city walls, near Porta Romana. Roadside rooms can be noisy.
Palazzo Ravizza
Pian dei Mantellini 34
Tel: 0577-280462
Fax: 0577-221597

www.palazzoravizza.it
Historic townhouse with frescoed ceilings, lovely gardens and a good restaurant. Well chosen antiques in the bedrooms. Welcoming public rooms.

Inexpensive (€)

Albergo Centrale
C. Angiolieri 26
Tel: 0577-280379

Fax: 0577-42152
Clean and spacious 2-star hotel.
Albergo Chiusarelli
Via Curtatone 15.
Tel: 0577-280562
Fax: 0577-271177
www.chiusarelli.it
Slightly decaying, genteel villa in a garden with a car park. Near the bus station.
Piccolo Hotel Etruria
Via delle Donzelle 3

Tel: 0577-288088
Fax: 0577-288461
www.hoteletruria.com
Friendly hotel with simple but clean rooms divided between two townhouses.
Tre Donzelle
Via delle Donzelle 5
Tel: 0577-280358
Fax: 0577-223933
Rooms are basic and a bit care-worn, but it's very near the Campo.

SOUTH OF SIENA

Bagno Vignoni

Albergo Posta Marcucci
Via Ara Urcea 43
Tel: 0577-887112
Fax: 0577-887119
www.hotelpostamarcucci.it
Hotel noted for its spa facilities, close to the famous medieval thermal pool. €€–€€€

Cetona

Locanda di Anita
Piazza Balestrieri, 5
Tel: 0578-239040
www.lalocandadianita.it
Charming little inn and cocktail bar set back from the main square with five tastefully decorated, air-conditioned upstairs rooms. €€

Chianciano Terme

Hotel Michelangelo
Via delle Piane
Tel: 0578-64004
Fax: 0578-60480
www.hotel-michelangelo.it
Modern 4-star hotel in a fine setting, with large grounds, a pool, sauna, tennis courts and good restaurants, including a rooftop restaurant in summer. Popular with Italians. Open Apr–mid-Oct. €€

Montalcino

Il Giglio
Via Saloni 5
Tel/fax: 0577-848167
www.albergoilmarzocco.it
Small family-run hotel suspended above the city walls. Its 12 rooms all offer fine views over the lush Val d'Orcia. €€
Il Marzocco
Piazza Savonarola 18
Tel: 0578-757262
Fax 0578-757530
www.albergoilmarzocco.it
Medieval *palazzo* with fine, if old-fashioned rooms, some of which have terraces. €

Montepulciano

Il Borghetto
Via Borgo Buio 7
Tel/fax: 0578-757535
www.ilborghetto.it
Three 16th-century *palazzi* in the heart of town, converted into a hotel. Rooms are small, but comfortable. Be sure to request one with views over the valley. Cosy sitting room with a big fireplace and resident cat. The owner is also a tour guide. €€
Palazzo Contucci
Via del Teatro 1
Tel: 0578-757006
www.residenzecontucci.it

This palatial 16th-century building designed by Sangallo still belongs to the aristocratic Contucci family. The Contessa rents out an apartment above the wine cellars. €€

Pienza

Antica Locanda
Corso Il Rossellino 72
Tel/fax: 0578-749509
www.anticalocanda.toscana.nu
Small bed and breakfast, with some rooms overlooking the valley. €
Piccolo Hotel
Via Circonvallazione 7
Tel: 0578 749402
Fax: 0578-749863
www.piccolohotellavalle.it
Popular, comfortable 3-star hotel with lovely views over the Val d'Orcia. €–€€
Hotel Corsignano
Via della Madonnina 11
Tel: 0587-748501
Fax: 0587-748166
www.hotelcorsignano.it
Modern hotel near the Duomo; not the most romantic of places but the welcome is very friendly. €–€€
Il Chiostro di Pienza
Corso Il Rosellino 26
Tel: 0578-748400
Fax: 0578-748440

www.relaisilchiostrodipienza.com
Beautifully converted medieval convent, with a quiet cloister, in the heart of Pienza. Also a restaurant. Very welcoming. €€€

Ripa d'Orcia

Castello di Ripa d'Orcia
Località Castiglione d'Orcia
Tel: 0577-897376
Fax: 0577-898038
www.casteloripadorcia.com
Peaceful medieval hamlet, dominated by a tower, parts of which

PRICE CATEGORIES

The price categories refer to the cost of a double room during high season, usually including breakfast.
€ = under €100
€€ = €100–200
€€€ = €200–300
€€€€ = more than €300

have been converted into hotel rooms and apartments. *Trattoria* with panoramic terrace views. Closed Dec–Feb. **€€–€€€**

Hotel Palazzuolo
Via Santa Caterina 43
Tel: 0577-897080
Fax: 0577-898264

www.hotelpalazzuolo.it
Surrounded by lush countryside, with terrace and pool; Tuscan cuisine a speciality. **€**

Sinalunga

Locanda dell'Amorosa
Località l'Amorosa
Tel: 0577-677211

Fax: 0577-632001
www.amorosa.it
Renaissance hamlet, complete with chapel, converted into a first-class hotel. Romantic setting; superb restaurant in adapted stables. Good facilities; high prices. **€€€–€€€€**

Sovicille

Borgo Pretale
Tel: 0577-345401
Fax: 0577-345625
www.borgopretale.it
Renovated fortified village divided into apartments and topped by a massive medieval tower. **€€€**

GROSSETO AND THE MAREMMA

Albinia

La Parrina
Km 146 Via Aurelia
Tel: 0564-862626
www.parrina.it
Genuine *agriturismo* set among vineyards, olive groves and orchards on the Maremman plains. It has retained the traditional décor of a country estate. Excellent buffet breakfast on garden terrace. Swimming pool, chapel, farm shop and bicycles. **€€**

Castiglione della Pescaia

L'Andana
Tenuta La Badiola
Tel: 0564-944800
www.andana.it
The former estate of Tuscan grand duke Leopold II has been transformed into a supremely refined hotel by one of France's most celebrated chefs, Alain Ducasse, who is also setting up his own winery here. The height of luxury. **€€€€**

Giglio

Pardini's Hermitage
Cala degli Alberi, Giglio Porto
Tel: 0564-809034
Fax: 0564-809177
www.finalserv.it/hermitage
Pleasant, secluded island retreat with 12 small rooms and well

tended gardens. Accessible by boat from Giglio Porto. Relaxed atmosphere, friendly welcome and good facilities. Half-board only. **€**

Montemerano

Villa Acquaviva
Strada Scansanese 10 Nord (2 km/ 1 mile from Montemerano). Tel: 0564-602890
Fax: 0564-602895
www.relaisvillaacquaviva.com
Family-run villa near Saturnia with a lovely garden and comfortable rooms. Mountain bikes available for hire. Swimming pool. **€€**

Porto Ercole

Don Pedro
Via Panoramica 7
Tel: 0564-833914
Fax: 0564-833129
www.hoteldonpedro.it
Long-established family-run hotel with views over the port below and a lovely summer terrace. The decor is rather old-fashioned, but it is well positioned. Half-board preferred. Open Easter–Sept. **€€**

Hotel Il Pellicano
Località o Sbarcatello
Tel: 0564-858111
Fax: 0564-833418
www.pellicanohotel.com
Chic hotel enjoying a superb, isolated clifftop position. Bedrooms are

housed in various buildings; terraces lead down to the private beach. Tennis courts and swimming pool. Weekly barbecues in summer. An expensive treat. **€€€€**

Porto Santo Stefano

Torre Di Cala Piccola
8km (5 miles) from Porto Santo Stefano on the Strada Panoramica, Argentario
Tel: 0564-825111
Fax: 0564-825235
www.torredicalapiccola.com
Charming cliff-top hotel, built around a 17th-century Spanish lookout tower. Rooms and apartments with private beach and superb sea views. Open Mar–Oct. **€€**

Saturnia

Hotel Villa Clodia
Via Italia 43
Tel: 0564-601212
Fax: 0564-601305
Centrally located three-star hotel with lovely view and swimming pool, within walking distance of the spa. Good value. **€**

Terme di Saturnia
Via della Follonata
Tel: 0564-600111
Fax: 0564-601266
www.termedisaturnia.it
Luxury hotel and spa resort. The thermal pool

and treatment centre is open to non-residents. **€€€–€€€€**

Sovana

La Scilla
Via Rodolfo Siviero 1–3
Tel: 0564-616531
Fax: 0564-614329
www.scilla-sovana.it
Eight bright and elegant rooms in a pretty tufa-stone hotel. **€€**

Albergo Ristorante Taverna Etrusca
Piazza del Pretorio
Tel: 0564-616183
Fax: 0564-614183
Excellent small restaurant with comfortable rooms. **€**

Talamone

Hotel Capo d'Uomo
Via Cala di Forno 7
Tel: 0564-887077
Fax: 0564-887298
Cliff-top hotel with balconies overlooking the sea and access to a private rocky beach. Within easy reach of the Parco dell'Uccellina. **€€**

AREZZO AND EASTERN TUSCANY

Arezzo

Continentale
Piazza G. Monaco 7
Tel: 0575-20251
Fax: 0575-350485
www.hotelcontinentale.com
A centrally located 3-star hotel, with good facilities, comfortable rooms and a lovely roof terrace. Popular among business travellers. €–€€

Hotel Patio
Via Cavour 23
Tel: 0575-401962
Fax: 0575-27418
www.hotelpatio.it
Innovative hotel in an old *palazzo* in the historic heart of Arezzo, not far from San Francesco. The colourful decor of each of the seven rooms was inspired by the writings of widely travelled novelist Bruce Chatwin. €€–€€€

Val di Colle
Località Bagnoro, Scopeto
Tel/fax: 0575-365167
www.valdicolle.it
A meticulously restored 14th-century house, 4 km (2½ miles) from the centre of Arezzo. There are eight elegant bedrooms with a rustic theme. Antique furniture sits harmoniously alongside the modern art. €€–€€€

Bibbiena

Albergo Borgo Antico
Via B. Dovizi 18
Tel: 0575-536445
Fax: 0575-536447
www.brami.com
Hotel-restaurant in the centre of Bibbiena, with comfortable, if non-descript bedrooms. Good base for exploring the Casentino area. €

Castiglion Fiorentino

Villa Schiatti
Località Montecchio 131
Tel: 0575-651440
Fax: 0575-651482
www.villaschiatti.it
Situated in the panoramic hills between Arezzo and Siena, equipped with pool, restaurant and terrace offering splendid views over the Tuscan countryside. €

Cortona

Il Falconiere
Località San Martino.
Tel: 0575-612679
Fax: 0575-612927
www.tuscany.net/falconiere
Luxurious country retreat set in olive groves 3 km (2 miles) above Cortona. First-class restaurant. €€€

Rugapiana Vacanze
Via Nazionale 63
Tel: 0575-630364
Fax: 0575-630447
www.tuscanytravel.net/rugapiana
Rooms and apartments for short or longer stays, in central Cortona. Guests can use the facilities at an *agriturismo* just outside town. €–€€

San Michele
Via Guelfa 15
Tel: 0575-604348
Fax: 0575-630147
www.hotelsanmichele.net
Centrally situated, comfortable hotel housed in an impressively restored Renaissance palace. €€

Foiano della Chiana

La Lodola
Via Piana 19
Tel: 0575–649 660
Fax: 0575–642521

Bed and breakfast in an 18th-century farmhouse. The rooms are lovingly decorated by the antique dealer owners – some of the furniture is for sale. €€

Gargonza

Castello di Gargonza
Monte San Savino
Tel: 0575-847021
Fax: 0575-847054
www.gargonza.it
Attractive fortified village near Arezzo, with a frescoed chapel and castle walls, converted into a hotel with separate apartments. The 13th-century buildings overlook the Val di Chiana. The restaurant, with large terrace, specialises in game. €€

Loro Ciuffenna

Villa Cassia di Baccano
Via Setteponti Levante 132
Tel: 055-9772310
Fax: 055-9772898
www.villacassiadibaccano.it
Stylishly converted villa 17 km (11 miles) from Arezzo, offering comfortable airy apartments on a weekly basis, and suites on a daily basis. Numerous services and a swimming pool. Lovely views. €€–€€€

Monterchi

B&B Il Colle
Località. Il Colle 4b
Tel: 0575-70749
www.bedandbreakfastilcolle.com
Former farmhouse which has been converted into a homely bed and breakfast. Living room, terrace and kitchen available. Open fire makes it cosy in colder weather. €

Sansepolcro

Relais Oroscopo
Via Togliatti 68
Tel: 0575-734875
Fax: 0575-759388
www.relaisoroscopo.com
Located on the outskirts of Sansepolcro, 3-star hotel with individually decorated rooms and a renowned restaurant. €€

Regello

Villa Rigacci
Vaggio 76
Tel: 055-8656718
Fax: 055-8656537
www.villarigacci.it
Country house hotel in a pleasant setting, off the scenic "Road of the Seven Bridges" and handy for the Rome–Florence motorway. Sophisticated Mediterranean food, extensive grounds and a swimming pool. Good base for designer outlet shopping – there are malls in nearby Leccio and Montevarchi. €€

TRANSPORT

ACCOMMODATION

ACTIVITIES

A – Z

LANGUAGE

ACTIVITIES

THE ARTS, NIGHTLIFE, FESTIVALS, SHOPPING AND SPECTATOR SPORTS

THE ARTS

Archaeological Sites

There are various places of archaeological interest in Tuscany. These include **Etruscan** (8th–2nd century BC) sites at Volterra, Fiesole, Arezzo, Chiusi, Vetulonia and on the island of Elba. There is an archaeological museum in Florence and other museums in Volterra, Chiusi, Cortona, Asciano, Grosseto and Massa Marittima.

Notable **Roman** (8th century BC– 5th century AD) remains can be seen at Fiesole, Cosa, Roselle, Volterra and Arezzo.

Art and Architecture

Art

Renaissance art is, of course, what Tuscany is most famous for. The most outstanding Renaissance collections are in Florence, in the **Uffizi Gallery**, the **Pitti Palace Gallery** and the **San Marco Museum**.

Works of art from the late Renaissance and Mannerist periods, the baroque, the neoclassical and romantic, and also the 20th century are exhibited at most galleries and museums in the main cities of the region.

Architecture

Tuscany is a treasure trove of architectural history *(see the feature on pages 54–59)*.

● Churches and civil buildings from the **Romanesque** period can be found at Pisa, Florence, Lucca, Siena, Pistoia and Arezzo.

● The most important **Gothic** buildings are in Florence, Siena, Pisa, Pistoia and Arezzo.

● Tuscany also abounds in religious and secular **Renaissance** buildings, Florence being the most important centre.

Sightseeing

Details of important museums and art galleries are in the *Places* section of this book. Be sure to take advantage of multi-entrance tickets where possible.

Florence

There are stands in shops and cafes where free leaflets detailing events and exhibitions can be picked up. Examples are *Informacittà* and *Vivi Firenze*.

The Friends of Florentine Museums Association (Via degli Alfani 39, tel: 055-293007) has 12,000 members. They arrange museum visits 9–11pm in the summer, with orchestral recitals.

Entry prices for museums and galleries vary greatly, with the Uffizi the most expensive. State

museums are closed on Monday while most other museums close on Tuesday or Wednesday. Most museums also close on 1 May.

Every year, in April or December, Florence has a "culture week" *(La Settimana di Beni Culturali)*, when all the state museums are free. Ask the tourist office.

Pisa

The main sites may be easily visited on foot or by local bus. Buy a joint ticket to see all the sights on the Campo dei Miracoli. A horse and carriage ride is a pleasant introduction to the city; prices are negotiable.

Siena

The tourist office can provide a list of authorised guides. With one week's notice, you can visit any of the *Contrada* (district) museums that celebrate the *Palio* and the ancient city traditions: the numbers are available on www.terresiena.it.

Listings

To find out what's on and what's new pick up Florence's monthly listings magazine *Firenze Spettacolo*. Although it is in Italian, the listings themselves are quite straightforward. Alternatively, obtain *Events*, another popular listings magazine, or you can check the entertainment pages of *La Nazione*, the regional newspaper, or the Tuesday edition of the national paper, *La Repubblica*. If you read Italian well, then get *Toscana Qui*, and *Firenze ieri, oggi, domani*.

Music, Ballet and Opera

Florence

The *Maggio Musicale* music festival (www.maggiofiorentino.it), held from mid-May to the end of June, is a big event with top names in concert, ballet and opera performing in various venues throughout the city. Tickets are available from the Teatro Comunale, Corso Italia 16, tel: 055-211158, and this is where most of the events are staged, although concerts are held throughout the summer in cloisters, piazzas and the Boboli Gardens.

The opera season opens at the end of September or beginning of October. During the *Estate Fiesolana* – Fiesole's summer festival – concerts, opera, ballet and theatre are held in the town's Roman amphitheatre. Classical concerts are also held in many of the city churches.

The principal venue for chamber music concerts in Florence is the **Teatro della Pergola**, Via della Pergola (tel: 055-2264335; www.pergola.firenze.it), a superb example of a 17th-century theatre (inaugurated in 1656). These concerts are generally held at weekends, and are well publicised.

The **Fiesole Music School** in San Domenico also holds a concert series (tel: 055-5978527; www.scuolamusica.fiesole.fi.it) and the Orchestra Regionale Toscana's lively concert series runs December–May.

Florence's **Teatro Verdi**, Via Ghibellina 99 (tel: 055-212320; www.teatroverdifirenze.it) is the venue for a wider range of entertainment, from light opera and ballet to jazz and rock concerts.

The Florence Dance Festival, held in late June/early July and again in December, features well-known national and international names along with up-and-coming dancers and choreographers (tel: 055-289276; www.florencedance.org for information).

Lucca

Puccini e la sua Lucca is a permanent festival dedicated to Giacomo Puccini, with concerts in the Basilica di San Giovanni. As well as Puccini, works by other composers are performed. Tickets available at the church on performance days from 6pm; www.puccinielasualucca.com.

Pisa

Pisa's opera season runs at the Teatro Verdi from September to February. Tel: 050-941111 or visit www.teatrodipisa.pi.it.

Siena

The **Accademia Musicale Chigiana** (Chigiana Academy of Music), Via di Città 89, 53100 Siena (tel: 0577-22091; www.chigiana.it) provides proficiency courses in July and August for young performers.

Public performances of rare, unpublished and new music are held in August each year during the Sienese Music Week. They include opera, symphonic concerts and chamber orchestras.

A theoretical and practical course in jazz music is held annually at the Seminari Nazionali Senesi. For details contact Siena Jazz (Associazione Siena Jazz, Fortezza Medicea, tel: 0577-271401, www.sienajazz.it).

Theatre

In addition to the main theatres, **Teatro della Pergola** *(see left)* and **Teatro Verdi** (Via Ghibellina 99; tel: 055-212320 www.teatroverdifirenze.it), there are numerous smaller companies performing regularly in Florence, but most productions are in Italian. The **Teatro Metastasio** in

Prato is another place to see high-quality drama productions (tel: 0574-6084; www.metastasio.net). Look out for the listings in *Firenze Spettacolo*.

Ticket Sales

Useful ticket agencies in Florence are **Agenzia Box Office**, Via Alamanni 39, tel: 055-210804; fax: 213112 (open Mon 3.30–7.30pm; Tues–Sat 10am–7.30pm); **Rinascente**, 4th Floor, Piazza della Repubblica, tel: 055-292508 (open Tues–Sat 1.30–7.30pm). In Prato, tickets can be purchased from **Dischi Niccoli**, Via Cairoli 19, tel: 0574-27890, fax: 0574-606726. It is best to go in person to buy tickets for all events from opera to rock music.

Cinema

Almost all films are dubbed into Italian, but there are a few cinemas that occasionally show original versions, screenings by organisations such as the British Institute and the odd film festival or special season which will use sub-titles rather than dubbing. The main cinema for foreigners is the **Odeon** (Piazza Strozzi, tel: 055-214068), which shows recent films in English on Mondays, Tuesdays and Thursdays and is packed with foreign students and expatriates. During the summer a number of films are shown in the open air – details of where and when can be sought from the tourist offices.

NIGHTLIFE

Tuscany's cities offer a wide variety of music and entertainment, especially in the summer when there are any number of festivals around the region *(see page 280)*; summer discos take place in resorts, and in Florence, bars and clubs are set up in the warm weather in several piazzas, often with live music. That said,

Florence is not New York. Once the restaurants have shut the majority of city streets empty. There are a number of late-night bars and clubs dotted around town, but most of the bigger discos are on the outskirts. Nightclubs come and go with some regularity, so it's best to ask around for recommendations.

The following places are all in Florence. Elsewhere, the local tourist offices *(see page 292)* are your best bet for finding out about local clubs and bars, concerts, festivals and other events. Note that most clubs close on Monday; very few get going before 10pm.

Bars and Live Music

Astor
Piazza del Duomo 20r, tel: 055-284305. Cocktail bar with dance floor, frequented by Americans.
Be Bop
Via dei Servi 76r. Cocktail bar with live music: country, blues and jazz.
Il Caffè
Piazza Pitti 9, tel: 055-2396241. Chic and refined: a cosy spot to chat to friends, day or evening.
Caffè Cibreo
Via del Verrocchio 5r, tel: 055-2345853. Annexe to the famous restaurant, this beautiful and intimate wood-panelled bar is ideal for anything from a morning coffee to a late-night *digestivo*. Snacks come from the Cibreo kitchen. Closed Sun and Mon.
Caruso Jazz Café
Via Lambertesca 14/16r, tel: 055-281940. Relaxed café with art exhibitions and live music Wed–Fri. Closed Sun.
Chiodo Fisso Club
Via Dante Alighieri 16r, tel: 055-2381290. Well-established club, with live music every night.
Dolce Vita
Piazza del Carmine, tel: 055-280 018; www.dolcevitaflorence.com. Fashionable and crowded bar located in the bohemian Oltrarno quarter.
Hemingway
Piazza Piattellina 9r, tel: 055-284781. Beautifully decorated

café where you can have a drink and a snack, or sample the superb chocolates. Comfy chairs and books to browse.
Jazz Club
Via Nuova dei Caccini 3, tel: 055-2479700. Relaxed basement bar with live music daily. Small fee to become a member.
Moyo
Via dei Benci 23r, tel: 055-2479738. Swanky cocktail bar in the Santa Croce area with outside seating and delicious cocktails.
Nova Bar
Via Martelli. Pleasant bar during the day, turns into a noisy cocktail bar with dance floor in the evening.
Piccolo Caffe
Borgo Santa Croce 23r, tel: 055-2001057. Primarily a gay bar, but also a friendly café which provides welcome relief from unwanted attention for women.
Il Rifrullo
Via San Niccolò 55r, tel: 055-2342621. The long bar groans with munchies during cocktail hour and there is an open fire in the back room. Great cocktails.
Roses
Via del Parione 26r, tel: 055-287090. Florence's first sushi bar; sophisticated, good for cocktails and long drinks.
I Visacci
Borgo Albizi 80r, tel: 055-2001956. Art café with friendly staff, relaxed music and a good selection of wines and cocktails.

Nightclubs

Central Park
Via Fosso Macinante 1, Parco delle Cascine, tel: 055-353505 Possibly the trendiest club in Florence. Open Thurs–Sat.
Dolce Zucchero
Via Pandolfini 36/38r, tel: 055-2477894. One of the few clubs in the city centre, it operates a drinks card whereby you pay on exit.
Escopazzo Garden
Lungarno Colombo 23r, tel: 051-676912. Popular with celebrities. Check the nature of the night's entertainment before turning up. Closed Mon.

Maracanà
Via Faenza 4, tel: 055-210298; www.maracana.it. A lively Latino club. Closed Mon.
Meccanò
Viale degli Olmi 1, tel: 055-331371. One of Florence's oldest and most famous discos. Vast dance floor, bar and lounge areas.
Space Electronic
Via Palazzuolo 37, tel: 055-293082; www.spaceelectronic.net Lasers and videos are the hallmarks; this is the usual hang-out of foreign teenagers and would-be Latin lovers.
Tabasco
Piazza Santa Cecilia 3, tel: 055-213000. Men only; this was the first gay bar in Italy.
Tenax
Via Pratese 46r, tel: 055-308160. Popular club and live music venue.
YAB
Via Sassetti 5r, tel: 055-215160; www.yab.it. Fashionable disco-pub.

FESTIVALS

Arezzo

First weekend of every month: Antique fair in the region.
Last Sunday in June & first Sunday in September: *Giostra del Saracino* – Mounted knights attack a wooden effigy of a Turk.

Cortona

July/August: Cortona Summer Festival with a full artistic programme.
15 August: *Sagra della Bistecca* – Feast of the Beefsteak.
September (first half of the month): antiques exhibition.

Florence

Easter Day: *Scoppio del Carro*, the Explosion of the "Carriage" (actually fireworks on a float) and the emergence of a dove. Colourful musical processions.
Ascension Day: *Festa del Grillo*, Festival of the Crickets in the Cascine park. Sale of crickets and sweets.

End of April: Flower Show, Parterre, near Piazza Libertà – a riot of colour.

May and June: *Maggio Musicale Fiorentino* – performances of opera, ballet and classical music to a high standard.

June–September: Estate Fiesolana in Fiesole (just outside Florence) – music, dance, opera, cinema and theatre.

24 June: *San Giovanni* – Florence's patron saint's day, with a holiday in the city and an evening firework display near Piazzale Michelangelo.

June–July: *Calcio in costume* (*Calcio Fiorentino*) – football in medieval costume in Piazza Santa Croce.

7 September: night festival of the *Rificolona* (lanterns) – procession of carts, lanterns and singers.

Livorno

Late July/August: *Effetto Venezia* – lively 10-day festival in the city's Venetian quarter. The little canals provide the setting for street theatre, music and food. The local fish stew (*cacciucco*) is on sale.

Lucca

July: Summer festival with big name bands in Piazza Anfiteatro.
September – first weekend. Festival of Flowers.
September: *Luminaria di Santa Croce* – a religious procession.

Lucignano

Last two Sundays in May: *Maggiolata Lucignanese* – festival that includes a procession of carts decorated with allegorical scenes in flowers.

Massa Marittima

Sunday following May 20 and the **second Sunday in August**: *Balestro del Girifalco* – crossbow competition.

Montalcino

Last Sunday in October: *Sagra del Tordo* – Thrush Festival. Pageant, costume ball, banquet and archery at the fortress.

Monticchiello

Last 15 days of July: *Il Teatro Povero* – "The Poor Theatre" presents a drama written and acted by everyone about the local history and culture of the farmer.

Pescia

September (even numbered years): Biennial Flower Show.

Pienza

August/September: "Meeting with a Master of Art" in the council chamber of the Town Hall.
First Sunday of September: *Fiera del Cacio* – a fair devoted to sheep's milk cheese – for which Pienza is renowned.

Pisa

May and **June**: concerts at various annual festivals and fairs, especially during the *Gioco del Ponte* on the last Sunday of June.

16–17 June: *Luminaria di San Ranieri* – thousands of candles displayed on buildings along the Arno creating a spectacle after dark. Boat race in the evening of the second day.

Last Sunday in June: *Gioco del Ponte*.

Mid-September to end October: The annual *Anima Mundi International Festival of Sacred Music* takes place in Pisa Cathedral. Tel: 050-3872229/210; fax: 050-3872245; www.opapisa.it.

Pistoia

25 July: *Giostra dell'Orso* – Joust of the Bear in Piazza del Duomo. A mock battle takes place between a wooden bear and 12 knights in costume.

San Gimignano

July–September: Summer Fair, Estate Sangimignanese – varied programme of artistic events, including ballet, concerts and cinema.

Siena

28-30 April: Feast of St Catherine.
2 July and **16 August**: *Palio* traditional horse race. For tickets and

hotel bookings, write to the tourist office six months in advance.
Mid-July–August: *Incontri in Terra di Siena* – chamber music festival featuring quality concerts held in stunning settings south of Siena.
August: Sienese Music Week – performances of opera, symphonies and chamber music.
13 December: Festa di Santa Lucia – ceramics festival.

Torre del Lago

July and **August**: Puccini Opera Festival, near the composer's villa on Lake Massaciuccoli.

Viareggio

February: *Carnevale* – one of the best carnivals in Italy.

Volterra

First Sunday in September: *Torneo di Tiro con la Balestra* – crossbow tournament in Piazza dei Priori.

OUTDOOR ACTIVITIES

Sources of Information

For information about green tourism and outdoor activities, first contact the nearest office of ENIT, the Italian national tourist board (*see page 292*).

For trekking or cycling routes (with map and suggested hostels and mountain refuges), request the *Turismo Natura Toscana* booklet from Regione Toscana, Via di Novoli 26, 50127 Firenze, tel: 055-4383822; fax: 055-04383064. (It also gives tips for other activities, from horse-riding to climbing and caving.)

In English, the most comprehensive guide to green tourism is *Wild Italy* (by Tim Jepson, Sheldrake Press, 2005). Recommended local guides (in various languages) are: *Italia a Cavallo (Italy on Horseback)* published by Edizioni Demomedia and available from bookstores (or tel: 055-282162; fax: 055-289063; or call 167-467692, a toll-free number from within Italy). The same publishers also produce *Toscana Verde (Green Tuscany), The Chianti* and *Il Mangia Firenze (Eating in Florence Province).*

Hiking

Hiking (usually called "trekking" in Italian) is a popular activity in Tuscany. Serious hikers can follow the Italian Alpine Club (CAI or Club Alpino Italiano: www.cai.it) paths, which criss-cross the region. There is a branch of the CAI in Florence (Via della Mezzetta 2m, tel: 055-6120467; www.caifirenze.it), or you can contact the local tourist office for information.

Two long-distance paths, **Apuane Trekking** (a four-day trek) and the **Grande Escursione Apenninica** (GEA, taking 25 days end to end), have well-marked trails and can be joined at various points. Shorter waymarked trails (such as those in the Maremma or Chianti regions) tend to be less well signposted, so take good local maps (such as those produced by CAI).

All walkers should bear in mind that there is no public right of way across private property. Be particularly vigilant during the hunting season, especially on Sundays. If travelling without a car, forward planning is required. City to city transport is generally fine (often quicker by bus than train) but rural transport is poor: either of the "two buses a day" variety or simply non-existent.

Areas to Explore

The following are guidelines to some of the more accessible areas of natural beauty.

Abetone and the Tuscan-Emilian border

Abetone makes a good base for exploring this forested mountain region, also known as the Alto Appennino. The town has a profusion of Swiss chalet-style hotels. The picturesque medieval centres of Fiumalbo and Cutigliano make good alternative bases but have fewer facilities and lack Abetone's more dramatic alpine views.

Transport: by public transport, it is quicker to reach Abetone by bus from Modena (in Emilia-Romagna) than by other routes.

Apuan Alps (Alpi Apuane)

Maps and information on mountain refuges are available from Massa, Carrara and most coastal tourist offices. Numerous one-day hikes are available through the Alps, with typical starting points being the villages of Stazzema and Levigliano on the western flanks of the mountains. Almost as appealing is a car journey along the winding mountain roads towards the interior.

Arezzo/Pratovecchio

The Parco Nazionale delle Foreste Casentinesi (www.parks.it) is one of Italy's newest national parks. The area straddles Tuscany and Emilia Romagna. The park headquarters is at Pratovecchio, Via G. Brocchi 7; tel: 0575-50301. Alternatively, contact the Arezzo tourist office for more information.

Lunigiana and Garfagnana

Serious hikers should request the *Trekking in Lunigiana* map, with long-distance trails beginning in Aulla, Fosdinovo, Frignoli and Sassalbo. To appreciate the rural atmosphere, avoid staying in such fashionable coastal resorts as Forte dei Marmi. Instead, choose the Garfagnana hinterland, where Castelnuovo di Garfagnana is picturesque, and Barga, the main town, makes a pleasant base. Both are convenient for Parco dell' Orecchiella, the national park, 15 km (9 miles) north of Castelnuovo di Garfagnana. San Pellegrino in Alpe, 16 km (9½ miles) north-east of Castelnuovo, is appealing in summer and winter.

Transport: coastal transport is good, with transport into the Garfagnana hinterland less so. If you are planning to explore Garfagnana and Lunigiana by train or bicycle, a small branch line connects Lucca with Aulla and allows bicycles to be transported on the train.

The Maremma

If you want to be by the sea, stay in Santo Stefano, Talamone or Orbetello. Otherwise, opt for a ranch or farm near the park.

Transport: visitors using public transport should go to Orbetello (by bus or train) or to Monte Argentario (by bus from Grosseto). To visit the nature reserve is trickier: by train to Alberese station (only a couple of trains a day, from Grosseto), then a taxi.

The Mugello

Up-to-date information is available at www.mugellotoscana.it. Alternatively, request the *Green Heart of Tuscany* booklet from tourist offices in the region.

Avoid staying in Borgo San Lorenzo, the main town, which is not very attractive, or in the semi-industrialised valleys. Instead, choose the countryside or such villages as Vicchio, where the landscape is in many ways lovelier than the over-rated Chianti.

Transport: for those who wish to explore the Mugello by train or bicycle, the Faenza–Florence train service stops at stations along the Apennine ridge (Vicchio, Marradi, Ronta), ideal places to begin trekking.

Green Sites

These include nature reserves, caves, botanical gardens and museums of rural life. The classification of Italian conservation areas is chaotic and confusing. In theory, the Arcipelago Toscano (Tuscan Archipelago, including Elba and the other islands) is a National Park but in reality much remains unprotected. Illegal hunting continues in the larger parks. The best-run sanctuaries tend to be the smallest, often those administered by the Worldwide Fund for Nature (WWF) or by LIPU, the Italian bird protection society (for which there is a great need).

Abetone

On the Tuscan-Emilian border Abetone is the main ski and summer resort in the northern Apennines *(see page 284)*. It is also the centre for information on GEA long-distance trails and shorter botanical rambles. For details, contact the Abetone tourist office.

The Apuan Alps and Lunigiana
The **Frignoli Botanical Gardens** near Sassalbo (tel: 0187-42259) have an arboretum and display the full range of plants grown in the Apuan Alps. In **Aulla**, in Lunigiana, there is an interesting natural history museum and ecological centre set in historic Brunella castle (open daily summer 9am–noon, 4–7pm; winter 9am–noon, 3–6pm; entrance fee; tel: 0187-400252), as well as neighbouring botanical gardens. From Aulla, visitors can organise tours of glacial moraines, karst gorges and caves.

Garfagnana
Here, **Parco dell'Orecchiella**, 15 km (9 miles) north of Castelnuovo di Garfagnana, is the chief regional park in the Lucca stretch of the Apennines. The main entry point is Corfino. There are also **botanical gardens** nearby, at Villa Collemandina, Pania di Corfino (tel: 0584-644911). The local visitors' centre (tel: 0583-619002) includes a civilised mountain refuge and suggested nature trails. For general information, contact the Comunità Montana Garfagnana (tel: 0583-644911) or the tourist office in Barga, the region's main town.

The **Orrido dei Bottri reserve** is a narrow gorge with sheer cliff faces that can be crossed by serious hikers.

Livorno Province
In Livorno, the **Oasi di Bolgheri** is the best bird and wildlife sanctuary, a mixture of scrub, scrub and marshy grasslands. This WWF reserve is home to native and migratory birds and small mammals such as wild boar. The reserve lies 10 km (6 miles) south of Cecina and is reached by train to Bolgheri. Contact Marina di

Cecina or Livorno provincial tourist offices for details.

Lucca Province
Bottaccio Wood, outside Castelvecchio di Compito, is a marshland nature reserve good for birds and best visited in spring (tel: 0583-65008).

The Maremma
In the Maremma region, the **Centro Visite Parco Naturale della Maremma**, or Parco dell'Uccellina (tel: 0564-407098) is closed to traffic. Entry points are Marina di Alberese (the coast) or Alberese (the landward side, with the park ticket office and small museum). The Marina entrance gives access to the park via the excellent beach. The Alberese entrance provides access to the park on foot or by means of the park shuttle bus. In addition to short trails, there are longer trails of 5 or 4 km (3 or 2½ miles, lasting about three hours). The waymarked paths are not wholly reliable. It is advisable to take drinking water and a picnic. In Alberese, canoes can be hired to explore the canals, and horse-riding is also available.

In the Maremma, **Lago di Burano** (tel: 0564-898829), further south, offers one of the best bird-watching opportunities in Tuscany. This is the southern-most of two lagoons (enclosing wildlife reserves) beside the peninsula of Monte Argentario. This WWF lagoon is home to falcons, cormorants, the black-winged stilt, purple and grey herons, with peregrines, ospreys and marsh harriers using the lagoons as feeding grounds. (By road, the reserve is 500 metres/yards from the Capalbio Scalo exit on the SS1; by rail, travel to the small Capalbio station.) For details of opening times, contact the Maremma national park (as above) or Grosseto provincial tourist office.

The Mugello
In the Mugello, the hamlet of Grezzano has **Casa d'Erci**, which is a farmhouse converted into a

museum of rural life and peasant culture, including early looms and a charcoal-burner's hut. Check opening times on 055-92519.

Pisa Province
Here, the lakeside habitat at **Lago di Massaciuccoli** is home to migratory and wintering wildfowl as well as native species, including flamingos, geese, ducks, cranes and terns. The region's lone surviving lagoon has suffered from intensive shooting but survives nonetheless. For details of opening times and organised tours, contact Pisa provincial tourist office.

For more information, see also Nature Parks, pages 64–5.

Horseriding

There are over 40 centres belonging to the National Association of Equestrian Tourism (FITETREC-ANTE; Piazza A. Mancini 4, 00196 Rome, tel: 06-32650230, www.fitetrec-ante.it) or to the Federazion Italiana Sport Equestri (Viale Tiziano 74, Rome, tel: 06-3233826, www.fise.it).

Here are some suggestions for riding near Tuscany's main cities: **Maneggio Belvedere**, Località Filetta 58010 Sorano (Grosseto), tel: 0564-615465, www.maneggio belvedere.it.
Club Ippico Senese, Località Pian del Lago, Siena, tel: 0577-318677.

For horse-riding centres elsewhere in Tuscany, call the **Centro Ippico Toscano**, Via Vespucci 5r, Florence, tel: 055-315621.

Fishing

Sport fishing can be practised both from the shore and from a boat. In some ports, a special permit is required from the Harbourmaster's Office. Fishing is prohibited within 500 metres/yards of a beach used by bathers and within 50 metres/yards of fishing installations and ships at anchor.

Freshwater fishing. Foreigners need a temporary membership of FIPS (Federazione Italiana della Pesca Sportiva) and a government licence issued by the Provincial Administration. Every provincial town has an office to give advice and notice of restrictions on fishing times and places.

Golf

There are some decent courses in Tuscany; the best include:
Golf Club Ugolino, Via Chiantigiana, Grassina; tel: 055-230 1009; www.golfugolino.it
Montecatini Golf and Country Club (18 holes), Via dei Brogi 32, Località Pievaccia, Monsummano Terme; tel: 0572-62218; www.montecatinigolf.com
Cosmopolitan Golf and Country Club, Viale Pisorno 60, Tirrenia-Pisa; tel: 050-33633; www.cosmopolitangolf.it
Golf Club Punta Ala, Tel: 0564-922121. www.puntaala.net/golf

Tennis

The Cascine Park in Florence has a club open to the public – or you could try these clubs:
Circolo Carraia, Via Monti alle Croci, Florence, tel: 055-2346353.
Zodiac, Via Grandi 2, Tavernuzze (near Florence), tel: 055-2022850.
Circolo Tennis Siena, Loc. Vico Alto, Siena, tel: 0577-335740.

Skiing

Tuscany has a major ski resort at Abetone in the Apennines, north of Pistoia, extending over four valleys with 30 km (19 miles) of trails. For information on ski passes, pistes, etc., call Azienda Autonoma Soggiorno e Turismo in Abetone, tel: 0573-630145.

Watersports

At all Tuscan sea resorts it is possible to water-ski and row with hired boats. Yacht chartering facilities are also available in the resorts of Marina di Pisa and Tirrenia, and Porto Azzurro, Elba.

Diving

Diving is very popular in Tuscany, the best areas being around the Argentario on the southern coast, and the islands Giglio, Giannutri, Elba and Capraia. There is red coral, a huge variety of Mediterranean underwater flora and even a couple of wrecks off Giannutri. Many of the seaside ports in the area have diving clubs which take boats out regularly.
Elba Diving Centre, Marciana Marina, tel: 0565-904256; www.elbadiving.it.
Giglio Diving Club, Via della Torre Campese, tel: 0564-804065; www.geocities.com/gigliodiving.

Swimming Pools

Many Tuscan hotels, villas and *agriturismo* places have swimming pools and there are public pools in most towns, although these often have limited opening hours. Public swimming pools in Florence:
Piscina Le Pavoniere, Viale della Catena 2, tel: 055-362233. Open during the summer. There is also a bar and pizzeria here.
Piscina Nannini, Lungarno Aldo Moro 6, tel: 055-677521. Olympic-size pool which is open air during the summer months.
Siena has its own **Piscina Comunale**, Piazza G. Amendola, tel: 0577-47496.

Spectator Sports

Football is the national sport. Almost every city and village has a team and the most important national championship is the "Serie A" (Premiership), the winner of which is eligible to play in the Champions' League, against other top European teams. If you want to see a game, check the newspaper listings, but it is difficult to get tickets for a big match.
Horse racing is also popular and there is a racecourse in Florence's Cascine park: **Ippodromo le Cascine**, tel: 055-226076.
For tickets for any sporting event, consult the local tourist office or, alternatively, buy the pink *Gazzetta dello Sport* newspaper, which gives the lowdown on what's on when and how to book.

SHOPPING

What to Buy

The quality of goods in Italy is very high and prices generally reasonable. Suggested buys are:
Fashions: dresses, suits, hats, gloves, linen, silk ties and shirts, knitwear, designer labels *(see outlet shopping below)* and jewellery.
Leather goods: prices are not rock bottom but the quality is often excellent and the designs appealing. Shoes and handbags are particularly good buys, but there are also boxes and belts, luggage, briefcases and wallets.
Cloth: silk, linen, wool and cotton.
Handicrafts: lace and tablecloths; pottery, ceramics and porcelain; gold and silver ware; alabaster and marble objects; woodwork; straw and raffia goods; glass and crystal work; art books and reproductions; marbled paper; rustic household goods; prints; antiques; reproduction furniture.
Alcohol: regional wines – along with the well-known Chianti, Montalcino and Montepulciano, wines from the coastal Maremma such as Sassicaia and Ornellaia, and other regions are gaining an international reputation; Italian spirits, liqueurs and aperitifs, such as Grappa or Liquore Strega.
Food: cold-pressed olive oil, herbs, locally made pasta, farmhouse cheeses, bottled vegetables, truffles, dried mushrooms, cured ham, salami, etc.

Shopping Hours

Food stores and general shops open 8.30am–1pm and 3.30 or 4–7.30pm. They stay open a little later in the summer. Many of the bigger supermarkets stay open through lunch and close at around 8.30pm. Department stores and other shops in bigger cities stay open all day (9.30am–7.30/8pm), and there is now limited Sunday opening in some places.

Food shops are usually closed on Wednesday afternoons in Tuscany, but this changes in the summer months, when early closing is usually on Saturday afternoon. Many clothing shops are closed on Monday mornings.

Where to Shop

Chain stores such as Upim and Standa can be found in most towns in Tuscany, and the upmarket Rinascente is in Florence. **Open-air markets** are held usually once or twice a week in almost all tourist resorts and towns. **Supermarkets** are found in most of the resorts and in all big towns, but are less common in smaller towns and villages. **Tobacconist's shops** (called *tabaccai*) sell postage stamps and *schede* (telephone cards), alongside cigarettes and tobacco.

Outlet Shopping

The Arno Valley is the cradle of many clothes factories for some of Italy's top designer labels. They tend to be located between Pontassieve and Incisa Val d'Arno and have retail outlets where there are bargains of up to 60 percent discount. Get there early for the best buys and be prepared to queue. Avoid weekends. The best retail outlets, within easy reach of Florence and Arezzo, include:
The Mall, Via Europe 8, Leccio Regello, tel: 055-865 7775. Gucci, Giorgio Armani, Sergio Rossi, Yves Saint Laurent, Bottega Veneta, Loro Piana, Agnona, Tod's, Hogan, La Perla group, Salvatore Ferragamo, Ungaro, Ermenegildo Zegna, Valentino.
Fendi, Via Pian dell'Isola 66, Rignano sull'Arno, tel: 055-834981. Especially good for accessories.

Dolce e Gabbana, Via Pian dell'Isola 49, Santa Maria Maddalena tel: 055-833 1300. Everything from accessories and clothes to household designer goods.
Prada, Località Levanella, Montevarchi tel: 055-91901. A good selection, but they operate a strict queuing system.

For more information on outlet shopping go to www.outlet firenze.com. Dedicated fashionistas might consider investing in a copy of *Lo Scopri Occasioni* (published in English as *Designer Bargains in Italy*), which has over 1000 outlet addresses. Visit www.scoprioccasioni.it.

Shopping in Florence

Despite tourism, consumerism and high labour costs, Florence still has a reputation as a city with high standards of craftsmanship in many spheres, from silver jewellery to marbled paper. If you wish to visit craftsmen at work, consult the tourist office and ask for their booklets on crafts; these will list the main craftspeople still practising in the city. For example, the **Santa Croce leather school**, on Piazza Santa Croce, is a popular place for visitors to watch skilled Florentine leather-workers.

Antiques

There are two main areas for antiques shops: Via Maggio and the surrounding streets in the Oltrarno and Borgo Ognissanti, west of the centre. There is a wide choice of goods, but you are unlikely to find a bargain.

Books

Edison, Piazza della Repubblica 27; tel: 055-213110; www.libreria edison.it. A large bookshop with an extensive range of language resources and guidebooks. Open daily until midnight.
Feltrinelli Internazionale, Via Cavour 12/20r; tel: 055-219524. The most comprehensive and respected bookshop in Florence, with a range of foreign language books and guides.

Seeber-Melbookstore, Via Cerretani 16r; tel: 055-287339; www.melbookstore.it. This bookshop has a range of books and music as well as a café.
The Paperback Exchange, Via Fiesolana 31r; tel: 055-2478154. North of the Santa Croce district, this is no ordinary bookshop: it stocks just about every book ever written on Florence. They also have a vast stock of quality second-hand English and American paperbacks.

Boutiques

Florence is full of top designer boutiques. The most elegant street is the Via de' Tornabuoni where Versace, Valentino and other big names in fashion have their outlets. Other exclusive streets are the Via Calzaiuoli and Via Roma (both have a stunning range of leather goods), Via della Vigna Nuova and Via del Parione.

The top designer shops are:
Giorgio Armani, Via della Vigna Nuova 51r; tel: 055/212081. For a more affordable Armani, visit Emporio Armani, Piazza Strozzi 14–16r, tel: 055-284315.
Brioni, Via Roma 1, tel: 055-282771. Classic men's style; exquisitely made clothes.
Dolce e Gabbana, Via della Vigna Nuova 27r, tel: 055-281003. Sexy, stylish, often outrageous clothes.
Enrico Coveri, Lungarno Guicciardini, tel: 055-216023. Flamboyant, colourful clothes.
Ferragamo, Via de' Tornabuoni 2, tel: 055-271121. The famous Florentine shoemakers have now branched out into accessories and clothes.
Gucci, Via de' Tornabuoni 73r, tel: 055-264011. The range has expanded, but belts and handbags remain their trademark.
Prada, Via de' Tornabuoni 51–55r and 67r, tel: 055-283439. Gorgeous accessories and shoes.
Emilio Pucci, Via de' Tornabuoni 20–22r, tel: 055-2958082.
Raspini, Via Roma 25r, tel: 055-213077.
Valentino, Via dei Tosinghi 52r, tel: 055-293142.

Versace, Via de' Tornabuoni 13r, tel: 055-296167. Haute couture by Donatella.

Also worth checking out are:

Echo, Via dell'Oriuolo 37r, tel: 055-2381149. An interesting selection of women's clothing arranged by colour.

Ethic, Borgo Albizi 37, tel: 055-2344413. One of the few trendy boutiques to offer clothing at reasonable prices, this shop has constantly changing stock.

Ceramics

Sbigoli Terracotte, Via Sant' Egidio 4r, tel: 055-2479713. Good choice of hand-painted ceramics in traditional and contemporary designs.

Fabrics

Antico Setificio, Via L. Bartolini 4, tel: 055-213861. Fabrics made traditionally, above all silk, still woven on 18th-century looms.

Casa dei Tessuti, Via de' Pecori, 20–24, tel: 055-215961. Fine silks, linens and woollens.

Gloves

Madova, Piazza San Felicità 4; tel: 055-210204. Every kind of glove you could imagine and all of them beautifully made.

Jewellery

There is still a flourishing jewellery trade in Florence (particularly on the Ponte Vecchio and in Oltrarno, on the south side of the river), though most gold jewellery is now made in Arezzo.

The following traditional goldsmiths and silversmiths remain:

Brandimarte, Via Bartolini 18r, tel: 055-239381. Handcrafted silver goods and jewellery in a large store. Good prices.

Marzio Casprini, Via Rosso Fiorentino 2a; tel: 055-710008. Silversmith.

Gatto Bianco, Borgo SS Apostoli 12r, tel: 055-282989. Contemporary designs in gold and silver.

Exclusive Jewellery

If you can afford to push the boat out, these two Florentine estab-lishments are well worth adding to your itinerary:

Buccellati, Via de' Tornabuoni 71r, tel: 055-2396579.

Torrini, Piazza del Duomo 10r, tel: 055-2302401.

Leather

Quality ranges from the beautifully tooled creations of local artisans to shoddy goods aimed at undiscerning tourists. For top-of-the-range quality (and prices), you should start with the designer boutiques in the Via de' Tornabuoni or shops in streets around the Piazza della Repubblica. Try the following outlets:

Raspini, Via Roma 25–29, tel: 055-213077. Superb leather bags and coats.

Il Bisonte, Via del Parione 31r, tel: 055-211976. Bags, luggage and other leather goods at high prices.

Furla, Via della Vigna Nuova 47r, tel: 055-281416. Bags and accessories in contemporary designs. There is also a branch in Siena in Via di Città.

For more down-to-earth prices, head for the **San Lorenzo market** northwest of the Duomo, where numerous street stalls sell shoes, bags, belts and wallets; you can also try the Santa Croce area.

Marbled Paper

Marbled paper is very closely associated with Florence and many of the designs echo ancient themes or Medici crests. With their beautiful colours, vibrant patterns and particular smells, the shops are a joy to visit.

Giulio Giannini e Figlio, Piazza Pitti 37r, tel: 055-280814. Florence's longest-established marbled paper shop.

Il Papiro, Via Cavour 55r; tel: 055-215262; Piazza del Duomo 27r, tel: 055-281628.

Il Torchio, Via de' Bardi 17, tel: 055-2342862. Cheaper than some other shops, you also see the artisans at work.

Markets

Many neighbourhoods have a weekly market. Try the following:

Straw Market (Mercato del Porcellino): hand-embroidered work, Florentine straw, leather goods, wooden objects and flowers.

Flea Market (Mercato delle Pulci, Piazza dei Ciompi): basically junk, but great fun.

Sant'Ambrogio (Piazza Ghiberti): fruit and veg, food and clothes.

San Lorenzo Market (Mercato di San Lorenzo, Piazza San Lorenzo): the covered market sells vegetables, fruit, meat and cheeses etc., while the surrounding streets are filled with stalls selling clothes, shoes, leather and jewellery.

Cascine Market (Mercato delle Cascine, Tuesday mornings only): produce, household goods and clothing.

Pharmacy

Officina Profumo Farmaceutica di Santa Maria Novella, Via della Scala 16, tel: 055-216276. Housed in a frescoed chapel, this fascinating shop was founded by monks in the 16th century. It sells herbal remedies, beautifully packaged perfumes, shampoos, lotions and room scents.

Shoes

Florence is still a good place to buy shoes at reasonable prices.

Cresti, Via Roma 9r, tel: 055-214150. Beautiful shoes at much lower prices than at Ferragamo.

Ferragamo, Via de' Tornabuoni 16r, tel: 055-292123. Italy's most prestigious shoemaker, providing hand-tooled shoes and beautifully crafted ready-to-wear collections.

Francesco, Via di Santo Spirito 62r, tel: 055-212428. Unpretentious hand-made shoes in classic designs tooled by a traditional craftsman.

The roads leading from the Duomo to Santa Maria Novella station have a good range of slightly cheaper shoe shops.

Shopping in Siena

Clothes and Shoes

The main shopping streets in Siena are Banchi di Sopra and Via di Città. They are lined with chain and individual stores selling a range of clothes and footwear.

Crafts

Wrought-iron and copper, ceramics, crystal and stained glass provide a wide choice. **Giogi Leonardo & Co**, at Antica Siena, Piazza del Campo 28, tel: 0577-46496, sells beautiful blue and yellow porcelain, while **Il Papiro** (Via di Città) sells handmade paper and gifts.

Food and Wine

Siena is known for its **confectionery**, particularly *panforte*, which is made from a sweet dough, flavoured with vanilla and full of candied citrus fruits. The most famous maker of such specialities is **Nannini**, at Piazza Matteotti 21 and Piazza del Monte 95/99, and **Bar Pasticceria Nannini** at Via Banchi di Sopra 24 (www.pasticcerienannini.it).

Siena Province produces a variety of good **wines** including Chianti, Brunello di Montalcino and Nobile di Montepulciano. The Permanent Italian Wine Exhibition in Fortezza Medicea (tel: 0577-288497, www.enoteca-italiana.it), was set up for the display and sale of regional wines.

OTHER ACTIVITIES

Children

Tuscany has much to offer children of all ages, from medieval castles to ice creams galore and plenty of child-friendly restaurants. There are several good parks, nature reserves and numerous opportunities for horse-riding, cycling and swimming. Much of the coast of Tuscany, particularly the well equipped resorts near Viareggio and the sandy beaches on islands such as Elba, is also great for children.

Tuscan festivals can be fun, especially the Lenten carnivals, the horse races, the jousting, boat pageants, and all the tiny food festivals *(see pages 280–1)*. To find out what's on, above all in summer, check the listings in *La Repubblica* or *La Nazione* as well as enquiring at the tourist offices. If you read Italian, buy *Firenze Spettacolo*, which has a good children's section: *Città & Ragazzi*.

Some of the suitable places in Tuscany for children are:
The Boboli Gardens *(Giardini di Boboli)* are fun for children to clamber around. There is an amphitheatre, strange statues and grottoes, and a handy café.
The Cascine, Florence's other main park, is popular with local families and at weekends is full of children, many of whom come to visit the tiny zoo.
Giardino dei Tarrocchi, near Capalbio, is a bizarre garden full of colourful fantasy figures.
Ludoteca Centrale, Via Fibbiai 2, Florence, tel: 055-2478386, is a fun children's centre with games, music and audiovisual equipment for the under-sixes.
Pinocchio Park *(Parco di Pinocchio)* at Collodi, near Pisa, is an obvious, if old-fashioned choice for children, tel: 0572-429342. Open 8.30am–sunset.
Pistoia Zoo, Via Pieve a Celle, Pistoia, tel: 0573-911219, www.zoodipistoia.it. Compact zoo, but one of the region's best.
Zoo Fauna Europa, just south of Poppi, tel: 0575-529079. A conservation centre for such breeds as the lynx and the Apennine wolf. Open 8am–sunset.
Canadian Island, Via Gioberti 15, Florence, tel: 055-677567. You can leave your children here if you (or they) are fed up with dragging around the sights. They can play with Italian children in an English-speaking environment.

Spas

Tuscany has a large number of spas, offering a range of health and beauty treatments from mud baths to hydro-massage or just the opportunity to relax in sulphurous hot springs. The cost and standard of accommodation and treatment ranges from basic to 5-star. The Italian Tourist Office (ENIT) has a complete list of facilities available; www.turismo.toscana.it (look at the *Terme e Benessere* section). The Consorzio Terme di Toscana, presso Terme di Chianciano(Via delle Rose 12, 53042 Chinciano Terme (Siena), tel: 0578-68111) also provides information.
Terme Jean Varraud, Piazza S. Martino 11, Bagni di Lucca, tel: 0583-87221, www.termebagnidilucca.it. Soak in the spa waters, have a massage or one of the many beauty treatments.
Terme di Bagno Vignoni, Hotel Posta Marcucci, tel: 0577-887112, www.piscinavaldisole.it. You can get an all-day ticket for the hotel's outdoor spa pool, which offers lovely views.
Terme di Casciana, Piazza Garibaldi 9, Casciana Terme (Pisa), tel: 0587-644461; www.termedicasciana.it. Thermal waters in the Pisan hills.
Terme di Chianciano tel: 0578-68292-3; www.chianciano terme.com. Spa town specialising in liver therapy
Terme di Monsummano, Grotta Giusti Hotel, Via Grotta Giusti 1411, Monsummano Terme (Pistoia), tel: 0572-51008/90771; www.grottagiustispa.com. Four-star treatment in a villa. Specialises in antrotherapy.
Terme di Montecatini, Viale Verdi 66 (tourist office); Montecatini Terme (Pistoia); tel: 0572-0572 7781; www.termemontecatini.it. Whole avenues of spa buildings dispensing waters and treatments from inhalation to mudbaths.
Terme di Montepulciano, Via delle Terme 46, Località S. Albino tel: 0578-7911. Especially good for asthma and bronchitis.
Terme di Saturnia, tel: 564 454527 (tourist information centre); www.termedisaturnia.it. Hotel Terme, Saturnia, tel: 0564-600800/600888/9. Pamper yourself in the luxury hotel or bathe free in the hot springs of the nearby Cascate del Gorello.

TRANSPORT

ACCOMMODATION

ACTIVITIES

A – Z

LANGUAGE

AN ALPHABETICAL SUMMARY OF PRACTICAL INFORMATION

Business Hours

Shops in the main cities open Monday to Friday 8.30am–1pm and 3.30–7.30pm. The majority open on Saturday, and several are open on Sunday too, especially in high season. Some shops in coastal resorts and tourist centres now stay open all day throughout the summer and have Saturday and Sunday opening.

Food shops are closed on Wednesday afternoons in winter and Saturday afternoons in summer. Clothes shops are closed on Monday mornings.

Offices are usually open 8am–1pm and 2–4pm, although many have more extensive opening hours.

On Italian national holidays, all shops and offices are closed.

Climate

The Tuscan climate is pleasantly mild in the spring and autumn, cool and wet in the winter, and very hot near the sea and on low-lying land in the summer, with a pleasant warmth in the hills. There is very little wind except for on the Tyrrhenian coastline around Marina di Pisa and Tirrenia, but surprise storms can be very heavy at any time of the year, and flooding in a number of places has caused severe damage in the past. The rainfall in Tuscany is generally higher than in most other parts of Italy. The temperature is slightly lower than in other areas, making it more agreeable in summer though somewhat colder in winter.

The weather in Florence can be extreme. The city is situated in a bowl, surrounded by hills, with the Arno cutting through it, and this accounts for the high degree of humidity that is often a feature of midsummer. The worst of the humidity is likely to occur between mid-July and mid-August with temperatures climbing well into the 30s Celsius (90s Fahrenheit).

Crime & Safety

Although violent crime is rare, in recent years, much crime in the north has tended to be gang- or drug-related. With increasing numbers of immigrants in Italy, the harassment of so-called "foreigners" (essentially immigrants from former Yugoslavia, Eastern Europe, Albania or Africa) is unfortunately on the increase in a country traditionally unused to dealing with immigrants.

CLIMATE CHART

- ☐ Maximum temperature
- ■ Minimum temperature
- — Rainfall
- ☼ Sunny months
- ☂ Rainy months

The main problem for tourists is petty crime, from pickpocketing and bag-snatching to the theft of objects left unattended in cars; it is wise to have insurance coverage against this and to take basic, sensible precautions against theft. If driving, lock your car and never leave luggage, cameras or other valuables inside. This applies particularly in major cities

If you are the victim of a crime (or suffer a loss) and wish to claim against your insurance, it is essential to make a report at the nearest police station as soon as possible and get documentation to support your claim. When you need a policeman, dial **113** (or **112** for the *Carabinieri*, the national police force).

Customs Regulations

Examination of luggage, passports, currency and hand baggage may take place on both entering and leaving Italy at airports, ports and borders. Formalities may also be also carried out on trains. Registered luggage may be sent to towns with Customs Offices: examination takes place at the destination.

It is no longer possible to buy duty-free or tax-free goods on journeys within the EU; VAT and duty are included in the purchase price. Shops at ports and airports will sell goods duty- and tax-paid to those travelling within the EU; in practice, many shops have chosen not to pass on price increases since the sale of duty-free goods within the EU was abolished.

There are no longer any limits on how much you can buy on journeys within the EU, provided it's for your own personal use. But there are suggested limits, and if you exceed them Customs may seize your goods if you can't prove they are for your own use. The guidance levels are:

- 3,200 cigarettes or 400 cigarillos or 200 cigars or 1 kg of smoking tobacco;
- 10 litres of spirits; 20 litres of fortified wine; 90 litres of wine; 110 litres of beer.

Duty-frees are still available to those travelling outside the EU.

Professional photographers must carry an ATA Carnet (issued in the UK through the London Chamber of Commerce, 33 Queen Street, London EC4R 1AP, tel: 020-7248 4444) for temporary importation of equipment.

D isabled Travellers

Despite difficult cobbled streets and poor wheelchair access to many tourist attractions and hotels, many people with disabilities visit Florence and Tuscany every year.

However, unaccompanied visitors will usually experience some difficulty, so it is best to travel with a companion.

Conditions and disability awareness are improving slowly in Tuscany (as well as in Italy in general), although the situation is certainly not ideal, and access is not always easy. More museums now have lifts, ramps and adapted toilets, newer trains and buses are accessible (although wheelchair users may need help when boarding), and recent laws require restaurants, bars and hotels to provide the relevant facilities. These laws, however, do not always cover access to those facilities. In 2004, Siena became the first Italian city to have an itinerary for the deaf. The brochure, *Siena in Lingua dei Segni*, is available from the tourist information centre, as is information about the facilities offered by sights and museums.

For drivers with disabilities, there are plenty of reserved parking places in towns, and these are free.

In the United Kingdom, you can obtain further information from RADAR, 12 City Forum, 250 City Road, London EC1V 8AF; tel: 020-7250 3222; www.radar.co.uk. In the United States, contact SATH, 5th Avenue, Suite 610, NY 10016; tel: (212) 447-7284; www.sath.org.

E lectricity

Italy uses 220v and two pin plugs. Adaptors for British three-pin appliances can be purchased from airports or departments stores in the city. You will need a transformer to use 100–120 volt appliances.

Embassies

Australian Embassy: Via Antonio Bosio 5, 00161 Roma; tel: 06-852721.
UK Embassy: Via XX Settembre 80a, 00187 Roma; tel: 06-42200001.

EMERGENCY NUMBERS

Fire Brigade: 115.
Medical Aid/Ambulance: 118.
Police Immediate Action: 112.
General Emergency: Fire, Police or Ambulance (replies are in foreign languages in the main cities): 113.
Automobile Club d'Italia (ACI):
- 24-hour breakdown: 803-116.
- 24-hour information line: 1518.

TRANSPORT

ACCOMMODATION

ACTIVITIES

A – Z

LANGUAGE

UK Consulate: Lungarno Corsini 2, 50123 Firenze; tel: 055-284133.
US Embassy: Via Vittorio Veneto 119a, 00187 Roma; tel: 06-46741.
US Consulate: Lungarno A. Vespucci 38, 50123 Firenze; tel: 055-266951.

Emergencies

Useful Florence Contacts

Heart Emergency Mobile Coronary Unit: 055-214444.
Ambulances (Misericordia) Piazza Duomo 19–20: tel: 188 or 055-212222.
Tourist Medical Service 24-hour home visits, with English- or French-speaking doctors: Via Lorenzo il Magnifico 59, tel 055-475411.
Lost Property Via Circondaria 17b, tel: 055-3283942.
Automobile Club d'Italia (ACI) tel: 055-24861.
Car pound – if your car is towed away - tel: 055-308249.
Police Headquarters (Questura) – the place to visit in the event of thefts, lost passports, etc., Via Zara 2, tel: 055-49771.
Tourist Police (Polizia Assistenza Turistica) are at Via Pietrapiana 50r, tel: 055-203911, and have interpreters on hand to assist.
Associazione Volontari Ospedalieri, Florence, tel: 055-2344567. This group of volunteers will translate (free) for foreign patients.

Useful Siena Contacts

Siena Hospital Nuovo Policlinico di Siena, Località le Scotte, Viale Bracci, tel: 0577-585111.
Police Station (Questura), Via del Castoro 6, tel: 0577-201111 – open 24 hours a day.
Pronto Soccorso (Misericordia), Via del Porrione 49, Siena, tel: 0577-21011, or dial 118 in an emergency.
Lost Property Via Casato di Sotto 23, tel: 0577-292426.

Associazione Volontari Ospedalieri, Siena, tel: 0577-247869.

Entry Requirements

Visas & Passports

Subjects from European Union countries require either a passport or a Visitor's Identification Card to enter Italy. A visa is not required. Holders of passports from most other countries do not require visas for stays of less than three months, except for nationals of Eastern European countries, who need to obtain visas from the Italian Embassy in their own country.

Police Registration

A person may stay in Italy for three months as a tourist, but police registration is required within three days of entering Italy. If staying at a hotel, the management will attend to the formality. Although this regulation seems to be rarely observed, it is advisable that you carry a set of passport photos in case you need them for registration.

You are legally obliged to carry a form of identification (passport, driving licence, etc.) with you at all times. This rule is often flouted but bear in mind that it would be unwise to call the police or attempt to report a problem (e.g. theft) unless you are carrying appropriate identification.

Etiquette

Tuscans are generally friendly and will appreciate efforts to speak the language. Any attempt to rush or pressure them, however, will be regarded as the height of bad taste, and whatever you want will take longer. Almost everything is done on the basis of personal favours or contacts so any personal recommendations you can muster will always come in useful.

H ealth

UK visitors are entitled to medical treatment in Italy provided they have a European Health Insurance Card (tel: 0845 606 2030, visit www.dh.gov.uk, or obtain an application form from the post office). There are similar arrangements for citizens of other European Union countries. As few Italians have faith in their own state health service, it may be advisable to take out insurance for private treatment in case of accident.

Vsitors from outside the EU are strongly advised to take out adequate holiday and medical insurance to provide full cover during their stay abroad.

In high summer, the weather can be very hot; sunscreen, shady hats and mosquito repellent are recommended.

Medical Services

Pharmacies: The staff in chemist's shops (farmacie) are usually very knowledgeable about common illnesses and sell far more medicines without prescription than in some other countries (even so, most drugs still require a prescription). Pharmacies are identified by a cross, often red or green and usually in neon.

Normal pharmacy opening hours are Mon–Fri 9am–1pm and 4pm–7pm. Every farmacia posts a list of the local chemists who are on emergency duty on to their pharmacy window. The following are chemist's shops which are open 24 hours in Florence:

Farmacia Comunale 13, in Florence station, tel: 055-216761.
Farmacia Molteni, Via Calzaiuoli 7r, tel: 055-215472.
Farmacia all'Insegna del Moro, Piazza San Giovanni 20r, tel: 055-211343.

In addition, you can call 800-420707 to find out which chemists are on the night rota.

First Aid Service (Pronto Soccorso) with a doctor is found at airports, railway stations and in all hospitals. See box on page 289 for numbers to call in an emergency.

M aps

Touring Club Italiano does a good fold-out map of the Tuscany region showing major and minor roads. The Siena and Florence tourist offices supply reasonable city maps. *Insight Guide Fleximaps* are also available for Florence and Tuscany.

Media

Each large Italian town has its own newspaper. *La Stampa, Il Corriere della Sera,* and *La Repubblica* also have a national following. *La Nazione* is the paper favoured by most Tuscans for regional matters.

Television is deregulated in Italy. In addition to the state network, RAI (which offers three channels), there are about 1,000 channels, of which the main ones are Canale 5, Rete 4, Italia 1, Telemontecarlo and Video Music.

There are several useful publications for visitors to Tuscany, including *Firenze Spettacolo*, a monthly listings magazine in Italian (with some listings also in English), focusing on nightlife, clubs, bars and the live arts in Florence.

Money Matters

In common with the other Eurozone countries of the EU, Italy's monetary unit is the Euro (€),

CALLING HOME

To call abroad from Italy, dial 00, followed by:
Australia 61
Canada 1
Ireland 353
New Zealand 64
UK 44
USA 1
Then dial the number, omitting the initial "0" if there is one.

which is divided into 100 cents. The currency is available in 500, 200, 100, 50, 20, 10 and 5 euro notes, and 2-euro, 1-euro, 50-cent, 20-cent, 10-cent, 5-cent, 2-cent and 1-cent coins.

Italy is a society that prefers cash to credit cards, except for large purchases, or, for instance, hotel bills. In the case of petrol stations, more modest restaurants and smaller shops, it is usual to pay in cash. Check beforehand if there is any doubt. Most shopkeepers and restaurateurs will not change money, so it is best to change a limited amount at the airport when you arrive, especially if it is the weekend, when banks are closed. Try to avoid changing money in hotels, where the commission tends to be higher than in banks.

Travellers' Cheques

Although travellers' cheques are gradually being replaced by credit cards, euro, dollar or sterling travellers' cheques are easy to cash, subject to a commission, but remember that you will be required to present your passport. In some cases they can be used in exchange for goods and services in shops and hotels.

Cash Machines and Credit Cards

Given the long queues for money-changing in Italy, it is simplest to get cash from cashpoint machines, which are now widely available. Most Maestro cards work in Italian machines, with your normal PIN number, as do credit cards, though you may sometimes have to look for particular "Bancomats" (cashpoint machines) that take your card.

In cities, many restaurants, hotels, shops and stores will take major credit cards, but in rural areas especially, you may be able to pay only in cash.

Banks

Banks offer the best exchange rates (small exchange booths often charge up to 3 percent

TIME ZONE

Italy works on GMT + 1 and switches to DST – daylight saving time, GMT + 2 – at the same time as the rest of Europe.

commission) and are normally open Mon–Fri 8.30am–1.30pm. Some banks also open in the afternoon 2.30pm–4.30pm. Outside these hours and at weekends you can use automatic exchange machines to change cash. There is a high concentration of banks in Florence, including foreign banks, to the west of Piazza della Repubblica, around Via Tornabuoni.

Florence
Banca Commerciale Italiana, Via Tornabuoni 16.
Banca d'America e d'Italia, Via Strozzi 16.
Banca d'Italia, Via dell'Oriuolo 37/39.
Banca Toscana, Corso 6.
Credito Italiano, Via Vecchietti 11.
Cassa di Risparmio di Firenze, Via Bufalini 6.

Siena
Banca Nazionale del Lavoro, Via Vittorio Veneto 43.
Banca di Roma, Via dei Termini 37.
Cassa di Risparmio di Firenze, Piazza Tolomei 11.
Monte dei Paschi di Siena, Via Banchi di Sopra 84.

Exchange Offices
Florence
Change Underground, Piazza Stazione 14, Int. 37 (under the station).
Post Office, Via Pellicceria 3 (1st floor), near Piazza della Repubblica. Open Mon–Sat 8.15am–7pm.

Siena
Viaggi Seti (Piazza del Campo 56) – changes notes and travellers' cheques.

TRANSPORT
ACCOMMODATION
ACTIVITIES
A – Z
LANGUAGE

Coop "Siena Hotels Promotion"
(Piazza San Domenico) – changes
notes and travellers' cheques.
Forexchange (Via di Città 80-82)
– changes notes and traveller's
cheques and processes Western
Union transfers.

P ostal Services

Main post offices in major towns
are open all day; otherwise the
hours are 8am–1.30pm
(12.30pm Saturday). Stamps are
sold at post offices and tobacconist's shops *(tabacchi)*.

There is also a courier service
for sending important documents
world-wide in 24/48 hours. This
service is only available at major
post offices. In Florence these
are at Via Pellicceria 3 (main post
office) and Via Alamanni 20r (by
the station).

Poste Restante

Correspondence addressed c/o
Post Office with FERMO POSTA
added to the name of the locality
will be held for collection (for 30
days). Letters are held at the
local Central Post Office and will
be handed over the Fermo Posta
counter on proof of identity – usually a passport – and a fee.

T elecommunication

Telephones

Most public telephones accept
phonecards *(carte telefoniche* or
schede telefoniche) and these
are available from tobacconists
or post offices in various denomi-
nations; few telephones now
accept coins. From some bars,
and from post offices, you can
call *scatti* (ring first, pay later
according to the number of units
or *scatti* used).

Italy has an extremely high
ownership of mobile phones and
in the major cities, such as Florence, it is possible to hire one.

For long-distance calls, the
cheapest time to telephone is
between 10pm and 8am Monday
to Saturday, and all day Sunday.

PUBLIC HOLIDAYS

● **1 January** – *Capodanno*
(New Year's Day).
● **6 January** – La Befana
(Epiphany)
● **Easter** – *Pasqua.*
● **Easter Monday** – *Pasquetta.*
● **25 April** – *Anniversario della
Liberazione* (Liberation Day).
● **1 May** – *Festa del Lavoro*
(Labour Day).
● **24 June** – *San Giovanni*
(St John the Baptist) – in
Florence only.
● **15 August** – *Ferragosto*
(Assumption of the Virgin
Mary).
● **1 November** – *Ognissanti*
(All Saints' Day).
● **8 December** – *Immacolata
Concezione* (Immaculate
Conception).
● **25 December** – *Natale*
(Christmas Day).
● **26 December** – *Santo
Stefano* (Boxing Day).

For directory enquiries dial 12.
For international enquiries, call
176 and to make a reverse
charges (collect) call, dial 170.

When dialling Italy from
abroad, dial the country code
(0039) and the area code
including the initial zero. In Italy,
when calling numbers either
inside or outside your area,
dialling must always be
preceded by the area code
including the zero. The area
code for Florence is 055 and for
Pisa the area code is 050.

E-mail, Internet and Fax

Most large hotels offer internet,
e-mail and fax facilities. There
are numerous internet cafés
around Florence, including the
chain Internet Train which allows
you to connect using their computers or your own laptop. Most
main post offices and stations
have fax facilities.

INTALCABLE provides international telegram services;
telegrams may be dictated over
the phone.

Tipping

Most Italian restaurants levy a
coperto of around €2 per person –
a cover charge for linen, bread
and service – and so tipping isn't
as common as in other countries.
However, in pricier places a tip of
around 10 percent is an appropriate indication of appreciation of
good service. Only in the finest
hotels, and for lengthy stays, is it
customary to tip bellboys, maids
and head waiters. You may wish to
note that according to Italian law,
you should keep the bill with you
until you are at least 100 metres
(300 ft) from the restaurant.

Tourist Board

The Italian State Tourist Board,
known as ENIT (Ente Nazionale per
il Turismo), provides tourist information. ENIT's headquarters are in
Via Marghera 2/6 Rome (tel: 06-
49711; www. enit.it).
In the UK, ENIT, 1 Princes Street,
London W1R 2AY; tel: 020-7408
1254; fax: 020-7493 6695.
In the US, ENIT, Suite 1565, 630
Fifth Avenue, New York, NY
10111; tel: 212-245 4822; fax:
212-586 9249. There are also
offices in Chicago, Los Angeles
and Canada.
Website: www.italiantourism.com

Tourist Offices

Tourist information is available at
the Azienda di Promozione Turistica (APT), the main tourist office
in each provincial capital. In addition, there is a tourist office *(Ufficio di Turismo)* in most towns. In
small places, the *Comune* holds
tourist information and some commercial banks and travel agencies
publish tourist guides. The Touring
Club Italiano (TCI), with offices in
almost every town, provides free
information about the area.

Arezzo Province

Arezzo: Piazza Risorgimento 116,
Arezzo, tel: 0575-23952; Piazza
della Repubblica 28, tel: 0575-
377678.

Cortona: Via Nazionale 42, tel: 0575-630352.
www.apt.arezzo.it

Florence Province

Florence: Via Manzoni 16, 50121 Firenze, tel: 055-23320; Via Cavour 1r, tel: 055-290832; Borgo Santa Croce 29r, tel: 055-2340444; and Piazza della Stazione 4, tel: 055-212245.
www.firenzeturismo.it
Fiesole: Via Portigiani 3/5, tel: 055-598720.

Grosseto Province

Grosseto: Via Fucini 43c, tel: 0564-414303; Viale Monterosa 206, tel: 0564-462611.
www.lamaremmafabene.it

Livorno Province

Livorno: Piazza Cavour 6, 57100, tel: 0586-898111. There is also the Harbour Information Office, Porto Mediceo, tel: 0586-895320.
www.costadeglietruschi.it
Elba: Calata Italia 26, 57037 Portoferraio, tel: 0565-914671.
www.aptelba.it

Lucca Province

Lucca: Piazza Guidiccioni 2, tel: 0583-91991; Piazza Santa Maria 35, tel: 0583-919931; Vecchia Porta San Donato, Piazzale Verdi, 55100, tel: 0583-442944.
www.turismo.provincia.lucca.it
Bagni di Lucca: Via E. Wipple, tel: 0583-804557.
Viareggio: Viale Carducci 10, tel: 0584-962233.

Massa-Carrara Province

Marina di Massa: Lungomare Vespucci 24, tel: 0585-240046.
Marina di Carrara: Via Garibaldi 41d, tel: 0585-632519.
www.aptmassacarrara.it

Pisa Province

Pisa: Via Pietro Nenni 24, tel: 050-929777; Via Duomo 1, tel: 050-560464;
www.pisa.turismo.toscana.it
Volterra: Piazza dei Priori 20, tel: 0588-87257.

Pistoia Province

Pistoia: Piazza del Duomo 1, tel: 0573-21622.
www.pistoia.turismo.toscana.it
San Marcello Pistoiese: Via Marconi 70, tel: 0573-630145.

Prato Province

Prato: Piazza Santa Maria delle Carceri 15, tel: 0574-24112.
www.prato.turismo.toscana.it

Siena Province

Siena: Piazza del Campo 56, 53100, tel: 0577-280551.
www.terresiena.it

W ebsites

Useful websites are given throughout the book. The following is just a selection of the many additional sites on Italy, Florence and Tuscany that are available on the web:

Tuscany Tourist Information: www.turismo.toscana.it.
Database on all Italian museums: www.museionline.com
Florence: www.firenzemusei.it, www.polomuseale.firenze.it.
Best routes in Italy: www.autostrade.it, www.rac.co.uk, www.theaa.com. Plan your journey from one Italian destination to another.
Piazze d'Italia: www.mediasoft.it/piazze Visit different squares in Italy, including virtual tours. Information plus hotels and restaurants: www.firenzeturismo.it.
Agriturismo **in Tuscany**: www.agriturismo.regione.toscana.it Official site giving information on rural farm stays in this popular area.
General Information: www.itwg.com www.charmingtuscany.com
Events: www.firenzespettacolo.it.

Weights and Measures

The metric system is used for weights and measures.

Multiply by the following:

Centimetres to inches	0.4
Metres to feet	3.3
Metres to yards	1.1
Kilometres to miles	0.6
Kilograms to pounds	2.2

Italians refer to 100 grams (about a quarter of a pound) as *un etto;* 200 grams are therefore *due etti.*
Liquid measurements are in litres. One litre is 1.75 imperial pints.
Temperatures are given in Celsius (Centigrade).

What To Bring

Towns like Florence, Lucca and Siena are sophisticated, so take something smart for shopping or dining out, although jackets and ties are rarely required for men. It can rain unexpectedly wherever you are, so a raincoat is an essential piece of clothing; it should be large enough to cover anything worn, and light enough to be folded and carried.
Decent dress is required when visiting religious buildings: men and women are expected to have their arms covered, and shorts are frowned upon. Women often carry a headscarf as a simple head covering. Sun hats are also recommended as protection.
Shoes need to be sturdy but comfortable and suitable for walking – especially on cobbled streets and for climbing steps.
Binoculars are a good idea for nature studies and viewing architectural details and frescoes.

LANGUAGE

UNDERSTANDING ITALIAN

Language Tips

In Tuscany, the Italian language is supplemented by regional dialects. In large cities and tourist centres you will find many people who speak English, French or German. It is well worth buying a good phrase book or dictionary, but the following will help you get started. Since this glossary is aimed at non-linguists, we have opted for the simplest options rather than the most elegant Italian.

Pronunciation and Grammar Tips

Italian speakers claim that pronunciation is straightforward: you pronounce it as it is written. This is approximately true but there are a couple of important rules for English speakers to bear in mind: *c* before *e* or *i* is pronounced "ch", e.g. *ciao, mi dispiace, coincidenza*. *Ch* before *i* or *e* is pronounced as "k", e.g. *la chiesa*. Likewise, *sci* or *sce* are pronounced as in "sheep" or "shed". *Gn* in Italian is rather like the sound in "onion", while *gl* is softened to resemble the sound in "bullion".

Nouns are either masculine *(il,* plural *i)* or feminine *(la,* plural *le).* Plurals of nouns are most often formed by changing an *o* to an *i*

and an *a* to an *e*, e.g. *il panino, i panini; la chiesa, le chiese.*

Words are stressed on the penultimate syllable unless an accent indicates otherwise, generally speaking.

Like many languages, Italian has formal and informal words for "You". In the singular, *Tu* is informal while *Lei* is more polite. For visitors, it is simplest and most respectful to use the formal form unless invited to do otherwise. There is, of course, rather more to the language than that, but you can get a surprisingly long way towards making friends with a few phrases.

Basic Communication

Yes *Sì*	
No *No*	
Thank you *Grazie*	
You're welcome *Prego*	
Alright/Okay/That's fine *Va bene*	
Please *Per favore* or *per cortesia*	
Excuse me (to get attention) *Scusi* (singular), *Scusate* (plural)	
Excuse me (to get through a crowd) *Permesso*	
Excuse me (to attract attention, e.g. of a waiter) *Senta!*	
Excuse me (sorry) *Mi scusi*	
Could you help me? (formal) *Potrebbe aiutarmi?*	
Certainly *Ma, certo*	

Can I help you? (formal) *Posso aiutarLa?*
I need ... *Ho bisogno di ...*
I'm sorry *Mi dispiace*
I don't know *Non lo so*
I don't understand *Non capisco*
Could you speak more slowly, please? *Può parlare piu lentamente, per favore?*
Could you repeat that please? *Può ripetere, per piacere?*
What? *Quale/come?*
When/why/where? *Quando/perchè/dove?*
Where is the lavatory? *Dov'è il bagno?*

Greetings

Hello (Good day) *Buon giorno*
Good afternoon/evening *Buona sera*
Good night *Buona notte*
Goodbye *Arrivederci*
Hello/Hi/Goodbye (familiar) *Ciao*
Mr/Mrs/Miss *Signor/Signora/Signorina*
Pleased to meet you (formal) *Piacere di conoscerLa*
Do you speak English? *Parla inglese?*
I am English/American *Sono inglese/americano*
Canadian/Australian *canadese/australiano*
How are you (formal/informal)? *Come sta/come stai?*
Fine thanks *Bene, grazie*

TRANSPORT

ACCOMMODATION

ACTIVITIES

A – Z

LANGUAGE

Telephone Calls

the area code il prefisso
May I use your telephone, please? Posso usare il telefono?
Hello (on the telephone) Pronto
My name's Mi chiamo/Sono
Could I speak to...? Posso parlare con...?
Can you speak up please? Può parlare più forte, per favore?

In the Hotel

Do you have any vacant rooms? Avete camere libere?
I have a reservation Ho fatto una prenotazione
I'd like... Vorrei...
  a room with twin beds una camera a due letti
  a single/double room (with a double bed) una camera singola/doppia (con letto matrimoniale)
  a room with a bath/shower una camera con bagno/doccia
for one night per una notte
for two nights per due notti
How much is it? Quanto costa?
Is breakfast included?
E compresa la prima colazione?
half/full board mezza pensione/pensione completa
Do you have a room with a balcony/view of the sea?
C'è una camera con balcone/con una vista del mare?
Is it a quiet room? E una stanza tranquilla?
Can I see the room? Posso vedere la camera?
Can I have the bill, please? Posso avere il conto, per favore?
Can you call me a taxi, please? Può chiamarmi un tassì/taxi, per favore?

Eating Out

Bar snacks and drinks

I'd like... Vorrei...
coffee un caffè (espresso: small, strong and black)
un caffellatte (like café au lait in France)
un caffè lungo (weak, served in a tall glass)
un corretto (laced with alcohol, probably brandy or grappa)
tea un tè
herbal tea una tisana
hot chocolate una cioccolata calda
orange/lemon juice (bottled) un succo d'arancia/di limone
fizzy/still mineral water acqua minerale gassata/naturale
with/without ice con/senza ghiaccio
red/white wine vino rosso/bianco
beer una birra
milk latte
a (half) litre un (mezzo) litro
ice cream un gelato
sandwich un tramezzino
roll un panino
Cheers Salute

In a Restaurant

I'd like to book a table Vorrei riservare una tavola
Have you got a table for...? Avete una tavola per ...?
I have a reservation Ho fatto una prenotazione
lunch/supper il pranzo/la cena
I'm a vegetarian Sono vegetariano/a
Is there a vegetarian dish? C'è un piatto vegetariano?
May we have the menu? Ci dia la carta?
wine list la lista dei vini
home-made fatto in casa
What would you like? Che cosa prende?
What would you recommend? Che cosa ci raccomanda?
home-made fatto in casa
What would you like as a main course/dessert? Che cosa prende di secondo/di dolce?
What would you like to drink? Che cosa desidera da bere?
a carafe of red/white wine una caraffa di vino rosso/bianco
the dish of the day il piatto del giorno
cover charge il coperto/pane e coperto
The bill, please Il conto per favore
Is service included? Il servizio è incluso?

Menu Decoder

Antipasti (hors d'oeuvres)

antipasto misto mixed hors d'oeuvres (including cold cuts, possibly cheeses and roast vegetables)
buffet freddo cold buffet
caponata mixed aubergine, olives and tomatoes
insalata caprese tomato and mozzarella salad
insalata di mare seafood salad
insalata mista/verde mixed/green salad
melanzane alla parmigiana fried or baked aubergine (with parmesan cheese and tomato)
mortadella/salame salami
peperonata grilled peppers (drenched in olive oil)

Primi (first courses)

Typical first courses include soup, risotto, gnocchi or numerous varieties of pasta in a wide range of sauces.
il brodetto fish soup
i crespolini savoury pancakes
gli gnocchi dumplings
la minestra soup
il minestrone thick vegetable soup
pasta e fagioli pasta and bean soup

EMERGENCIES

Help! Aiuto!
Stop! Fermate!
I've had an accident Ho avuto un incidente
Watch out! Attenzione!
Call a doctor Per favore, chiama un medico
Call an ambulance Chiama un'ambulanza
Call the police Chiama la Polizia/i Carabinieri
Call the fire brigade Chiama i pompieri
Where is the telephone? Dov'è il telefono?
Where is the nearest hospital? Dov'è l'ospedale più vicino?
I would like to report a theft Voglio denunciare un furto

il prosciutto (cotto/crudo) **ham** (cooked/cured)
i tartufi **truffles**
la zuppa **soup**

Secondi (main courses)

Typical main courses are fish-, seafood- or meat-based, with accompaniments *(contorni)* that vary greatly from region to region.

La carne (meat)
allo spiedo **on the spit**
arrosto **roast meat**
al ferro **grilled without oil**
al forno **baked**
al girarrosto **spit-roasted**
alla griglia **grilled**
stufato **braised, stewed**
ben cotto **well-done** (steak, etc.)
al puntino **medium** (steak, etc.)
al sangue **rare** (steak, etc.)
l'agnello **lamb**
il bresaolo **dried salted beef**
la bistecca **steak**
il maiale **pork**
il manzo **beef**
l'ossobuco **shin of veal**
il pollo **chicken**
la salsiccia **sausage**
saltimbocca (alla romana) **veal escalopes with ham**
le scaloppine **escalopes**
lo stufato **stew**
il sugo **sauce**

Frutti di mare (seafood)
Beware the word *"surgelati"*, meaning frozen rather than fresh.
affumicato **smoked**
alle brace **charcoal grilled/ barbecued**
alla griglia **grilled**
fritto **fried**
ripieno **stuffed**
al vapore **steamed**
le acciughe **anchovies**
l'aragosta **lobster**
il branzino **sea bass**
i calamari **squid**
i calamaretti **baby squid**
i crostacei **shellfish**
le cozze **mussels**
il fritto misto **mixed fried fish**
i gamberi **prawns**
i gamberetti **shrimps**
il granchio **crab**
il merluzzo **cod**
le ostriche **oysters**

il pesce **fish**
il pesce spada **swordfish**
il polipo **octopus**
il risotto di mare **seafood risotto**
le sarde **sardines**
la sogliola **sole**
le seppie **cuttlefish**
la triglia **red mullet**
la trota **trout**
il tonno **tuna**
le vongole **clams**

I legumi/la verdura (vegetables)
a scelta **of your choice**
i contorni **accompaniments**
ripieno **stuffed**
gli asparagi **asparagus**
la bietola **similar to spinach**
il carciofo **artichoke**
le carote **carrots**
i carciofini **artichoke hearts**
il cavolo **cabbage**
la cicoria **chicory**
la cipolla **onion**
i funghi **mushrooms**
i fagioli **beans**
i fagiolini **French (green) beans**
le fave **broad beans**
il finocchio **fennel**
l'insalata mista **mixed salad**
l'insalata verde **green salad**
la melanzana **aubergine**
le patate **potatoes**
le patatine fritte **French fries**
i peperoni **peppers**
i piselli **peas**
i pomodori **tomatoes**
le primizie **spring vegetables**
il radicchio **red lettuce**
la rughetta **rocket**
i ravanelli **radishes**
gli spinaci **spinach**
la verdura **green vegetables**
la zucca **pumpkin/squash**
gli zucchini **courgettes**

I dolci (desserts)

al carrello **(desserts) from the trolley**
un semifreddo **semi-frozen dessert (many types)**
la bavarese **mousse**
la cassata **Sicilian ice cream with candied peel**
un gelato **ice cream**
una granita **water ice**
una macedonia di frutta **fruit salad**

il tartufo (nero) **(chocolate) ice cream dessert**
il tiramisù **cold, creamy rum and coffee dessert**
la torta **cake/tart**
lo zabaglione **dessert made with eggs and Marsala wine**
lo zuccotto **ice cream liqueur**
la zuppa inglese **trifle**

La frutta (fruit)
le albicocche **apricots**
le arance **oranges**
le banane **bananas**
il cocomero **watermelon**
le ciliege **cherries**
i fichi **figs**
le fragole **strawberries**
i frutti di bosco **fruits of the forest**
i lamponi **raspberries**
la mela **apple**
il melone **melon**
la pesca **peach**
la pera **pear**
il pompelmo **grapefruit**
le uve **grapes**

Basic foods

l'aceto **vinegar**
l'aglio **garlic**
il burro **butter**
il formaggio **cheese**
la frittata **omelette**
la grana **parmesan cheese**
i grissini **bread sticks**
l'olio **oil**
la marmellata **jam**
il pane **bread**
il pane integrale **wholemeal bread**
il parmigiano **parmesan cheese**
il pepe **pepper**
il riso **rice**
il sale **salt**
le uova **eggs**
lo zucchero **sugar**

Si può visitare? **Can one visit?**
Suonare il campanello **ring the bell**
aperto/a **open**
chiuso/a **closed**
chiuso per la festa **closed for the festival**
chiuso per ferie **closed for the holidays**
chiuso per restauro **closed for restoration**

Is it possible to see the church?
E possibile visitare la chiesa?
Where can I find the custodian/sacristan/key?
Dove posso trovare il custode/il sacristano/la chiave?

At the Shops

What time do you open/close?
A che ora apre/chiude?
Closed for the holidays (typical sign) *Chiuso per ferie*
Pull/push (sign on doors) *Tirare/spingere*
Entrance/exit *Entrata/uscita*
Can I help you? (formal) *Posso aiutarLa?*
What would you like? *Che cosa desidera?*
I'm just looking *Sto soltanto guardando*
How much does it cost? *Quant'è, per favore?*
Do you take credit cards?
Accettate carte di credito?
I'd like... *Vorrei...*
this one/that one *questo/quello*
I'd like that one, please *Vorrei quello lì, per cortesia*
Have you got ...? *Avete ...?*
We haven't got (any) ... *Non (ne) abbiamo...*
Can I try it on? *Posso provare?*
the size (for clothes) *la taglia*
What size do you take? *Qual'è Sua taglia?*
the size (for shoes) *il numero*
expensive/cheap *caro/economico*
It's too small/big *E troppo piccolo/grande*
I (don't) **like it** *(Non) mi piace*
I'll take it/I'll leave it *Lo prendo/Lo lascio*
This is faulty. Can I have a replacement/refund? *C'è un difetto. Me lo potrebbe cambiare/rimborsare?*
Anything else? *Altro?*
Give me some of those *Mi dia alcuni di quelli lì*
a (half) kilo *un (mezzo) chilo*
100 grams *un etto*
200 grams *due etti*
more/less *più/meno*
with/without *con/senza*
a little *un pocchino*
That's enough *Basta così*

Types of shops

bank *la banca*
bureau de change *il cambio*
chemist's *la farmacia*
food shop *l'alimentari*
leather shop *la pelletteria*
market *il mercato*
news-stand *l'edicola*
post office *l'ufficio postale*
supermarket *il supermercato*
tobacconist *il tabaccaio*
travel agency *l'agenzia di viaggi*

Travelling

Transport

airport *l'aeroporto*
arrivals/departures *arrivi/partenze*
boat *la barca*
bus *l'autobus/il pullman*
bus station *l'autostazione*
car *la macchina*
ferry *il traghetto*
first/second class *prima/seconda classe*
flight *il volo*
left luggage office *il deposito bagagli*
motorway *l'autostrada*
no smoking *vietato fumare*
platform *il binario*
railway station *la stazione (ferroviaria)*
stop *la fermata*

At the station

Can you help me please? *Mi può aiutare, per favore?*
Where can I buy tickets? *Dove posso fare i biglietti?*
at the ticket office/at the counter *alla biglietteria/allo sportello*
What time does the train leave? *A che ora parte il treno?*
What time does the train arrive? *A che ora arriva il treno?*
Can I book a seat? *Posso prenotare un posto?*
Is this seat free/taken? *E libero/occupato questo posto?*
I'm afraid this is my seat *E il mio posto, mi dispiace*
You'll have to pay a supplement *Deve pagare un supplemento*
Do I have to change? *Devo cambiare?*

Where does it stop? *Dove si ferma?*
You need to change in Firenze *Bisogna cambiare a Florence*
Which platform does the train leave from? *Da quale binario parte il treno?*
The train leaves from platform one *Il treno parte dal binario uno*
When is the next train/bus/ferry for Pisa? *Quando parte il prossimo treno/pullman/traghetto per Pisa?*
How long does the crossing take? *Quanto dura la traversata?*
What time does the bus leave for Siena? *Quando parte l'autobus per Siena?*
Next stop please *La prossima fermata per favore*
Is this the right stop? *E la fermata giusta?*
The train is late *Il treno è in ritardo*
Can you tell me where to get off? *Mi può dire dove devo scendere?*

Directions

right/left *a destra/a sinistra*
first left/second right *la prima a sinistra/la seconda a destra*
Turn to the right/left *Gira a destra/sinistra*
Go straight on *Va sempre diritto*
Go straight on until the lights *Va sempre diritto fino al semaforo*
opposite/next to *di fronte/accanto a*
up/down *su/gìu*
traffic lights *il semaforo*
Where is ...? *Dov'è ...?*
Where are ...? *Dove sono ...?*
How do I get there? *Come si può andare?* (or: *Come faccio per arrivare a ...?*)

On the Road

petrol *la benzina*
petrol station/garage *la stazione servizio*
oil *l'olio*
Fill it up please *Faccia il pieno, per favore*
lead free/unleaded/diesel *senza piombo/benzina verde/diesel*
My car won't start *La mia macchina non s'accende*
My car has broken down *La macchina è guasta*

FURTHER READING

Art and History

The Architecture of the Italian Renaissance, by Peter Murray. Thames and Hudson.
Autobiography, by Benvenuto Cellini. Penguin Classics.
Catherine de Medici: a Biography by Leonie Frieda. Phoenix
A Concise Encyclopedia of the Italian Renaissance, edited by J.R. Hale. Thames and Hudson.
Etruscan Places, by D.H. Lawrence. Olive Press.
The Florentine Renaissance and *The Flowering of the Renaissance* by Vincent Cronin. Fontana.
The High Renaissance and *The Late Renaissance and Mannerism*, by Linda Murray. Thames and Hudson.
The Italian Painters of the Renaissance, by Bernard Berenson. Phaidon Press.
Lives of the Artists, vols. 1 & 2, by Giorgio Vasari. Penguin Classics.
Machiavelli, by Anglo Sydney. Paladin.
The Merchant of Prato, by Iris Origo. Penguin.
Painter's Florence, by Barbara Whelpton Johnson.
The Rise and Fall of the House of Medici, by Christopher Hibbert. Penguin.
Siena: A City and its History, by Judith Hook. Hamish Hamilton.

Travel Companions

A Room with a View, by E.M. Forster. Penguin.
D.H. Lawrence and Italy, by D.H. Lawrence. Penguin.
The Italians, by Luigi Barzini. Hamish Hamilton.
Italian Hours, by Henry James. Century Hutchinson.
Love and War in the Apennines, by Eric Newby. Picador.
The Love of Italy, by Jonathan Keates. Octopus.
Pictures from Italy, by Charles Dickens. Granville Publishing.
The Stones of Florence, by Mary McCarthy. Penguin.

FEEDBACK

We do our best to ensure the information in our books is as accurate and up-to-date as possible. The books are updated on a regular basis, using local contacts, who painstakingly add, amend and correct as required. However, some mistakes and omissions are inevitable and we are ultimately reliant on our readers to put us in the picture.
We would welcome your feedback on any details related to your experiences using the book "on the road". Maybe we recommended a hotel that you liked (or another that you didn't), as well as interesting new attractions, or facts and figures you have found out about the country itself. The more details you can give us (particularly with regard to addresses, e-mails and telephone numbers), the better. We will acknowledge all contributions, and we'll offer an Insight Guide to the best letters received.

Please write to us at:
Insight Guides
PO Box 7910
London SE1 1WE
United Kingdom
Or send e-mail to:
insight@apaguide.co.uk

Under the Tuscan Sun and the sequel *Bella Tuscany*, by Frances Mayes. Bantam
The Villas of Tuscany, by Harold Acton. Thames and Hudson.

Other Insight Guides

Europe is comprehensively covered by over 400 books published by Apa Publications. They come in a variety of series, each tailored to suit different needs.
Insight Guides, the main series of guides that Apa publishes, provide the reader with a cultural background, plus comprehensive travel coverage linked to photography and maps.
The series includes titles on Italy, Southern Italy and Northern Italy, Sicily, Tuscany and Sardinia. Italian destinations in Insight's highly successful **City Guides** series include Rome, Florence and Venice.
The itinerary-based **Insight Pocket Guides**, written by local hosts, come complete with a pull-out map. Titles include The Italian Lakes, Florence, Tuscany, Umbria, Rome, Bologna and the Bay of Naples. **Insight Compact Guides** give you the facts about a destination in a very digestible form and feature numerous Italian titles.

ART & PHOTO CREDITS

GENERAL INDEX